MYTH AND POETICS

A series edited by
GREGORY NAGY

THE TRAFFIC IN PRAISE

Pindar and the Poetics of Social Economy

LESLIE KURKE

CORNELL UNIVERSITY PRESS

ITHACA AND LONDON

First published 1991 by Cornell University Press.

International Standard Book Number 0-8014-2350-3
Library of Congress Catalog Card Number 90-55722
Printed in the United States of America
*Librarians: Library of Congress cataloging information
appears on the last page of the book.*

⊗The paper in this book meets the minimum requirements
of the American National Standard for Information Sciences—
Permanence of Paper for Printed Library Materials, ANSI Z39.48-1984.

Contents

Foreword

GREGORY NAGY

The Traffic in Praise: Pindar and the Poetics of Social Economy, by Leslie Kurke, represents a subtle broadening in the scope of the Myth and Poetics series. My goal, as series editor, is to encourage work that helps to integrate literary criticism with the approaches of anthropology and pays special attention to problems concerning the nexus of ritual and myth. The first two books in the series, Richard P. Martin's *The Language of Heroes* (1989) and my own *Greek Mythology and Poetics* (1990), set the groundwork for a broadened understanding of the very concepts of myth and ritual as reflected in the specific cultural context of ancient Greek poetics. *The Traffic in Praise* now expands the horizon further by confronting a question so fundamental that it subsumes even the problem of defining the pervasive interaction of myth and ritual in early Greek society. The question is: what exactly is value?

Leslie Kurke's book seeks answers in the poetics of a prime representative of ancient Greek values, a figure who flourished in the first half of the fifth century before our era, the poet Pindar. The poetry of Pindar is represented primarily by the epinikion or victory odes, a body of praise poems composed for choral performance on specific occasions celebrating the athletic victories of aristocrats who competed in the Panhellenic games. In this context, myth implies ritual in the very performance of myth by way of poetry. The myths deployed in these compositions of Pindar are in many cases demonstrably relevant to the ritual dimensions of athletics, in that the efforts of athletes participating in the games are viewed as stylized ordeals that serve as ritual compensation for corresponding ordeals endured by heroes in the remote past of myth. The athletes' ordeals in turn are viewed as requiring the compensation of the poet's creative efforts as realized in the performance of the victory ode, which in its own turn, as praise poetry, requires honorific material compensation for the poet. This whole chain of compensation, ideologically grounded in myth and realized in ritual, is a matter of value.

If there is a single Greek word that can best capture for us such a value, such a driving social force behind Pindar's poetics, that word is surely *oikonomiā*, ancestor of our borrowed English terms *economy* and *economics*. For Pindar, *oikonomiā* is not merely a material concern—which is what we might have inferred from our usage of *economy*. Rather, it is for him a sacred trust that transcends as well as embraces the material world. In the traditional poetics of Pindar, the reciprocity between poet and patron, which is the *oikonomiā* or "traffic" of praise poetry, depends on a world view that places the ultimate value on the notion that value itself is sacred. It is this same world view that accepts the ultimate authority of myth and ritual.

Yet Pindar's "real world" has moved beyond the inherited world view of Pindar's traditional poetics. Just as the authoritativeness of myth and ritual has become destabilized in this real world, so also the very concept of value, by becoming desacralized, has lost its own stability. In this brave new world, the desacralization of value and the destabilization of the poetics that embodies this value go hand in hand. These developments threatened to redefine the patron–poet relationship, shifting away from a reciprocity where poem and material compensation could serve as the vehicles through which the prestige of praise poetry flows, and toward a more straightforward exchange of wealth and products between two principals.

This crisis of poetics is dramatically articulated by the poetry of Pindar. Although the poetry treats the notion of material compensation for the composition of a Pindaric poem as a positive value, it is clear that the picture of a Muse who is described as "profit-loving" and "working for wages" in *Isthmian* 2 is a foil for the even more positive value of the honorific reciprocity between the poet and his subject. Leslie Kurke argues that the contemporary model of a "mercenary Muse" is transformed, in the course of Pindar's poetic elaboration, into a positive value through the appropriation of the idealized old-fashioned model of the nonprofessional Muse. In the poetry of Pindar, the *misthos* or "wage" of compensation for song is equated with *kharis*, the beauty and pleasure of reciprocity between the poet and the subject of his praise (*Pythian* 1.75–77). This more positive value of compensation is simultaneously materialistic and transcendent, *because it is sacred*: inside the framework of Pindaric poetry, the notion of compensation for poetic composition remains sacred so long as it stays within the sacred context of such ritual occasions as the celebration of an athletic victory.

Outside the framework of Pindaric poetry, of course, in the real world of Pindar, compensation for artisans, including poets, is becoming a purely material value. It is this outside reality that makes it possible for Pindar's poetry to set up the "mercenary Muse" as a foil for its own transcendence. In this real world, the system of reciprocity within the community at large, as represented by the polis or city-state, is breaking down. It is an era when individuals can achieve the wealth and power to overreach the polis itself, and the pattern of overreaching extends to the realm of song. The craft of song is in danger of shifting from an expression of community to an expression of the individual whose wealth and power threatens the community, a shift that Leonard Woodbury has aptly described as a diverting of the poetic art: "Before the end of the [fifth] century choral poetry was divested of its traditional connections with the festivals of cult . . . and diverted to the praise of the great. The change meant that the expense of the poet's fee and the choral production was assumed by a wealthy patron, with whom lay the power of decision in regard to all questions relating to the performance of the ode. The Muse, in Pindar's phrase, had grown fond of money and gone to work for the living."[1]

Leslie Kurke's *Traffic in Praise* confronts these historical realities as well as examining the traditional forms and ideologies of Pindar's poetics. In its methodology, it draws both on the historicism of earlier Pindaric scholars such as Ulrich von Wilamowitz-Moellendorff and on the formalism of more recent experts such as Elroy Bundy, without wholly aligning itself with either approach. In its judicious eclecticism, Kurke's book transcends the internal battles of Pindaric scholarship, applying a wide enough variety of empirical approaches to do full justice to the complexity of the problem it addresses, the question of value in Pindar's world. Besides a solid grounding in Pindaric philology, Kurke displays a keen appreciation of empirical perspectives provided by such distinct fields as anthropology, sociology, and economics. She offers us thereby a poet of great interest to classicists, many of whom now find Pindar inaccessible, and general readers alike. In her breadth of vision, Leslie Kurke resembles the very best of the "New Historicists."

---

[1]L. Woodbury, "Pindar and the Mercenary Muse: *Isthmian* 2.1–13," *Transactions of the American Philological Association* 99 (1968): 535.

Acknowledgments

I am grateful to my teachers Richard Martin, Anne Carson, and Froma Zeitlin, who guided and meticulously criticized an earlier version of this work. All three have profoundly influenced the way I read and think about texts. I have often had the feeling as I revised that I was exposing the argument that lay just under the surface of what I had written. To Richard Martin, Gregory Nagy, and Richard Hamilton, who understood what I was up to long before I did, I owe special thanks for encouragement and guidance. Many other readers along the way have been generous with their time and insights: Andrew Garrett, Greg Crane, Thomas Cole, Carol Dougherty-Glenn, Leonard Muellner, Lisa Maurizio, Steven White, and Ian Rutherford. Thanks also to David Halperin for suggesting my title, and to Naomi Rood for her invaluable assistance with the manuscript.

I owe a special debt of gratitude to the Harvard Society of Fellows, where I wrote the book. In addition to material support, this community furnished an intensely stimulating intellectual environment. For that, I thank Seth Schwartz, Andrew Cohen, Laura Quinney, William Flesch, Joseph Koerner, Lisbet Rausing Koerner, Robin Fleming, Charles Bailyn, Juliet Fleming, Rogers Brubaker, Dwight Reynolds, and Maren Niehoff.

Pindar is a difficult author, and therefore any discussion of his work must concern itself with basic problems of interpretation. I have tried to relegate all purely philological discussion to the footnotes, where it is available to the specialist, but not intrusive for the general reader. All translations are my own. Their aim is not elegance but merely a literal rendition of the sense (insofar as this is possible within the limits of English syntax). I have despaired of consistency in the spelling of Greek words and names. For proper names familiar in their Latinized form (such as Thucydides, Sophocles, and Corinth), I have used that form. For less familiar names and transliterated Greek words, I have followed a compromise system, closer to the Greek spelling, with k for κ, ch for χ, and y for υ.

LESLIE KURKE

Cambridge, Massachusetts

Abbreviations

AJA	American Journal of Archaeology
AJP	American Journal of Philology
CA	Classical Antiquity
CJ	Classical Journal
CP	Classical Philology
CQ	Classical Quarterly
CSCA	California Studies in Classical Antiquity
DK	Diels and Kranz 1951–52
FGrH	Jacoby 1923–1958
GRBS	Greek, Roman, and Byzantine Studies
I.	Isthmian
ICS	Illinois Classical Studies
IG	Inscriptiones Graecae
JHS	Journal of Hellenic Studies
LP	Lobel and Page 1955
LSJ	Liddell, Scott, and Jones 1940
MH	Museum Helveticum
MW	Merkelbach and West 1967
N.	Nemean
NC	Numismatic Chronicle
O.	Olympian
P.	Pythian
PCPS	Proceedings of the Cambridge Philological Society
PMG	Page 1962
QUCC	Quaderni Urbinati di Cultura Classica
REA	Revue des Etudes Anciennes

REG	*Revue des Etudes Grecques*
RhM	*Rheinisches Museum*
SIG	*Sylloge Inscriptionum Graecarum*
SM	Snell and Maehler 1970 or Snell and Maehler 1975, as appropriate
TAPA	*Transactions of the American Philological Association*
W	West 1971–1972
WS	*Wiener Studien*

THE TRAFFIC
IN PRAISE

Genre, Poetics, and
Social Change

In ancient Greek society, all poetry was composed for public performance—whether at a symposium before a small select group or at a religious festival before the entire city. Thus, the lyrics of Alcaeus were performed at symposia before the members of a single aristocratic *hetaireia*, or political club, in sixth-century Mytilene, and Attic tragedy and comedy played before an estimated fifteen thousand citizens and visitors at the Great Dionysia.[1] For such a milieu, we must crucially modify the terms in which we conceptualize poetry. To begin with, we must correlate genre with performance: if we define genre as the set of audience expectations which shapes and constrains each individual composition, we must take into account the nature of the audience *and* the occasion that informed their expectations.[2] This reorientation implicates genre in a whole set of social, political, and religious issues, since different occasions were designed for audiences of different classes and different political persuasions, and often the occasions were specifically religious in nature. We must also reorient our notion of poetics, the "making" of poetry, the conception that underlies its production, and the function for which it is made. Just as genre depends upon performance, poetics depends upon the broader social context, for given its setting, we must believe that such poetry fulfilled a *social* function.

[1]On the performance context of monodic poetry in general and Alcaeus in particular, see Rösler 1980, Herington 1985.31–39, 195–200, Gentili 1988.72–104, 197–215. For the context of Attic tragedy and comedy, see Pickard-Cambridge 1968.57–126, 263–278, Herington 1985.87–99.
[2]For considerations of genre which take more account of social context, see Todorov 1978.44–60, Bakhtin 1986.60–102, Martin 1984, 1989.10–88, and Nagy 1990.8–9, 114–115, 362–363, 397–400.

I

What then is the function of poetry in such a culture? In a society where poetry and its performance are completely embedded in the social fabric, how is poetry conceptualized and what purposes does it serve? Work done recently to recontextualize Attic tragedy considers both its specific performance setting and its broader social implications.[3] For the first, Simon Goldhill has called attention to the complex interplay between tragedy and the pre-play ceremonials at the Great Dionysia. His findings support the more general formulation of Jean-Pierre Vernant and Pierre Vidal-Naquet that tragedy provides the city the opportunity to put itself and its values on trial:

> The performance of tragedy is not only an art form, it is a social institution to which the city, by founding the tragic competitions, gives status along with its political and legal instruments. By establishing, under the authority of the *archon eponymos* in the same civic arena and following the same institutional norms as the assemblies or the popular tribunals, a performance open to all citizens, directed, played, and judged by qualified representatives of the various tribes, the city makes itself into a theater; in a way it becomes an object of representation and plays itself before the public. But if tragedy, therefore, appears to be . . . rooted in social reality, that does not mean that it is its reflection. It does not reflect reality; it expresses the entire problematics of this reality. In presenting society as torn and divided against itself, tragedy makes it profoundly questionable.[4]

Vernant and Vidal-Naguet suggest that tragedy is, at least in part, a reaction to and examination of a contemporary cultural development—the rise of the democratic polis. These findings raise another intriguing question: within a traditional society how does poetry respond and adapt to cultural change? The archaic period in Greece is one of great upheaval, for it sees, in addition to the rise of the polis, the development of tyrannies, the invention of coinage and the beginnings of a money economy, the crisis of the aristocracy, the slow spread of literacy, and the trend toward Panhellenism.[5] How does a socially embedded, occasional poetry come to terms with these developments?

---

[3]On the specific performance setting, see Goldhill 1987; on the broader social implications of tragedy, see Vernant and Vidal-Naquet 1981.viii–x, 1–27, 65–86, Loraux 1981, Zeitlin 1986, and the other essays collected in Euben 1986.

[4]Vernant and Vidal-Naquet 1969.107–108.

[5]On the profound developments of the archaic period in general, see Snodgrass 1980; on tyranny, see Andrewes 1956, Berve 1967, Mossé 1969. On the invention and use of coinage, see Robinson 1951 and 1956, Kraay 1976, Austin and Vidal-Naquet 1977.56–58; on the crisis of the aristocracy, see Jaeger 1945.185–222, Donlan 1980.35–111, Gernet

It is the object of this book to apply such questions to the odes of Pindar, in an attempt to restore to them their social dimension. The composition of the odes (to the best of our knowledge) covers a span from 498 to 446 B.C.—from the end of the archaic into the classical period, roughly coeval with the development of Attic tragedy.[6] It seems likely that the major social developments of the archaic period would have left some mark on these poems composed for public performance. But before addressing this question, we must know a bit more about the genre and the poetics of Pindar's odes.

Of the forty-five poems preserved in the manuscript tradition, all but one belong to the genre of epinikion.[7] Epinikion was occasional poetry and we know a fair number of specifics about its occasion (much more so than about prosodion or paean, for example). These were poems written on commission for victors at athletic games and usually performed at the site of the games or at the victor's home in the context of a victory celebration.[8] Athletic games in general were the province of the aristocracy because training for the games, making the trip, and competing required both leisure and wealth.[9] Most of Pindar's epinikia were written for victors at Panhellenic contests—the Olympian, the Pythian, the Isthmian, and the Nemean.[10] Of all the games, these Panhellenic

---

1981b.279–288. On orality and literacy, see Gentili 1988.3–23 and the essays collected in Detienne 1988; on the trend toward Panhellenism, see Nagy 1979.7–11.

[6]The traditional date for the establishment of tragic contests is 534 B.C. (see Marm. Par. ep. 43, Pickard-Cambridge 1968.72), though West 1989 has underscored the unreliability of the ancient evidence. The earliest datable epinikion was composed by Simonides for Glaukos of Carystus in 520 B.C. (see Bowra 1961.311–312).

[7]I ignore here that phantom of Pindaric scholarship, the "literary epistle." There are in fact no grounds for believing that such a form could exist in archaic Greece, in spite of Wilamowitz. See Woodbury 1968.540 n. 20, Nisetich 1980.168, Young 1983.31–33, and Herington 1985.26, 30, 189–191. The passages listed by Herington make very clear that certain poems were sent by the poet *to be performed*. Only Nemean 11 is not an epinikion in the technical sense: it is rather a poem in celebration of Aristagoras' inauguration as *prytanēs* of Tenedos. Still, it includes mention of the victories Aristagoras won at local contests as a boy.

[8]For a discussion of the conventional setting of the epinikion, see Slater 1984, Gelzer 1985, and Heath 1988.

[9]I say "in general" because Young (1984.107–170) has challenged the traditional scholarly view that participation in the games was essentially monopolized by the aristocracy in the archaic and classical periods. Young's caveats are important: we cannot just assume, as scholars have tended to do, that athletic victors must be noblemen *because* they are athletic victors. On the other hand, the number of victors in this period who are certainly not aristocrats is very small; see the discussions of Kyle 1985 and Poliakoff 1989 reviewing Young. For a general discussion of the demographics and sociology of athletic victors, see Pleket 1974 and 1975.

[10]The order of the list reflects the relative prestige of the Panhellenic games, based on their relative antiquity (Olympian games traditionally founded 776, Pythian 582, etc.)

contests had the greatest prestige at the time when Pindar was composing. All four were designated "crown-bearing" contests, at which the prize was a wreath whose value was symbolic, not monetary.[11] The ideology behind the prestige of the crown-bearing contests is adumbrated by a story in Herodotus: during the Persian invasion, the Persian commanders inquired of some Greek informants what their countrymen were currently doing. On being informed that they were celebrating the festival at Olympia and competing in the games, a Persian nobleman asked what the prize was. Herodotus goes on,

> They said a crown of olive was given. At that point, Tritantaichmes, the son of Artabanus, incurred the charge of cowardice from the king by making an observation which was in fact a most noble saying [γνώμην γενναιοτάτην]. For having heard that the prize was a crown, not money, he could not keep silent, but exclaimed before them all, "Alas, Mardonius, what sort of men have you led us here to fight, who compete not for money but for honor!" [οὐ περὶ χρημάτων . . . ἀλλὰ περὶ ἀρετῆς]. (Herodotus 8.26)

What is translated as "honor" in this passage is aretē—literally "excellence" or "prowess." In this context, aretē is still very much a competitive virtue and a virtue of the aristocracy.[12] The disparaging tone toward money also reflects the aristocratic perspective behind the exclamation, a perspective Herodotus confirms, praising it as a γνώμη γενναιοτάτη, "a most noble saying."[13] Indeed, the great Panhellenic games were, to quote one scholar, "a conspicuous arena for demonstrations of the superiority of the ruling class."[14]

The Olympian and Pythian games occurred every four years, the Isthmian and Nemean every two years. The only poems among the preserved epinikia which clearly do not commemorate Panhellenic victories are N.9, N.10, and N.11. The two former were composed to celebrate victories at epichoric (i.e., local) games.

[11]This is not to say that athletic victors did not reap monetary rewards: we know of direct cash prizes and special privileges (e.g., free meals for life in the prytaneum) awarded by cities to victorious citizens. But officially the prize at the four great games was only a wreath, no matter what incentives and subsequent awards the cities chose to confer. See Robert 1967, Young 1984.128–133.

[12]On these aspects of aretē, see Jaeger 1945.5–10, 105, Adkins 1960.31–60, 153–171, Rose 1974.154–155.

[13]Compare the sneer of Euryalus, at Odyssey 8.159–164, that Odysseus looks not like an athlete but rather like a trader who "scrounges for profits."

[14]Rose 1974.155. Rose 1982.55 aptly compares the games of this period with jousting in fourteenth-century Europe and notes that "the phenomenon . . . results from a similar cause: compensation for the relative eclipse of the aristocratic monopoly of military force." In spite of the revisionism of Young 1984, such texts as the story in Herodotus confirm that in this period the games were aristocratic in ideology, even if not completely

At these crown-bearing contests, the interests of the individual households, the cities, and the aristocracy from the entire Greek world intersected, for every noble house was competing with all the others, and every city was eager to have its representatives win. Indeed, the involvement of these three concentric social circles was emblematized in the victory announcement, which traditionally heralded the victor's name, his patronymic, and his city before the Panhellenic audience of the games.[15] In its broadest terms, the audience for Pindar's celebratory odes embraced these same three spheres. The poem was usually commissioned at the expense of the house of the victor but performed by a chorus of his fellow citizens before an audience that would include many of his countrymen and perhaps noble visitors.[16] After their initial performance, Pindar's poems circulated fairly widely through solo performances at symposia. Their diffusion and, indeed, their survival attest to their popularity with the social stratum that tended to perform poetry at symposia—generally speaking, the upper classes.[17] On the other hand, we are told that one of Pindar's epinikia, which narrates the birth of Rhodes from the sea, was inscribed in golden letters and dedicated in the temple of Athena of Lindos on Rhodes. Whether the story is true or not, it was conceivable to its audience, suggesting that the cities as well as the aristocracy found something in Pindar's poems to support their ideology.[18] How is it that Pindar's odes satisfied their heterogeneous audience? How did they juggle the interests, so often in tension if not in open conflict, of *oikos*, aristocracy, and polis?

---

in practice. For my purposes, the level of ideology, of self-representation and aspiration on the part of poet, victor, and audience, is more important than the reality.

[15]On the traditional form of the victory announcement, see Nisetich 1980.4.

[16]The traditional theory of choral performance has recently been challenged by Lefkowitz 1988 and Heath 1988, but see the responses of Burnett 1989 and Carey 1989a.

[17]On solo reperformance at symposia, see N.4.13–16, Aristophanes *Clouds* 1355–1358, Irigoin 1952.8–20, Herington 1985.28. The distribution of attestations of Pindar in fifth- and fourth-century Athens is very revealing. In his comedies, Aristophanes quotes and parodies poems that would have been well known to a civic audience: the dithyramb for Athens and a couple of poems written for Panhellenic celebrities (e.g., a hyporcheme for Hieron). In contrast, Plato refers nine times to poems not cited in earlier sources. Of these, five references come from poems that are not extant, and four from the epinikia (O.1, O.2, P.3, I.1). Irigoin notes that three of these four were written for Sicilian tyrants and suggests that these poems were known in Athens because their addressees were celebrities. Still, Plato shows great familiarity with Pindar, including a knowledge of Isthmian 1, a poem written for a private individual in Thebes (Irigoin 1952.12–18). This familiarity suggests that part of Plato's aristocratic *paideia* was a thorough exposure to the Theban poet.

[18]The story is recorded in the scholia to O.7 (Drachmann 1903.195), citing the historian Gorgon (probably second century B.C.).

The question of interests and ideology takes us from the level of genre and audience to that of poetics. What social function of epinikion, broadly conceived, motivated the particulars of its performance? Explicitly, the epinikion set out to commemorate and thereby immortalize the victory. Poet and audience conceptualized the poem as the completion of victory, which meant in social terms the reincorporation of the victor and his achievement. Thus a few critics have recently suggested that Pindar's epinikia served to reintegrate the victor, who had isolated himself by his achievement, back into his community. Kevin Crotty, for example, compares the athlete's journey to the games and his competition to initiation rituals in Greece and elsewhere. He concludes: "The victory ode . . . purports to be an effective kind of poetry. . . . [T]he ode effects [its] praise by reintroducing the victor into the *koinōnia* of good men that he left behind in order to compete. To offer praise is to include the athlete in a community; the epinician is an 'act of inclusion.' "[19] But what constitutes the victor's community? One of the weaknesses of Crotty's work is that he is fairly vague about the nature of this community. If the phrase "the *koinōnia* of good men" is any indication, he seems to be thinking narrowly of the aristocratic class.[20] Yet the set of the victor's "communities" must be equivalent to the heterogeneous audience of epinikion. The victor must be reintegrated into his house, his class, *and* his city, and it is the task of Pindar's poem in performance to accomplish this reintegration.

Let us then locate epinikion in the conceptual landscape we have already mapped out. Generically, Pindar's odes were poised between the sympotic poetry of Alcaeus, composed for an elite audience of aristocratic *hetairoi*, and the civic space of Attic tragedy and comedy. Pindar's poems had to participate in both spheres and speak to both audiences. At the same time, in terms of its poetics, epinikion was the antitype to tragedy. Tragedy, as I have said, explored the tensions inherent in civic ideology, allowing its heroic protagonists to confront the choral community and often depicting the clash of *oikos* and polis.[21] Everything in epinikion aimed at the defusion and resolution of these

[19]Crotty 1982.121, and see 112–122. See also Fitzgerald 1987.1, 19–20.

[20]In his more explicit formulations (1974.149–155 and 1982.52, 55–58), Rose clearly sees the aristocracy as Pindar's sole audience and as the group that validates the victor's achievement (and is validated by it in turn).

[21]Vernant and Vidal-Naquet 1981.1–5 see the ambiguities of tragedy emblematized by the split between the mythic protagonist and the chorus. Jones 1962.193–200, Goldhill 1987.74 (with bibliography listed in n. 67) consider the confrontation of *oikos* and polis as a staple of tragedy.

same tensions, for its goal was the successful integration of the athlete into a harmonious community. Thus, whereas tragedy pitted the realm of mythic heroes against the civic community (in the form of protagonists and chorus), epinikion fused the two, embedding the central mythic section within the ode performed by a chorus of the victor's fellow citizens. And rather than dramatize the conflict of *oikos* and polis, epinikion skillfully assimilated the interests of these two spheres.

I want to consider in detail how the poet occupied this ambiguous space between public and private performance and how he achieved his task of reintegration, for these questions will take us to the very heart of Pindar's social poetics. But also essential to our understanding is a thorough exploration of the issue of payment. A tradition preserved in the scholia to Isthmian 2 tells us that Simonides was the first to compose epinikia "at a wage."[22] Though this story may not be true, recent studies of the beginning and development of coinage have pushed down the probable dates for the real use and circulation of money to the period 580–550 B.C.[23] (Simonides' traditional dates are 556–468 B.C.) Whoever introduced the practice, epinikion was certainly poetry for pay by Pindar's time, and such payment must have been a fairly recent development, given the dates for the development of coinage. The economic aspect of Pindar's poetry is important, though unfortunately it has engendered much anachronistic commentary from modern critics.[24] To understand the social dimension of Pindar's odes we must make sense of their economics, for he composed at a time when the economy was largely embedded in various social, political, and religious structures and institutions.[25] Precisely because coinage was a relatively new phenomenon, we can observe in Pindar's poetry the tensions and conflicting reactions it created. Specifically, how did the poet's working "for hire" alter his status? How were his relations to the house of the victor and to the victor's city conceptualized, and how did the fact of payment affect his ability to reintegrate the victor?

[22]Drachmann 1926.214. As is clear from the context in which this assertion is made (in reference to the proem of Isthmian 2), a monetary wage is meant.

[23]See Kraay 1976, Figueira 1981.80–97, 108, and Kroll and Waggoner 1984.

[24]At the extreme, M. I. Finley observes in a review of Bowra 1964, Pindar "never forgets that he is the hireling of powerful, capricious and pitiless men. . . . More than 2,000 years before Brecht, Pindar knew it was a crime . . . not to have money. It is hard on occasion to resist the word 'toady', but Sir Maurice, too kind and excusing, manages to do so" (Finley 1968.40). For other anachronistic discussions, see Gzella 1969–1970a and b, and 1971.

[25]For the concept of an embedded economy, see Polanyi 1968 passim, Austin and Vidal-Naquet 1977.8–11.

In a sense, the question of poetry for pay is only a part of a much broader issue: the systems of exchange in which poet, patron, and audience were enmeshed. Like any other form of symbolic interaction, economic systems of exchange are ideologically fraught. As we shall see, during the time Pindar was composing, different systems coexisted and different groups consciously defined themselves by the type of exchange they practiced. Thus the charting of various economic systems that operate within the epinikia will expose the networks of interest and interaction in the poet's audience.

In the embedded economy of ancient Greece, exchange went far beyond concrete economics. As Pierre Bourdieu has argued, in such a society we must apply economic analysis in the broadest possible sense to comprehend all the exchanges and negotiations that occur. Money is only a single counter in a system in which each household tries to acquire the greatest stock of honor and prestige—what Bourdieu terms "symbolic capital."[26] We might say epinikion was the marketplace for the negotiation of symbolic capital. What I have defined as the function of Pindar's praise—the reintegration of the victor—can be construed as a whole series of social exchanges whose goal is the management and reapportionment of an influx of this precious commodity. My focus is on exchanges of all sorts: hence the title of this book, "The Traffic in Praise," is deliberately ambiguous. On one level, it designates poetry for pay as an emblem of the varied economic systems in which the poem participated. On another level, it refers to the complex negotiations among interest groups—the social traffic—which transpired in the space of the epinikian performance.

By focusing on the interaction of the different social groups that comprised the poet's audience and the victor's community, I hope to construct a sociological poetics of Pindar—that is, to observe in detail how the poet satisfied his audience and reintegrated the victor and how he accommodated social developments within his program. The first step is to restore the minimal social unit of Greek society—the individual household, or *oikos*—to Pindar's economy. I can offer no better definition of the *oikos* than that formulated by John Jones for his study of the importance of the household in Aeschylus' *Oresteia*:

> "House" (the Greek *oikos* and its synonyms) is at once house and household, building and family, land and chattels, slaves and domestic animals,

[26]Bourdieu 1977.171–183.

hearth and ancestral grave: a psycho-physical community of the living and the dead and the unborn.[27]

This definition draws attention to the many different spheres in which the *oikos* participated: it structured economic and social life as well as the individual's religious experience and his relation to past and future. As W. K. Lacey observes, the *oikos* was absolutely central to every aspect of life in antiquity.[28] It defined the individual, and through it he interacted with the larger social spheres of the aristocracy and the city. Thus Aristotle observed that the polis is made up not of individuals but of households (*Politics* 1253b1).

We shall consider first how the *oikos* of the victor itself figures in the epinikia, to determine what the household required of the individual. Then we shall trace the depiction of the relation of the house to the outside world. The interaction between houses will reveal to us the closed circle of the aristocracy, and the confrontation of the house with the city will expose the tensions inherent in a relatively new civic ideology. Thus we can use the *oikos* as our tracking device within the poetry of Pindar, since its appearances often pinpoint moments of strain engendered by the demands of competing or conflicting ideologies that the poet must reconcile.

Finally, a word about methodology. In 1962 Elroy Bundy published his terse, magisterial *Studia Pindarica* and thereby revolutionized the study of Pindar. Bundy was an uncompromising formalist who insisted that all the elements of epinikion be understood as conventional topoi that contribute to the poem's primary function of praising the victor.[29] Thus with a single stroke he rejected a venerable tradition of naive historicism, whereby scholars attempted to explain Pindar's obscurities of thought by fabricating biographical or political detail to motivate the poet.[30] The work of Bundy and those who follow him has been absolutely essential for the proper understanding of the genre and conven-

[27]Jones 1962.83–84. Note that Jones's parenthesis, "the Greek *oikos* and its synonyms," designates my interests as well. Thus I include οἶκος, δόμος, δῶμα as well as the adverbial derivatives of οἶκος (οἴκοι, οἴκοθεν, and οἴκαδε) in my consideration of Pindar. Of the first two terms, Benveniste observes, "Far from constituting two distinct social units, Gr. *domos* and *(w)oikos* signify practically the same thing, 'house'" (Benveniste 1973.240). See Benveniste 1973.239–261 for the complex prehistory of these terms; for their etymologies, see Chantraine 1968.292–293 and 781–782.

[28]Lacey 1968.9.

[29]Bundy 1962 passim.

[30]See Young 1970a.9–11, 20–21, 38–43, 52–56, for details.

tions the poet took for granted.[31] This work is particularly important in
the case of Pindar, who took a great deal for granted. What earlier
scholars had read as obscure historical allusion or sheer incoherence, we
have learned to recognize as the masterful ellipses, manipulations, and
baroque elaborations of a consummate poet composing for an audience
that shared his complete familiarity with the conventions of praise.

But no tradition can be completely understood by formalism in a
vacuum. The biographical critics had given a bad name to attempts to
set the poet in his historical context, but more recently there has been a
trend away from narrowly formalist readings toward a different kind of
contextualization.[32] First, there has been much discussion of the actu-
alities of performance and attention to the details of Pindar's language
which link the poem to its particular occasion.[33] More broadly, Peter W.
Rose has called for a reading of Pindar's myths which takes into account
their investment in aristocratic ideology.[34] Other scholars have focused
on imagery drawn from different spheres of social life, demonstrating
the cultural and poetic coherence of the poet's use of marriage imagery
and certain types of legal language.[35]

I follow this last group of scholars in focusing on the concrete details
of Pindar's images and the social contexts from which they are drawn.
Yet this does not mean that I shall ignore the methods and advances of
Bundy and his followers. A sociological poetics must be thoroughly
grounded in the formal analysis of Pindar's odes, for only by knowing
what is narrowly conventional in literary terms can we identify a surplus of meaning or imagery. This surplus must also be motivated, and I
would explain it by a certain set of relations between the poetry and its
social context. Implicit in this approach is the assumption, first, that the
spheres from which the poet's imagery was drawn were coherent cultural systems.[36] This assumption has certain methodological implications, for it suggests that the poet, as a participant in the culture,

[31]See, for examples, Young 1968, 1971, Thummer 1968, Köhnken 1971, Hamilton
1974, Greengard 1980, Carey 1980, Race 1982, 1983, 1987, Miller 1981, 1983, Pelliccia
1987.
[32]This trend in Pindar studies in fact parallels the trend in Greek history away from a
narrow focus on politics and biography to interest in social and economic history and to
more anthropological approaches. See Austin and Vidal-Naquet 1977.xii, 3–4.
[33]On performance, see Floyd 1965, Mullen 1982, Slater 1984, Heath 1988; on language
and occasionality, see Nisetich 1975, 1977a.
[34]Rose 1974 and 1982.
[35]On marriage imagery, see Woodbury 1982, Carson 1982, Brown 1984; on legal
language, see Stoddart 1990.
[36]See Geertz 1973 and 1983 passim.

intended to evoke the whole system when he used any part of it. Thus, for example, we may not always find explicit mention of a household, but instead the poet may endow some figure within a poem with the attributes of ταμία, "the housekeeper," or κληδοῦχος, "the keyholder" (P.8.1–5, P.9.55–57). These figures did not stand in isolation—structurally they were elements of the *oikos* and its management, and we must understand them as such when we interpret the poems.[37]

My second assumption is that the evocation of different cultural systems in Pindar's imagery was meaningful to the poet and his audience. This statement requires a disclaimer. It has always been fashionable to argue that the poet used imagery from different cultural spheres (especially religious practice or ceremonial) to enhance the emotional charge of the poem. In reality this is a nonexplanation, for as Clifford Geertz observes in his discussion of ideological symbols, affects are also culturally determined and largely public.[38] Given a sophisticated enough methodology for the interpretation of such symbols, Geertz insists, we should be able to explain the emotional charge generated by a particular image in a particular culture. Thus by *meaning* I do not designate merely a local emotive effect. Rather I wish to suggest that as a participant in the culture speaking to other participants, the poet incorporated various cultural symbols and thereby transmitted a coherent message to his audience through his imagery.[39]

We can go a step farther: precisely because the poet's imagery was culturally grounded and meaningful to his audience, it was systematically deployed in the service of the poetic program. Thus we must see Pindar's images as a set of systems constitutive of the poetry's social effects. Therefore my approach to Pindar's imagery will be twofold. First, I shall compare images in different poems to establish the cultural register from which they were drawn and to fill in the ellipses poet and audience took for granted. Second, I shall attempt to connect imagery drawn from the same sphere within a single poem in order to decode the message different systems of imagery sent to the poet's audience.

There is a potential objection to the second approach. Pindar's odes are densely metaphoric, and he shifted and mixed his images rapidly and repeatedly. Thus, for example, at the close of the myth in Pythian 10:

---

[37]See Xenophon *Oeconomicus* 9.11–13.
[38]Geertz 1973.215–216.
[39]I use *symbol* here as it is defined by Geertz, as "any physical, social, or cultural act or object that serves as the vehicle for a conception" (Geertz 1973.208 n. 19).

Check your oar and swiftly fix the anchor in the earth from the prow, as a defense against the rocky reef. For the peak of encomiastic hymns flits from topic to topic like a honeybee. (P. 10. 51–54)

Given this dense texture of different metaphors in rapid succession, what right do I have to connect images separated by long distances in individual poems? Could the poet's original audience have done so?

It is a fallacy, however, to assume that imagistic density precludes imagistic coherence; even if different images appear in rapid succession, it would still be possible for an audience to detect and associate metaphors drawn from the same sphere which were temporally distant from each other. To use a musical analogy, in a classical symphony the same theme is recognizable (even with variation) over long distances, though other themes have intervened. Formal analysis can also come to our aid, for often images that are linked thematically are also associated structurally by the poet. Thus, for example, imagery of voyaging often serves as both the lead-in and the break-off formulas of the central myth.[40] Such structural correspondences support a reading that would organize thematically related images into a coherent system. But ultimately I can argue only for the *possibility* of such interpretive strategies on the part of the poet's original audience. The proof lies in the interpretation of individual poems and in the conviction individual readings inspire. So finally, it devolves upon the reader to decide if this approach makes sense of the epinikia in their social context.

[40]For the terminology, see Schadewaldt 1928.268, 286, 312, and Hamilton 1974.36–38, 46 (I call "lead-in" what Hamilton calls "transition").

PART I

THE ECONOMY OF *KLEOS*: SYMBOLIC CAPITAL AND THE HOUSEHOLD

CHAPTER I

The Loop of *Nostos*

In some parts of Greece during the archaic and classical periods, the most extreme punishment—reserved for murderers, traitors, and tyrants—was the ritual destruction of the wrongdoer's house, the *kataskaphē domōn*.[1] Where this punishment was recorded, it was accompanied by a series of provisos that affected the entire household of the miscreant: death or banishment for the current representative of the house, seizure of property, banishment for all succeeding generations, and sometimes the disinterment and expulsion from the territory of the bones of his ancestors. Thus the first-century B.C. historian Nikolaos of Damascus recorded the punishments imposed on the last representative of the Kypselid tyranny in Corinth. When the tyrant had been killed in an insurrection, "the people razed the houses of the tyrants and confiscated their property; threw Kypselos, unburied, over the border; and digging up the bones of his ancestors, cast them out."[2] Indeed, Gustave Glotz maintains that the bones of the Alkmeonidai were *twice* exhumed and cast beyond the boundaries of Attica, once in the seventh century and once in the sixth, after their pious restoration by the surviving family members.[3]

This punishment, by its thoroughgoing transgression of the norm, reveals to us a great deal about the concept of the house in archaic and classical Greece. The house itself is in some sense the unit of integrity, the individuals who constitute it only its appendages or members. Furthermore, that such punishments as banishment and disinterment

[1] Connor 1985. See also Glotz 1904.456–492.
[2] *FGrH* 90 F60, quoted by Connor 1985.81. I have adapted Connor's translation of the passage. As Connor notes (83), this story may well not be historical but would have been fabricated along the lines of traditional punishments.
[3] Glotz 1904.461.

were so closely linked with the actual destruction of the building suggests that for the Greeks of this period the symbolic aspects of the house were inseparable from the literal edifice. For them the spatial dimension of the house embraced not just the building but also the ancestral tombs (though these were not usually situated on family land).[4] The representative of the house was bound to this space. He was also bound in a chain of ancestors and descendants, for as we can see from the elements of this punishment, the house also had a temporal dimension. The murderer, tyrant, or traitor uprooted his entire family line from its fixed residence and inheritance. By contrast, the situation to which every household aspired was survival in perpetuity in a spot fixed by the coordinates of house, family land, and ancestral graves. The spatial imperative of the house demanded the presence in the same spot of at least one representative of the house, and the temporal imperative imposed on the current representative a responsibility to the future—to procreate—and to the past—to maintain the tombs of his ancestors with the periodic offerings due to them.[5]

Yet the nature of Greek society also exerted a centrifugal pull on the individual through the constant rivalry of aristocratic households for achievement and prestige—for all that was summed up by the single word *kleos*, "glory" or "fame." Thus Jakob Burckhardt, in his monumental *Griechische Kulturgeschichte*, designated the archaic period the age of the "agonale Mensch," the "agonistic man."[6] *Kleos* could be won only in what we might describe as a zero-sum game—in war or in agonistic contests in which there was a clear winner and loser. Such competition could not take place within the household because, as we have seen, the house itself was the minimal unit of integrity. (For this reason, tragedy, an essentially transgressive genre, played out the many permutations of intrafamilial strife.) Barred from competition within the house, the individual was inevitably driven from home in search of glory.

The tension between these two forces, between the spatial and temporal imperatives of the household and the centrifugal force of the competitive search for prestige, shaped a cultural pattern that looped out from the house and back again.[7] This cultural pattern finds its fullest

---

[4]See Humphreys 1983.79–130. Humphreys challenges the claim of Fustel de Coulanges 1980.24–25, that the ancestors were originally buried beneath the family hearth.

[5]I shall discuss these imperatives further in Chapter 3.

[6]Burckhardt 1952.3.65–86.

[7]For a fascinating discussion of domestic and external space in the mythological register, see Vernant 1983.127–175.

expression in Homer's *Odyssey*, the tale of Odysseus' *nostos*, or "return home," after years of war and wandering. Although Odysseus' own story emphasizes only the latter half of the loop, the story of his son, Telemachus, narrated in the first four books of the epic, supplies the first half—the departure from home in search of adventure. At the moment of his coming of age, the goddess Athena visits Telemachus in disguise and finds him sitting in his father's house daydreaming (*Ody.* 1.113–118, 281–283=2.214–217). She inspires him to leave home to search for the *kleos*, or "report," of his father, thereby earning his own *kleos*, or "glory" (*Ody.* 1.95, 3.77–78, 13.422).

This doubling of the *kleos* of father and son depends on two different meanings of the word, both derived from the verb *kluein*, "to hear." Yet "rumor" and "fame" are not so far apart; at one point, Telemachus says, "I am pursuing the broad report [κλέος εὐρύ] of my father" (*Ody.* 3.83). The epithet "broad" is striking, for it is the standard epithet for *kleos* meaning "fame."[8] The diction of epic, at least, does not distinguish the two. This homonymy suggests that the quest for *kleos* is a familial, not a personal concern. As long as Odysseus fails to return and there is no word of him, his house does not have the benefit of his achievements to add to its store of prestige.[9] Thus Telemachus observes sadly to Athena:

> μέλλεν μέν ποτε οἶκος ὅδ' ἀφνειὸς καὶ ἀμύμων
> ἔμμεναι, ὄφρ' ἔτι κεῖνος ἀνὴρ ἐπιδήμιος ἦεν·
> νῦν δ' ἑτέρως ἐβόλοντο θεοὶ κακὰ μητιόωντες,
> οἳ κεῖνον μὲν ἄϊστον ἐποίησαν περὶ πάντων
> ἀνθρώπων—ἐπεὶ οὔ κε θανόντι περ ὧδ' ἀκαχοίμην,
> εἰ μετὰ οἷς ἑτάροισι δάμη Τρώων ἐνὶ δήμῳ
> ἠὲ φίλων ἐν χερσίν, ἐπεὶ πολεμον τολύπευσε.
> τῷ κέν οἱ τύμβον μὲν ἐποίησαν Παναχαιοί,
> ἠδέ κε καὶ ᾧ παιδὶ μέγα κλέος ἦρατ' ὀπίσσω—
> νῦν δέ μιν ἀκλειῶς ἅρπυιαι ἀνηρείψαντο.
> οἴχετ' ἄϊστος, ἄπυστος, ἐμοὶ δ' ὀδύνας τε γόους τε
> κάλλιπεν·

(*Odyssey* 1.232–243)

This house was likely to have been rich and blameless once, as long as that man was still at home. But now the gods, contriving evil, have wished

---

[8]Εὐρύ as epithet of κλέος meaning "fame": *Odyssey* 1.344, 3.204, 4.726, 4.816; εὐρύ with κλέος ambiguous: *Odyssey* 3.204, 19.333; εὐρύ where κλέος must mean "report": *Odyssey* 3.83, 23.137. Κλέος εὐρύ meaning "broad fame" appears to be a formula of Indo-European antiquity: see Schulze 1968.35, Schmitt 1967.19–20, 72–74, 88, and West 1973.187–188.

[9]For the sociology of epic *kleos*, see Redfield 1975.30–35.

otherwise. They have made that one invisible beyond all men—since I would not have grieved thus for him, though he were dead, if he had been overcome among his companions in the land of the Trojans or in the arms of his friends. In that case, all the Achaians would have made a tomb for him, and he would have won great glory also for his son afterward. But [as it is] now, the storm winds have snatched him away so that there is no word of him. He is gone, invisible, unknown, but for me he has left behind sorrows and lamentations.

Telemachus makes very clear that achievement and fame are familial property; his first concern is the welfare of the house. When Odysseus was home, the house was "rich and blameless," but now, he implies, its reputation, like its substance, wastes away (cf. *Ody.* 1.250–251). Furthermore, as he says, Odysseus' *kleos* would also have benefited his son after him. As it is, Odysseus is gone, ἀκλειῶς, and his house is debilitated, not so much by his absence in this formulation, as by the loss to his house of his *kleos*. And thus it becomes the son's quest to seek and win back his father's *kleos*—in quest of a quest, winning glory by retrieving the glory that has somehow disappeared. In some way or other, the glory must be brought home, either with the father or in his place, in a report of his death and the whereabouts of his grave.

In the doubling of the quest, the *Odyssey* distills to its purest form the problematic relationship of the aristocratic household with the world: every trip out aims at regaining the ancient prestige of the house as new prestige. In a sense, every quest is a displacement of this quest, for whatever its literal object, its ultimate goal is always the renewal of the father's glory. But such a system implies that stasis is always loss: there is an inevitable entropy of *kleos*.[10] Thus, even while the integrity of the house requires spatial and temporal continuity, it also necessitates the continual renewal of the family's achievements by each new generation. These antithetical imperatives generate an oscillating system, an economy of *kleos* in which each noble house participates. We might say that the winning of *kleos* is a cottage industry that aims at but never quite achieves complete thesaurization. The house seeks to hoard *kleos*, but in order to do so, it must exchange with the outside world. The *oikos* sets

[10]In practical terms, one important reason for the entropy of *kleos* is the relatively short collective memory of a largely oral culture. In such a culture, a family must periodically renew its conspicuous public achievements to be remembered at all. For a detailed discussion of the largely oral nature of family tradition down through the fifth century in Athens, see Thomas 1989.95–155. Cf. modern anthropological analyses of the constant jockeying and competition for prestige: Campbell 1964.204–212, 284, Bourdieu 1977.67–68, 181–182, and Herzfeld 1985.3–91.

its integrity at risk, relinquishing its sons to the world so that it may receive them back enriched with glory.

The *Odyssey* reveals a culture pattern centered on the *oikos* and structured as a repeating loop of departure and return. To what extent does this same culture pattern (and the centrality of the house within it) inform Pindar's poetry? Judging from most modern Pindar criticism, one would be inclined to say that the house plays only a very minor role. Most critics who address the issue of the poet's patrons focus relentlessly on the individual. The reasons for this are twofold. In the first place, there is the general modern tendency to overemphasize personal agency and autonomy in the reading of archaic texts (a tendency that has frequently been deplored by modern critics of Greek tragedy).[11] This general tendency has been exacerbated by the rhetoric of much modern Pindar criticism, which pictures the athletic victor haloed by the terrible isolating brilliance of his achievement. Elroy Bundy's work, which has done much to dispel the haze of sentimental criticism, has unfortunately also contributed to the almost obsessive focus on the individual victor. This focus results, first, from his general principle that everything in the ode must function to praise the victor and, second, from the terms in which his analyses are couched.[12] Here, for example, is a passage chosen almost at random from Bundy's discussion of Isthmian 1:

> The glory of Herodotos is enhanced by his inclusion in the hymn to Kastor and Iolaos. The background becomes richer, deeper, more layered, but remains firmly structured. The laudator is in perfect control of the scene. The figures emerge and recede to take their place in the perspective, leaving always in the foreground that single figure to whom our eyes must return, Herodotos, victorious charioteer at the Isthmos.[13]

As a counter to this vision of the splendid isolation of the Pindaric victor, let us shift the perspective and focus on an element Bundy places firmly in the background—the house of the victor.

Restoring to the house the symbolic fullness implied by the contemporary punishment of *kataskaphē domōn*, let us consider where this complex of family, property, and spatial continuity surfaces in the odes. I count thirty-seven separate passages, including both naming of the victor and victory catalogs, in which victories of other family members

[11]E.g., Jones 1962.29–46, 82–137, Goldhill 1986.79–106.
[12]For criticism of Bundy's work along similar lines, see Rose 1974.149–155.
[13]Bundy 1962.47.

are included with the victor's as a matter of course, over against twenty-eight in which the victor stands alone.[14] Scholars have of course noted this preponderance of relatives and explained *family praise* as a sub-category of *victor praise*: Pindar corroborates his claims about *phyē*, about the hereditary nature of excellence, by enumerating a noble family's past successes.[15] This interpretation keeps the family firmly in the background, but it does not account for every case. Consider, for example, the naming of the victor in Olympian 8:

> Τιμόσθενες, ὔμμε δ᾿ ἐκλάρωσεν πότμος
> Ζηνὶ γενεθλίῳ· ὅς σὲ μὲν Νεμέᾳ πρόφατον,
> ᾿Αλκιμέδοντα δὲ πὰρ Κρόνου λόφῳ
> θῆκεν ᾿Ολυμπιονίκαν.

(O.8.15–18)

Timosthenes, fate has allotted you to ancestral Zeus, who made you renowned at Nemea and [made] Alkimedon Olympic victor beside the hill of Kronos.

As L. R. Farnell notes, the scholia assume that this poem was written for two brothers together, along with their trainer Melesias. Thus the ancient commentators recognize the equal weight given to each brother's achievement in the poem, though they are at a loss to explain it.[16] But such handling becomes explicable as soon as we conceive of the *oikos*, rather than its individual members, as the acting unit.

Then there is the practical question of the poet's contract. The mechanics of commissioning are completely lost to us, but it is generally

---

[14]O.2.48–51, O.3.37–38, O.6.71–81, O.7.15–17, O.8.15–17, 67–76, O.9.83–99, O.13.1–2, 29–46, 97–113, P.6.5–6, 45–46, P.7.13–18, P.8.35–38, P.9.71–72, P.10.11–16, P.11.13–14, 43–50, N.2.17–24, N.4.73–90, N.5.41–46, 50–54, N.6.11–22, 25–26, 31–44, 58–63, N.8.16, N.10.33, N.11.19–20, I.2.28–32, I.3.9–17b, I.4.1–5, 25–29, I.5.17–19, I.6.3–7, 57–62, I.8.61–66 versus O.1.18–21, O.4.8–12, O.5.1–3, O.7.80–87, O.10.1–3, O.11.11–14, O.12.17–18, O.14.17–20, P.1.30–33, P.2.5–6, P.3.73–74, P.4.1–3, 66–67, P.5.20–22, P.8.78–84, P.9.97–103, P.12.5–6, N.1.5–7, N.3.15–18, 83–84, N.7.6–8, N.9.4–5, 51–53, N.10.24–28, I.1.52–63, I.4.69–71b, I.7.21–22, I.8.1–5.

[15]Thummer 1968.1.38–54. See also Bowra 1964.101, Rose 1974.152.

[16]See Farnell 1930.2.59, and Drachmann 1903.236–237. Carey 1989b.1–6 suggests that the scholiasts' statement that Timosthenes is Alkimedon's brother is mere conjecture. He proposes that Timosthenes is in fact Alkimedon's grandfather, mentioned again in lines 70–71. Whichever theory we prefer, the point remains the same: the naming complex designates two victors, members of the same household, as joint objects of celebration. Many more examples of odes that appear to celebrate multiple victories by members of the same family (O.13, P.7, P.11, N.8, I.5, I.8) are discussed by Hamilton 1974.104–106.

assumed that the athletic victor as an individual commissioned the poet. Yet as many as one-third of Pindar's extant epinikia may have been written for boy victors who were not yet old enough to enter into contracts. In these cases we must assume that the poem was commissioned by the head of the household, as representative of the corporate body.[17] The three odes for the sons of Lampon, for example, seem to form a clear unit, commissioned by the head of the house to celebrate all the current victories of the *oikos*.[18] The case of the ten to fourteen poems for boy victors raises a question about all the rest. Even when the athletic victor himself commissioned the ode, in what capacity did he do so? Was he acting as an individual or as *kyrios* of his household, acquiring for his house an enduring treasure?[19] It may not ever be possible to answer this question, but we should at least consider the possibility of a system completely alien to our assumptions.

These are largely external arguments for the primacy of the household in Pindar. But what of the evidence of the poet's diction and imagery? To what extent do the household's imperatives of survival and achievement structure Pindar's representation of the victor's experience? The three chapters of Part I will consider two systems of imagery which have the *oikos* as their center: spatial imagery that loops out from the house and back, and temporal imagery of funeral libations and new birth. Through both these systems Pindar's imagery tends to subsume the victor's achievement as family property. By the deployment of both spatial and temporal metaphors, the poet secures the present victory for the house and "brings home" the memory of past victories. Thus, epinikion itself accomplishes the thesaurization of *kleos* which is the goal of all individual activity. And thus Pindar endorses the ideology

[17]The eighth edition of the Teubner text titles ten poems παίδι or ἀγενείῳ ("for a boy" or "for a beardless youth"): O.8, O.10, O.11, P.10, P.11, N.5, N.6, N.7, I.6, and I.8. Hamilton 1974.106–110 considers four other poems that various scholars have suggested are for boy victors (O.14, P.8, N.4, and I.7); so the total may be as high as fourteen. On the inability of minors to enter into contracts in Greek law, see MacDowell 1978.84–86, 91. One exception to the hypothesis that the poem was commissioned by the head of household is P.10, which we know to have been commissioned by the victor's friend Thorax.

[18]N.5, I.6, I.5. Note especially the prominent praise of the father Lampon at I.6.66–73.

[19]The observations of Lacey 1968.23 may be relevant in this context: "Inalienability of land . . . is a limitation on the power even of a *kyrios*. It is also a reminder that modern notions of ownership may be misleading, and suggests that we should not look on the *kyrios* of an *oikos* as an individual owner, but as the present custodian of what belongs to his family, past, present and, if he is successful in procreating a son, future."

of household integrity which also underlies the ritual punishment of *kataskaphē domōn* and the narrative structure of the *Odyssey*.[20]

This chapter and the next address certain aspects of Pindar's spatial imagery. As Otfrid Becker noted in his book-length study of the image of the road in early Greek thought, Pindar is the first extant Greek poet to make substantial use of road metaphors.[21] Becker found a great profusion of images of roads and of land, sea, and air travel in Pindar's epinikia, and he attempted to catalog them, categorizing them as the road of achievement, the road of fame, the road of the ancestors, and the road of song.[22] Most subsequent critics of Pindar's imagery have followed Becker's system.[23] The problem with such an approach is that it atomizes the poet's imagery, isolating it from its context and from other categories of roads, literal and metaphorical, within the same ode. I would like to try a different tack by considering Pindar's paths as much as possible as a single system and by asking where the poet's roads lead. That is to say, identifying and labeling the different roads may be less instructive than establishing the landscape they occupy and the circuit they trace.

Let us begin by considering Pindar's metaphorical geography, what Becker described as the road of achievement. It has often been observed that the geographic ends of the earth figure prominently in epinikion as an image for the limitations set on human achievement.[24] The Hyperboreans, the Nile or the Ethiopians, most commonly the Pillars of Herakles—every reader of Pindar is familiar with these as the boundaries beyond which a mortal cannot pass.[25] But it is rarely noted that the

[20]For a very different treatment of *nostos* in Pindar, see Crotty 1982.104–138. My discussion is intended to complement that of Crotty, who considers athletic competition as an initiatory experience for the athlete who leaves and returns. As Redfield (1982.185–188) has observed, every rite of passage is both a transformation and a transferral. Crotty's concern is the transformation—the experience of the individual athlete. My focus is the transferral—the victor's journey out and back from the perspective of the *oikos* from which he leaves and to which he returns.

[21]Becker 1937.54.

[22]Becker 1937.54–100.

[23]Exceptions are Bernard 1963.13–15, Simpson 1969a, and Hubbard 1985.1–60. I would, however, add a diachronic narrative element to Hubbard's structural analysis. The reason, I suggest, that "near" is valorized on some occasions and "far" on others (as Hubbard observes) is that the representative of the house must first leave home and then return "with the goods."

[24]See Becker 1937.59–61, Bundy 1962.43–44 (on the hounds of Geryon), Young 1971. 29 n. 94, Fränkel 1973.493, Peron 1974.67–89, Carey 1980.154–155, Carne-Ross 1985.71–72, 77–78, Steiner 1986.95.

[25]The Hyperboreans: O.3.31–32, P.10.28–30, I.6.22–23; the Nile: N.6.48–50; the Ethiopians: I.2.39–42, I.6.22–23; the Pillars of Herakles: O.3.43–45, N.3.21–23, N.4.69–72, I.4.12–13.

house largely organizes this space: that the ends of the earth are perceived from and set in relation to the victor's *oikos*. In Olympian 3
Pindar ends his ode to Theron with the assertion

> νῦν δὲ πρὸς ἐσχατιὰν Θήρων ἀρεταῖσιν ἱκάνων ἅπτεται
> οἴκοθεν Ἡρακλέος σταλᾶν. τὸ πόρσω δ' ἐστὶ σοφοῖς ἄβατον
> κἀσόφοις.

> (O.3.43–45)

But now Theron, coming to the limit by his achievements, fastens onto
the Pillars of Herakles from home. But that which is farther is impassable
for the wise and the foolish.

And again in Isthmian 4 he says of the family of the Kleonymidai,

> ἀνορέαις δ' ἐσχάταισιν
> οἴκοθεν στάλαισιν ἅπτονθ' Ἡρακλείαις
> καὶ μηκέτι μακροτέραν σπεύδειν ἀρετάν·

> (I.4.11–13)[26]

But by extreme acts of courage they have fastened onto the Pillars of
Herakles from home so as not to haste after longer achievement.

We must take this οἴκοθεν, "from home," seriously, for the poet need
not have included the word for his metaphor to be understood; yet he
employs it emphatically in the same context in two different poems.[27]
The house itself seems to organize this landscape, pointing its members
to the ends of the earth. And insofar as they go out "from home," these
victors are not completely free agents; they are rather the representatives of a corporate body that requires their achievement.

Furthermore, when the members of the *oikos* reach the limits of
achievement, the house seems to draw them back. In Nemean 3, the
limit of Pindar's Herakles "digression" is this description of his reaching
Gades:

> ἰδίᾳ τ' ἐρεύνασε τεναγέων
> ῥοάς, ὁπᾷ πόμπιμον κατέβαινε νόστου τέλος,
> καὶ γᾶν φράδασε.

> (N.3.24–26)

[26]On the divergence of the punctuation given from that of Snell-Maehler's Teubner
text see Farnell 1930.2.350.
[27]For the translation "from home" in both passages, see Farnell 1930.2.29 and 350.
There seems to be a great deal of critical resistance to taking οἴκοθεν in the most natural

And on his own he found the streams of the shallows, where he disembarked at the end that led him back home, and he made known the land.

Here, the geographic limit is characterized entirely by its relation to the hero's home: it is the πόμπιμον . . . νόστου τέλος, "the end [of the voyage] that led him back home."[28] Herakles serves as Pindar's paradigm for the victor (here and elsewhere) because he made it to the ends of the earth and chose to return home. The failure to reach this *telos* that escorts back home has drastic consequences, as the poet shows us in the contrasting portrait of the "obscure man":

ὃς δὲ διδάκτ᾽ ἔχει, ψεφεννὸς ἀνὴρ ἄλλοτ᾽ ἄλλα πνέων οὔ ποτ᾽ ἀτρεκεῖ
κατέβα ποδί, μυριᾶν δ᾽ ἀρετᾶν ἀτελεῖ νόῳ γεύεται.

(N.3.41–42)

But he who has [only] what he has been taught, an obscure man aspiring
to different things at different times—he never disembarks with sure foot
but tastes of countless achievements with ineffectual intention.

way to mean "from home." Critics have a number of strategies for denying it any significance within the poet's geographical metaphor.

One strategy is to assert that οἴκοθεν has lost all concrete force by Pindar's time, that it means merely, "from one's own resources, by nature" (thus the scholiast's διὰ τῶν οἰκείων ἀρετῶν [Drachmann 1930.126]; compare German *von Haus aus*). Norwood finds no good evidence for this meaning (Norwood 1915.1). Furthermore, the critics who make this claim are the same ones who believe that Pindar's "meaning" is no more than a prose summary of his thought, stripped of metaphor. But in these passages where the Pillars of Herakles figure as a metaphor for the limit of human achievement, the poet has chosen a word that works within his metaphorical geography. That is to say, even if οἴκοθεν could "mean" φυά, the poet has taken the trouble to define that quality in terms of the *oikos*, and we must respect his imagistic choice.

Other critics claim that οἴκοθεν means "at home": the victor, they say, has gone to the limit of achievement "without leaving home" (thus Bury 1892.65; see also Hubbard 1985.12–15). Norwood (1915.2) and Peron (1974.77–78) refute this interpretation, pointing out that if οἴκοθεν means "at home" the presence of ἱκάνων at O.3.43 is inappropriate.

Finally, Norwood (1915.1) suggests that οἴκοθεν means "on the homeward side"—on the near side of the Pillars of Herakles. But there is no other evidence for such a meaning, and it would make the concluding warnings in each passage otiose.

The critical effort to efface οἴκοθεν from the text is significant, for it reveals what is at stake in modern interpretations. The prominence of the victor's house in these passages threatens the perception of the victor as an autonomous agent.

[28]Thus I cannot agree with the suggestion of Von der Mühll 1968.229–230, seconded by Verdenius 1969.195, that νόστος here means simply "voyage." This interpretation completely fails to account for πόμπιμον: how can the end of a journey be "an escort for" the journey itself? Von der Mühll senses the difficulty and claims that the adjective is transferred from νόστος to τέλος. But as an epithet of νόστος meaning "journey," the adjective is flat and prolix. Of course the journey escorts out—what else would it do?

Κατέβα (42) echoes Herakles' κατέβαινε (25), and ἀτελεῖ νόῳ (42) picks up and contrasts the hero's successful τέλος (25). These verbal parallels draw the two passages together. W. J. Slater glosses κατέβα here as "*met*. arrive, win through, attain one's goal," and the echo of the earlier passage suggests that the source of the metaphor is sea travel.[29] Unlike Herakles, the ψεφεννὸς ἀνήρ "never disembarks with sure foot," never achieves any *telos* at all. In this context, as Deborah Steiner has recently observed, the participle πνέων also contributes to the seafaring imagery, evoking the inconstant, shifting winds that keep the sailor from his goal.[30] The man with no natural talent pursues a whole host of accomplishments but never brings any to fulfillment. For this very reason he is ψεφεννός, "in darkness": the different winds of his impulses, out of control, blow him right off the map of the poet's metaphorical landscape into oblivion.[31]

The model of the house and the ends of the earth clarifies and universalizes the trajectory of the victorious athlete. At the most obvious level, we can ground geographic metaphor in agonistic fact: if you never leave home, you can't win any prizes. Pindar articulates this truism most clearly in Olympian 12, in a contrafactual statement about what would have happened to the victor, had civil war not driven him from his homeland:

> υἱὲ Φιλάνορος, ἤτοι καὶ τεά κεν
> ἐνδομάχας ἅτ' ἀλέκτωρ συγγόνῳ παρ' ἑστίᾳ
> ἀκλεὴς τιμὰ κατεφυλλορόησε(ν) ποδῶν,
> εἰ μὴ στάσις ἀντιάνειρα Κνωσίας σ' ἄμερσε πάτρας.
>
> (O. 12.13–16)

Son of Philanor, indeed also the honor of your feet would have shed its leaves without glory, like a cock fighting within beside its hereditary

---

[29]Slater, 1969a, s.v. καταβαίνω. On the traveling imagery here, see Becker 1937.66.
[30]Steiner 1986.69.
[31]The ψεφεννὸς ἀνήρ functions as negative foil not only for the Herakles paradigm that precedes but also for the Achilles myth that follows. In contrast to the one who has only the things he has been taught, Achilles possesses both inherited excellence and a noble education (43–58). The various winds of the obscure man's impulses (ἄλλοτ' ἄλλα πνέων [41]) contrast with the winds that carry Achilles to Troy (θαλασσίαις ἀνέμων ῥιπαῖσι πεμφθείς [59]). Together, Herakles and Achilles play out the heroic options between which Odysseus is suspended in Telemachus' speech: Herakles returns; Achilles dies abroad and gets a tomb from which light shines back to his home (64). The light from Achilles' tomb fixed on the Hellespont (τηλαυγὲς ἄραρε φέγγος Αἰακιδᾶν αὐτόθεν) provides the final contrast to the shifting obscurity of the ψεφεννὸς ἀνήρ. Pindar uses strikingly similar imagery to characterize his own poetic activity at N.4.37–38, a passage I shall discuss in Chapter 2.

hearth, if hostile civil war had not deprived you of your Knossian fatherland.

The image of the rooster, enclosed in his line between ἐνδομάχας and παρ' ἑστίᾳ, dramatically expresses the waste of a young man who sits at home beside his hereditary hearth.[32] Indeed, the home-fighting cock is doubly enclosed—within his own line and then also within the ring of τεά . . . τιμά. Τιμά, in turn, is surrounded by the adjective and verb that negate it: without *kleos* your honor would have lost its leaves. This claustrophobic picture of the prize cock who never gets to strut his stuff underscores the athlete's need to leave home.[33]

The poet can express the same concept in terms of going and returning, as he does in Nemean 11. This poem, written to celebrate the accession of Aristagoras to the office of *prytanēs* in Tenedos, mentions his victorics as a boy in the local games. As the poet informs us, Aristagoras' parents would not send him to the great games at Olympia and Delphi:

> ἐλπίδες δ' ὀκνηρότεραι γονέων παιδὸς βίαν
> ἔσχον ἐν Πυθῶνι πειρᾶσθαι καὶ Ὀλυμπίᾳ ἀέθλων.
> ναὶ μὰ γὰρ ὅρκον, ἐμὰν δόξαν παρὰ Κασταλίᾳ
> καὶ παρ' εὐδένδρῳ μολὼν ὄχθῳ Κρόνου
> κάλλιον ἂν δηριώντων ἐνόστησ' ἀντιπάλων,
>
> (N. 11.22–26)

But the too hesitant hopes of his parents checked the force of the child from making trial of contests in Pytho and at Olympia. For on oath, in my opinion, had he gone beside Kastalia and beside the beautiful-leaved hill of Kronos he would have returned home more nobly than his contending wrestling opponents.

The loop that is the proper shape of achievement is rapidly sketched in the last two lines. Had Aristagoras gone out to Olympia, he would have returned enhanced with the prestige of victory. And it is no accident that the emphasis of the poet's oath, marked by the finite verb ἐνόστησ(ε) after the participle μολών, is on the victor's return home.

---

[32]On the image contained in κατεφυλλορόησε(ν) and its literary pedigree, see Nisetich 1977b.

[33]Compare the remarks of Bourdieu 1970.158, based on his fieldwork among the Kabyle in North Africa: "The man who stays too long in the house during the day is either suspect or ridiculous: he is 'the man of the home,' as one says of the importunate man who stays amongst the women and who 'broods at home like a hen in the henhouse.'"

The same imperative of achievement is implicit in his compliment to
the victor's family in Nemean 10:

ἀξιωθείην κεν, ἐὼν Θρασύκλου
Ἀντία τε σύγγονος, Ἄργεϊ μὴ κρύπτειν φάος
ὀμμάτων.

(N. 10. 39–41)

I would have deemed it worthy, if I were of the family of Thrasykles and
Antias, not to hide the light of my eyes in Argos.

The light imagery here recalls the ψεφεννὸς ἀνήρ of Nemean 3. The
one reaches no fixed shore on his journey out; the other never leaves
home at all. The result is the same: both are hidden in obscurity. If
Theaios were never to leave home, he would condemn himself to
perpetual darkness, hiding the light of his eyes in Argos.[34]
    Thus both metaphorically and literally the poet advocates what I have
called the imperative of achievement. That is, he repeatedly expresses
the necessity to leave home in search of glory. For Pindar and his
contemporaries, agonistic competitions represent the most common
forum for the winning of *kleos*. But the poet reveals the ideology of the
quest in its purest form in the mythic narratives he incorporates into the
poems. Thus, in Pythian 4 the poet says that Hera inspired the heroes
with longing for the ship Argo,

μή τινα λειπόμενον
τὰν ἀκίνδυνον παρὰ ματρὶ μένειν αἰῶνα πέσσοντ᾽, ἀλλ᾽ ἐπὶ καὶ θανάτῳ
φάρμακον κάλλιστον ἑᾶς ἀρετᾶς ἅλιξιν εὑρέσθαι σὺν ἄλλοις.

(P. 4. 185–187)

in order that no one, left behind, wait nursing a life without risk beside
his mother, but even at the cost of death find the noblest drug for his
virtue together with the rest of his age-mates.

[34]Thus I do not follow the scholia, who take these lines to mean, "Were I the relative of
such athletic victors, I would not look down in shame in my native city [of Argos]"
(Drachmann 1926.175–176). The issue is not the victor's bearing at home but his
aspirations abroad. The poet has just prayed for an Olympic victory for Theaios (29–33),
and now goes on to catalog his relatives' victories throughout Greece (41–48). In
context, in an ode that celebrates victories at the local Argive games, the point is surely
that the victor should not restrict himself only to epichoric contests; he should "show the
light of his eyes" in other places, including Olympia. As parallels for φάος here, compare
I. 1.20 and O. 1.90.

Just as in the *Odyssey*, death abroad in the context of heroic enterprise is preferable to a life without *kleos*. But though they risk the fate of Odysseus, the young men the poet describes share the status of Telemachus: Hera, like Athena in the *Odyssey*, wants to save them from a life spent at home. To be left behind beside one's mother is the negation of heroic achievement.

In Olympian 1 we find very similar diction in Pelops' formulation of a wasted life:

> θανεῖν δ᾽ οἷσιν ἀνάγκα, τά κέ τις ἀνώνυμον
> γῆρας ἐν σκότῳ καθήμενος ἕψοι μάταν,
> ἁπάντων καλῶν ἄμμορος;
>
> (O. 1.82–84)

But for those for whom it is necessary to die, why would anyone sitting in darkness stew a nameless old age in vain, without a share of all good things?

Pelops' assertion that "great risk does not take a cowardly man" (ὁ μέγας δὲ κίνδυνος ἄναλκιν οὐ φῶτα λαμβάνει [O. 1.81]) parallels the "life without risk" (τὰν ἀκίνδυνον . . . αἰῶνα) described at Pythian 4.186. And both passages use the imagery of cooking to designate idling away life in safety: καθήμενος ἕψοι in Olympian 1 is the equivalent of μένειν . . . πέσσοντ᾽ in Pythian 4. This similarity of diction suggests that Pelops is also imagining himself sitting at home for his whole life. Ἐν σκότῳ (in darkness), then, appears to stand here in the place of παρὰ ματρί (beside his mother).[35]

As in Nemean 10, staying at home is conceived as sitting in darkness, and Pelops tells us clearly what that darkness consists of. He would "stew" in the center, surrounded by alpha-privatives—with no name and "without a share of all good things." Ἁπάντων καλῶν spans a continuum from concrete possessions to honors won to the pleasures of the symposium and the songs that attend it.[36] Together, the two negative adjectives ἀνώνυμον and ἄμμορος reveal by contrast all the hero is seeking when he leaves home.

But if the first rule of this competitive ideology is the necessity of leaving home, the second is surely the equally compelling need to

---

[35]I shall return to the equivalence of these phrases in Chapter 3.

[36]For the concrete usage, see I.1.4b; for honors or achievements, P.8.33, O.10.91, O.13.45, P.5.116, N.7.59; for symposium and song, O.1.104, O.11.18.

return with the "goods" (in all the senses in which Pelops uses the term
καλά).[37] In Isthmian 1, for example, Pindar opens his "hymn to Castor
and Iolaos"[38] with a description of their athletic successes:

ἔν τ᾽ ἀέθλοισι θίγον πλείστων ἀγώνων,
καὶ τριπόδεσσιν ἐκόσμησαν δόμον
καὶ λεβήτεσσιν φιάλαισί τε χρυσοῦ,
γευόμενοι στεφάνων
νικαφόρων· λάμπει δὲ σαφὴς ἀρετά
ἔν τε γυμνοῖσι σταδίοις σφίσιν ἔν τ᾽ ἀσπιδοδούποισιν ὁπλίταις δρόμοις,
(I.1.18–23)

> And in contests they laid hold of the most events, and they adorned their
> house with tripods and cauldrons and phiales of gold, tasting of vic-
> torious crowns; but achievement shines clear for them both in the naked
> furlong races and in the shield-thumping races in armor.

The first line ("And in contests they laid hold of the most events")
informs us only that they entered competitions.[39] That they won is
expressed obliquely in the lines that follow: "they adorned their house
with tripods and cauldrons and phiales of gold." The fact of victory is
expressed by its result. This odd periphrasis reveals the real purpose of
competition—to take the prizes home and set them up in the house as
visible symbols of one's achievement. The continuum of καλά is expressed here by the light imagery, which effectively merges these
golden prizes with their symbolic value. The heroes' "achievement
shines clear" because these vessels reflect it.

The description of their success in contests is framed by the heroes'
emphatic location at home. Thus the hymn begins with the specifica-
tion, "For those men were born best charioteers of heroes in Lac-
edaemon and in Thebes" (I.1.17) and ends (with chiastic inversion),[40]

---

[37]We have in fact observed both halves of the loop of *nostos* already at N.3.24 and
N.11.26. What I wish to draw attention to in I.1 and the following examples is the
emphasis on the victor's bringing home the *kala* to incorporate them in the substance of
the house.

[38]Bundy 1962.44–47.

[39]I follow Farnell 1930.2.337 and Slater 1969a (s.v. θιγγάνω) in taking the genitive
ἀγώνων as the object of θίγον, rather than the dative ἀέθλοισι (contra Thummer
1968.2.16–17). It is true that elsewhere Pindar always uses a dative object with θιγγάνω,
but a genitive object is perfectly normal Greek practice, while the preposition ἐν is
problematic for Thummer's interpretation (notice that he has no parallels for θιγγάνω +
ἐν + dat.).

[40]Bundy 1962.47.

"Both by the streams of Dirce and near by Eurotas they appeared frequently crowned with clustered shoots, the child of Iphikles, of the same people as the race of sown men, and the child of Tyndareos, inhabiting [οἰκέων] the lofty seat of Therapne in Achaia." It appears, then, that the inset hymn replicates the model I have postulated in its very structure. The heroes progress from home to agonistic competition, then back home, bearing with them the light of their achievement made tangible as golden prizes.

In other contexts referring to actual victors, Pindar catalogs their successes by telling us what prizes they brought home from the games. Thus in Nemean 4, he announces the victories of the Theandridai at Olympia, the Isthmus, and Nemea simply by saying that they "did not come home without glorious-fruited crowns" (οἴκαδε κλυτοκάρπων οὐ νέοντ᾽ ἄνευ στεφάνων [N.4.76–77]). In a negative version of the same motif in Nemean 11, the too hesitant expectations of his parents have deprived Aristagoras of the opportunity to return home "more nobly than his . . . opponents" (κάλλιον ἂν . . . ἐνόστησ᾽ N.11.26). Aristagoras' experience leads Pindar to general reflections; one man, he observes, is overambitious, while another's hesitancy robs him of his οἰκεῖα καλά:

> τὸν δ᾽ αὖ καταμεμφθέντ᾽ ἄγαν
> ἰσχὺν οἰκείων παρέσφαλεν καλῶν
> χειρὸς ἕλκων ὀπίσσω θυμὸς ἄτολμος ἐών.
>
> (N.11.30–32)

But a spirit without daring has knocked another man astray of the goods that properly belonged to his house, drawing [them] back from his hand—another man who blamed his strength too much.

Slater glosses the adjective οἰκεῖος here (and throughout Pindar) as "one's own," but the pattern of usage in authors down through the fifth century suggests that the etymological meaning "of one's household" was still operative.[41] Pindar's own usage elsewhere reveals that the house is still central to his notion of οἰκεῖος. Thus in Nemean 1, the

[41]Cf. Hesiod *Works & Days* 457; Bacchylides 1.167; Aeschylus *Agamemnon* 1220, *Prometheus Bound* 396; Sophocles *Antigone* 661, 1187, 1249, *OC* 765, *OT* 1162, *Trachiniae* 757; Euripides *Andromache* 986, *Bacchae* 1250, *IT* 1140, 1171, *Phoenissae* 374, 1107; Herodotus 1.45, 2.37, 3.65, 4.65, 5.5; Andocides 4.15; Thucydides 1.9, 2.40, 2.51; Lysias 13.41; Xenophon *Oeconomicus* 9.18. See Eernstman 1932.1–14. The common translation "one's own" reflects the same bias toward the individual as the basic unit that Jones criticizes in Aeschylean scholarship (Jones 1962.82–111). On the opposition οἰκεῖον/ἀλλότριον, see Hubbard 1985.33–60.

poet uses the adjective substantively in the gnomic observation, "Still, what is *oikeion* oppresses one entirely" (τὸ γὰρ οἰκεῖον πιέζει πάνθ' ὁμῶς [N.1.53]). The context of the gnome makes the force of τὸ . . . οἰκεῖον quite clear; what presses upon Amphitryon is his fear for his sons (and hence for the continuity of his house). That οἰκεῖος embraces the house and not just the individual is also clear from its opposite term, ἀλλότριος. For, as Pindar tells Hieron's son Deinomenes in Pythian 1, "A father's victory is no foreign joy" (χάρμα δ' οὐκ ἀλλότριον νικα-φορία πατέρος [P.1.59]). Thus it is at least possible that we should understand *oikeia kala* as "household goods." The man who doubts his strength has been knocked astray of the good things he would have won and incorporated in the substance of the house.

Indeed, the poet shows us the result of bringing home the *kala* in his final picture of Pelops in Olympian 1. Pindar's description of the hero cult of Pelops at Olympia is striking for its systematic inversion of the "nameless old age" the youthful Pelops rejected in his speech to Posei-don:

> νῦν δ' ἐν αἱμακουρίαις
> ἀγλααῖσι μέμικται,
> Ἀλφεοῦ πόρῳ κλιθείς,
> τύμβον ἀμφίπολον ἔχων πολυξενωτάτῳ παρὰ βωμῷ· τὸ δὲ κλέος
> τηλόθεν δέδορκε τᾶν Ὀλυμπιάδων ἐν δρόμοις
> Πέλοπος,
>
> (O.1.90–95)

But now he is mixed with shining blood-offerings, reclining on the way of Alpheus, having a much-visited tomb beside the altar most frequented by strangers. And the glory of Pelops shines from afar in the courses of the Olympic games.

Recall that the poet has designated the entire Peloponnese as the "set-tlement" of Pelops (Λυδοῦ Πέλοπος ἀποικία [O.1.23]). Within his ἀποικία, the hero reclines upon the way of the Alpheus as on a banquet-ing couch (Ἀλφεοῦ πόρῳ κλιθείς). In this new home, Pelops enjoys all the *kala*—a sympotic setting, offerings, company (ἀμφίπολον), fame (κλέος), and light (ἀγλααῖσι, τηλόθεν δέδορκε)—once he has com-peted and won the chariot race.

Thus we can say that the house in Pindar organizes a moral landscape: out to achievement, success, the winning of prizes, and then back. Light imagery makes this circuit clear. Never to leave home or never to reach the end of achievement leaves the individual shrouded in obscurity (N.10, O.1, N.3). In contrast, success and return generate a radiance that shines from afar (I.1, O.1).[42] This pattern suggests the limitations of Becker's mode of analysis, for the "road of achievement" appears not as an isolated image but as one element in a system, and the principle that organizes the system is *nostos*. The prominence of *nostos* within the epinikia has implications, in turn, for the status of the household and the victor's relation to it. Conceptualizing victory in terms of success and return (as Pindar does) locates the house rather than the individual at the center. The athlete departs from home (οἴκοθεν [O.3, I.4]) and returns to home (οἴκαδε [N.4]), contributing his achievement to the household's stock (οἰκείων . . . καλῶν [N.11]). Thus the poet's representation endorses the ideology of *oikos* integrity and incorporates the victor's achievement within the substance of the house.

To conclude this survey of *nostos* in Pindar, let us consider Olympian 12, which offers a good model for the whole complex of ideas I have been tracing—the heroic or agonistic necessity for the individual to leave home and to return bearing the glory he has won. Here Pindar goes to the length of attributing to saving Fortune (σώτειρα Τύχα) the victor's expulsion from his original home. In explanation, the poet asserts that the "honor of [the victor's] feet would have shed its leaves without *kleos*" had civil war not driven him from his Cretan homeland. But Pindar could not regard the loss of one's homeland as advantageous, even if it is the precondition of the athlete's competing. The real reason he regards Tyche as a savior is given only in the poem's final lines:

νῦν δ' Ὀλυμπίᾳ στεφανωσάμενος
καὶ δὶς ἐκ Πυθῶνος Ἰσθμοῖ τ', Ἐργότελες,
θερμὰ Νυμφᾶν λουτρὰ βαστάζεις ὁμιλέων παρ' οἰκείαις ἀρούραις.
                                                         (O.12.17–19)

But now having been crowned at Olympia and twice from Pytho and at the Isthmus, Ergoteles, you lay hold of the warm baths of the Nymphs, living in company beside your own fields.

She is a benevolent "saving" goddess because she has given Ergoteles, first, the occasion to leave home and win *kleos* and, then, a home to which he can return. We should notice in this context the emphatic final

[42]See Becker 1937.61–62.

words, οἰκείαις ἀρούραις. Only with these words is the victor's return completed. And the adjective οἰκείαις implies that the victor is not an isolated individual, for his holdings in Sicily constitute an *oikos*.[43]

But if this is a literal homecoming (to a new home), it is also a metaphor that shapes the entire poem. The dominant imagery of strophe and antistrophe, as critics have noted, is that of sea travel.[44] As if inspired by the literal ships he mentions, "piloted on the sea by Fortune" (3–4), Pindar ends the strophe with a bleak image of mortal hopes:

αἵ γε μὲν ἀνδρῶν
πόλλ᾽ ἄνω, τὰ δ᾽ αὖ κάτω
ψεύδη μεταμώνια τάμνοισαι κυλίνδοντ᾽ ἐλπίδες·

(O. 12. 5–6a)

The hopes of men are whirled, some up, some down again on many occasions, cleaving vain lies.

This is in fact an image of ships whirled helpless in a storm at sea. Again, Pindar fills the last two and a half lines of the antistrophe with imagery drawn from the same realm:

οἱ δ᾽ ἀνιαραῖς
ἀντικύρσαντες ζάλαις
ἐσλὸν βαθὺ πήματος ἐν μικρῷ πεδάμειψαν χρόνῳ.

(O. 12. 11–12a)

But those who have met with grievous storms in a little time have changed from trouble to deep good.

Here, as he modulates from the most general statement to the specific application to the victor, Pindar alters the nautical image. Βαθύ still suggests the open sea, but calm rather than storm.[45] These men have

[43]Fränkel argues quite persuasively from the end of Olympian 12 and other sources for the significance of this bathing in the final line; it marks the end of Ergoteles' wanderings: "It is clear that a bath could be perceived as the emblem of coming to rest, after the conclusion of misfortune or the accomplishment of a strenuous task. In particular, a bath in the spring or river water of a place can serve to indicate that journeying has ended and that the weary traveler has come to rest in the land where he wishes to remain" (Fränkel 1968.97–98, my translation).

[44]Gildersleeve 1890.224–225. See also Peron 1974.122–131, 296–297, Steiner 1986.68, 71.

[45]Pindar uses the adjective βαθύς with various nouns to designate the open sea at P.1.24, P.3.76, P.5.88, and N.4.36. On its metaphorical cast in this context, see Peron 1974.296–297.

survived, but they're not home yet. Then the epode and the entire poem
end with a different kind of water, the warm baths of the Nymphs.[46]

The sense of relief and well-being which pervades this picture draws
its peculiar force from the metaphorical development of the poem: we
feel that the victor is not only literally home but "home safe" from the
delusory hopes and vicissitudes that make all human life a dangerous sea
voyage. In this context, it is tempting to see in the "warm baths of the
Nymphs" not only a reference to a geographic feature of Himera but
also an allusion to the most famous *nostos* of all. For the most salient
features of the Cove of Phorkys, where the Phaiakians deposit the
sleeping Odysseus in Book 13 of the *Odyssey*, are a wild olive tree and
the Cave of the Nymphs, "in which the waters are ever flowing" (ἐν δ᾽
ὕδατ᾽ ἀενάοντα [*Ody.* 13.109]). And it is to these Nymphs that Odysseus addresses his first prayers when he finally recognizes his homeland
(*Ody.* 13.353–60). If there is an echo of this scene in Olympian 12, it
transforms the little poem in retrospect into a mini-*Odyssey* and contributes to our sense of joy and relief at its ending. This metaphorical
elaboration of *nostos* as an image for the attainment of perfect peace and
security depends on the compelling ideological power the concept has
for the poet and his audience. In the next chapter, we shall explore
further the cultural complex of which *nostos* forms a part and chart the
traces of this system in Pindar's imagery.

[46]Anne Carson points out to me the significance of different kinds of water in Pindar's
poetry. The poet often marks the arrival home by the mention of a native spring or river.
Freshwater seems to symbolize restoration and reward in many poems. Compare
O.1.90–92, O.5.11–12, O.6.28, 85–86, O.14.1–5, P.4.294–299 (note the two springs
marking the end points of Damophilos' journey), N.1.1–4, I.1.28–29 (and see Duchemin 1955.252–254, Steiner 1986.72).

CHAPTER 2

The Economics of *Nostos*

Pindar endorses a model of achievement which sends the victor out
from home and leads him back again. I have described the loop of *nostos*
but not explained it, for thus far the discussion has been limited to the
nostos of the individual victor or hero. Why insist that Aristagoras' *oikeia
kala* and Ergoteles' *oikeiai arourai* are family property? Why not consider
the impetus to achievement as personal and individual? Yet embracing
the model of the individual leaves the motivation to return home somewhat obscure. Why does the poet endorse *nostos* so emphatically, high-
lighting it with the image of light shining from the house? What is at
risk if a victory is won but not "brought home"?

The answer lies in the familial quality of *kleos*. For Pindar, as for
Homer, achievement and reputation are hereditary. They are not simply
the possessions of an individual; they are rather treasures for the household, and therefore they must be installed at home to be made available
as community property. Thus in Pythian 11, the poet affirms:

εἴ τις ἄκρον ἑλὼν ἡσυχᾷ τε νεμόμενος αἰνὰν ὕβριν
ἀπέφυγεν, μέλανος {δ'} ἂν ἐσχατιὰν
καλλίονα θανάτου ⟨στείχοι⟩ γλυκυτάτᾳ γενεᾷ
εὐώνυμον κτεάνων κρατίσταν χάριν πορών·

(P. 11.55–58)

If a man who has taken the highest peak [of achievement], dwelling in
peace, flees dread *hybris*, he would go to a better end of black death, since
he has granted to his sweetest offspring the grace of a good name as the
best of possessions.

35

As D. C. Young argues, ἄκρον ἑλών probably refers to athletic victory, though in terms general enough to apply to any achievement.[1] The man who has reached the limit of achievement dies a better death *because* he knows that he has passed on to his descendants "the grace of a good name as the best of possessions." The darkness of death (μέλανος . . . θανάτου) stands in implicit contrast to the radiant reputation the achiever leaves behind.

In this context, the phrase εὐώνυμον κτεάνων κρατίσταν χάριν is striking. The notion that a father leaves behind his good name as an inheritance for his children, that it inheres in the *oikos*-substance, is common in fiercely competitive shame cultures.[2] Thus J. K. Campbell describes a very similar notion of honor among the Sarakatsani, the modern mountain dwellers of rural Epirus: "Objectively, . . . honour is an aspect of the integrity and social worth of the family as this is judged by the community; subjectively it represents the moral solidarity of the family, an ideal circle that must be defended against any violation by outsiders. . . . all Sarakatsani are born with honour. But it is constantly threatened; and its conservation is, in effect, a struggle to maintain an ideal equality. When a life or the virtue of a woman has been taken away, something equivalent must be taken back if a family is not to fall forever from grace and social reputation."[3] Indeed, what I have designated the economy of *kleos* (and traced in Pindar as the *oikeia kala*) is what Pierre Bourdieu characterizes as "symbolic capital"—"the prestige and renown attached to a family and a name."[4] As Bourdieu emphasizes, there is perfect interconvertibility of symbolic and real capital, with the result that we must extend an economic analysis of preindustrial societies to those spheres we consider "spiritual" or disinterested. The concept of symbolic capital accounts for the continuum of *kala* we have observed; both concrete and abstract "goods" are designated thereby because both participate in a single economy of exchange.[5] What seems to us the striking concretization of εὐώνυμος . . . χάρις as "the best of possessions" reveals the continuity of *oikos*-substance.[6]

[1]Young 1968.21.
[2]Stoddart 1990.12–14 considers the notion of an inheritance of good repute in the context of the polis, citing parallel images from the Attic orators. I take the phrase *oikos*-substance in this sense from Jones 1962.92.
[3]Campbell 1964.193.
[4]Bourdieu 1977.179.
[5]Bourdieu 1977.177–183. Note that for Bourdieu, as for Pindar here, "symbolic capital . . . is perhaps *the most valuable form of accumulation*" in such a culture (179).
[6]Compare the observations of Jones 1962.92–95, 109–110, on the theme of *oikos*-substance in the *Oresteia*. If, allowing for the difference in genre, we read "hereditary

Thus a father leaves his reputation to his children. But precisely because achievement and the prestige it earns are family property, the enhancing effect of glory can work in the opposite direction as well. In Nemean 6, Pindar says of the current victor's paternal grandfather:

κεῖνος γὰρ Ὀλυμπιόνικος ἐὼν Αἰακίδαις
ἔρνεα πρῶτος ⟨ἔνεικεν⟩ ἀπ᾽ Ἀλφεοῦ,
καὶ πεντάκις Ἰσθμοῖ στεφανωσάμενος,
Νεμέᾳ δὲ τρεῖς, ἔπαυσε λάθαν
Σαοκλείδα᾽, ὃς ὑπέρτατος
Ἀγησιμάχοι᾽ ὑέων γένετο.
ἐπεί οἱ τρεῖς ἀεθλοφόροι πρὸς ἄκρον ἀρετᾶς
ἦλθον, οἵ τε πόνων ἐγεύσαντο.

(N.6.17–24)

For that one as Olympic victor first bore shoots from Alpheus for the Aiakidai, and having been crowned five times at the Isthmus and three times at Nemea, he ended the oblivion of Soklides, who turned out to be the best of the sons of Hagesimachos, since three prize-winners came to the peak of achievement for him, and they tasted of toils.

Here, the glorious achievements of three sons redeem the reputation of their father Soklides from oblivion. Though he accomplished nothing notable himself, he has become in retrospect "the best of the sons of Hagesimachos" *because* his house possesses the largest share of prestige from athletic victories.[7]

Indeed, Pindar goes on immediately to assert:

ἕτερον οὔ τινα οἶκον ἀπεφάνατο πυγμαχία ⟨πλεόνων⟩
ταμίαν στεφάνων μυχῷ Ἑλλάδος ἁπάσας.

(N.6.25–26)

Boxing has proclaimed no other house as steward of more crowns in the hollow of all Greece.

---

glory" for "hereditary guilt," we can take Jones's characterization as a very apt description of the Pindaric economy of *kleos*: "Family guilt is as much collective as inherited, in that the dead of the group form one enduring community with the living. . . . The morality of the *Oresteia* . . . is one with the great arc which its action describes, from the watchman perched on the palace roof to the acquitted Orestes whose response to deliverance from the Furies is a corporate thanksgiving: 'O Pallas, O saviour of my house!' . . . We have paused over the murder of Agamemnon to indicate the gross distortion caused by the severance of morality from *oikos*-focussed action in an attempt to make it serve the king's single fate" (94–95).

[7]I follow the interpretation of Bury 1890.107 for the sense of ὑπέρτατος and γένετο at N.6.21.

The prestige of victory merges with its physical emblems, the crowns, as the common treasure of the house. Thus Soklides and his entire patriline (including the current victor) benefit from the household's acquisitions. And as in Pythian 11, the poet's language blurs the family's real and symbolic capital by the use of the concrete word ταμίαν (like κτεάνων at P.11.58). The ταμίας is the steward who oversees the management of the family property.[8] Here, the house as a whole acts as "steward of crowns," ensuring their proper management and transmission to each new generation.

The language of Pythian 11 and Nemean 6 suggests that the source of the spatial imagery we have been considering is essentially economic. The poet's metaphoric geography maps the exchanges transacted between the house and the world. Thus, the voyage out to achievement is the means of production of symbolic capital, but that capital is not available until it is properly lodged in the house. For this reason, the loop of *nostos* is a recurrent image in the epinikia, for by this pattern the poet "brings the victory home"—that is, integrates it into the substance of the house.

The Pindaric economy of *kleos* is essentially a household concern. We have seen in Olympian 12 how Pindar evokes the return of Odysseus as a model for the victor's *nostos*. But what of the model of Telemachus, setting out to pursue his father's *kleos* and thereby to renew it as his own? Is there in epinikion a familial loop of *nostos* which corresponds to the familial stockpiling of prestige? Indeed, on occasion, Pindar's imagery echoes Telemachus's succinct description of his quest, πατρὸς ἐμοῦ κλέος εὐρὺ μετέρχομαι (*Ody.* 3.83). In Pythian 8, for example, Pindar says in praise of the victor Aristomenes, "For, hunting after [ἰχνεύων] your mother's brothers in wrestling, you did not shame Theognetos at Olympia or the bold-limbed victory of Kleitomachos at the Isthmus" (P.8.35–37). The same image occurs in Nemean 6, when Pindar says of the boy victor Alkimidas:

> παῖς ἐναγώνιος, ὃς ταύταν μεθέπων Διόθεν αἶσαν
> νῦν {τε} πέφανται
> οὐκ ἄμμορος ἀμφὶ πάλᾳ κυναγέτας,
> ἴχνεσιν ἐν Πραξιδάμαντος ἑὸν πόδα νέμων
> πατροπάτορος ὁμαιμίοις.
>
> (N.6.13–16)

[8]See Xenophon *Oeconomicus* 9.10–13. Notice that the name of Odysseus's *tamia* is Eurykleia!

A child taking part in the games, who, pursuing this lot from Zeus, is now revealed as a hunter not without a share in wrestling, plying his foot in the kindred traces of Praxidamos, his father's father.

Here the evocation of hunting in ἰχνεύων (P.8.35) is expanded in μεθέπων . . . κυναγέτας; Alkimidas, seeking the same glory as his grandfather (Διόθεν αἶσαν), tracks it down by following his route.

The metaphor of the victor's following in his grandfather's footsteps replaces the bleak image with which Nemean 6 begins. Pindar opens the poem by contrasting the race of the gods with the race of men: "The one is nothing, while the other the brazen heaven awaits as ever-safe seat. But in some way still we approximate to divinity,"

> καίπερ ἐφαμερίαν οὐκ εἰδότες οὐδὲ μετὰ νύκτας
> ἄμμε πότμος
> ἄντιν' ἔγραψε δραμεῖν ποτὶ στάθμαν.

(N.6.6–7)

although we do not know what course fate has inscribed for us, along which we run by day or through the nights.[9]

We do not even know along what course we are running by day or by night: the individual simply gropes along blindly into oblivion. How then, is it that mortals "approximate to divinity"? Pindar answers by shifting from the individual to the familial level, replacing the unknown, unmarked course of the opening with another. Thus ἴχνεσιν . . . ἑὸν πόδα νέμων (14) picks up the image of στάθμαν (3) and transforms it. The generations of a family replace the brief night and day of the individual's course, and the victor runs a track that is known because it was traveled by his ancestors before him. This is the image Becker describes as the "road of φυά." But again, Becker fails to note that the shape of this track is a loop—out to the sites of the games, "the peak of achievement" (N.6.11–12, 18), and then home with a bounty of crowns (N.6.25–26).[10]

The poet's most thoroughgoing representation of victory as part of a familial loop occurs in Nemean 2, a brief ode for an Acharnian pancration victor. The poem ends with the mention of the *nostos* of the victor, Timodemos:

[9]For στάθμα here as "course" rather than "goal," see Mezger 1880.415, Bury 1890.104–105, Stoneman 1979.75–77, Most 1987.576–577 with note 56; and cf. P.6.45.
[10]Becker 1937.65–68. Becker does note, however, that the "road of φυά" replicates the road of achievement.

τόν, ὦ πολῖται, κωμάξατε Τιμοδήμῳ σὺν εὐκλέι νόστῳ·
ἁδυμελεῖ δ᾽ ἐξάρχετε φωνᾷ.

(N.2.24–25)

Him [Zeus], O citizens, celebrate together with the glorious return for
Timodemos; but begin with sweet-sounding voice.

Here νόστος describes the victor's literal return from the games, while
the adjective εὐκλεής can be taken to refer to the effect of the poem
itself. Timodemos's return is glorious *because* it is celebrated by Pindar's
song.[11] But we do the poem an injustice if we understand the victor's
nostos as completely personal. The meaning of *nostos* here cannot be
considered in isolation, for it has been conditioned by the preceding
lines of the poem, whose theme is how the victor properly re-presents
his city and especially his family. Even the elaborate opening simile,
with its assertion that the victor's Nemean prize is only the beginning,
depends on the notion of hereditary excellence, τὸ συγγενές; Pindar can
be sure Timodemos will go on to greater things because of his family
history,

πατρίαν
εἴπερ καθ᾽ ὁδόν νιν εὐθυπομπός
αἰὼν ταῖς μεγάλαις δέδωκε κόσμον Ἀθάναις,

(N.2.6–8)

if indeed a life leading him straight along the road of his ancestors has
given him as an ornament to great Athens.

Note the images through which the poet chooses to express his cer-
tainty. Ancestral achievements have marked out a clear course for the
victor to follow. And implicitly that course leads him out to achievement and back to Athens, where his newly won prestige will adorn the
entire city.

At this point, Pindar introduces a mythological and cosmological
parallel to justify his expectations for the victor:

[11]Pindar implies the importance of song to *nostos* in his description of the negative
version, the νόστος ἔχθιστος suffered by the defeated athletes, at O.8.67–69. Notice that
the attributes of the "hateful return" which the poet chooses to mention are exactly the
negation of the *kōmos*, which goes conspicuously through the main streeets, and of the
vaunting song that attends it. For another, similar picture of the negative *nostos* of the
defeated, see P.8.81–87.

ἔστι δ᾽ ἐοικός
ὀρειᾶν γε Πελειάδων
μὴ τηλόθεν Ὠαρίωνα νεῖσθαι.

(N.2.10–12)

But it is fitting that Orion circle not far from the mountain Pleiades . . .

As Friedrich Mezger and J. B. Bury note, the force of this analogy depends on the word play of ὀρειᾶν and Ὠαρίωνα; as Bury puts it, "Timodemos follows as naturally in the wake of the Timodemids, as the mountain-hunter follows the mountain Doves." Furthermore, as Bury also notes, νεῖσθαι here has a double force, describing the motion of stars through the sky and also, as the verbal form of *nostos*, the return home.[12] Pindar has effectively mapped the πατρίαν . . . ὁδόν among the stars, implying that the circling course of the victor in the wake of his ancestors is as sure and eternal (at least in song) as the circuit of the constellations.[13]

Thus Pindar represents the victor's *nostos* as replicating the shape of his ancestors' achievements. Indeed, after the name pun of the central myth, Pindar explicitly describes the Timodemids' victories in terms of *nostos*:

παρὰ μὲν ὑψιμέδοντι Παρνασσῷ τέσσαρας ἐξ ἀέθλων νίκας ἐκόμιξαν·

(N.2.19)

Four victories from contests beside Parnassos ruling on high they conveyed safely home.

We should pay particular attention to ἐκόμιξαν here. For κομίζω is a verb Pindar favors, using it frequently in one of two meanings: "to preserve" or "to convey safely home."[14] As a verb of motion, κομίζω

[12]Bury 1890.30, following Mezger 1880.322–324. In spite of his unnecessary emendation Ὠαρίων᾽ ἀνεῖσθαι, his observation on the double meaning of the verb is still valid. It is tempting in this context to apply the linguistic model Douglas Frame has worked out for the *Odyssey*—the etymological and semantic connection of *nostos* with *noos*—for immediately before using the verb νεῖσθαι in a poem that hinges on *nostos*, Pindar names the victor as Τιμονόου παῖδ᾽ (N.2.10). If indeed we may regard this as the preservation of an extremely old association, the implication would be that Timodemos knows how to achieve an "honorable return" because he is the child of Timonoos. See Frame 1978.28–33.
[13]See Krischer 1965.34–35.
[14]"To preserve": O.2.14, P.5.51, and perhaps P.8.99; "to convey safely home":

can also denote metaphorical conveyance, as in Pythian 3, where Asclepius "conveyed back from death a man who had already been taken" (P.3.56–57). Slater considers the use of the verb here figurative, since its object is the abstract "four victories at Delphi."[15] But we are by now used to the blurring of concrete and abstract terms in descriptions of *oikos*-substance. So here, four victories represent an enormous gain in prestige which must be conveyed home to be added to the household's symbolic capital. As in Nemean 4, the announcement of victory is formulated in terms of the return home.

What is more, the poem's structure, its very spatial configuration, reinforces the generational continuity of achievement and *nostos*. Many commentators have noted the elaborate ring composition that structures the ode.[16] The victor's projected triumphs are echoed with inversion by the family's past victories, building a complete circle round the central cosmological image:

Nemean (line 4)
Isthmian (line 9)
Pythian (line 9)
Pythian (line 19, with responsion)
Isthmian (line 20)
Nemean (line 23).

Thus the victories, future and past, themselves form a loop that leads to the victor's *nostos* in the final lines. In addition, as Hermann Fränkel perceived, the end and beginning of the poem form a perfect grammatical loop, audible when the poem was sung repeatedly in the course of a procession:[17]

O.13.59, P.3.56, P.4.159, N.2.19, N.3.48, N.7.28, N.8.44. Pindar's usage is exceptional in that whenever he uses κομίζω as a verb of motion it seems to designate conveyance *back* or *home*. There are parallels for this usage in Herodotus, for example (1.67.4, 1.153.3, 2.121γ2, 4.179.3), but Herodotus also uses the verb for any kind of careful conveyance (1.188.2, 2.73.3,4, 2.86.1, 2, 2.140, 2.175.1, 3, 3.6.2, 3.98.1, 3.111.3, 4.33.1, 2, etc.). On the etymology and meaning of κομίζω, see Chantraine 1968.2.560 (s.v. κομέω), Frisk 1960.1.908, Wackernagel 1916.219, Hoekstra 1950.103–104, and Jebb 1894.152 (on Sophocles *Electra* 1113).

[15]Slater 1969a, s.v. κομίζω. I would like to add N.6.30 to Slater's class of figurative uses.

[16] See Shepphard 1922, Krischer 1965.37–38, and Newman and Newman 1984.110–111.

[17]Fränkel 1973.429 n. 6, Heath 1988.192.

τὰ δ' οἴκοι μάσσον' ἀριθμοῦ,
Διὸς ἀγῶνι. τόν, ὦ πολῖται, κωμάξατε Τιμοδήμῳ σὺν εὐκλέι νόστῳ·
ἀδυμελεῖ δ' ἐξάρχετε φωνᾷ.

(N.2.23–25)

Ὅθεν περ καὶ Ὁμηρίδαι
ῥαπτῶν ἐπέων τὰ πόλλ' ἀοιδοί
ἄρχονται, Διὸς ἐκ προοιμίου, καὶ ὅδ' ἀνήρ . . .

(N.2.1–3)

And [victories] at home more than number, at the contest of Zeus. Him [Zeus], O citizens, celebrate together with the glorious return for Timodemos; but begin with sweet-sounding voice. . . . From the very point where also the Homeridai, the singers, begin the majority of their stitched-together songs, from the prooimion of Zeus, also this man . . .

Even grammatically, the ancestors' τέλος—their victories at home at the contest of Zeus—become the present victor's ἀρχή. The cycle of *nostos*–achievement–*nostos* loops without end in the performance of the poem.

In Nemean 2, the poet takes the victor's achievement and inserts it in a familial pattern. The circuit out to the games and back home becomes the "ancestral road" along which his life will "guide him straight" (εὐθύπομπὸς αἰών [7–8]). But it is crucially Pindar's poem that gives the individual's *nostos* this aspect, for the current victory provides the occasion for the poet's commemoration of all the family's past victories and *nostoi*. The evocation of the former glories of the house is necessary because, as Pindar says, "ancient grace sleeps, and men are forgetful, [of] whatever does not arrive at the highest peak of poetic skill yoked with glorifying streams of songs" (I.7.16–19). In other words, the entropy of *kleos* results in a continual pressure to achieve: the house's reputation wanes if it is not periodically renewed. By the same token, each new achievement, properly publicized, reactivates all the symbolic capital of the house. Thus it is the poet's task to celebrate the current victory and recall the family's past achievements in order to consolidate and renew its stock of glory.

On occasion, the poet represents the act of commemoration itself as *nostos*, as the "bringing home" of the ancestors' achievements. Thus in Nemean 6, Pindar prays for sufficient poetic power to celebrate the victor's house:

εὔθυν' ἐπὶ τοῦτον, ἄγε, Μοῖσα,
οὖρον ἐπέων
εὐκλέα· παροιχομένων γὰρ ἀνέρων,
ἀοιδαὶ καὶ λόγοι τὰ καλά σφιν ἔργ' ἐκόμισαν·

(N.6.28–30)

Guide straight upon this [house],[18] Muse, a favoring breeze of songs
which make glorious, for of men who have gone by, songs and words
[alone] convey safely home their noble deeds.

The poet frames his prayer in spatial imagery: may the Muse "guide
straight" upon this house a "favoring breeze" of words. Then, in his
explanation for the prayer, Pindar continues that imagery. He speaks of
the dead as παροιχόμενοι, "those who have gone by." It is usually
assumed that the participle represents an ordinary way of designating
the dead, but in fact it is more likely to have seemed a striking metaphor
to Pindar's audience. Homer and Herodotus both use παροίχομαι
metaphorically to designate things that are temporally past, but only in
cases where the word could have no literal meaning. Thus the participle
is a standard epithet of time, of the night, or (as a neuter substantive) of
"past events" generally.[19] In spite of what the dictionaries say, the use of
οἴχομαι or its compounds absolutely to designate the dead is extremely
rare in extant Greek. Within the fifth century (outside of Pindar),
οἴχομαι occurs with this meaning once in a choral ode of Aeschylus'
Persians and once in a lyric exchange in Sophocles' *Electra*. Like the
Pindaric context here, both of these passages are densely metaphoric
and so should not be invoked to establish idiomatic usage.[20] Accordingly, we should not assume that παροίχομαι here is a "dead" metaphor devoid of imagistic force.

[18]Οἴκον implied from line 25; see Bury 1890.108 and Thummer 1968.1.129. As a
parallel for οὖρον ἐπέων εὐκλέα, cf. σὺν εὐκλεῖ νόστῳ at N.2.24.

[19]*Iliad* 10.252; Herodotus 1.209, 2.14, 3.86, 6.107, 7.120, 9.58, 9.60. See also Xenophon *HG* 1.4.17, *Anabasis* 2.4.1, *IG* I².90.15.

[20]Most of the passages listed in LSJ for οἴχομαι, ἀποίχομαι, and παροίχομαι meaning "to be dead" are not used absolutely. Either the author explicitly designates the goal
of the journey (as in "he went to the house of Hades," *Iliad* 22.213; cf. *Iliad* 23.101;
Aristophanes *Frogs* 83–85; Plato *Phaedo* 115d), or he adds a participle or adjective that
indicates the finality of the "going" (as in "having died, he is gone" Sophocles *Philoctetes*
414; cf. Euripides *Helen* 134). Furthermore, contra LSJ, compounds of οἴχομαι do not
mean "to have perished" in Aeschylus *Suppliants* 738 (see Friis Johansen and Whittle
1980.3.95–96) or Euripides *Herakles* 134. Once we have removed all these passages from
LSJ's lists, we are left with Pindar N.6.30, P.1.93, P.3.3 (on which see Young 1968.31,
35, 43 and Pelliccia 1987.54–58); Aeschylus *Persians* 546; Sophocles *Electra* 145–146; and
one third-century B.C. inscription (*SIG* 1219.10).

The juxtaposition of a favoring breeze that drives home with men who have gone by strongly evokes the motif of *nostos*, and indeed, one *nostos* in particular. For the obvious precursor for Pindar's use of compound forms of οἰχόμενος as epithets for men is the diction of the *Odyssey*. There οἰχόμενος and ἀποιχόμενος occur absolutely twenty-two times, always in the genitive and almost invariably as epithets of Odysseus.[21] The Homeric usage is not metaphorical: it is not a euphemistic way of saying that Odysseus is dead (like our "dear departed"). He is simply "gone," vanished from the world of men with no report, no *kleos*, to locate him. Thus the participles οἰχόμενος and ἀποιχόμενος express the same condition as Telemachus' plaint, οἴχετ᾽ ἄϊστος, ἄπυστος (*Ody.* 1.242). And it is Odysseus' condition, stranded in the limbo of obscurity, which Pindar's participle παροιχομένων evokes.[22]

In this context of opposing motions (the drift of the ancestors outward and the favoring breeze of song leading home), the logic of the metaphor demands that ἐκόμισαν also be taken as a verb of motion. Songs and words, the poet asserts, "convey safely home" the noble deeds of men who are gone. If the current victor knows the way to achievement because his ancestors have marked out the road, the converse is also true. His new success rescues their past glories from the oblivion of forgetfulness. Or as Pindar puts it here, since the celebration of victory is the means of commemoration, song itself brings home the family's past achievements. In both cases, the continuity of past and present is mapped spatially, expressed through the metaphors of departure, travel, and return.

Again in Nemean 8, Pindar expresses the continuity of memory in spatial terms. At one point he turns to address the victor's dead father:

> ὦ Μέγα, τὸ δ᾽ αὖτις τεὰν ψυχὰν κομίξαι
> οὔ μοι δυνατόν· κενεᾶν δ᾽ ἐλπίδων χαῦνον τέλος·
> σεῦ δὲ πάτρᾳ Χαριάδαις τ᾽ ἐλαφρόν

[21]*Odyssey* 1.135, 253, 281, 2.215, 264, 3.77, 4.164, 393, 14.8, 144, 376, 450, 15.270, 355, 17.296, 18.313, 19.19, 20.216, 290, 21.70, 395, 24.125. The only time the participle is used as an epithet of another character in the *Odyssey*, it designates Menelaus in the context of his own wandering (at 4.393).

[22]The same argument could be made for the deliberately ambiguous use of οἴχομαι in the first lines of Aeschylus *Persians* (τάδε μὲν Περσῶν τῶν οἰχομένων / Ἑλλάδ᾽ ἐς αἶαν πιστὰ καλεῖται). It may be that οἰχομένων here, like Pindar's uses of the compounds, resonates with Odysseus' standard epithet. If so, Aeschylus uses this Odyssean ambiguity in the service of dramatic irony: the chorus thinks that the Persians are "gone to Greece," while the audience knows that they are simply "gone."

ὑπερεῖσαι λίθον Μοισαῖον ἕκατι ποδῶν εὐωνύμων
δὶς δὴ δυοῖν.

(N.8.44–48)

O Megas, to convey your soul home again is not possible for me; but the
end of empty hopes is idle. But it is easy to set up a stone of the Muses for
your clan and for the Chariadai, thanks to the feet of two, twice glorious.

In context here, κομίξαι cannot mean "preserve": it would be nonsense
to say "I cannot preserve again" the soul of a dead man. It must be taken
as a verb of motion: I cannot convey your soul safely home again.[23] The
son's achievement, celebrated in Pindar's song, cannot secure the father's literal *nostos*. Instead, the son's victory provides the poet the
opportunity to erect a monument for Megas. As a λίθον Μοισαῖον, the
song itself becomes the father's *sēma*. We recognize the alternatives
desired by Telemachus in his speech to Athena—either to have the
father home or to ground his *kleos* in a tomb. The poet's words evoke a
minimal landscape: the house of the victor and the tomb of the father,
with the family's *kleos* arcing between them.

On occasion, the poet extends this temporal use of *nostos* imagery
from the continuity of past and present to the future. Thus the voyage
to the ends of the earth and back becomes a metaphor for the victor's
relation to posterity. Consider, for example, the play of imagery in
Pythian 1. In the second triad, Pindar introduces the notion of *nostos* as a
metaphor for the future glory of the newly founded city of Aitna.
Hieron's chariot victory is like "the first grace for seafaring men":

ναυσιφορήτοις δ᾽ ἀνδράσι πρῶτα χάρις
ἐς πλόον ἀρχομένοις πομπαῖον ἐλθεῖν οὖρον· ἐοικότα γάρ
καὶ τελευτᾷ φερτέρου νόστου τυχεῖν,

(P.1.33–35)

And [it is] the first grace for seafaring men as they begin the sailing that a
favoring breeze come to escort them. For it is likely also in the end [that
they will] happen upon a better return home.

Hieron's proclamation of his newly founded city at the site of the
games, like a favoring breeze when one sails out, augurs a better return
for the city's voyage into the future. The loop of *nostos* imposes itself
compellingly as the proper shape of achievement.

[23]Cf. P.3.56 and P.4.159, where the soul of Phrixos can be conveyed home (κομίξαι)
by the repossession of the golden fleece.

Pindar then picks up this seafaring imagery in the last triad, using it to
exhort Hieron to kingly virtues.[24] First briefly, the poet enjoins him,
"Guide your people with just rudder" (νώμα δικαίῳ πηδαλίῳ στρατόν
[P. 1.86]), and then he offers an extended image:[25]

εἴπερ τι φιλεῖς ἀκοὰν ἀδεῖαν αἰεὶ κλύειν, μὴ κάμνε λίαν δαπάναις·
ἐξίει δ' ὥσπερ κυβερνάτας ἀνήρ
ἱστίον ἀνεμόεν {πετάσαις}. μὴ δολωθῇς, ὦ φίλε, κέρδεσιν
    ἐντραπέλοις· ὀπιθόμβροτον αὔχημα δόξας
οἷον ἀποιχομένων ἀνδρῶν δίαιταν μανύει
καὶ λογίοις καὶ ἀοιδοῖς.

(P. 1.90–94)

If indeed you love always to hear a sweet hearing [i.e., to be well spoken
of], do not toil too much over expenditures, but let go your sail to the
wind just like a steersman. Do not be deceived, friend, by [the prospect
of] profits that turn you from your course; only the acclaim of men to
come, consisting of glory, reveals the way of life of men who have passed
away, by means of both chroniclers and poets.

In these lines, the poet elaborates a consistent system of imagery. Again,
Hieron is the pilot, but this time, it seems, of the ship of his own fame.
The poet's injunction to let the sail out to the wind recalls the "favoring
breeze" (πομπαῖον . . . οὖρον) of the second epode. In effect, Pindar
urges Hieron to sail boldly for the ends of the earth in expenditure,
implicitly promising him the return to future glory which figures in the
earlier passage. For ἀποιχομένων here, like παροιχομένων in Nemean
6, conjures up the model of the *Odyssey*. Within this metaphorical
landscape, men of the past are like Odysseus, stranded beyond the reach
of memory. Only the acclaim of men to come rescues these shipwrecks
from oblivion. Thus, the endurance of their fame into the future becomes their safe harbor, their welcoming hearth. And it is poets and
chroniclers who accomplish the *nostos* of "bygone" men by conveying
their glory to future generations.

The same pattern of the victors' reaching the metaphorical limits of
the earth and the poet's carrying them home again seems to generate the
imagery of the opening triad of Isthmian 4. At the end of the first
strophe Pindar speaks of the ἀρεταί of the Kleonymidai,

[24]That these injunctions are addressed to Hieron, not his son Deinomenes, is without
doubt. See Köhnken 1970.1–13 and Puelma 1972.86–109 for the relationship of poet and
king in advice contexts.
[25]On the progression of naval images, see Peron 1974.111.

αἶσι Κλεωνυμίδαι θάλλοντες αἰεί
σὺν θεῷ θνατὸν διέρχονται βιότου τέλος. ἄλλοτε δ᾽ ἀλλοῖος οὖρος
πάντας ἀνθρώπους ἐπαΐσσων ἐλαύνει.

(I.4.4–6)

with which the Kleonymidai, blooming ever with the god, go through to
the mortal end of life. But at different times, different winds rushing up
drive all men.

The poet's language here implies successful accomplishment (δι-,
τέλος), but accomplishment ultimately circumscribed by mortality
(θνατόν, wind imagery for vicissitude—cf. O.7.94–95). But in the
same metrical position at the end of the first antistrophe Pindar revises
this position:

ὅσσα δ᾽ ἐπ᾽ ἀνθρώπους ἄηται
μαρτύρια φθιμένων ζωῶν τε φωτῶν
ἀπλέτου δόξας, ἐπέψαυσαν κατὰ πᾶν τέλος· ἀνορέαις δ᾽ ἐσχάταισιν
οἴκοθεν στάλαισιν ἅπτονθ᾽ Ἡρακλείαις·

(I.4.9–12)

But however many witnesses of boundless fame of men living and dead
are blown among men, they have attained [them] according to every end;
and by extreme deeds of prowess they have fastened onto the Pillars of
Herakles from home.

The imagery has shifted imperceptibly: the winds of vicissitude have
been replaced by the winds of song, which blow the reputation of the
living and the dead back from the limits of the world to men. The
family's manly virtues alone, limited as they are by mortality, might
leave them stranded at the Pillars of Herakles, the farthest shore of
achievement, but song will bring their glory safely home.[26]
    In all these cases, the temporal continuity of the household—the
endurance of its reputation from past to future—is figured spatially.
The Odyssean loop of departure and return comes to represent the
oscillation of the family's *kleos*, as the achievements of one generation
fade, only to be renewed by those of the next. Given the occasion of the
present victory, poetry accomplishes a metaphorical *nostos* of the noble
deeds of the past. It is true that the ancestors as *bodies* require no return:

[26]For a somewhat different interpretation of this imagistic complex, see Peron
1974.198–200.

they are planted in their native soil for all time. But the memory of their achievements fades if not perpetually revived: in spatial terms, they drift from the *oikos*, their center, to the edges of memory.

But we must take one final turn on *nostos*. Perhaps because it is such an important element in the epinikian system, *nostos* also functions as a structuring principle in a number of odes, generating what seems to be one of the preferred shapes for the poems themselves—the loop. In a spatial mimesis of the victor, the poet enforces the metaphorical boundaries of achievement as aesthetic limits or turning points for the poem as well. In Nemean 3, for example, the poet's assertion that Aristokleides has reached the Pillars of Herakles in achievement first generates a brief explanatory narrative about these markers,

> ἥρως θεὸς ἃς ἔθηκε ναυτιλίας ἐσχάτας
> μάρτυρας κλυτάς· δάμασε δὲ θῆρας ἐν πελάγεϊ
> ὑπερόχους, ἰδίᾳ τ' ἐρεύνασε τεναγέων
> ῥοάς, ὁπᾷ πόμπιμον κατέβαινε νόστου τέλος,
> καὶ γᾶν φράδασε.
>
> (N.3.22–26)

which the hero god set up as glorious witnesses of the farthest sailing; but he mastered violent wild beasts in the sea, and on his own he found the streams of the shallows, where he disembarked the end which guided him back home again and he discovered the land.

This narrative, in turn, immediately evokes from the poet the dismayed exclamation,

> θυμέ, τίνα πρὸς ἀλλοδαπάν
> ἄκραν ἐμὸν πλόον παραμείβεαι;
> Αἰακῷ σε φαμὶ γένει τε Μοῖσαν φέρειν.
>
> (N.3.26–28)

My spirit, to what foreign shore have you led my voyage astray? I tell you to bring the Muse for Aiakos and his race.

The πόμπιμον . . . νόστου τέλος has in effect turned the poet back to his "home" subject, just as it sent Herakles home originally (note especially οἴκοθεν μάτευε [31]). Thus, the topos of the Pillars of Herakles functions structurally in the poem as a pivot, a turning point from praise of the victor (14–21) to the central mythic narrative of the Aiakidai (31–

64).[27] It is worth noticing how subtly Pindar accomplishes this transition; the Pillars of Herakles first appear as a reference to the victor and his achievements, then modulate imperceptibly into an aesthetic boundary for the poem itself.[28] Such smooth shifts from victor or hero to poet, as well as from topic to topic, seem to occur frequently at the spatial boundaries Pindar builds into his poems, encouraging us to perceive space as a fundamental structuring principle of the odes themselves.[29]

Nemean 4 contains a very similar transition. Pindar breaks off his narrative of the blessedness of Peleus—the Olympian gods themselves attended his wedding—by matter-of-factly observing, "The part of Gades toward darkness is not to be passed" (Γαδείρων τὸ πρὸς ζόφον οὐ περατόν [N.4.69]). But the poet continues immediately,

> ἀπότρεπε
> αὖτις Εὐρώπαν ποτὶ χέρσον ἔντεα ναός·
> ἄπορα γὰρ λόγον Αἰακοῦ
> παίδων τὸν ἅπαντά μοι διελθεῖν.
>
> (N.4.69–72)

Turn the equipment of the ship back again to the dry land of Europe; for it is impossible for me to go through the entire tale of the children of Aiakos.

What begins as a gnome referring to Peleus and the extraordinary divine favor he enjoyed becomes almost immediately an aesthetic injunction by the poet to himself, marking the boundary of the myth and the poet's return to the victor and his family as subject matter.[30] Indeed, the poet's "return" to the victor's *oikos* is made quite explicit:

> Θεανδρίδαισι δ' ἀεξιγυίων ἀέθλων
> κάρυξ ἑτοῖμος ἔβαν
> Οὐλυμπίᾳ τε καὶ Ἰσθμοῖ Νεμέᾳ τε συνθέμενος,
>
> (N.4.73–75)

[27]See Carey 1980.153–162 for a formal analysis of this passage.

[28]See Becker 1937.72, Peron 1974.34–35 and 79–81, and Steiner 1986.75. For such shifts from "subjective" to "objective" referent in transitions, see Hubbard 1985.133–162.

[29]In addition to the poems discussed in this section (N.3, N.4, P.10, I.6, N.6, O.13) and earlier sections (I.1, N.2), notice Pindar's tendency to name Memnon/the Ethiopians as the final entry in catalogs of Achilles' victims, from which he pivots back to praise of the victor (O.2.83, N.3.63; Memnon is the penultimate entry at I.5.40–41).

[30]Peron 1974.46 and 81–82. Becker 1937.71 sees these lines as simply a break-off formula, but Carey 1980.155 notes the shift of referent.

But I have come as ready herald of limb-exalting prizes for the Theandridai, having contracted at Olympia and at the Isthmus and at Nemea.

The aorist ἔβαν locates the poet at the house of the Theandridai, where
he has come as "ready herald" to announce the family's victories.

What is more, the transition through the Pillars of Herakles motif
participates in a system of imagery which structures the entire ode. The
poem forms a perfect loop: of twelve identical strophes, the first three
are devoted to the victor and his family, the central six to myths of the
Aiakidai (with a self-referential interlude by the poet), and the last three,
with a number of chiastic responsions, back to the victor's *oikos*.[31] The
transitions into and out of the myth are significant within this scheme.
At the end of the third strophe, describing Timasarchos' victories at the
games in Thebes, Pindar says,

> φίλοισι γὰρ φίλος ἐλθών
> ξένιον ἄστυ κατέδρακεν
> Ἡρακλέος ὀλβίαν πρὸς αὐλάν.

(N.4.22–24)

For having come as a friend for friends, he looked down on the host city,
toward the blessed court of Herakles.

The mention of Herakles gives the poet his lead-in to the myth (σὺν ᾧ
ποτε Τροΐαν κραταιὸς Τελαμὼν πόρθησε [25–26]). But essentially the
frame of the myth is spatial; it begins at Herakles' *oikos* and ends at
Gades, the farthest limit of the hero's wanderings.[32] Within these geographic transitions, the central myth is a poetic voyage through all the
lands conquered and ruled by Aiakids. Pindar pursues the Aiakid saga
to the Pillars of Herakles and then returns to the victor's *oikos*.

Even within this catalog of hegemony, Pindar maintains the metaphor of a journey for his poetic enterprise. He urges himself on,

> ἔμπα, καίπερ ἔχει βαθεῖα ποντιὰς ἅλμα

[31]On the structure of the ode, see Miller 1983; on the parallelism of the first and last
three strophes, see Köhnken 1971.191, 214–215.
[32]Up to line 53 we could take the organizing principle of the myth as chronological,
progressing through the generations of Aiakids. But note that at 54 Pindar backtracks
from Neoptolemus to Peleus and devotes as many lines to his story as to those of all the
other Aiakids combined. One of the consequences of placing Peleus at the end is the
opportunity it provides the poet of using the break-off formula of the limits of human
happiness (N.4.69).

μέσσον, ἀντίτειν᾽ ἐπιβουλίαις· σφόδρα δόξομεν
δαΐων ὑπέρτεροι ἐν φάει καταβαίνειν·

(N.4.36–38)

Still, although the deep saltwater of the sea holds you about the middle,
hold out against plots; we will be seen to disembark in the light very
much superior to enemies.[33]

In the middle of the myth Pindar is in midvoyage, surrounded by deep
sea (βαθεῖα ποντιὰς ἅλμα). Yet he expects, by completing his narration, to make a successful landing (καταβαίνειν).[34] And the poet will
disembark "in light" (ἐν φάει), in contrast to another man:

φθονερὰ δ᾽ ἄλλος ἀνὴρ βλέπων
γνώμαν κενεὰν σκότῳ κυλίνδει
χαμαὶ πετοῖσαν.

(N.4.39–41)

But another man with niggardly regard whirls an empty intention that
falls to the ground in darkness.

The man who stints his praise whirls an empty thought in darkness.
The image in γνώμαν κενεὰν σκότῳ κυλίνδει recalls the "obscure
man" in Nemean 3: ψεφεννὸς ἀνὴρ ἄλλοτ᾽ ἄλλα πνέων οὔ ποτ᾽
ἀτρεκεῖ κατέβα ποδί (N.3.41–42).[35] The parallel is significant. The
mean-spirited man here, like the ψεφεννὸς ἀνήρ, never lands at the
fixed shore of achievement, and therefore he languishes "in darkness."
By contrast, the poet who undertakes the full mythical "voyage" is
irradiated by the light of his accomplishment. But ἐν φάει stands in
contrast to another term as well. At the end of the myth, as we have

[33]Against Norwood 1945.270 n. 57, Farnell 1930.2.266, and Köhnken 1971.211,
Peron 1974.92–100 insists that these lines do not reflect Pindar's literal journey to Aigina
but continue the maritime metaphor. On these lines in general, see Miller 1983.
[34]The language of these lines is complicated by the presence of another image: the poet
wrestles with opponents as did the victor himself (ἔχει . . . μέσσον, ἀντίτειν᾽). I do not,
however, consider καταβαίνειν to be a wrestling image (as do Willcock 1982.4–10 and
Lefkowitz 1984.5–12), because such an interpretation would leave βαθεῖα ποντιὰς
ἅλμα isolated and completely unmotivated. That is, if Pindar wished to use only
wrestling imagery, he need not have introduced the sea at all. That it is here suggests that
a poetic voyage is implicit in these lines. See Carne-Ross 1985.115, 119, who connects
the sea here with the Pillars of Herakles at the end of the myth and concludes that the
image represents the sea of Aiakid legend.
[35]Bury 1890.72 and Miller 1983.209–210 cite this passage as a parallel.

seen, Pindar refers to the far side of Gades as "the part toward darkness" (τὸ πρὸς ζόφον). Thus it appears that the poet's course, like the victor's, is circumscribed and marked out by light—to the limits of achievement or myth (but no farther), then back to the victor's house.

A similar spatial conceit contributes to the poem's structure in Pythian 10. Instead of the Pillars of Herakles, the land of the Hyperboreans functions as the geographic boundary at which the poem pivots to and from the myth. Pindar closes the initial praise of the victor and his father with a geographic metaphor:

> ὅσαις δὲ βροτὸν ἔθνος ἀγλαΐαις ἁπτόμεσθα, περαίνει πρὸς ἔσχατον
> πλόον· ναυσὶ δ' οὔτε πεζὸς ἰὼν ⟨κεν⟩ εὕροις
> ἐς Ὑπερβορέων ἀγῶνα θαυμαστὰν ὁδόν.

> (P. 10. 28–30)

But however many glories we, the mortal race, fasten onto, he crosses to the farthest sailing. But neither with ships nor going on foot would you find the marvelous road to the gathering of the Hyperboreans.

But what begins as a topos of human limitation becomes the lead-in to the myth, which is in fact the story of Perseus' visit to the Hyperboreans. When the poet has concluded this mythic narrative (clearly marking its end by the verbal echo of θαυμαστὰν ὁδόν [30] by θαυμάσαι [48] in the same metrical position)[36] he enjoins himself:

> κώπαν σχάσον, ταχὺ δ' ἄγκυραν ἔρεισον χθονί
> πρῴραθε, χοιράδος ἄλκαρ πέτρας.
> ἐγκωμίων γὰρ ἄωτος ὕμνων
> ἐπ' ἄλλοτ' ἄλλον ὥτε μέλισσα θύνει λόγον.

> (P. 10. 51–54)

Check your oar and swiftly fix the anchor in the earth from the prow, as a defense against the rocky reef. For the peak of encomiastic hymns flits from topic to topic like a honeybee.

The geographic metaphor now applies not to the victor but to the poet and the course of the poem, as he turns from the myth to another λόγος, or topic (cf. N.4.71–72: λόγον Αἰακοῦ παίδων).[37] The closing triad

---

[36]For the verbal echo marking ring composition, see Illig 1932.92 n. 2.

[37]Peron (1974.68–71) notes the structural importance of maritime imagery in introducing and closing the myth in Pythian 10. See also Becker 1937.71.

then immediately returns to Thessaly, conjuring up a chorus of Thessalians who will "pour forth my sweet song around Peneius"—a *kōmos* to celebrate future victories. These lines (55–58) repeat the victor's name juxtaposed to the mention of the poet's voice from the opening strophe, Ἱπποκλέᾳ θέλοντες ἀγαγεῖν ἐπικωμίαν ἀνδρῶν κλυτὰν ὄπα ("wishing to lead the celebratory voice of men which makes glorious for Hippokleas" [5–6]). The echo of the festal occasion after the break-off from the myth reinforces the sense of Pindar's poetic return to the victor and his *oikos*.

In the poems we have been looking at, Pindar makes smooth transitions of referent within a single geographic image. In Isthmian 6, he sets up instead two parallel tracks of imagery, creating concentric circles of *nostos* which structure the poem. In the first triad he makes a general statement that seems to fit both the victor and his father:

εἰ γάρ τις ἀνθρώπων δαπάνᾳ τε χαρείς
καὶ πόνῳ πράσσει θεοδμάτους ἀρετάς
σύν τέ οἱ δαίμων φυτεύει δόξαν ἐπήρατον, ἐσχατιαῖς ἤδη πρὸς ὄλβου
βάλλετ᾽ ἄγκυραν θεότιμος ἐών.

(I.6.10–13)

> For if someone of men, rejoicing in both expense and toil, accomplishes god-built achievements and the daimon plants lovely glory together with him, already he has cast his anchor at the limits of blessedness, being honored by the gods.

The poet then picks up and completes this spatial metaphor in the last triad, at the end of a catalog of the family's victories:

ἀνὰ δ᾽ ἄγαγον ἐς φάος οἵαν μοῖραν ὕμνων·
τὰν Ψαλυχιαδᾶν δὲ πάτραν Χαρίτων
ἄρδοντι καλλίστᾳ δρόσῳ,
τόν τε Θεμιστίου ὀρθώσαντες οἶκον τάνδε πόλιν
θεοφιλῆ ναίοισι·

(I.6.62–66)

> And they have brought back to the light what sort of share of hymns, and they water the clan of the Psalychiadai with the most beautiful dew of the Graces, and having set upright the house of Themistios, they inhabit this city dear to the gods.

Slater lists this passage under his definition "a. bring up, raise, awaken" for ἀνάγω.[38] But forming the transition as it does between the sites of the family's victories and the mention of their clan, house, and city, the verb is perhaps better translated "they have brought back."[39] If we allow ourselves this translation, the logic of the passage immediately becomes much clearer; lines 63–66 are then an elaboration of 62, detailing the different groups within Aigina which benefit from the family's "share of hymns." Thus, the poet says, they water with the most beautiful dew of the Graces their *clan*, and having set their *house* upright, they inhabit this *city*.

Again, light attends the victors' successful return home, and the phrase ὀρθώσαντες οἶκον makes explicit the effect of their achievements on the house. The winning of new *kleos* is a prop or support for the *oikos*, which would otherwise sink into oblivion.[40] And here, as in Nemean 6, Nemean 8, Pythian 1, and Isthmian 4, song is the intermediary that ensures this continuity of glory for the household. For the poet says not what a share of *victories* but what a share of *hymns* they have led back to the light. Thus the poet picks up the image of the "limits of blessedness" and accomplishes a "return" of the family's glories home through poetry.

Within the ring of this familial *nostos*, Pindar has set another, purely poetic one. In the first epode, he breaks off from praise of the victor to address the Aiakidai:

> ὕμμε τ᾽, ὦ χρυσάρματοι Αἰακίδαι,
> τέθμιόν μοι φαμὶ σαφέστατον ἔμμεν
> τάνδ᾽ ἐπιστείχοντα νᾶσον ῥαινέμεν εὐλογίαις.
> μυρίαι δ᾽ ἔργων καλῶν τέτμανθ᾽ ἑκατόμπεδοι ἐν σχερῷ κέλευθοι
> καὶ πέραν Νείλοιο παγᾶν καὶ δι᾽ Ὑπερβορέους·
>
> (I.6.19–23)

I affirm that it is my clearest ordinance, whenever I come to this island, O gold-charioted Aiakidai, to sprinkle you with praises. And ten thousand roads of noble deeds are cut, a hundred feet wide in succession, both beyond the springs of the Nile and through the Hyperboreans.

The image of ten thousand roads of noble deeds starts out as a hyper-

---

[38]Slater 1969a s.v. ἀνάγω.

[39]See LSJ, ἀνάγω II.

[40]Cf. Aeschylus *Agamemnon* 897–898, where Clytemnestra describes Agamemnon's successful return home as ὑψηλῆς στέγης στῦλον ποδήρη, "the fixed pillar of the lofty roof."

bolic expression of the extent of Aiakid fame.[41] But again, the poet uses the geographic ends of the earth as a pivot to the myth:

> οὐδ' ἔστιν οὕτω βάρβαρος οὔτε παλίγγλωσσος πόλις,
> ἅτις οὐ Πηλέος ἀίει κλέος ἥρωος, εὐδαίμονος γαμβροῦ θεῶν,
> οὐδ' ἅτις Αἴαντος Τελαμωνιάδα
> καὶ πατρός· τόν. . . .

(I.6.24–27)

Nor is there any city so barbarous or perverse of tongue which does not hear the report of the hero Peleus, blessed son-in-law of the gods, or of Ajax the son of Telamon and his father; him. . . .

The Nile and the Hyperboreans, the farthest barbarian cities, offer the poet the pretext for beginning his mythic narrative (which starts with the relative τόν).

Then, after narrating the story of Herakles' visit to Telamon and his prophecy of Ajax's birth and achievements, Pindar breaks off from the myth:

> ἐμοὶ δὲ μακρὸν πάσας ⟨ἀν⟩αγήσασθ' ἀρετάς·
> Φυλακίδᾳ γὰρ ἦλθον, ὦ Μοῖσα, ταμίας
> Πυθέᾳ τε κώμων Εὐθυμένει τε·

(I.6.56–58)

But [it would be] long for me to go through all their achievements, for I have come, O Muse, as steward of *kōmoi* for Phylakides and Pytheas and Euthymenes.

Slater translates ⟨ἀν⟩αγήσασθ' as "relate," but he notes that Pindar plays on the verb's literal meaning, "drive onward" in Olympian 9: εἴην εὑρησιεπὴς ἀναγεῖσθαι πρόσφορος ἐν Μοισᾶν δίφρῳ ("May I be fluent in verse, so as suitably to drive onward/narrate in the chariot of the Muses" [O.9.80–81]).[42] I would suggest that Pindar is taking advantage of both meanings here as well. He began the myth with the assertion that there are innumerable roads cut a hundred feet wide in succession to praise the Aiakidai. He ends the myth with a disclaimer framed in the same imagery: "[it would be] long for me to go through

---

[41]Cf. I.4.1–3, Bacch. 5.31–33.

[42]Slater 1969a s.v. ἀναγέομαι. ⟨ἀν⟩αγήσασθ' is Mingarelli's universally accepted correction for the MSS' ἀγήσασθ'.

[drive along/narrate] all their achievements."[43] The reason the poet offers for breaking off his mythic narrative contributes significantly to the metaphorical framework, "for," he says, "I have come . . . as ταμίας . . . κώμων for Phylakides and Pytheas and Euthymenes."[44] Pindar represents himself as a servant of the house of the victors and implies in breaking off that his responsibilities lie there, not chasing Aiakids all over the map. The myth has itself become a distant land from which the poet must return to the victor's *oikos*.

But of course, Pindar's disclaimer is qualified, since his journey into myth benefits the house just as the victor's journey to achievement does. By his divagation into myth at the center of the ode, the poet appropriates the prestige of the heroic past for the household he celebrates. The myth itself becomes part of the symbolic capital of the victor's *oikos*. On one occasion, the poet explicitly acknowledges this act of appropriation. In Nemean 6, Pindar frames an abbreviated Aiakid myth with spatial imagery very similar to that of Isthmian 6. The poet introduces the Aiakidai:

> πλατεῖαι πάντοθεν λογίοισιν ἐντὶ πρόσοδοι
> νᾶσον εὐκλέα τάνδε κοσμεῖν· ἐπεί σφιν Αἰακίδαι
> ἔπορον ἔξοχον αἶσαν ἀρετὰς ἀποδεικνύμενοι μεγάλας,
> πέταται δ' ἐπί τε χθόνα καὶ διὰ θαλάσσας τηλόθεν
> ὄνυμ' αὐτῶν· καὶ ἐς Αἰθίοπας. . . .
>
> (N.6.45–49)

There are broad roads from everywhere for chroniclers to adorn this island so that it is glorious. Since the Aiakidai have given them an exceptional share [of glory], displaying great achievements, and their name flies afar over the earth and through the sea. Even to the Ethiopians. . . .

The mention of the Ethiopians provides the pretext for a brief narrative of Achilles' duel with Memnon. But almost immediately, the poet turns from the myth with an extended image of roads: "And these things older [poets] found as a highway [ὁδὸν ἀμαξιτόν]. And I too follow

---

[43]Note that the adjective μακρόν suits both meanings of the verb, since it can designate both temporal and spatial length (cf. I.4.13, P.4.247).
[44]Cf. N.4.73–75, and see Burnett 1989.292 n. 28 for the implications of ταμίας . . . κώμων.

diligently. But they say that the wave whirling beside the ship [τὸ δὲ παρ ποδὶ ναός] most of all moves the spirit" (N.6.53–57). These lines are in fact an elaborate break-off formula, justifying the poet's attention to "that which is beside his foot." By now we are very familiar with the poet's excuse for sidestepping the high road of epic narrative:

> ἑκόντι δ᾽ ἐγὼ νώτῳ μεθέπων δίδυμον ἄχθος
> ἄγγελος ἔβαν,
> πέμπτον ἐπὶ εἴκοσι τοῦτο γαρύων
> εὖχος ἀγώνων ἄπο, τοὺς ἐνέποισιν ἱερούς,
> Ἀλκίμιδα, τέ γ᾽ ἐπαρκέσαι
> κλειτᾷ γενεᾷ·

(N.6.57–61)

But undertaking with willing back a double burden, I have come as messenger, announcing that you, Alkimidas, have provided your glorious family this twenty-fifth boast from the contests that [men] call holy.

These lines recall both Isthmian 6.56–58 and Nemean 4.73–75. Always in the same position, after a geographic transition from the myth, all three passages share the image of the poet coming to the victor's *oikos* (ἔβαν, ἦλθον) in some concrete capacity of service (ἄγγελος, ταμίας, κάρυξ). Two of the three even emphasize his willingness to perform this service (ἑκόντι . . . νώτῳ, ἑτοῖμος).[45]

But one element in these lines is unparalleled in the other two passages: the poet's assertion that he has come bearing a "double burden" (δίδυμον ἄχθος). What is this burden and why is it double? The commentators suggest that ἄχθος is the weight of praise or glory the poet bears to the victor's house, in an image drawn from the import and export of cargo (cf. N.6.32–33, P.2.67–68). Bury and Farnell also suggest that the poet's double cargo refers to praise of both the Aiakidai

---

[45]See Becker 1937.80–82. A very similar transition from the myth occurs in Olympian 13. In contrast to Pegasos, who remains in heaven (where he bears Zeus's lightning bolts [Hesiod *Theogony* 285–286]), the poet is responsible for other bolts: ἐμὲ δ᾽ εὐθὺν ἀκόντων / ἱέντα ῥόμβον παρὰ σκοπὸν οὐ χρή / τὰ πολλὰ βέλεα καρτύνειν χεροῖν. / Μοίσαις γὰρ ἀγλαοθρόνοις ἑκών / Ὀλιγαιθίδαισίν τ᾽ ἔβαν ἐπίκουρος ("I must not discharge too many bolts from my hands, sending forth the straight whirl of spears beside the mark, for I have come as willing helper for the shining-throned Muses and the Oligaithidai" [O.13.93–97]). Note γάρ (like I.6.57), ἐπίκουρος (like ἄγγελος, ταμίας, κάρυξ), ἑκών, and ἔβαν of the poet's return from the myth in heaven to the house of the victor. The similarities in these passages suggest that the poet's "*nostos* from the myth" is such a fundamental conception that it has already generated its own conventional topoi within epinikion (and cf. fr. 94b 31–41 for a similar topos in another genre).

and Alkimidas and his family.[46] Thus, the image of a freight of glory represents concretely the symbolic capital that victory and its celebration add to the house of the victor, while διδυμον acknowledges that the poet's voyage into myth contributes to that familial cargo.

We can corroborate the implication of Pindar's image with a story from the life of Simonides, the inventor of epinikion. The story is preserved only in late sources, but with a pedigree suggesting that versions of it were much older.[47] It is said that Simonides composed an epinikion for Scopas of Thessaly, in which he included much about Castor and Pollux. His patron, Scopas, annoyed by the poet's digressions, declared that he would pay only half the fee agreed on for the song and bid Simonides collect the other half from the Tyndaridai. Shortly afterward, during the banquet celebrating the victory, Simonides was summoned out by a messenger who told him that two young men urgently wished to speak to him outside. When he went outside, the poet found no one, but while he was looking the roof of the banqueting chamber collapsed, killing all within. Indeed, the banqueters were so badly crushed that they could not be identified by their relatives for proper burial. Simonides alone was able to identify them by recalling the order in which they had reclined at the banquet. And this experience, according to the story, inspired Simonides to invent his memory system, whereby one remembers things by mentally locating them in a particular sequence in space.[48]

This is the tale as Cicero narrates it in *De oratore*, as a prelude to the discussion of the part played by memory in rhetoric. For Cicero's purposes, the first half of the story—Scopas' stinginess and Simonides' "payment" by the Dioscuri—is unnecessary; all that is required for the

---

[46]Bury 1890.101, 112, Farnell 1930.2.286, and Hubbard cited in Nagy 1990.16 n. 44.

[47]The full story is recounted by Cicero *De oratore* 2.86; Quintilian *Inst.* 11.2.11–16; and Phaedrus *Fabulae* 4.25 (without names for the protagonists). We also find allusions to the tale in Callimachus fr. 64 Pfeiffer; Ovid *Ibis* 509–510; Valerius Maximus 1.8. Ext. 7; Alciphron *Epistulae* 3.32.2; Aristides *Orationes* 50.36; Aelian fr. 78 Hercher; and Libanius *Orationes* 5.53. Quintilian also offers a pedigree of different versions of the story which extends all the way back to "some passage in Simonides" (Quintilian *Inst.* 11.2.14). This is not to claim with Molyneux 1971 that we can extract historical data from the fantasies of ancient biography. Rather, I assume that the stories that accrete around ancient poets are symptomatic of the culture that invented them. Slater (1972.236–238) regards the story as no older than the late fourth century, but, as I hope to demonstrate, the underlying assumptions of the story seem to suit an older context. Slater (1972.238) makes the intriguing suggestion that "somewhere Simonides sang of the fall of a house, and this was taken literally."

[48]For the tradition and the method, see Yates 1966.1–49.

invention of the memory system is the collapse of the roof with Simonides outside. Given the contextual irrelevance of the first half of the story, Cicero's impulse to narrate it suggests a coherence that has nothing to do with rhetoric. Indeed, we can read the entire narrative as a parable about the relation of the epinikian poet to the house of his patron. Within the logic of epinikion, the tale of the Dioscuri is essential because it provides the *cause* for the second half of the story: the collapse of the roof is the direct result of Scopas' rejection of the mythic half of Simonides' ode. The poet attempts to enhance the patron's glory by incorporating into his poem a myth of the Dioscuri, but his mean-spirited patron will not accept the poet's "double cargo."[49] Instead, Scopas is willing to pay only "half" (*dimidium*) for his half of the poem. As a result of Scopas' too-narrow definition of *oikeios*, his house collapses and his line is (literally) effaced. The rest of the story, then, literalizes other motifs we have traced through Pindar's imagery, for in this anecdote, as in Pindar's odes, only the memory of the poet rescues the family's dead from oblivion. By securing their proper burial, the poet enables the family's name and glory to continue.[50]

It is the epinikian economy of *kleos* which makes sense of Cicero's narrative. In a double movement, the poet secures the symbolic capital of the victor's house: first, trying to augment it with the glory of the Dioscuri, then providing the faceless Scopadai with tombs to anchor their name. In a different register, this same economic model explains the poet's spatial mimesis of the victor, for the reason that the road of song traces the same circuit as the road of achievement and the road of the ancestors is that all three serve and express the economic interests of the house.[51] The victor's ultimate goal in winning *kleos* is to bring it home, to set it in the house as a renewal of past achievements and an inspiration to future glories. If it is not set within this temporal framework, accessible to all the generations of the family—which means metaphorically within the spatial framework of the *oikos*—the *kleos* won has no fixity. In order to win glory, the individual athlete follows in

---

[49]For an interpretation of Cicero's narrative along similar lines, see Miller 1983.210 n. 30.

[50]Gzella 1971.194–195 and Svenbro 1976.170–172, against Slater 1972, take the story as archaic and interpret it as a warning to the poet's patrons not to renege on his fee. Such an interpretation, however, does not account for Scopas' reason for withholding only *half* his fee nor for the particular form his "punishment" takes. As for the relation of burial to remembrance, I shall consider it in greater detail in Chapter 3.

[51]Becker 1937.84 notes the equivalence of metaphorical paths: "Achievement, glory, song—somehow they all go the same road" (my translation).

the footsteps of his ancestors, out to achievement and back again. Thus the road of achievement and the road of the ancestors are one. In like manner, the road of song enables the poet to follow in the footsteps of his (poetic) ancestors in order to convey the fruit of his efforts to the victor's house. And thus all three interconnected images function within epinikion to assert the central importance of the house in athletic victory and its celebration.

CHAPTER 3

Funeral Rites and New Birth

Through the imagery of departure and return, Pindar represents the traffic between the house and the world. Another set of images allows the poet to depict victory and its celebration in terms of the household's internal economy—as the perpetuation of funeral ritual and as the birth of an heir for the house. In the classical Greek polis, the right of inheritance carried with it the duties of proper burial and the maintenance of funeral cult.[1] Ideally, this system guaranteed the commemoration of the dead within the *oikos*. Periodic grave offerings—libations of milk, honey, oil, wine, or water and wreaths to adorn the gravestone— were believed to nourish and sustain the dead of the household, providing them with some kind of continued existence and participation in the life of the family.[2]

The obligation to one's ancestors was also an obligation to the future, for the duty of maintaining the funeral cult made it essential that the *oikos* continue. As Walter Burkert observes, "The cult of the dead remains the foundation and expression of family identity: the honour accorded to forebears is expected from descendants: from the remembrance of the dead grows the will to continue."[3] Thus we find in Greek

---

[1]Nilsson 1968.1.181, Fustel de Coulanges 1980.26–31, 40–86, Burkert 1985.192–194, Stoddart 1990.5–13, Humphreys 1983.83–84. We can say further that the duty to the ancestral graves imposed not only temporal but also spatial continuity on the *oikos*, for the representative of the house had to go home to care for his ancestors' tombs.

[2]For offerings, see Stengel 1920.146–149, Kurtz and Boardman 1971.148, and Burkert 1985.194. For wreaths and crowns, see also Aeschylus *Choephori* 95. For the nourishing effect of offerings on the dead, see Onians 1951.271–279, Jones 1962.98.

[3]Burkert 1985.194.

thought an intimate connection between the family's cult of the dead and the obligation to procreate—to carry the family's property and name into the future. W. K. Lacey aptly characterizes this association of ideas:

An *oikos* without children was also not fully an *oikos*. Every Greek family looked backwards and forwards all the time. It looked backwards to its supposed first founder, and shared a religious worship with others with a similar belief; it also looked forwards to its own continuance, and to preservation for as many future generations as possible of the cult of the family which the living members practised in the interest of the dead. The son of a house was therefore . . . under a strong obligation to marry and procreate an heir for the *oikos* in order to keep the *oikos* alive. . . . An *oikos* was . . . a living organism which required to be renewed every generation to remain alive; it supported its living member's needs for food, and its deceased members' needs for the performance of cult rituals. A childless *oikos* was visibly dying—no man's life-span is all that long—so we may appreciate the joy with which a child, and especially the first-born son of a family, was received.[4]

Pindar explicitly articulates this same position on one occasion, in a fragment conventionally taken to be a partheneion:[5]

ἀθάναται δὲ βροτοῖς
ἀμέραι, σῶμα δ᾽ ἐστὶ θνατόν.
ἀλλ᾽ ᾧτινι μὴ λιπότεκνος σφαλῇ πάμπαν οἶκος βιαίᾳ δαμεὶς ἀνάγκᾳ,
ζώει κάματον προφυγὼν ἀνιαρόν·

(fr. 94a SM, 14–20)

The days are immortal for men, but the body is mortal. But for whomever the house is not tripped up entirely, mastered by violent necessity by being deprived of children, he lives having escaped grievous toil.

"The days are immortal for men, but the body is mortal." Here the kind of immortality Pindar offers is not personal but familial. Because his house is not tripped up by being bereft of children, a man "lives having escaped grievous toil." The subject of the last line lives though he is dead; he survives not in body, but through the continuity of his *oikos*.[6] This double obligation of the heir to the past and the future con-

[4]Lacey 1968.15–16.
[5]On the problems of taking this poem as a partheneion, see Kirkwood 1982.333.
[6]See Gundert 1935.17, 112 esp. nn. 46, 47. Compare Aeschylus *Choephori* 504–507.

stitutes what I have called the temporal imperative of the household. And just as Pindar takes up the model of spatial continuity and deploys it in metaphor, so also he makes use of imagery drawn from funeral cult and new birth. Thus the poet can represent victory and celebratory song as funeral libations poured to the dead ancestors and as the birth of a new heir for the house. Various scholars have recognized and attempted to explain the image of funeral libations of song. Gerhard Wilhelmi, in his study of liquid imagery for speech in Greek literature, notes the image and suggests that it arises from Pindar's representation of his song as "Muses' wine." Once poetry is wine, according to Wilhelmi, it can serve all the same functions literal wine serves.[7] But this is to invert cause and effect in the analysis of metaphor: Pindar does not use the image of funeral libations *because* he has represented his song as wine. Rather, the images of song as wine and as funeral libation are both effects of an association of phenomena by poet and audience, based on analogous social functions. Thus we cannot explain one image simply by referring to another that is equally symptomatic.[8]

Charles Segal discusses the image as a form of communication between the living and the dead. As he observes, the metaphor of song as funeral libation is a way of bringing the past into the present and establishing "the continuity that is one of [Pindar's] main poetic goals."[9] Segal is fairly vague, however, about exactly which community is involved in the poet's establishment of continuity.[10] Finally, Robert Stoddart has considered the image within the context of inheritance—as part of the rights and duties of the heir of the house. Stoddart alone of modern critics has recognized the close link between the image of funeral libations and that of the birth of an heir.[11] This association of images reveals the context in which both must be understood: it is the continuity of the *oikos* which generates Pindar's imagery. What makes these metaphors possible is the isomorphism of the terms within the life of the house. Each new victory and celebration, like the maintenance of cult or the birth of an heir, guarantees the survival in memory of all the family's past achievements. Just like a literal libation or the literal birth of an heir, athletic success and epinikion preserve and renew the vitality

[7]Wilhelmi 1967.41, 48–49.

[8]For a very different treatment of the overlap of triumphal and funerary imagery, see Duchemin 1955.269–296.

[9]Segal 1985.206–209 (quotation from 207).

[10]But see Segal 1985.210, where he notes "the emphasis on family solidarity" in O.8.74–84.

[11]Stoddart 1990.5–15.

of the house. Thus I wish to follow and extend Stoddart's interpretation, setting both images within the sphere of intrafamilial exchanges, for as we shall see, inheritance is only one half of a reciprocal exchange between ancestors and descendants.

Consider the final triad of Olympian 8, which describes in some detail the effect of victory on the victor's *oikos*. Pindar begins by characterizing the response of the victor's paternal grandfather:

> πατρὶ δὲ πατρὸς ἐνέπνευσεν μένος
> γήραος ἀντίπαλον·
> Ἀΐδα τοι λάθεται
> ἄρμενα πράξαις ἀνήρ.
>
> (O.8.70–73)

> But he inspired in his father's father strength to wrestle with old age; to be
> sure, when he has accomplished fitting things, a man forgets Hades.

On his triumphal return, the victor inspires in his grandfather the "strength to wrestle against old age." Ἀντίπαλον is an appropriate metaphor, for the victor is a wrestler, but perhaps a bit surprising in this context since it seems to invert Pindar's usual idea of hereditary excellence, τὸ συγγενές or *phyē*.[12] Usually the victor's hereditary quality and the example of his ancestors' triumphs instill in him the force needed to win. Here, the victor's triumph infuses his grandfather with renewed strength. Indeed, these lines suggest a more reciprocal relation between ancestors and descendants: the former transmit to the latter their quality, *aretē* or strength; then the latter reinfuse their ancestors with these qualities once they have won by virtue of them. The gnomic observation Pindar adds is surprisingly slippery when we look at it closely, for the victor must be the ἀνήρ who has accomplished fitting things, but his grandfather is the one who "forgets Hades." The blurred reference of the sentence replicates the exchange of μένος, superimposing grandfather and grandson.[13]

But the *oikos* embraces not only the living ancestors but also the dead, and they too are affected by the triumphal return of the individual. Pindar continues:

[12]On ἀντίπαλον, see Renehan 1969b.218 and Carey 1989b.4.
[13]I hope to consider the ambiguity of this passage in greater detail in a forthcoming article.

ἀλλ᾽ ἐμὲ χρὴ μναμοσύναν ἀνεγείροντα φράσαι
χειρῶν ἄωτον Βλεψιάδαις ἐπίνικον,
ἕκτος οἷς ἤδη στέφανος περίκειται φυλλοφόρων ἀπ᾽ ἀγώνων.
ἔστι δὲ καί τι θανόντεσσιν μέρος
κὰν νόμον ἐρδομένων·
κατακρύπτει δ᾽ οὐ κόνις
συγγόνων κεδνὰν χάριν.
Ἑρμᾷ δὲ θυγατρὸς ἀκούσαις Ἰφίων
Ἀγγελίας, ἐνέποι κεν Καλλιμάχῳ λιπαρὸν
κόσμον Ὀλυμπίᾳ, ὅν σφι Ζεὺς γένει
ὤπασεν.

(O.8.74–84)

But it is fitting for me, awakening remembrance to declare the epinikian
peak of hands for the Blepsiadai, whom now a sixth wreath from the
crown-bearing contests surrounds. But there is also some share to the
dead of rites performed according to custom; and the dust does not hide
the dear grace of relatives. And Iphion, having heard from Angelia,
daughter of Hermes, could report to Kallimachos the shining ornament
at Olympia, which Zeus has bestowed on their race.

The present victory rouses remembrance of past triumphs (74–76) and
its report will go even to the dead ancestors (81–84). Set between these
two assertions is Pindar's observation that "there is also some share to
the dead of rites performed according to custom; and the dust does not
hide the dear grace of relatives." As Gildersleeve and Farnell note, κὰν
νόμον ἐρδομένων refers to ritual offerings to the dead; the offerings are
called τὰ νόμιμα or τὰ νομιζόμενα, while ἔρδειν has a special ritual
sense.[14] Pindar's four-line reference to such grave offerings is more than
a parenthesis to justify his belief that the dead are conscious and so take
an interest in their descendants' doings, as Farnell would have it.[15] More
than that, Pindar seems to be setting up a kind of parallelism: as the dead
have a share in the rites their living descendants perform, so also they
partake of their heirs' athletic victories and the song that commemorates

[14]Gildersleeve 1890.199, Farnell 1930.2.66; see Kurtz and Boardman 1971.147–148
and LSJ, s.v. ἔρδω, 2.
[15]Farnell 1930.2.66: "The dead have their share in the νόμιμα ἱερά, which shows that
they are conscious; and therefore they may well be interested in the triumphs of their
living kindred." Gildersleeve 1890.199–200 perceives the analogy Pindar sets up: "As the
dead are not insensible of rites paid in their honor, so they are not blind to the glory
gained by their kindred."

them. As the grave offerings somehow infuse new life into the dead, so too new triumphs "awaken" the old ones for the household.[16]

The analogy the poet sets up is enhanced by the use of χάρις in this context. In the diction of epinikion, *charis* can be used to designate the grace of victory, and so we can understand it here.[17] But, occurring right after κὰν νόμον ἐρδομένων, it may also refer to funeral offerings, as it does three times in Aeschylus' *Choephori*.[18] On a fourth occasion in Aeschylus' play, it designates not funeral offerings but the lamentation sung over the grave, in a passage that has much in common with Olympian 8:

> σκότῳ φάος ἀντίμοιρον, χάριτες δ' ὁμοίως
> κέκληνται γόος εὐκλεὴς
> †προσθοδόμοις† Ἀτρείδαις.

(Choephori 319–322)

The realm of light is opposed to the realm of darkness, but still the lamentation that makes glorious is called graces to the Atreidai who formerly resided in/ruled the house(?)[19]

Like Orestes, Pindar recognizes the barrier between living and dead (κόνις) but asserts that it does not prevent communication and the exchange of *charis* (κατακρύπτει δ' οὐ . . . χάριν). And like Pindar's epinikion, Orestes' song of lamentation confers glory upon the dead Agamemnon (εὐκλεής is causative).

Charis, as always, designates a willing and precious reciprocal exchange.[20] It is used in the context of funeral offerings because, as Numa

---

[16]For the notion that the dead need to be awakened, see Aeschylus *Choephori* 318, 495 and Vermeule 1979.24–26, 41.

[17]Slater 1969a, s.v. χάρις 1.a. Cf. Segal 1985.210: "*charis*, the honor of the victory as a shared joy in the reciprocal relations of the family: hence κεδνὰν χάριν."

[18]At Aeschylus *Choephori* 41 and 517, Clytemnestra's funeral offerings to Agamemnon (χοαί) are designated as χάριν ἀχάριτον and δειλαία χάρις respectively, while at *Choephori* 180, Electra designates Orestes' offering of a lock of hair as χάριν πατρός. See LSJ s.v. χάρις V.2, Schadewaldt 1932.317–318, Gundert 1935.43 and 125 n. 200, Garvie 1986.90–91, 130, 186.

[19]For the interpretation of these lines, see Schadewaldt 1932.316–319 and Garvie 1986.129–131. Here, as in my interpretations of Pindar, I assume that there is no substantive difference in meaning between *charis* singular and *charites* plural (except that Pindar uses only the plural to designate his songs).

[20]On the semantics of *charis*, see Wilamowitz 1922.152–153, Stenzel 1926.203–204, Stenzel 1934.92, Hewitt 1927, Schadewaldt 1928.268, 277–278, 287 n. 5, 294 n. 2,

Denis Fustel de Coulanges observes, "there was a perpetual interchange of good offices between the living and the dead of each family. The ancestor received from his descendants a series of funeral banquets, that is to say, the only enjoyment that was left to him in his second life. The descendant received from the ancestor the aid and strength of which he had need in this. The living could not do without the dead, nor the dead without the living. Thus a powerful bond was established among all the generations of the same family, which made it a body forever insepar-able."[21] The crown "laid around" the Blepsiadai (O.8.76) serves as the concrete representation of the *charis* that is both victory and funeral offering. In this case the poet exploits the homology of ritual symbols, for a crown is both the symbol of victory at the games and an ornament placed on the ancestral tomb.[22]

Pythian 5 contains a similar passage on the effect of a new victory on the ancestors. Note the emphasis on the *oikos* in Pindar's statement early in the ode that Arkesilaos has been restored to prosperity by Castor,

> εὐδίαν ὃς μετὰ χειμέριον ὄμβρον τεάν
> καταιθύσσει μάκαιραν ἑστίαν.

(P.5.10–11)

who sheds good weather after wintry storm over your blessed hearth.

It is significantly Arkesilaos' hearth, the center and symbol of his *oikos*, upon which Castor sheds "good weather after storm." The play of darkness and light at the hearth symbolizes the family's fortunes and thereby represents victory as a concern to the entire *oikos*.[23]

Pindar returns to the theme of the house in the poem's last triad:

> ἄτερθε δὲ πρὸ δωμάτων ἕτεροι λαχόντες Ἀίδαν
> βασιλέες ἱεροί
> ἐντί· μεγαλᾶν δ' ἀρετᾶν
> δρόσῳ μαλθακᾷ
> ῥανθεισᾶν κώμων {θ'} ὑπὸ χεύμασιν,
> ἀκούοντί ποι χθονίᾳ φρενί

Gundert 1935.30–45, 55–58, Maehler 1963.88–92, Latacz 1966, Carne-Ross 1985.59–64.

[21]Fustel de Coulanges 1980.28.

[22]See Duchemin 1955.275–278.

[23]On the motif of storm and good weather, see Bundy 1962.48–52, Bernard 1963.76 n. 40, Bowra 1964.249–250, Young 1971.26.

σφὸν ὄλβον υἱῷ τε κοινὰν χάριν
ἔνδικόν τ' Ἀρκεσίλᾳ·

(P. 5.96–103)[24]

But apart before the houses are the other holy kings who have been
allotted Hades; but when great achievements have been sprinkled with
gentle dew by the pourings of *kōmoi*, they hear somehow with chthonic
mind their good fortune and the grace which is common to them and the
proper possession of their son Arkesilaos.

The implicit analogy of Olympian 8 has been compressed into metaphor; as Mezger noted, "the expression recalls funeral libations."[25] The
kōmoi that accompany the victor home are a libation poured to the
ancestral dead, "the holy kings" who lie "before the houses." The richly
figural language of lines 99–100 combines the revitalizing power of dew
with the sprinkling (ῥανθεισᾶν) and pouring (χεύμασιν) that characterize the ritual offering of fluids.[26] And again Pindar uses *charis* in a
context of funeral libations to designate the grace of victory. We should
pay particular attention to the adjectives that modify this *charis*: it is
"common" to the king and his ancestors and the "legitimate possession"
of Arkesilaos. Behind this conjunction of qualities lies the notion of
inheritance and the duties of the heir. Arkesilaos wins because of the
excellence (and wealth) he has inherited from his ancestors; hence the
victory is his legitimate property. But the victory is also "common"

[24]I follow the eighth edition of the Teubner text here, though omitting the comma at
the end of line 101. Most other editors and commentators—Heyne, Turyn, Bowra,
Mezger, Farnell, Gildersleeve—read μεγάλαν δ' ἀρετάν . . . ῥανθεῖσαν (the MSS have
μεγάλαν δ' ἀρετᾶν . . . ῥανθεισᾶν). Though it makes no difference to the argument
presented here, I have a slight preference for the genitive plural, simply to avoid the
monotony of seven accusative singulars, all presumably direct objects of ἀκούοντι. As
Farnell points out, however, if we read genitive plural we must understand it as a
genitive absolute, not as object of ἀκούοντι, since that would leave the accusatives of
lines 102–103 with no construction in the sentence (Farnell 1930.2.180). Thus we cannot
punctuate with a comma at the end of line 101 as the Teubner text does.

[25]Mezger 1880.232. So also Lefkowitz 1985.52–53, 57, Segal 1985.205–208. We
should note in this case that the dead kings are not just ancestors but recipients of hero
cult (see Lefkowitz 1985.52 with note 58, Segal 1985.207). The distinction between
funeral cult and hero cult is important, especially in the democratic polis. See Nagy
1986a. I consider this passage in the context of ancestor cult because the lines
are specifically addressed to the dead kings as Arkesilaos' *forebears* (hence υἱῷ P. 5.102). That
is, in this case, the distinction of ancestor cult and hero cult collapses.

[26]On the life-giving properties of dew in Greek poetry, see Boedeker 1984; on this
passage in particular, pp. 96–97. It may be that Pindar's use of χεῦμα here suggests the
etymologically related χοαί, which designate almost exclusively funeral libations (see
LSJ s.v. χοή, Stengel 1920.103–104, 143, 148–149, Citron 1965.69–70).

because the king renders part of the glory won, like a funeral libation, back to his forefathers.

The image of celebratory song as grave offering is suggestive for other Pindaric contexts. In Pythian 9, for example, the poet says at the close of the victory catalog:

ἐμὲ δ' οὖν τις ἀοιδᾶν
δίψαν ἀκειόμενον πράσσει χρέος, αὖτις ἐγεῖραι
καὶ παλαιὰν δόξαν ἑῶν προγόνων·

(P.9.103–105)

But someone exacts a debt from me, curing the thirst for songs, in turn to rouse also the ancient glory of his ancestors;

After the account of the victor's achievements, the obligation to remember the dead ancestors is felt, and it seems to generate the imagery of thirst appeased by song.[27] I take these lines to mean that Pindar feels he has already quenched the "thirst for songs" of Telesikrates' own deeds: the καί of line 105 signifies that "someone" (presumably Telesikrates) now requires him to do the same for his ancestors' past glories as well. The notion of awakening the past reputation of the ancestors recalls Olympian 8.74 (μναμοσύναν ἀνεγείροντα), while the liquid imagery implicit in ἀοιδᾶν δίψαν reminds us of Pythian 5.[28] Together these images suggest that the ancient glory of Telesikrates' forebears is roused by a liquid offering of song on the occasion of the current victory.

The imagery we have been tracing, of light restored to the hearth and libations poured to the dead, suits another context besides the athlete's victorious return: it is also the imagery used for the birth of an heir.[29]

---

[27]I take ἀοιδᾶν as objective genitive with δίψαν—with LSJ, contra Mezger, Gildersleeve, and Farnell. I can see no justification in Pindar's language for Farnell's elaborate metaphorical construct: "Pindar has in mind the chariot of the Muses; he knows that when horses come in tired, they want a drink. . . . Pindar was just going to unyoke and refresh his tired horses when someone requires him to yoke them again for a second journey" (Farnell 1930.2.212).

[28]Emily Vermeule's comments on "the thirsty dead" are very interesting in this context: "The dead in many cultures are rumored to be thirsty, and our communication with them is more commonly by toast and libation than by food. The 'thirsty ones,' the *di-pi-si-jo-i* of a few Pylos Linear B texts are sometimes interpreted as the dead, in a local euphemism, although the word may as easily represent a place name" (Vermeule 1979.57; and see 225 n. 28). See Gundert 1935.43 and n. 198. See also Onians 1951.255–256 on the dead as "the dry ones."

[29]For the birth of an heir represented as light at the hearth, see Gernet 1981b.326–327.

The overlap of imagery makes a great deal of sense, for both the bringing home of victory and new birth crucially guarantee the survival of the *oikos*. Kevin Crotty notes that, as in initiation rituals, the return of the victor is symbolically a new birth or rebirth.[30] I would extend the implications of this observation from the individual to the entire *oikos*. It is not just in the initiatory context that victory is equivalent to (re)birth: it plays the same role structurally in the life of the *oikos*. In the context of this analogy we can now understand the imagery we observed earlier, of darkness associated with staying in the house and light with returning triumphant. For he who "sits at home" in one sense never actualizes his birth (thus also, in Pythian 4, παρὰ ματρί substitutes for ἐν σκότῳ), whereas he who returns victorious "comes to birth"—that is, "into the light"—for his house.[31]

Thus in a sense, the heir of the house is born (as far as epinikion is concerned) only when he fulfills in action the promise, the potential of his birth. It is perhaps for this reason more than any other that Nemean 7 opens with an elaborate prayer to Eileithyia, the goddess of childbirth. Modern critics have pointed out the fallacy of the ancient scholiasts' question "What is Eileithyia's particular relevance to Sogenes?" and rejected the biographical fantasies this question engendered.[32] But current explanations of the proem of Nemean 7 seem to go too far in the opposite direction, replacing the particularity of her relation to Sogenes with the universal truism "we are all born." Yet this interpretation does not account for the end of Pindar's prayer to Eileithyia:

σὺν δὲ τίν
καὶ παῖς ὁ Θεαρίωνος ἀρετᾷ κριθείς
εὔδοξος ἀείδεται Σωγένης μετὰ πενταέθλοις.

(N.7.6–8)

But distinguished by his achievement with your help, also the child of Thearion, Sogenes, is sung of as glorious with the pentathlon.

As Glenn Most observes, the aorist participle κριθείς denotes the moment of victory,[33] and Pindar associates Eileithyia's assistance specifi-

[30]Crotty 1982.113, 117.
[31]Compare the observations of Bourdieu 1970.165 on the Berber house: "A man who has respect for himself should leave the house at daybreak, morning being the day of the daytime, and the sallying forth from the house in the morning, being a birth."
[32]Drachmann 1926.116–117, Fränkel 1961.391–394, Young 1970b.633–643, Most 1985.134–140.
[33]Most 1985.140.

cally with that moment by the phrase σὺν δὲ τίν. Thus somehow Eileithyia was involved in Sogenes' victory. Perhaps then, the association with Eileithyia occupies a middle ground between complete generality (we are all born) and complete specificity (Sogenes' particular link to the goddess). That is to say, perhaps athletic victory in general could be associated with the maieutic powers of Eileithyia. As far as the house is concerned, the athlete first emerges into the light at the moment of victory. And in this particular case, Pindar's invocation implies, Sogenes "comes to birth" for his house by winning at the great games, thereby actualizing his inherited *aretē*.[34]

Thus the victor can be represented as newborn, or by a transfer of the metaphor, the epinikion itself becomes the heir whose emergence into the light saves the house from oblivion. In Isthmian 4, for example, we find birth imagery combined with the other metaphors we have been tracing. Describing the fortunes of the Kleonymidai, Pindar says:

> ἀλλ᾽ ἁμέρᾳ γὰρ ἐν μιᾷ
> τραχεῖα νιφὰς πολέμοιο τεσσάρων
> ἀνδρῶν ἐρήμωσεν μάκαιραν ἑστίαν·
>
> (I.4.16–17b)

But in fact, in a single day, a harsh snowstorm of war deprived the blessed hearth of four men.

This is a negative version of the same image as in Pythian 5, and again Pindar focuses the metaphorical storm at the hearth of the house. The literal loss of four men and the metaphorical "snowstorm of war" combine to darken the ancestral hearth. But now, Pindar continues, the family fares better by the favor of Poseidon:

> τόνδε πορὼν γενεᾷ θαυμαστὸν ὕμνον
> ἐκ λεχέων ἀνάγει φάμαν παλαιὰν
> εὐκλέων ἔργων· ἐν ὕπνῳ γὰρ πέσεν· ἀλλ᾽ ἀνεγειρομένα χρῶτα λάμπει,
> Ἀοσφόρος θαητὸς ὣς ἄστροις ἐν ἄλλοις·
>
> (I.4.21–24)

[Poseidon] by granting this marvelous hymn to the family leads forth from its beds the ancient repute of glorious deeds; for it has fallen in sleep.

---

[34]Indeed, the association of victory and birth may have been encoded in the very geography of Olympia, where, Pausanias tells us, there was a shrine to Olympian Eileithyia on the northern foot of Kronion (Pausanias 6.20.2).

But awakened it shines in flesh, wonderful like the morning star among
the other stars.

Φάμαν παλαιάν and ἀνεγειρομένα echo the contexts of grave offerings in Olympian 8 (ἀνεγείροντα [74]) and Pythian 9 (ἐγεῖραι καὶ
παλαιὰν δόξαν [104–105]), while ἐκ λεχέων ἀνάγει again suggests the
slumber and awakening of the family's former glories. Then λάμπει
and the simile of the morning star seem to restore the light snuffed from
the ancestral hearth.[35] Indeed, line 23 may carry the imagery even
farther in χρῶτα, "flesh" or "body." This is the only occasion on which
the word occurs metaphorically in Pindar, and it is usually ignored by
commentators and translators.[36] What does it mean to say that the
ancient repute, roused, "shines in flesh"? What restores the light to a
house if not a new heir, a replacement for the men lost in war, a "re-
incarnation" of his dead ancestors? But here, this new embodiment that
brings light to the house is not a literal heir but the ancient repute roused
from sleep by Pindar's song. As each new birth rescues the family from
oblivion, so a new victory commemorated in song recalls and revital-
izes its past glories.

But the mediation of song is crucial for the process, as Pindar observes:

τοῦτο γὰρ ἀθάνατον φωνᾶεν ἕρπει,
εἴ τις εὖ εἴπῃ τι· καὶ πάγκαρπον ἐπὶ χθόνα καὶ διὰ πόντον βέβακεν
ἐργμάτων ἀκτὶς καλῶν ἄσβεστος αἰεί.
προφρόνων Μοισᾶν τύχοιμεν, κεῖνον ἅψαι πυρσὸν ὕμνων
καὶ Μελίσσῳ, παγκρατίου στεφάνωμ᾽ ἐπάξιον,
ἔρνεϊ Τελεσιάδα.

(I.4.40–45)

For this goes immortal, speaking, if anyone says anything well. And over
the all-fruited earth and across the sea goes the beam of noble deeds,
unquenchable always. May we happen upon kindly disposed Muses to
kindle that torch of hymns, a worthy crown of the pancration, also for
Melissos, the scion of Telesiades.

---

[35]For somewhat different treatments of light imagery in I.4, see McNeal 1978 and
Segal 1981.

[36]Χρώς is used literally at P.1.55, N.8.28, and fr. 43 SM. Χρῶτα is simply ignored in
the commentaries of Farnell and Thummer, and omitted from the translations of Woodbury 1947.369, Lattimore 1976.143, and Nisetich 1980.307.

The light imagery in λάμπει and Ἀοσφόρος is picked up here in "the beam of noble deeds, unquenchable always." The two passages correspond, since both describe the power of song. The poet then focuses this light on the house of the victor, praying for the poetic power to kindle that firebrand of hymns also for Melissos. The conflation of the death of its men, darkness, and the hearth of the house in lines 16–17b implies that the men of the house constitute the light at its hearth. Here the poet replaces the darkness and desolation of the hearth with a firebrand of hymns. Indeed, the word he chooses to characterize Melissos in relation to his father, ἔρνεϊ (shoot or scion), reinforces the identification of the men of the house as its source of light.[37]

The diction of Aeschylus' *Choephori* again offers a parallel for this sequence of imagery. In the parodos, the chorus of *choēphoroi* (libation bearers) sings what A. F. Garvie describes as "a θρῆνος in honour of Agamemnon, the dirge which was denied him at his funeral."[38] As part of this dirge, the singers lament:

> ἰὼ πάνοιζυς ἑστία
> ἰὼ κατασκαφαὶ δόμων·
> ἀνήλιοι βροτοστυγεῖς
> δνόφοι καλύπτουσι δόμους
> δεσποτᾶν θανάτοισι.
>
> (*Choephori* 49–53)

Alas for the all-unhappy hearth, alas for the destruction of houses! Sunless glooms hateful to men cover the house with the deaths of its masters.

Here, the darkness of the hearth implicit in Pindar's "harsh snowstorm of war" is clearly described and emphatically linked to the death of the master of the house. Then, in order to heal the house, Electra prays as she pours the funeral libations:

> λέγω καλοῦσα πατέρ᾽, ἐποίκτιρον τ᾽ ἐμὲ
> φίλον τ᾽ Ὀρέστην φῶς ἄναψον ἐν δόμοις.
>
> (*Choephori* 130–131)

Summoning my father I say, "Pity me and kindle dear Orestes as a light in the house."[39]

[37]For the topos of the men as the light of the hearth, see Fustel de Coulanges 1980.17, 24–25, 29, Gernet 1981b.326–327, Vernant 1983.133–134. On the vegetal imagery in ἔρνος, see Segal 1981.76.

[38]Garvie 1986.54.

[39]I follow Wilamowitz 1896.62, reading φῶς ἄναψον ἐν for M's πῶς ἀνάξομεν, rather

As far as Electra is concerned, the only thing that can restore light to the house is the return and repossession of the rightful heir, Orestes. The striking verbal parallels between Aeschylus and Pindar suggest that both are drawing on traditional images for the ruin and well-being of the house.[40] But Pindar has subsumed the whole system into metaphor in Isthmian 4, for within the epinikian context it is not the birth or return of an heir which kindles light for the house but the performance of celebratory song.

Very similar images cluster together in Isthmian 7. Pindar ends his catalog of Thebes's glories thus:

ἀλλὰ παλαιὰ γὰρ
εὕδει χάρις, ἀμνάμονες δὲ βροτοί,
ὅ τι μὴ σοφίας ἄωτον ἄκρον
κλυταῖς ἐπέων ῥοαῖσιν ἐξίκηται ζυγέν·
κώμαζ’ ἔπειτεν ἀδυμελεῖ σὺν ὕμνῳ
καὶ Στρεψιάδᾳ· φέρει γὰρ Ἰσθμοῖ
νίκαν παγκρατίου, σθένει τ’ ἔκπαγλος ἰδεῖν τε μορφάεις, ἄγει τ’
ἀρετὰν οὐκ αἴσχιον φυᾶς.
φλέγεται δὲ ἰοπλόκοισι Μοίσαις,
μάτρωί θ’ ὁμωνύμῳ δέδωκε κοινὸν θάλος,

(I.7.16–24)

But ancient grace sleeps, and men are forgetful, whatever does not arrive as the choice peak of poetic skill yoked with streams of words that make glorious. Celebrate the *kōmos* then with sweet-sounding hymn also for Strepsiades; for both terrible in strength and handsome to see, he bears a pancration victory at the Isthmus, and he leads achievement no baser than his inherited quality. But he is set ablaze by the violet-tressed Muses, and he has given to his like-named maternal uncle a common shoot.

The first lines, "But ancient grace sleeps, and men are forgetful," refer back to Thebes, but also ahead to the family of the two Strepsiadai. For *charis* here recalls the reciprocal exchange of good offices between ancestors and descendants we observed in Olympian 8 and Pythian 5. And as in Olympian 8, Pythian 9, and Isthmian 4, such *charis* sleeps (εὕδει) until it is awakened by new streams of song. In context there may be a

than the reading of Page 1972, φῶς τ’ ἄναψον (the emendation of "Philologus" 1844). On the various readings, their advantages and disadvantages, see Garvie 1986.77–78.

[40]Cf. Aeschylus *Choephori* 808–811, 934, *Persians* 169, 300, *Agamemnon* 900; Sophocles *Antigone* 600, *Electra* 1354–1355; Euripides *Ion* 1464–1467, *Bacchae* 1308, *Orestes* 243. See also Artemidorus 2.10 (quoted by Vernant 1983.147) and Alexiou 1974.187–189.

faint echo of the imagery of grave offerings in the "*streams* of words that make glorious" (recall the γόος εὐκλεής of *Choephori* 321).

The image with which Pindar ends this section is strikingly reminiscent of Isthmian 4.42–44: "He is set ablaze by the violet-tressed Muses, and he has given to his like-named maternal uncle a common θάλος." Again, the victor returns home irradiated by light (φλέγεται) and causes streams of song to be poured for his ancestors' achievements. In this context, θάλος is an extraordinarily bold usage. For this passage alone in the epinikia and for a single fragmentary passage in Dithyramb 1, Slater offers the definition "flowering garland, crown *met*."[41] But the dithyramb fragment does not provide sufficient context to decide how Pindar is using the word and so must be left out of account. In all its other appearances in Pindar, as in Homer, θάλος means "offspring, child" and I believe that that meaning must play a part here.[42] In metaphor Strepsiades' victory and return, when they are celebrated in song, kindle light for the house and produce an heir to preserve the memory of the dead ancestors.

Furthermore, the play of darkness and light linked to the fortunes of the family recurs in Isthmian 7. The battle in which the elder Strepsiades died is described as "this cloud [of war]," in which he "fended off the hail of blood for the sake of his dear homeland" (ἐν ταύτᾳ νεφέλᾳ χάλαζαν αἵματος . . . ἀμύνεται [I.7.27]). Then, in the words that close the description of the heroic death of Strepsiades, Pindar replaces the storm of war with "good weather:"

> ἔτλαν δὲ πένθος οὐ φατόν· ἀλλὰ νῦν μοι
> Γαιάοχος εὐδίαν ὄπασσεν
> ἐκ χειμῶνος.

(I.7.37–39)

I have endured sorrow unspeakable. But now the Earthshaker has bestowed on me good weather after storm.

This passage combines the image of "good weather after storm" (εὐ-

---

[41] Slater, 1969a, s.v. θάλος.

[42] Cf. O.2.45, O.6.68, N.1.2, and Παρθ. 2.36. On the etymology of θάλος and its equivalence to ἔρνος see Lowenstam 1979.128–129; on its exclusively metaphorical meaning, see Chantraine 1968.2.420 and Rose 1974.163 with n. 53. Pace Renehan 1969b.221–223, without independent evidence, I would not take the meaning "flowering garland" from I.7.24 and apply it elsewhere, for the reasons offered in the text. I agree with Renehan that θάλος is used ambiguously in I.7; I would simply construe the ambiguity differently.

δίαν . . . ἐκ χειμῶνος), which we also saw in Pythian 5. 10–11, with the agency of Poseidon, as in Isthmian 4. 19–23. As Young has argued, the source of the poet's grief is the death of the uncle, whereas the good weather bestowed by Poseidon refers to the Isthmian victory of his nephew. Here, as in Isthmian 4, the alternation of obliterating storm and clear daylight charts the family's setbacks and successes.[43] And, as in Isthmian 4, the death of family members in war is compensated *not* by a new birth but by a new athletic victory celebrated in song.

Up to this point, the argument for victory and celebratory song conceived as a birth for the house may seem tenuous, ultimately dependent as it is on the metaphorical significance of two words, χρῶτα in Isthmian 4 and θάλος in Isthmian 7. Could Pindar really have conceptualized athletic victory or epinikian song in these terms? The end of Olympian 10 gives us a clear answer:

> ἀλλ' ὥτε παῖς ἐξ ἀλόχου πατρί
> ποθεινὸς ἵκοντι νεότατος τὸ πάλιν ἤδη, μάλα δέ οἱ θερμαίνει
>   φιλότατι νόον·
> ἐπεὶ πλοῦτος ὁ λαχὼν ποιμένα
> ἐπακτὸν ἀλλότριον
> θνᾴσκοντι στυγερώτατος·
> καὶ ὅταν καλὰ {μὲν} ἔρξαις ἀοιδᾶς ἄτερ,
> Ἀγησίδαμ', εἰς Ἀίδα σταθμόν
> ἀνὴρ ἵκηται, κενεὰ πνεύσαις ἔπορε μόχθῳ βραχύ τι τερπνόν. τὶν δ'
>   ἁδυεπής τε λύρα
> γλυκύς τ' αὐλὸς ἀναπάσσει χάριν·

> (O. 10. 86–94)

But as a child, long desired, from his wife for a father who has already come to the opposite of youth, very much warms his mind with affection (since wealth allotted to a foreign shepherd is most hateful to the one who is dying); just so, whenever a man comes to the dwelling of Hades, having accomplished noble things without song, Hagesidamos, having breathed empty things, he has given [only] brief pleasure to his toil. But upon you the sweet-speaking lyre and the sweet aulos sprinkle grace.

Here, the song that celebrates and preserves achievement is explicitly likened to the son and heir born to an old man. Furthermore, Pindar links the image of the birth of an heir with that of funeral libations. As

---

[43]See Young 1971.25–26, who notes that lines 27 and 37–39 form "a unified pattern of imagery, despite their distance from one another"—a pattern he compares to I.4.15–19.

Stoddart observes, "Like the old man, the boy victor Hagesidamos has
an estate to leave behind—the glory he won at Olympia; he too has no
heir to receive his bequest and care for his soul, until Pindar's ode
secures the same sort of immortality a son brings his father: when
Hagesidamos is dead, the lyre and flute will 'sprinkle grace' upon him
(that is, upon his tomb), like a libation."[44] The final word of the
passage, χάριν, after the verb of sprinkling, collapses tenor and vehicle
in a single radiant offering. For here, as in Olympian 8 and Pythian 5,
charis evokes the funeral libations to the dead of the house but also
designates the grace bestowed by epinikion.[45]

An interesting parallel for Olympian 10 is Isthmian 6, in which a
hoped-for Olympic victory is equated with the birth of an heir not
explicitly in simile but by the analogy of myth. As Pindar prays for an
Olympic victory for the family of Lampon (I.6.7–9, 16–18), so Herakles in the myth prays for the birth of a son to Telamon (I.6.42–49).
Even the language in which Pindar's prayer for Lampon is couched
supports the analogy:

> τοίαισιν ὀργαῖς εὔχεται
> ἀντιάσαις Ἀΐδαν γῆράς τε δέξασθαι πολιόν
> ὁ Κλεονίκου παῖς· ἐγὼ δ' ὑψίθρονον
> Κλωθὼ κασιγνήτας τε προσεννέπω ἑσπέσθαι κλυταῖς
> ἀνδρὸς φίλου Μοίρας ἐφετμαῖς.

> (I.6.14–18)

The child of Kleonikos prays to receive Hades and grey old age when he
has obtained [his wishes] by such dispositions; but I invoke Klotho and
her sister Fates to follow the glorious behests of a dear man.[46]

Lampon prays to die only when the Fates have granted him certain
conditions. The poet then intercedes on his behalf with the Moirai. We

---

[44]Stoddart 1981.313. See Stoddart 1990.5–14.

[45]See Slater 1969a, s.v. χάρις 1.b.α.

[46]The syntax of lines 14–16 is not completely clear. Farnell (1930.2.358) and Thummer
(1968.1.181) take Ἀΐδαν γῆράς τε . . . πολιόν as direct objects of both ἀντιάσαις and
δέξασθαι. But this interpretation seems to me to leave τοίαισιν ὀργαῖς with no clear
construction or meaning in the sentence: it cannot mean "in solchem Glück," as Thummer translates it. Rather, this phrase must be connected with a verb in some way,
whether we wish to take it as a dative object with ἀντιάσαις (so Bury 1892.108, Slater
1969a.57) or as an instrumental dative, with ἀντιάσαις used absolutely to mean "having
obtained [his wishes]" (so LSJ). Whichever alternative we choose, I take τοίαισιν ὀργαῖς
to refer back to δαπάνᾳ τε χαρεὶς καὶ πόνῳ (10–11, cf. I.2.35–42); ἀντιάσαις to
πράσσει θεοδμάτους ἀρετάς (11). Lines 14–16 are then the particular application of the
general statement of 10–13: in effect, Lampon prays to die only when he has reached the
limit of human blessedness—i.e., had a family member win at the Olympic games.

should pay particular attention to the topos of conditionally accepting death, for it is conventionally associated with certain desires. What are Lampon's conditions? An unexpected parallel from Pythian 11 will clarify the situation these lines imply:

> εἴ τις ἄκρον ἑλὼν ἡσυχᾷ τε νεμόμενος αἰνὰν ὕβριν
> ἀπέφυγεν, μέλανος {δ'} ἂν ἐσχατιὰν
> καλλίονα θανάτου ⟨στείχοι⟩ γλυκυτάτᾳ γενεᾷ
> εὐώνυμον κτεάνων κρατίσταν χάριν πορών·

> (P.11.55–58)

If a man who has taken the highest peak [of achievement], dwelling in peace, flees dread *hybris*, he would go to a better end of black death, since he has granted to his sweetest offspring the grace of a good name as the best of possessions.

A man welcomes going to the limit of death, or at least regards it as "better" (καλλίονα) only when he has "the grace of a good name" *and* the offspring to whom to bequeath it. In Isthmian 6 Pindar wishes for the former for Lampon through the metaphor of the latter. For the language of lines 16–18 is that of a man wishing for an heir: the Μοῖραι as the Fates, plural, always appear in the context of birth in Pindar, and Klotho, "she who spins the thread of our lives," appropriately heads the list.[47]

Only an Olympic victory would fulfill the aspirations of Lampon: then his life would be complete. But even without this crowning achievement, Pindar represents the house of Lampon as rich in metaphorical heirs, for he concludes the family's victory catalog thus:

> ἀνὰ δ' ἄγαγον ἐς φάος οἵαν μοῖραν ὕμνων·
> τὰν Ψαλυχιαδᾶν δὲ πάτραν Χαρίτων

---

[47]For the Moirai, see O.6.42, O.10.52, and N.7.1; for Klotho, O.1.26; for Lachesis, O.7.64, Πα. 12.17. See also Most 1985.137–138, esp. n. 5. P.4.145 is no exception; there "the Fates would turn away," as Jason says, because he and Pelias would not be acting with the proper respect due their birth into the same family (note especially τρίταισιν δ' ἐν γοναῖς [143], ὁμογόνοις [146]). The imagery of the lines that immediately follow in I.6 may be significant in this context. After wishing for a metaphorical child for Lampon, the poet turns to the duty he owes to the Aiakidai: ὕμμε τ', ὦ χρυσάρματοι Αἰακίδαι, / τέθμιόν μοι φαμὶ σαφέστατον ἔμμεν / τάνδ' ἐπιστείχοντα νᾶσον ῥαινέμεν εὐ-λογίαις ("I affirm that it is my clearest ordinance, whenever I come to this island, O gold-charioted Aiakidai, to sprinkle you with praises" [I.6.19–21]). Just as his son's Olympic victory would pour libations of song for Lampon even after his death, it is the poet's duty to sprinkle the island of Aigina with praises of the Aiakidai. Thus the poet fulfills for the heroes of myth the same role as a son plays for his father.

ἄρδοντι καλλίστᾳ δρόσῳ,
τόν τε Θεμιστίου ὀρθώσαντες οἶκον τάνδε πόλιν
θεοφιλῆ ναίοισι·

(I.6.62–66)

And they have brought back to the light what sort of share of hymns, and
they water the clan of the Psalychiadai with the most beautiful dew of the
Graces, and having set upright the house of Themistios, they inhabit this
city dear to the gods.

We have already noted the motif of *nostos* in ἀνὰ δ᾽ ἄγαγον. We are now
in a better position to understand ἐς φάος. By this little phrase Pindar
infuses these lines with a rich double meaning, since in Greek "to come
to the light" means to be born; hence, "to lead to the light" is to cause to
be born.[48] The metaphor inherent in the next two lines is also clearer
now. Through victory hymns, associated with *nostos* and new birth, the
sons of Lampon "water the clan of the Psalychiadai with the most
beautiful dew of the Graces"—that is, they offer songs like funeral
libations to give new life to the glories of their forebears. Here as in
Pythian 5, the image of funeral libations is conflated with that of dew to
underscore the revitalizing effect on the ancestral dead of these liquid
offerings of song.[49] Given the metaphors that play through these lines,
it is no surprise that Pindar closes this section with the assertion that the
victorious sons of Lampon have "set upright the house of Themistios"
(τόν τε Θεμιστίου ὀρθώσαντες οἶκον).

I hope to have shown that a common complex of ideas and images
links the passages we have considered from Olympian 8, Pythian 5,
Pythian 9, Isthmian 4, Isthmian 7, Olympian 10, and Isthmian 6. These
seven poems share some or all of the following motifs: the slumber of
ancient glory, the rousing effect of song, poetry as a liquid offering,
charis between ancestors and descendants, the shifting darkness and
light of the family's fortunes, and finally, the birth of an heir for the
house. I have claimed that the only context that makes sense of all these
motifs is the temporal continuity of the household, represented by
funeral libations and new birth. Thus a single ideological system underlies an apparently disparate series of images.

[48]Cf., for example, O.6.42–44 (ἦλθεν δ᾽ ὑπὸ σπλάγχων ὑπ᾽ ὠδίνεσσ᾽ ἐραταῖς
Ἴαμος ἐς φάος) and N.1.35–36 (θαητὰν ἐς αἴγλαν παῖς Διὸς ὠδῖνα φεύγων διδύμῳ
σὺν κασιγνήτῳ μόλεν).
[49]See Boedeker 1984.31, 50, 95, 122.

In other terms, we can understand Pindar's use of the family's temporal imperative as an economic system. If the poet's spatial imagery represents the exchanges of the house with the world, his temporal imagery expresses all the intrafamilial exchanges involved in competition, victory, and its celebration. For in Pindar's world, the athlete never competes alone. If he has the quality to win, it is because he has inherited it from his ancestors. And his victory is not just a personal triumph: it is a renewal of strength, of $\mu\acute{\epsilon}\nu o\varsigma$, for all his ancestors, living and dead.[50] Thus the athlete, when he "comes into his inheritance" of *phyē* and *aretē* by his victory, reciprocates the gifts of his ancestors by including them in his celebration and pouring out for them a libation of song which is at once occasional and everlasting.

Within this household economy, hereditary excellence—*phyē* or $\tau\grave{o}$ $\sigma\upsilon\gamma\gamma\epsilon\nu\acute{\epsilon}\varsigma$—represents only half of an ongoing series of reciprocal exchanges and services between ancestors and descendants, which Pindar again and again designates as *charis* in the passages we have been considering (O.8.80, P.5.102, I.7.17, O.10.94, and notice the "dew of the Charites" at I.6.64–65). In these contexts, *charis* can simultaneously denote funeral offerings and the grace bestowed by victory and song because these phenomena serve the same function in the life of the house.

From the perspective of the household, this economy of intrafamilial exchanges can be reduced to a simple accountancy of the hearth. In Isthmian 4 and, to a lesser extent, in Isthmian 7 and Pythian 5, Pindar indulges in such stark accounting. Four men are dead in war and the hearth is darkened, while an Isthmian victory causes a torch of the Muses to be kindled for the scion of Telesiades. Commentators take the poet's addition and subtraction in stride, dismissing the family's misfortunes as "negative foil" for the victor's current success.[51] But in so doing, they fail to apprehend the model that underlies Pindar's arithme-

[50]Cf. the remarks of Cole 1987.566: "Victory in Pindar's world springs from a complex set of circumstances: inherent ability, training, toil and effort, chance, the favor of the gods. Ability is always inherited; chance and divine favor operate to the benefit of nations and families quite as often as to that of individuals; training is received from older friends and kinsmen; effort and toil are impossible without the example and inspiration of one's predecessors. It is hard to conceive of a victory the credit for which could not with good reason be distributed among several people; and this means that, in varying degrees and various ways, victory belongs to them as well as to the single athlete whose name the herald proclaims."

[51]Bundy 1962.14, 47–53, Thummer 1968.1.66–81, Lee 1978.66–70. An exception to such dismissal is Young's sensitive reading of the relation of the Strepsiadai in Isthmian 7 (Young 1971.34–46).

tic: if the death of men darkens the hearth, it is new birth that restores light to it.

The designation of Pindar's accountancy as "negative foil" also insists on the primacy of the individual victor, though the current of the poet's imagery seems to go in another direction. Assimilating athletic victory to the rhythm of funeral cult and new birth puts the house at the center of the victor's experience, integrating his achievement into the life cycle of the family. At the beginning of this chapter we considered a fragment of a partheneion, in which the poet represented immortality in familial terms: "the days are immortal for men, but the body is mortal." In the epinikia, the route to immortality is explicitly through the winning of *kleos*. But here too, I would contend, Pindar's conception of *kleos* is not personal: it is inextricably bound to the *oikos* as a social entity and as the space that defines that entity. I believe that the strands of imagery we have traced, separately and as they intertwine, lead inevitably to the conclusion that this *kleos* depends on and aims at the preservation and glorification of the *oikos*.

PART II

THE ECONOMY OF PRAISE
IN THE ARISTOCRATIC
COMMUNITY

CHAPTER 4

The Ideology of
Aristocratic Exchange

We have seen how the imagery that clusters around the *oikos* is deployed for the reintegration of the victor into his family unit. The system of images involving the house expresses the individual's responsibility to that corporate entity and endorses a model of behavior. Ideally, the individual representative of the house leaves it to win *kleos*, then returns to enrich the entire household with his booty and his dutiful presence. Thereby, the victor contributes to the symbolic capital of the house, while assuring its spatial and temporal integrity.

This model requires for its functioning no more than the single house and the site of the games, or in metaphorical terms, the house and the ends of the earth. But in reality, the atomic unit of the household exists within the context of the larger social organization, and the poet must also reintegrate the victor into his aristocratic group and into his civic community. Can we isolate different strategies within the poetry for reintegration into these broader circles of community? Again, it may help to distinguish the social units involved and to identify the lines of force among them, for praise is always a communal activity, and as such it travels along the culture's customary avenues of exchange. Can we find a community and a system of exchange which stand outside the circle of the victor's polis? If so, these may guide us to an understanding of the workings of praise within the aristocratic group.

Let us focus on the interaction between houses, where the polis appears to play no part. A fragment of Pindar affirms that every house participates in what we may call an economy of praise: ὁ γὰρ ἐξ οἴκου ποτὶ μῶμον ἔπαινος κίρναται (fr. 181 SM),[1] "For praise from home is mixed with blame." As Gordon Kirkwood has recently argued, this line cannot mean "for praise is by nature mixed with blame," as Gregory Nagy would have it, but rather that "self-praise, or partisan praise, is no praise at all or worse. Alternatively, the words may mean that 'praise from home' will inevitably bring an answering censure and hence be 'mixed with blame.'"[2] Praise is part of an exchange system, for the same house that produces achievements cannot also manufacture their glorification. Praise must come from outside in order that the surrounding community not be alienated, or put positively, the value of achievement is the prestige it has in the eyes of that community, so that praise must come from the larger group.[3]

What community does ἐξ οἴκου imply, and what is its dominant mode of exchange? This fragment is preserved in the scholia to Nemean 7, as a gloss on the lines,

> ξεῖνός εἰμι· σκοτεινὸν ἀπέχων ψόγον,
> ὕδατος ὥτε ῥοὰς φίλον ἐς ἄνδρ' ἄγων
> κλέος ἐτήτυμον αἰνέσω·
>
> (N.7.61–63)

I am his guest-friend; holding back dark censure, I shall praise, leading true fame like streams of water to a man who is a friend.

Ξεῖνος and ἐξ οἴκου suggest the community the poet wishes to draw into the praise of the victor, for they evoke the great households and elaborate guest-friendship systems of the Homeric poems. In Homeric epic, the powerful households of local kings and nobles treat with each other in isolation, establishing complex networks of distant guest-friends.

In his seminal work, *The World of Odysseus*, Moses Finley observes that such guest-friendship systems were part of functioning networks

---

[1]Drachmann 1926.128.

[2]Kirkwood 1984.21–22. It is worth quoting Kirkwood's argument against the Detienne/Nagy interpretation: "Pindar says ὁ ἐξ οἴκου ἔπαινος: Nagy translates ὁ ἔπαινος . . . ἐξ οἴκου. Pindar is saying something not about praise in general but about a specific form of praise, praise 'from home.' Detienne quotes only the three words μῶμον ἔπαινος κίρναται and gives, as a translation of them, 'L'éloge touche au blâme.' Detienne quotes from Puech's Budé edition and uses Puech's translation for these words. He does not mention the additional words in Puech's translation, 'Quand il vient de notre propre maison.'"

[3]See Crotty 1982.55–60.

of aristocratic gift exchange within the Homeric poems. Praise in Pindar's system functions like treasure in the Homeric model as Finley describes it:

> With their flocks and their labour force, with plentiful stone for building and clay for pots, the great households could almost realize their ideal of absolute self-sufficiency. . . . But there was one thing which prevented full self-sufficiency, a need which could neither be eliminated nor satisfied by substitutes, and that was the need for metal. . . . Metal meant tools and weapons, but it also meant something else, perhaps as important [— treasure]. . . . The Greek word customarily rendered as "treasure" is *keimelion*, literally something that can be laid away. In the poems treasure was of bronze, iron, or gold, less often of silver or fine cloth, and usually it was shaped into goblets, tripods, or cauldrons. Such objects had some direct use value and they could provide aesthetic satisfaction, too . . . but neither function was of real moment compared to their value as symbolic wealth or prestige wealth. The twin uses of treasure were in possessing it and in giving it away.[4]

The analogy between praise in epinikion and *keimelia* in the Homeric world is not fortuitous, as we shall see.

It may be objected that the society for which Pindar composed his songs in the first half of the fifth century is very far from the "world of Odysseus." Is gift exchange still a viable model for the poet and his audience? We need not accept Finley's thesis whole to make use of his valuable observations about gift exchange. Finley argues that the Homeric poems reflect a historical society that existed in the tenth or ninth century B.C., before the appearance of the polis.[5] Ian Morris has recently challenged this position, contending first that the nature of a living oral tradition would preclude the perfect preservation of a vanished system for a hundred years or more. He also maintains that the polis and other institutions of which Finley saw no trace in the Homeric poems have, in fact, left their mark on the epics. Finally and most significantly for our purposes, Morris suggests that the Homeric poems did not accurately reproduce any historical society but instead depicted the ideal of the eighth-century aristocratic audience for which they were composed. Indeed, Morris has proposed that the poems were recorded

---

[4]Finley 1977.60–66, quotation from 60–61. On the uses of treasure, see further Finley 1977.120–121, Lacey 1968.45.
[5]Finley 1977.26–50.

in the eighth century because they served so well the ideological needs of a beleaguered aristocracy.[6]

However this may be, for many centuries the Homeric poems continued to provide models for conscious emulation by Greek aristocrats. Eric Havelock has observed that Homeric epic served as a central educative tool down to Plato's time, especially, as Walter Donlan has emphasized, for Greek aristocrats. In a sense, the very thing that crystallized the text of Homer in the first place, according to Morris, ensured its prominence in Greek *paideia*: it offered a model for aristocratic self-definition in the face of encroachment and change. Thus W. K. Lacey observes that *xenoi* remained an important part of the aristocratic *oikos*, especially under the influence of Homer.[7]

But gift exchange survived not just because of conscious emulation of Homer. For gift-exchange categories and modes of thought endured tenaciously, even after the spread of money and commodity exchange.[8] As Victor Turner notes,

> The culture of any society at any moment is more like the debris, or "fallout," of past ideological systems, than it is itself a system, a coherent whole. Coherent wholes may exist . . . but human social groups tend to find their openness to the future in the variety of their metaphors for what may be the good life and in the contest of their paradigms. If there is order, it is seldom preordained . . . ; it is achieved—the result of conflicting or concurring wills and intelligences, each relying on some convincing paradigm.[9]

Archaic Greece offers a fine example of a society in which there were a variety of operative metaphors and a contest of paradigms. Gift exchange remained a compelling paradigm for a segment of the population. Thus a line of Solon preserves the sentiment "Happy is he who has . . . a *xenos* in foreign parts" (fr. 23W), and Herodotus reports that Croesus and the Spartans exchanged guest-gifts to establish an alliance (Herodotus 1.69–70).[10] Historians have even begun to take seriously Herodotus' statement that the Spartans assisted the Samian exiles

[6]Morris 1986b.81–129.

[7]For the general influence of Homer on aristocrats, see Havelock 1963.36–96, Donlan 1980.1–2, 183 n. 1, and cf. Morris 1986b.125 n. 246. For specific areas of influence (attitudes toward *xenoi*), see Lacey 1968.31–32.

[8]Morris 1986a.3–13, Herman 1987.

[9]Turner 1974.14.

[10]These examples are cited by Morris 1986a.6, Cartledge 1982.250, and Finley 1977.100. See also Herman 1987.73–161.

against Polykrates because of a long-standing relationship of reciprocal goodwill. In this case, the basis for international relations was a special bond of guest-friendship between certain influential Spartans and Samian aristocrats. And, it appears, this special relationship endured well into the fifth century.[11]

Herodotus provides evidence that gift exchange continued to play an important part in patterning international relations. It also endured among private citizens, developing along two diverging paths that reflect the "conflicting or concurring wills" to which Turner refers. On the one hand, the polis appropriated and adapted gift exchange for the public sphere, transforming it into a system of liturgies imposed upon its richest citizens. The ideology of lavish, visible expenditure remained, but it was diverted to different objects and a different audience. Thus the proxeny system replaced private *xenia*, and spending on public sacrifices, *choregiai*, and trierarchies was encouraged.[12]

Alongside the public track of the liturgical system, the closed circuit of aristocratic gift exchange endured. Its objects of expenditure were the same as they had always been: weddings, funerals, long-distance ties of guest-friendship. Indeed, it appears that in this period participation in this older form of gift exchange became a polemical gesture, a way for aristocrats to define themselves to themselves and to differentiate themselves from their fellow citizens.[13] The existence of this sphere of exchange is revealed by legislation attempting to regulate it—sumptuary laws against lavish displays at weddings and funerals.[14] As Louis Gernet observes, expenditure on such closed aristocratic occasions was rightly perceived by the polis as a challenge to its communal ideology: "It is instructive that the ruling polis, which encourages expenditures on the part of the nobility in certain areas, puts limits on them in others, even by legislation. This is the case with marriages, but even more so with funerals. . . . by its nature the city opposes any special code of behavior that would contribute to the maintenance of a household's unity, the unity between households, and the prestige of the whole order."[15]

[11]Cartledge 1982.
[12]On proxeny, see Cartledge 1982.250, Herman 1987.130–142; on the development in general, see Gernet 1981b.285, Humphreys 1978.219.
[13]Donlan (1980.52–75, 155–171) and Herman (1987.161–165) note the need for aristocrats to differentiate themselves by their extravagant lifestyle.
[14]For the evidence of such legislation, see Pleket 1969.48–50.
[15]Gernet 1981b.285. On the democratic nature of such sumptuary legislation, see Mazzarino 1947.193–194, 214–222, and Will 1955.512–514.

90   The Economy of Praise

We find the same opposition between private gift exchange and civic solidarity articulated from the aristocratic perspective in a speech put into the mouth of Xerxes by Herodotus. After the battle of Thermopylae, the Great King asks Demaratus of Sparta how to defeat the Lacedaemonians. His advice is to split the Persian fleet and send a contingent to harry the Peloponnese. Achaimenes, the commander of the Persian fleet, denounces Demaratus' advice and questions his good faith. The Greeks, he says, love to envy good fortune and hate that which is stronger (Herodotus 7.236.2). Xerxes accepts the advice of Achaimenes, but defends the goodwill of Demaratus:

ὅτι πολιήτης μὲν πολιήτῃ εὖ πρήσσοντι φθονέει καὶ ἔστι δυσμενὴς τῇ σιγῇ, οὐδ' ἂν συμβουλευομένου τοῦ ἀστοῦ πολιήτης ἀνὴρ τὰ ἄριστα οἱ δοκέοντα εἶναι ὑποθέοιτο, εἰ μὴ πρόσω ἀρετῆς ἀνήκοι· σπάνιοι δὲ εἰσι οἱ τοιοῦτοι· ξεῖνος δὲ ξείνῳ εὖ πρήσσοντί ἐστι εὐμενέστατον πάντων, συμβουλευομένου τε ἂν συμβουλεύσειε τὰ ἄριστα. (Herodotus 7.237.2–3)

The fact [is] that a citizen envies a fellow citizen when he does well, and is hostile in silence, nor would a citizen advise the things that seem best when a fellow-citizen asks his advice, unless he attain to the extreme of virtue. But such men are rare. Now, a guest-friend, on the other hand—he is the most well disposed of all things to a guest-friend when he fares well, and he would give the best advice to one seeking his council.

The observation that one's fellow citizens are envious of one's success seems a bit incongruous in the mouth of the Great King of Persia. In this case, as often in Herodotus, a barbarian dynast expresses what is essentially a Greek aristocratic position—that you cannot trust your fellow citizens, but you can trust your guest-friends.[16] Given the constraints of his heterogeneous audience and the essentially integrative function of his art, Pindar can never be so explicit in opposing aristocratic gift exchange to the ideology of the polis. But the unselfconscious formulation of the aristocratic position in Herodotus makes clear that the opposition was still very much alive in Pindar's era.[17]

In this period of two diverging models of gift exchange, athletic competition participated in both. Competition at the Panhellenic games figured in catalogs of prestigious liturgies from the fifth and fourth

[16]Cf. Herodotus 1.153, on which see Kurke 1989.
[17]Slater (1979a.82 n. 40) notes the relevance of this Herodotus passage for the motif of xenia in Pindar. He compares O.4.4 and N.7.69.

centuries, and the custom of feasting athletic victors in the prytaneum shows that they were regarded as public benefactors. But as we have seen, the time and expense of training and competing limited participation almost exclusively to wealthy aristocrats. Thus the Panhellenic games also provided a forum for aristocratic self-presentation and differentiation from their civic communities.[18] Because of the ambiguity of athletic competition, hovering between these two models, the epinikian poet can represent victory either as a public benefaction or as an element in aristocratic gift exchange. When he chooses to represent it as the latter, therefore, we must conclude that he is embracing aristocratic ideology. In such cases, the poet's choice of metaphor cannot be neutral, for it participates in a conflict of ideologies.

This argument requires a disclaimer. The opposition of public and private spheres of gift exchange is already an oversimplification, for the polis itself is a complex institution and reflects the same "fall-out" of past ideologies which Turner describes. If one strand of polis ideology is reflected in sumptuary legislation regulating aristocratic weddings and funerals, another strand is the diffusion or generalization of aristocratic values throughout the civic community. As Gernet observes, "The very revolution that ended the nobility's power did not completely suppress the concept of their kind of life. What the revolution did was diffuse such an idea. The citizen has a quality of human pride which is comparable to that of a nobleman, and his enduring contempt for things mercantile reflects the nobility's prejudices."[19] It is significant in this context that Gernet chooses to single out the citizen's "contempt for things mercantile," for this is essentially a gift-exchange attitude. Gernet's observation should warn us, then, that aristocratic ideology may not always be coextensive with the aristocratic group.

Still, it appears that gift exchange is not only an available model but a preferred one for a certain segment of the poet's audience. By representing the economy of praise as gift exchange, the poet marks himself and the victor as aristocrats and speaks compellingly to those who participate in aristocratic ideology. But to what extent does the poet actually avail himself of the model of gift exchange in the epinikia? To answer, let me cite Finley once more, this time from his essay on "Marriage, Sale, and Gift in the Homeric World": "Although gift-giving went on in a great variety of situations, three particular contexts were of such special

---

[18]Thus Rose 1982.55, Starr 1961.308–309.
[19]Gernet 1981b.288; see also Donlan 1980.xiii, 178–179.

significance that an individualised terminology was developed for the respective gifts. One was the gifts of compensation for a wrong— *apoina*; a second the gifts of guest-friendship—*xeineia*; and the third the gifts of marriage—*hedna*."[20] These same three spheres of terminology figure prominently in the epinikia as metaphors for the relationship between the poet and the victor. All three represent exchange between houses, in which the polis played only a secondary part. Thus recompense, marriage, and guest-friendship circumscribe a field of imagery directed primarily at an aristocratic audience. But why are these three particular spheres of imagery chosen? That is to say, what is the "special significance" that makes them a set for Pindar? And how, within this metaphorical field, does the poet accomplish the reintegration of the victor into his aristocratic group? To answer these questions, we must examine in detail the imagery drawn from the three spheres of recompense, marriage, and guest-friendship in the epinikia. But first we must pause to flesh out our understanding of gift exchange as a functioning social system in primitive and archaic cultures.

Perhaps the best introduction to the social realities and the psychological underpinnings of gift exchange is Marcel Mauss's *Essai sur le don* (1925, translated into English in 1954 as *The Gift*). Mauss's thought-provoking essay has stimulated much anthropological research and analysis of gift-exchange cultures. For our purposes, it is worth summarizing the observations of Mauss and others on gift exchange as it functions in a number of different societies.

We should first emphasize the totality of the system in gift-exchange cultures: the model pervades every aspect of social life, establishing and maintaining the social order:

> In the systems of the past we do not find simple exchange of goods, wealth and produce through markets established among individuals. For it is groups, and not individuals, which carry on exchange, make contracts, and are bound by obligations. . . . Further, what they exchange is not exclusively goods and wealth, real and personal property, and things of economic value. They exchange rather courtesies, entertainments, ritual, military assistance, women, children, dances, and feasts.[21]

[20]Finley 1953.240–241.

[21]Mauss 1967.3. In a footnote to this passage, Mauss cites the opening of Olympian 7 (though he uses very little Greek material otherwise): observing "The whole passage still reflects the kind of situation we are describing. The themes of the gift, of wealth, marriage, honour, favour, alliance, of shared food and drink, and the theme of jealousy in marriage are all clearly represented" (Mauss 1967.84 n. 7).

There is nothing that does not partake of the system of gift exchange. As Pierre Bourdieu points out, there is "perfect interconvertibility of economic capital (in the narrow sense) and symbolic capital."[22] Indeed, the distinction capitalism makes between economic interest and some "disinterested" realm of the spiritual does not exist in such a culture. Every social interaction, every act of exchange, can be assimilated to the model of reciprocal gift giving. And as we shall see, Pindar incorporates into this system every step of the epinikian process—the games themselves, their foundation by men, the divine favor that bestows victory, the resultant dedications, the celebratory *kōmos*, and the contract between victor and poet.

In contrast to commodity exchange, gift exchange depends on a personalized relationship between transaction partners which endures over time.[23] Within such an operative gift-exchange system, there are three crucial obligations: giving, receiving, and repaying.[24] Thus, for example, in the gift-exchange ceremony of the Trobriand Islanders, "pains are taken to show one's freedom and autonomy as well as one's magnanimity, yet all the time one is actuated by the mechanisms of obligation which are resident in the gifts themselves."[25] The one who receives must make a return that is equal or superior to the original gift: "The obligation of worthy return is imperative. Face is lost for ever if it is not made or if equivalent value is not destroyed."[26]

Mauss suggests the reason for the threefold obligation of giving, receiving, and repaying when he observes, "To refuse to give, or to fail to invite, is—like refusing to accept—the equivalent of a declaration of war; it is a refusal of friendship and intercourse."[27] Marshall Sahlins, in an essay devoted to Mauss's treatise, elaborates this notion, seeing in the gift "the primitive analogue of social contract":

In posing the internal fragility of the segmentary societies, their constituted decomposition, *The Gift* transposes the classic alternatives of war and trade from the periphery to the very center of social life, and from the occasional episode to the continuous presence. This is the supreme importance of Mauss's return to nature, from which it follows that primitive society is at war with [Hobbesian] Warre, and that all their dealings are treaties of peace. All the exchanges, that is to say, must bear in their

22Bourdieu 1977.177.
23Mauss 1967.34–35, Bourdieu 1977.171.
24Mauss 1967.37–41.
25Mauss 1967.21.
26Mauss 1967.41.
27Mauss 1967.11.

material design some political burden of reconciliation. Or, as the Bush-
man said, "The worse thing is not giving presents. If people do not like
each other but one gives a gift and the other must accept, this brings a
peace between them. We give what we have. That is the way we live
together."[28]

Thus gift exchange makes and preserves peace; gift giving is not merely
a material transaction but also a way of binding giver and receiver
together. Far more important than their functional value as objects, gifts
connect people and groups: they create community.

In practice, such a pervasive system of gift exchange not only creates
community; it sustains it. As E. E. Evans-Pritchard observes, "This
habit of share and share alike is easily understandable in a community
where everyone is likely to find himself in difficulties from time to time,
for it is scarcity and not sufficiency that makes people generous, since
everybody is thereby ensured against hunger. He who is in need today
receives help from him who may be in like need tomorrow." Or again,
succinctly, "In general it may be said that no one in a Nuer village
starves unless all are starving."[29]

Thus gift exchange serves a crucial integrative or constitutive function in the culture that practices it. But the circulation of gifts can
contribute to social differentiation as well as to community, for there
exists a higher tier of gifts which confer particular status and prestige.
This function depends on a notion of value very different from that of
monetary systems: in many gift-exchange cultures objects of exchange
are ranked hierarchically. Goods are organized into "spheres of exchange," which, as Morris observes, are "valued not cardinally but
ordinally."[30] "Top-rank goods," usually objects which are precious and
rare, cannot be "traded down" for any quantity of goods of lesser rank.
Raymond Firth describes the situation: "It is as if, allowing for the
obvious differences, in our society gold, silver and copper were used as
media of exchange in three series of transactions but there was no
accurate means of rendering them in terms of each other."[31]

Within such a system of spheres of exchange, the social occasion
determines the rank of gifts to be given and received. The circulation of
top-rank gifts is confined to the most important occasions, which vary
in different cultures but generally include "rites of passage and institu-

---

[28]Sahlins 1972.169, 182, and see 186–187.
[29]Evans-Pritchard 1940.85 and 1951.132, quoted in Sahlins 1972.210 and 213.
[30]Morris 1986a.8; cf. Gregory 1982.48–50.
[31]Firth 1965.341.

tionalised competition," according to Morris. He applies this model to
the Homeric poems and concludes that the top-ranked gifts in Homer
are "women, cattle and finished objects of metal."[32] This last is the
category Finley designates as *keimelia* and Louis Gernet considers under
the rubric *agalmata*.[33] Morris identifies the appropriate contexts for the
exchange of top-rank gifts as "marriages, funeral games and within
guest-friendship arrangements."[34] Indeed, Gernet anticipated the anthropological analysis of spheres of exchange when he observed,

> The objects given as prizes [in funeral games] belong to a category both
> extensive and definite, relatively at any rate. Such objects or their ana-
> logues occur in several different but parallel contexts: traditional pres-
> ents, gifts between guest-friends, offerings to the gods, grave-goods and
> objects placed in the tombs of princes. As a class of goods, they are the
> *medium of aristocratic intercourse.* They are classified implicitly as different
> from another sort of goods which are both inferior in nature and distinct
> in function.[35]

As Gernet noted, the circulation of *agalmata* in high-prestige contexts is
limited to "aristocratic intercourse" in Homer. The monopoly on such
goods secures for the Homeric heroes their elite standing within society.

Thus control of top-rank goods can establish and maintain one class
within a hierarchical system. These same goods can also be used by
members of the top class to establish preeminence within that group,
for within a highly competitive culture, property can be deployed in the
struggle for honor. As Finley observes of the Homeric system: "Gift-
giving too was part of a network of competitive, honorific activity. . . .
One measure of a man's true worth was how much he could give away
in treasure."[36] It is the unmatched expenditure or even destruction of
top-rank goods which establishes the preeminence of a family within
the nobility. Mauss discusses the extreme form of such a system when
he considers the potlatch of the Northwest Indians. Potlatch, the conspicuous destruction of enormous quantities of precious objects, occurs
only among the nobles in order to establish their rank within the
hierarchy.[37] As might be expected of such a ranking system, the potlatch is highly competitive:

[32]Morris 1986a.8, 9, with the sources he cites.
[33]Finley 1977.60–61, Gernet 1981a.
[34]Morris 1986a.9.
[35]Gernet 1981a.113 (my italics).
[36]Finley 1977.120–121.
[37]Mauss 1967.4–5, Meillassoux 1968.

Nowhere else is the prestige of an individual as closely bound up with
expenditure, and with the duty of returning with interest gifts received in
such a way that the creditor becomes the debtor. Consumption and
destruction are virtually unlimited. . . . The rich man who shows his
wealth by spending recklessly is the man who wins prestige. The principles of rivalry and antagonism are basic. Political and individual status in
associations and clans, and rank of every kind, are determined by the war
of property, as well as by armed hostilities, by chance, inheritance,
alliance or marriage. But everything is conceived as if it were a war of
wealth.[38]

Paradoxically then, it appears that gift giving both creates community
and divides it; that there is a "war of property" as well as a "war with
Warre" inherent in the system of gift exchange.

Finally, we should consider what we might call the metaphysics of
gift exchange. Within a functional gift exchange system, the cosmos
itself is perceived to run by the same rules. Therefore, gifts must be
rendered to the gods and the dead, for as Mauss observes, "They are the
real owners of the world's wealth. With them it was particularly necessary to exchange and particularly dangerous not to; but, on the other
hand, with them exchange was easiest and safest."[39] This projection of
gift exchange onto the cosmos naturalizes the system, so that it cannot
be recognized for what it is—simply one possible mode of exchange
among many. As Bourdieu notes, gift exchange endures by misrecogni-
tion, by repression of the fact that it is an economic system.[40]

The link to the cosmos applies to the whole system, but particularly
to top-rank goods. Thus within the Greek context, Louis Gernet articulates a gift-exchange concept when he notes that *agalmata* had a special
connection with another world, whether the sea, the underworld, or the
land of dreams: "Like other mythical objects which are related to them
in the Greek imagination, precious objects, traditional symbols of opu-
lence, are ineluctably related—indeed, in a way especially related—to
that other world presupposed by the religious mind: now they go down
to it, and now they journey back."[41] Cross-culturally it appears that
top-rank gifts, objects of special status, are particularly likely to be
linked to the past, to the gods or founding heroes. Such objects often
have a pedigree that enhances their value. For example, in the *kula*, the
great institutionalized cycle of exchanges among the Trobriand Is-

[38]Mauss 1967.35.
[39]Mauss 1967.13.
[40]Bourdieu 1977.171–177.
[41]Gernet 1981a.131.

landers, the most precious objects of exchange have "a name, a person-
ality, a past, and even a legend attached to them, to such an extent that
people may be named after them."[42] Just as gift exchange creates community by forging a bond between exchange partners, precious objects
form a chain through time as well. More than that, in certain cultures
each new exchange of top-rank goods seems to represent or reincarnate
the first passing-on, putting the living in touch with the gods and their
dead ancestors. The potlatch, for example, "is more than a legal phenomenon; it is one of those phenomena we propose to call 'total.' It is
religious, mythological and shamanistic because the chiefs taking part
are incarnations of gods and ancestors, whose names they bear, whose
dances they dance and whose spirits possess them."[43] The special link
between top-rank goods and the gods or heroes supports the privileged
status of those who control their circulation. As the metaphysics of gift
exchange tends to support the whole system by projecting it onto the
cosmos, the pedigrees of top-rank gifts, their links to the past, ratify the
ranking of exchange spheres and the social hierarchy such ranking
makes possible. The links with gods and ancestors affirm that the
society's system of value is not contingent but natural.

With Mauss's "shamanism" and Sahlins's "war with Warre" we may
seem to have wandered very far from Pindar's bright epinikian world.
What application do these anthropological analyses have for Pindar's
odes? We might recognize Mauss's "obligation to repay" in the χρέος
motif of epinikion. According to this topos, the victor's achievement
puts the poet under an obligation to celebrate him.[44] Bundy's discussion
of the χρέος motif clearly evokes the "obligation of worthy return"
which Mauss describes:

> Both passages depend on the notion that ἀρετά creates a debt that must
> be paid in the true coin of praise. . . . The metaphor is frequent in still
> other forms and is one of the set conventions of the genre. . . . ἀγάνορα
> κόμπον is a "lordly" vaunt to match "lordly" deeds. The epithet obeys
> that common enkomiastic imperative "to match the deed in words."
> "Praise to match" is the overt point of κόμπον τὸν ἐοικότα ("the vaunt
> they deserve," i.e., a lordly one) in I.5.26 (cf. also ποτίφορος . . . μισθός
> in N.7.63, and πρόσφορον / . . . κόμπον in N.8.48f.).[45]

---

[42]Mauss 1967.22.
[43]Mauss 1967.36.
[44]See Schadewaldt 1928.277–280, Bundy 1962.10–11, 54–59, Maehler 1963.85.
[45]Bundy 1962.57–59.

What is the precise nature of the poet's debt? We can say first what *chreos* is not. It does not designate the poet's contractual obligation, for in *chreos* contexts poet and victor are presented as equals and the fact of payment is completely suppressed.[46] Wolfgang Schadewaldt suggests that the poet undertakes his debt as a representative of the civic community, which regards the victor as εὐεργέτης.[47] But as Gundert notes with some discomfort, εὐεργέτης never occurs in civic contexts in the epinikia; it occurs, rather, in contexts of private gratitude and gift exchange.[48] This distribution is significant: it supports our earlier conclusions that the language and imagery of gift exchange are ideologically loaded and directed primarily at the aristocracy. Schadewaldt's explanation, then, appears to conflate two different segments of the poet's audience and thereby to obscure the poet's diverse strategies for dealing with each. Let us instead attempt to understand the *chreos* motif within the model of gift exchange between houses.

We must first take a step backward to consider the source of the poet's obligation: athletic victory itself. Epinikion often represents athletic victory as pure, unrivaled expenditure, of both money and effort, on the part of the victor. The praise of such expenditure is frequently linked with the notion of competition or striving. Thus, in Olympian 5, the poet observes appreciatively,

αἰεὶ δ᾽ ἀμφ᾽ ἀρεταῖσι πόνος δαπάνα τε μάρναται πρὸς ἔργον
κινδύνῳ κεκαλυμμένον·

(O.5.15–16)

But always about achievements effort and expenditure strive toward the deed obscured by risk.

Or again, in Isthmian 4, Pindar characterizes the victor's noble family,

οὐδὲ παναγυρίων ξυνᾶν ἀπεῖχον
καμπύλον δίφρον, Πανελλάνεσσι δ᾽ ἐριζόμενοι δαπάνᾳ χαῖρον ἵππων.

(I.4.28–29)

They have never kept their curved chariot from the common assemblies, but vying with all the Greeks, they rejoiced in expenditure on horses.

[46]See the discussion of Maehler 1963.85–88.
[47]Schadewaldt 1928.277–278.
[48]Gundert 1935.32 and 121 n. 134. Cf. O.2.94, P.2.24, P.4.30, P.5.44, I.1.53, and I.6.70 (εὐεργεσίαις).

Μάρναται and ἐριζόμενοι mark the expenditure of wealth and effort as competitive activities: each noble family vies with every other throughout Greece (notice Πανελλάνεσσι). In these passages, the poet represents athletics as a kind of potlatch, a competition for prestige based on the lavish expenditure of wealth, physical exertion, and time.[49] This incorporation of athletic competition into the system of top-rank gift exchange is surely no mere poetic conceit. It is rather a conceptual model shared by the poet and his aristocratic audience. Competition at the Panhellenic games, largely limited to the nobility, who were thereby distinguished from their fellow citizens, provided a forum for aristocrats to vie for preeminence within their own class.[50] The poet frequently acknowledges athletic expenditure as "competitive honorific activity" in which the victor has revealed himself and his family as "the best."[51]

But if the games are conceptualized as "potlatch," as competitive, honorific expenditure of top-rank goods, the poet's debt and his acceptance thereof transform the "war of property" into community, for as we have seen, the obligation to repay represents a choice against war in segmentary societies. Pindar enacts a similar choice on a couple of occasions, when he explicitly describes his obligation in negative terms— what he must *avoid* doing. We should not dismiss these passages as mere litotes, for they show us each act of praising as a deliberate choice not to blame. This binary choice of praise or blame corresponds to the alternatives Sahlins perceives between gift exchange and war. Thus Pindar tells us emphatically in Nemean 7:

[49]Besides the passages quoted, see I.5.54–58. Though the meaning of the passage is obscured by corruption, it combines the notion of striving with some kind of statement about *ponos* and *dapane*. For theoretical discussions of athletics as potlatch or sacrificial expenditure, see Huizinga 1950.58–75 and Sansone 1988.

[50]Finley (1977.120) sees the Panhellenic games as the natural continuation of aristocratic competiton in the Homeric poems. The analogy between athletic competition and potlatch also allows us to reconcile the positions of Starr 1961.309 and Rose 1982.70–71. Rose criticizes Starr's analysis of the Panhellenic games in terms of competition *within* the aristocracy, preferring to emphasize the aspect of aristocratic solidarity in Panhellenic competition. But both aspects are explained by the analogy of potlatch: such enormous expenditure is both limited to the nobility and a means of establishing standing within that class.

[51]Cf. O.10.64, O.13.43, P.3.74, and N.11.13–14, where Pindar expresses this concept by the use of the verb ἀριστεύειν, or consider the many examples Slater (1969a) lists under ἀρετά b, c, d. In these passages, as in Herodotus 8.27, ἀρετά designates a fiercely competitive, aristocratic virtue. This competitive conception of "virtue" may also account for Pindar's brutal presentation of the shame of the defeated at O.8.67–69 and P.8.81–87.

> ξεῖνός εἰμι· σκοτεινὸν ἀπέχων ψόγον,
> ὕδατος ὥτε ῥοὰς φίλον ἐς ἄνδρ᾽ ἄγων
> κλέος ἐτήτυμον αἰνέσω·
>
> (N.7.61–63)

I am his guest-friend; holding back dark censure, I shall praise, leading
true fame like streams of water to a man who is a friend.

Here *xenia*, a relation of private gift exchange, obligates the poet to offer
praise for the victor's achievement.

In the most extended rejection of blame in the epinikia, the poet
implies by contrast the reasons he chooses praise over blame:

> ἐμὲ δὲ χρεών
> φεύγειν δάκος ἀδινὸν κακαγοριᾶν.
> εἶδον γὰρ ἑκὰς ἐὼν τὰ πόλλ᾽ ἐν ἀμαχανίᾳ
> ψογερὸν Ἀρχίλοχον βαρυλόγοις ἔχθεσιν
> πιαινόμενον·
>
> (P.2.52–56)

But it is necessary for me to flee the relentless bite of evil speaking. For
being far away, I have seen censorious Archilochus often in a state of
resourcelessness, fattening himself on heavy-worded hatreds.

Here the poet's obligation (ἐμὲ δὲ χρεών) is specifically described as the
need to flee blame.[52] In the person of Archilochus as archetypal blame
poet, Pindar represents blame as the complete breakdown of a community of poetic exchange.[53] Archilochus is completely isolated; Pindar
emphasizes that he views him from "far away." Archilochus must
"fatten himself" (πιαινόμενον middle) on [his own] "heavy-worded
hatreds": because he is unwilling to share with others the poetic nour-
ishment of praise, no one else will share his substance with him.[54] And

[52]Both the context and Pindar's usage elsewhere (cf. P.9.92) argue for the interpretation that the poet himself is choosing not to blame, rather than fleeing his own censurers.
See Nagy 1979.224–225 and Miller 1981.136–139.

[53]On Archilochus' generic quality here, see Nagy 1979.224 and Miller 1981.139–140.

[54]Compare with Pindar's tone here the observation of Lévi-Strauss: "The action of
the person who, like the woman in the Maori proverb, *Kai kino ana Te Arahe*, would
secretly eat the ceremonial food, without offering any of it, would provoke from his or
her near relatives irony, mockery, disgust and even anger, according to the circumstances
and persons" (Lévi-Strauss 1969.58). For a somewhat different interpretation of πιαινόμενον, see Nagy 1979.225–226.

by his self-imposed isolation, the blame poet casts himself into a condition of poetic resourcelessness and poverty (τὰ πόλλ' ἐν ἀμαχανίᾳ).[55]

As the opposite of Archilochus, Pindar always derives his own *eumachania*—his poetic resources—from outside, from choosing to take part in an exchange economy of praise. Thus he tells the victor Melissos in the opening lines of Isthmian 4:

> Ἔστι μοι θεῶν ἕκατι μυρία παντᾷ κέλευθος,
> ὦ Μέλισσ', εὐμαχανίαν γὰρ ἔφανας Ἰσθμίοις,
> ὑμετέρας ἀρετὰς ὕμνῳ διώκειν·
>
> (I.4.1–3)

There are for me, by the grace of the gods, ten thousand paths in every direction, O Melissos, for you have revealed resources at the Isthmian [games], to pursue your achievements with song.

And thus he declares in Pythian 9 that he has "glorified this city three times," thereby escaping what Andrew Miller glosses as "poverty of subject matter such as results, and inevitably must result, in speechlessness" (σιγαλὸν ἀμαχανίαν . . . φυγών [P.9.92]).[56] The victor provides the poet with subject matter, the poet quenches the victor's "thirst for song" (N.3.6–7; cf. P.9.103–104), and both are nourished by the exchange.[57] Thus by accepting the debt, by choosing to praise, the poet creates a bond with the victor, as well as saving himself from isolation and starvation. The community the poet creates by his act of praise extends beyond the single link between poet and victor, however, for the poem, like the victory, is a public act that addresses an audience and implicates them in its obligation to praise.

[55]Contra Svenbro 1976.178, it seems best to take ἀμαχανία metaphorically rather than literally, since πιαινόμενον is clearly metaphorical. So Miller 1981.140: "Thus the point of Pindar's reference to Archilochos seems to be that a poet who, for whatever reason, restricts his professional activity to the negative exercises of censure and blame, *psogos* and *kakagoria*, will eventually find himself afflicted by a kind of poverty of poetic resource, a sterility or barrenness of *inventio*." Compare Mauss's remarks on the rationality of gift exchange: "It is by opposing reason to emotion, by setting up the will for peace against rash follies of this kind, that peoples succeed in substituting alliance, gift and commerce for *war, isolation and stagnation*" (Mauss 1967.80; my italics).

[56]Miller 1981.140, following Fennell 1893.256. Miller quotes I.4.1–3 and P.9.90–92 to support his interpretation of *amachania* in Pythian 2 as poetic resourcelessness (Miller 1981.139–140). I would add only that *amachania* and *eumachania*, thus used, are metaphors drawn from the sphere of concrete material survival and would emphasize that Pindar's "resources" are always a gift conferred from outside.

[57]This is the poet's side of ὁ γὰρ ἐξ οἴκου ποτὶ μῶμον κίρναται: he must find subject matter for praise outside his own "house."

On the basis of the workings of *chreos* within the epinikia, we can anticipate the conclusions of the detailed analysis of different spheres of gift exchange. It appears that the poem itself modulates from the hierarchical, ranking function of gift exchange to its integrative function. As a "war of property," athletic victory establishes the preeminence of the victor and his family by putting his whole class in his debt. The poet acknowledges and accepts the debt, and by his gift of praise he reconstitutes the community. The movement from the victory as unrivaled expenditure to the reconstitution of the group by means of the poem is clearly articulated in a passage from Isthmian 1:

εἰ δ᾽ ἀρετᾷ κατάκειται πᾶσαν ὀργάν,
ἀμφότερον δαπάναις τε καὶ πόνοις,
χρή νιν εὑρόντεσσιν ἀγάνορα κόμπον
μὴ φθονεραῖσι φέρειν
γνώμαις. ἐπεὶ κούφα δόσις ἀνδρὶ σοφῷ
ἀντὶ μόχθων παντοδαπῶν ἔπος εἰπόντ᾽ ἀγαθὸν ξυνὸν ὀρθῶσαι καλόν.
                                                        (I.1.41–46)

> But if a man expends himself for achievement in every impulse, both
> with expenditures and toils, it is fitting to bear a lordly boast for those
> who find it with ungrudging purpose. Since it is a light gift for a skilled
> man in exchange for all sorts of toils, by saying a good word, to set up a
> common ornament.

The first two lines describe athletic competition as the total expenditure of resources for the sake of preeminent achievement (ἀρετᾷ). Χρή introduces the notion of the poet's debt: "to match the deed in words," as Bundy says, for those who win (νιν [= ἀρετὰν] εὑρόντεσσιν). In this context, the adjective ἀγάνορα, "proud" or "lordly," is significant. It is predominantly a Homeric epithet, used of the θυμός or "spirit" of heroes. In the *Iliad* it occurs most commonly in speeches, as a form of heroic self-presentation. Thus, when a character claims that "his proud spirit bids him" act in a certain way, he is implicitly asserting that he has made the proper *heroic* decision.[58] Applied here to the boast owed to victors, it is almost a challenge to its aristocratic audience, for it asserts that such ungrudging praise can be offered only by the truly "lordly." There must be nothing mean in the response to victory. The gift of

[58]For the use of ἀγήνωρ in dialogue, see *Iliad* 2.276 (ironically applied to Thersites), 9.398, 635, 699–700, 10.220, 244, 319, 24.42. For similar contexts in narrative, see *Iliad* 12.300, 20.174, 406.

praise should be offered μὴ φθονεραῖσι . . . γνώμαις. Φθόνος is
excluded from the charmed circle of gift-exchange partners. Thus the
poet extends the obligation to praise to the entire aristocratic community.[59] The imagery of heroic gift exchange speaks to the aristocracy
and extorts their ungrudging goodwill. Precisely insofar as they are
committed to gift exchange as an aristocratic system, the nobles in the
audience are confronted with the same binary choice as the poet—praise
or blame, community or isolation. If they wish to maintain the aristocratic system, they must follow the poet's example and choose praise.[60]

Thus we can say that the poet's *chreos* attends the representation of
athletic victory as potlatch; his stance of indebtedness to the victor
implies the choice of community or dissolution. But we should notice
the modulation from obligation to freely offered gift in the progression
from χρή to κούφα δόσις. As Mauss observes, gift giving is an obligation in the guise of magnanimity.[61] The *chreos* motif acknowledges the
obligation, but this same bond can be represented as a relationship
freely entered into by willing and generous exchange partners. Such is
the implication of κούφα δόσις here; elsewhere, when the poet wishes
to emphasize the freedom of his gift, he designates his relationship with
the victor simply as *charis*.[62] Wilamowitz observed astutely, "Again and
again Pindar represents his art as the gift of the Charites, precisely when
he composes for others."[63] Praise poetry is by its very nature a gift

[59]Notice that Pindar supplies no personal object for χρή here (vs. ἐμὲ δὲ χρεών at
P.2.52). As a result, the obligation to praise extends to all those who consider themselves
ἀγήνορες, "lordly."
[60]In the final lines of the passage, the poet extends the community once more. The
gift-exchange imagery continues in κούφα δόσις and ἀντὶ μόχθων παντοδαπῶν, but
now the poet implies that the entire civic community benefits from the victor's achievement. For this is the force of ξυνόν in the epinikia, while ὀρθῶσαι καλόν participates in
the imagery of the civic virtue of *megaloprepeia* (to which I shall return in a later chapter).
The apparently effortless expansion of the community included and the easy modulation
from gift exchange to its civic counterpart are characteristic of the poet's fluid rhetoric.
[61]Mauss 1967.1–3, 21.
[62]See Gundert 1935.31–32, 40–41 (following Stenzel 1926, 1934) and Maehler
1963.88. Both emphasize the elements of freedom and generosity in *charis* in the epinikia.
[63]Wilamowitz 1922.152 (my translation). See, for examples, O.4.8–9, O.9.25–27,
P.5.45, P.6.1–3, P.8.21, P.9.89a–90, N.4.7–8, N.9.53–54, N.10.1–2, I.5.21–22, and
I.8.16–16a. It is not my purpose here to undertake a comprehensive survey of the
meaning of *charis* in Greek (for which see Wilamowitz 1922.152–153, Stenzel 1926.203–
204, Stenzel 1934.92, Hewitt 1927, Latacz 1966) or even within Pindar's poetry (see
Wilamowitz 1922.152–153, Schadewaldt 1928.268, 277–278, 287 n. 5, 294 n. 2, Gundert
1935.30–45,55–58, Maehler 1963.88–92, Carne-Ross 1985.59–64). I hope, rather, by a
series of analogies from gift-exchange cultures to approximate the meaning and connotations of *charis* as it appears in certain gift-exchange contexts in the epinikia.

exchanged, and the Charites are the special patrons of Pindar's epinikia because these poems are specifically composed "for others," born out of a particular relationship of goodwill between poet and victor. Thus Pindar can even refer to the poems themselves as χάριτες and to the genre of epinikion as the ἐπωνυμίαν χάριν νίκας, "the grace named for victory" (O. 10.78–79).[64]

But *charis* in the epinikia designates both sides of the relationship between poet and victor, for Pindar frequently represents the victory itself as *charis*, a precious gift bestowed on the victor by the gods or the Charites. Thus victors at the Olympic and Pythian games are described as those "on whom flourishing Charis gazes" (O.7.10–11). In another context, Pindar designates the chariot victories of Theron and his brother simply by saying "the common Graces led the blooms of four-horse chariots" for them (O.2.49–50).[65] The representation of victory as divine grace deemphasizes the element of conflict or competition involved in athletic success. In contrast to the potlatch model for athletic achievement, *charis* retrojects the community-building function of gift exchange to the moment of victory. Athletic competition is conceptualized not as a "war of property" but as the context for human-divine gift exchange. This construction of the cosmos as a community of exchange partners ratifies the aristocratic system and thereby imposes itself even more compellingly on the interested portion of the poet's audience. We might say that epinikian *charis* co-opts the metaphysics of gift exchange to serve the social functions of the genre, for investment in the gift-exchange system compels the aristocracy's acceptance of the victor's achievement once the poet has framed it within the terms of divine generosity.

But as with the potlatch model, the construction of victory as divine *charis* can occur only because victory and its celebration are top-rank occasions. As we have seen, it is top-rank objects, *agalmata*, which are particularly associated with the gods and founding heroes. Cross-culturally and traditionally in Greece, funeral games, like marriages and guest-friendships, were occasions for the exchange of top-rank gifts among the nobility.[66] At some point in their evolution, the games that

[64]For the poems as χάριτες, see Slater, 1969a, s.v. χάρις 1.b.β. There is some dispute about the reference of O.10.78–79. Gildersleeve understands χάριν as appositional to βροντάν in line 79 (Gildersleeve 1890.219, so also Nassen 1975.235). Gundert (1935.44) and Slater (1969a, s.v. ἐπωνύμιος) take it to designate epinikion.

[65]Cf. O.6.76, O.8.8, 57, 80, P.5.102, N.10.30, I.2.19. In all these passages, *charis* designates the victory as the gift of some deity; at O.10.17, *charis* denotes the gratitude the victor owes to his trainer for the victory.

[66]See *Iliad* 23, Gernet 1981a.

were institutionalized as the most prestigious Panhellenic contests no longer involved precious objects as prizes: instead, they conferred only wreaths, but they remained top-rank occasions in terms of their prestige.[67] Thus Pindar frequently represents wreaths from the Panhellenic games as *agalmata* or *keimelia*, and thus he identifies epinikian poetry as an *agalma* bestowed on the victor, persistently concretizing song as a precious object. In Olympian 11, for example, Pindar refers to his song as a "sweet-sounding ornament upon a crown of golden olive" (κόσμον ἐπὶ στεφάνῳ χρυσέας ἐλαίας ἀδυμελῆ [O.11.13–14]). Thus he transforms the olive crown to gold, the most precious of gifts, and then adds the ornament of his epinikion on top of it. In Nemean 7, the poet reciprocates the gift of the victory crown with one of his own:

> εἴρειν στεφάνους ἐλαφρόν, ἀναβάλεο· Μοῖσά τοι
> κολλᾷ χρυσὸν ἔν τε λευκὸν ἐλέφανθ᾽ ἁμᾶ
> καὶ λείριον ἄνθεμον ποντίας ὑφελοῖσ᾽ ἐέρσας.

(N.7.77–79)

It is easy to weave crowns—begin! The Muse cobbles gold and white ivory together, having taken up as well the lilylike flower of marine dew.

Pindar represents the victory ode as a crown offered to the victor, fashioned out of the most precious materials imaginable (gold, ivory, and coral). Thus epinikion has it both ways: it is a crown and an *agalma*.[68]

Charis is prominent in this sphere of prestige exchanges, for the element of gratuity is particularly stressed in the circulation of the culture's most valued gifts. Thus *charis* seems to designate in Pindar the "grace" or "glamour" that particularly infuses those occasions on which top-rank gifts are exchanged. On such occasions, *charis* irradiates all the participants and their gifts. Thus Pindar can identify victors at the great games simply as "those on whom . . . Charis sprinkles glorious form" (οἷς ποτε . . . αἰδοία ποτιστάξῃ Χάρις εὐκλέα μορφάν O.6.75–76). This *charis* of the occasion inspires the poet to make his precious gift of song, as in Olympian 1:

[67]On the evolution of the games, see Meuli 1941.189–190. Herodotus reveals the mystique of the "crown-bearing" contests among the Greeks in the earlier-quoted anecdote of the Persian Tritantaichmes (Herodotus 7.26.2–4).

[68]For the victory crown as *agalma*, see O.3.13, O.11.13–14, P.2.10, N.4.17, N.6.25–26, I.8.66–67, and Παρθ.2.48. Pindar specifically designates the poem an *agalma* at N.8.16; cf. Bacchylides 5.4, 10.11, fr. 20B5 SM.

ἀλλὰ Δωρίαν ἀπὸ φόρμιγγα πασσάλου
λάμβαν᾽, εἴ τί τοι Πίσας τε καὶ Φερενίκου χάρις
νόον ὑπὸ γλυκυτάταις ἔθηκε φροντίσιν,

(O.1.17–19)

But take the Dorian lyre from its peg, if at all the *charis* of Pisa and
Pherenikos has set your mind under sweetest thoughts.

The poet's song enhances the *charis* of the victor (O.10.94, N.7.75,
I.3.8, I.4.72), while the giving of it allows him to participate in the great
prestige of the occasion (O.9.25–29, N.9.54, I.5.21).

Thus it appears that *charis* and *chreos*, two notions that are fundamental to Pindar's program of praise, operate within a system of aristocratic
gift exchange. They are two sides of the same coin, for both characterize
the relationship of poet and victor, but with different emphases. As a
result, *charis* and *chreos* represent two slightly different strategies for
achieving the victor's reintegration into the aristocratic group. The
chreos motif forges a community of praise in response to the victor's
competitive expenditure by exposing the risk of disintegration which
gift exchange forestalls. *Charis* works more insidiously, pretending that
such a community already exists and that the victory is its token. Both
representations exploit the aristocracy's investment in gift exchange to
compel its acceptance of the victor's achievement, figured as potlatch or
as divine grace.

Furthermore, both representations of the relationship of poet and
victor presuppose that athletic competition and its celebration are top-
rank occasions, privileged spheres of aristocratic exchange. This status,
in turn, provides the explanation for Pindar's use of recompense, marriage, and guest-friendship imagery. In light of recent anthropological
work, we can characterize more concretely the "special significance"
Finley detected in these three spheres. It is their character as *top-rank
occasions* which makes a natural set of *apoina*, *hedna*, and *xenia*, and it is
their top-rank status that seems to evoke Pindar's use of these occasions
in metaphor to represent victory and celebration. Recompense, marriage, and hospitality provide the poet with conceptual models to con-
cretize and explore the obligations and gratuities of aristocratic exchange. Detailed consideration of these metaphorical systems will
reveal how the poet deploys the model of gift exchange between houses
to reconcile the victor to his aristocratic group. In the next chapter,

then, we shall chart the uses of *apoina* and marriage imagery, and in Chapter 6 examine the metaphorical sphere of *xenia*.[69]

[69]In addition to Finley's three top-rank spheres of exchange, Gernet lists funeral offerings and dedications to the gods. Although Pindar makes use of these as analogies for epinikian *chreos* and *charis*, they do not participate in the system of exchange between houses, and therefore they will not be considered in Part II. Funeral offerings have already been discussed under the rubric of intrafamilial exchanges. Dedications, which partake of the world of the polis, will be examined in the context of the victor's civic community.

CHAPTER 5

Recompense and Marriage: Models of Community

In this chapter, we shall consider the two spheres of *apoina* and *hedna*. The analysis will reveal a set of systems and strategies which we may then apply to the consideration of *xenia*, the most extensive sphere of gift-exchange imagery in the epinikia. In a sense, *apoina* and marriage form a complementary set, for both of these top-rank occasions, though contracted privately, have repercussions for the survival and stability of the entire community. *Apoina* protects the community from the threat of a destructive past, and marriage exchange guarantees the successful future of the group. The poet's use of these two highly charged occasions as analogies for the victory celebration serves the interests of aristocratic ideology, for these analogies depict the whole community's well-being as contingent on the smooth workings of aristocratic exchange. Thus, in a sense, Pindar coerces the approval of two groups at once: those who adhere to aristocratic ideology respond to the representation of victory as gift exchange, while the wider community is induced to believe that such aristocratic exchange serves its interests as well.

Ἄποινα and its synonyms, ποινή, λύτρον, and the adjective λυτήριος, all come from the legal or penal sphere. In that context, they express the obligation of requital or satisfaction—recompense for wrong done, wergild, or ransom.[1] As Pierre Chantraine notes, ποινή in Pindar's work is "exceptionally used positively" (as opposed to its nor-

[1] See Frisk 1960.2.573–574, Chantraine 1968.3.925, LSJ.

mally negative meaning), referring to the poem itself as "recompense" for the victor's efforts.[2] *Apoina* and its synonyms offer perhaps the best model of the community-building function of epinikian gift exchange, for in its penal context *apoina* recompenses great loss—murder or captivity—and thereby keeps the society from self-destructing. Specifically in the case of murder, the most serious threat to a fragile society is an endless cycle of blood vengeance. *Apoina* interrupts such a cycle, replacing it with a single exchange. As Ajax puts it to the intransigent Achilles in the *Iliad*,

> καὶ μέν τίς τε κασιγνήτοιο φονῆος
> ποινὴν ἢ οὗ παιδὸς ἐδέξατο τεθνηῶτος·
> καί ῥ’ ὁ μὲν ἐν δήμῳ μένει αὐτοῦ πόλλ’ ἀποτείσας,
> τοῦ δέ τ’ ἐρητύεται κραδίη καὶ θυμὸς ἀγήνωρ
> ποινὴν δεξαμένῳ·

(*Iliad* 9.632–636)

And a man accepts recompense from the slayer of a brother or of a child dead, and the one man remains in his land, having paid much, but the heart and lordly spirit of the other are checked when he receives the recompense.

The giving of compensation allows the wrongdoer and the family of the victim to live peaceably and honorably in the same community. It is appropriate here that Ajax specifically mentions son and brother, for such penal recompense remains the concern of the *families* involved, long after the polis has established its authority in other spheres.[3] *Apoina* is essentially private justice. The phrase πόλλ’ ἀποτείσας is also significant, as Gustave Glotz observes, for the paying of recompense is possible only for the very wealthy: "The murderer must relinquish a veritable fortune. If poor, he flees or resigns himself to inevitable death. If rich, he counts himself lucky to 'remain in his land' when he has renounced a good part of his fortune. . . . The ποινή is a great, sometimes perhaps a total dispossession of the offender in favor of the injured party. One escapes just death only by financial ruin."[4]

All these characteristics of *poinē* and *apoina* in their social context are

[2]Chantraine 1968.3.925. There are only two other (nonmetaphorical) occurrences of ποινή in Pindar (O.2.58 and P.4.63). In both these contexts it has a clear sense of "punishment" or "recompense" within a reciprocal framework. On λύτρον and λυτήριος, see Crotty 1982.78.

[3]Glotz 1904.117–122.

[4]Glotz 1904.129, my translation.

relevant for their metaphorical application within the epinikia. Because *apoina* represents private justice between families, it can participate in the gift exchange imagery directed toward the aristocrats in Pindar's audience. That is, this sphere of imagery implies a noncivic relationship between exchange partners. Poet and victor are conceived instead as the representatives of two noble houses, treating with each other. Furthermore, the immense sums involved mark the exchange of *apoina* as a top-rank occasion and therefore a suitable analogue for the offering of epinikion at the victory celebration. But most significant for our understanding of *apoina* imagery in Pindar is its socially reintegrative function. We must not underestimate the force a term like *apoina* carries with it from its proper context. It must imply to its audience a critical exchange that rescues the community from the threat of internal violence and disintegration. The danger which *apoina* implies in these contexts, even as it averts it, represents the victor's just recompense as a crucial concern to the entire community, for though it is private justice, the privilege of the wealthy, the giving of recompense ensures the stability of the group as a whole.

Significantly, *apoina* and its synonyms occur most often in the epinikia when the poet is emphasizing the enormous cost of victory, both in wealth and in toil or suffering. Thus the metaphorical occurrences of these terms are evenly divided between poems celebrating success in boxing or the pancration and those that commemorate chariot victories.[5] The first two were the most grueling of the "heavy events," in which injuries were common and athletes were sometimes even killed in the course of the contest.[6] The pancration, in which biting and gouging alone were forbidden, was extremely dangerous but was not considered as punishing as boxing. Thus it is recorded by Pausanias that a man who wished to compete in both pancration and boxing at Olympia requested that the usual order of the events be reversed: that the pancration take place "before he got wounded in the boxing."[7] Pindar's use of *apoina* imagery in the context of these heavy events acknowledges the suffering and even the risk of death involved. Thus the poem is a "glorious requital of toils" (λύτρον εὔδοξον . . . καμάτων) for the pancration victories of Kleandros in Isthmian 8 or simply the "recompense for boxing" (πυγμᾶς ἄποινα) for Diagoras in Olympian 7.[8]

[5]Boxing and pancration: O.7.16, I.8.1, 4; chariot racing: P.1.59, P.2.14, P.5.106; pancration and horse racing: I.3.7; pentathlon: N.7.16.
[6]Poliakoff 1987.54–88. For death in pancration, see Peek 1955.1.680, Philostratus *Imagines* 2.6.
[7]Pausanias 6.15.5, cited by Poliakoff 1987.63 and 85.
[8]Slater (1969a) considers ἄποινα here (as at P.2.14, I.3.7, and I.8.4) to be accusative

If pancration and boxing require the greatest expenditure of effort, chariot racing demands an enormous outlay of wealth. In Athens, for example, J. K. Davies estimates that of the class wealthy enough to perform liturgies, only a small proportion could afford to keep and race horses at international contests.[9] Pindar acknowledges the enormity of such expenditure when he refers to his poem as "recompense of four-horse [chariots]" (ποινὰν τεθρίππων) in Pythian 2 or simply as "requital for expenditures" (λυτήριον δαπανᾶν) in Pythian 5.[10] *Apoina* imagery, it appears, tends to gravitate to the sphere of athletics conceptualized as the competitive expenditure of self and property—as potlatch. Athletic victory requires unrivaled outlay, and as such, it is damage and loss that the poem alone can recompense. Thus far, the negative connotations of *apoina* and its synonyms seem to endure in epinikion, suggesting that the communal danger unleashed by the failure of *apoina* also haunts these epinikian contexts.

Perhaps to palliate the negative associations of *apoina*, Pindar frequently grounds his desire to offer the victor the "recompense" of the poem in the relationship of *charis* which exists between laudator and laudandus. Thus in Pythian 2, Pindar first makes the general statement,

> ἄλλοις δέ τις ἐτέλεσσεν ἄλλος ἀνήρ
> εὐαχέα βασιλεῦσιν ὕμνον ἄποιν᾽ ἀρετᾶς.
>
> (P.2.13–14)

But different men have accomplished for different kings the beautiful-sounding hymn as recompense of achievement.

Then, with a μέν, he offers Kinyras as one specific instance of the statement and continues, with a δέ: ἄγει δὲ χάρις φίλων ποί τινος ἀντὶ

---

fixed as preposition (+ gen.), which he defines as "in reward for." It is true that Pindar favors the fixed form, accusative + genitive, but we should not suppose that the fixity of the phrase reflects a blunting of the metaphorical force of the term. The very similar uses of ποινή (acc. + gen.) at P.1.59 and N.1.70 argue against a loss of metaphorical force and suggest that in the case of both words the accusative stands as *appositio ad sententiam*, characterizing the whole activity of celebration in song as a "recompense" for the victor.

[9]Davies 1981.29, 31, 99–102, 167, cf. Anderson 1961.128–139 and Young 1984.111 with n. 6.

[10]Gundert notes this correlation of Pindar's use of *apoina* with contexts of extraordinary *ponos* or *dapane*: on one occasion he refers to the poem as "recovery and recompense for toils" (Gundert 1935.23) and elsewhere he elaborates, "For toils and expenditure the *charis* of song is the finest indemnity: ἄποινα, ἀμοιβά or λύτρον καμάτων, μόχθων, πόνων (or δαπανᾶν)" (Gundert 1935.43, my translations). Note that in the single case in which *apoina* occurs for an event other than a heavy contest or horse racing (in N.7), it still emphasizes the element of toil or effort. There Pindar designates praise poetry as ἄποινα μόχθων, "recompense of toils" (N.7.16), for Sogenes' pentathlon victory.

ἔργων ὀπιζομένα· ("But grace guides [us], showing regard in exchange for the dear achievements of someone" [P.2.17]). Thus the origin of the poet's *chreos* is located in the relationship of *charis* between friends.

Again we find a collocation of *apoina* and *charis* in Isthmian 3:

> εὐκλέων δ' ἔργων ἄποινα χρὴ μὲν ὑμνῆσαι τὸν ἐσλόν,
> χρὴ δὲ κωμάζοντ' ἀγαναῖς χαρίτεσσιν βαστάσαι.

> (I.3.7–8)

As recompense for glorious achievements it is fitting to hymn the noble man, and fitting to exalt the one celebrating the *kōmos* with gentle graces.

In these two lines, the poet equates his debt, the *apoina* owed to the victor's toil, with the χάριτες that exalt the victor. As in Pythian 1, *charis* makes clear the friendship that exists between poet and victor, but it also registers the participation of a larger group in the transformation of debt into pleasure. For the participle κωμάζοντ'—used absolutely of the victor "celebrating a *kōmos*"[11]—indicates the means by which he will be "exalted." The recompense for toil is not just the poem, but the poem in its festal context (ἀγαναῖς χαρίτεσσιν): it is the celebration that causes the victor to forget his struggles. The widening community of praise within these lines may account for the poet's emphatic χρὴ μέν and χρὴ δέ to distinguish what J. B. Bury terms "two parts of the same process." The first obligation, "to hymn the noble man," can be taken narrowly to apply to the poet's duty, while χρὴ δέ in the second line expands the circle of obligation to all those participating in the festivities.[12]

The same association of *apoina* with the *kōmos* celebration is very clear in the opening of Isthmian 8:

> Κλεάνδρῳ τις ἁλικίᾳ τε λύτρον εὔδοξον, ὦ νέοι, καμάτων
> πατρὸς ἀγλαὸν Τελεσάρχου παρὰ πρόθυρον
> ἰὼν ἀνεγειρέτω
> κῶμον, Ἰσθμιάδος τε νίκας ἄποινα, καὶ Νεμέᾳ
> ἀέθλων ὅτι κράτος ἐξεῦρε·

> (I.8.1–5)

Let someone, O young men, for Kleandros, going to the shining portal of his father Telesarchos, awaken the *kōmos*, as glorious requital of toils

[11]Slater 1969a, s.v. κωμάζω.
[12]Bury 1890.60. For the distinction between festivity and the poet's song, see Bundy 1962.2, 22–23. For other collocations of *apoina* terms and *charis*, cf. P.1.59 and P.5.105–106.

for his youth and as recompense for his Isthmian victory, and because he found the winning of contests at Nemea.

With the vocative ὦ νέοι, Pindar draws the victor's age-mates into the celebration of his victories. Indeed, the vague τις . . . ἀνεγειρέτω causes the scripted performance to call for its own improvisation, making it appear that the chorus that has just begun does so spontaneously, of its own volition.[13] Meanwhile, the two images of penal recompense which frame the injunction to "awaken the *kōmos*" (λύτρον . . . καμάτων and νίκας ἄποινα) imply that there is danger for the whole community in failing to celebrate Kleandros' remarkable achievements.

The *kōmos* celebration enforces a kind of horizontal community—a community of age-mates. But the poet has another strategy for exacting the approval and participation of the victor's aristocratic circle. On occasion, the connection between *apoina* and the *kōmos* celebration leads in turn to the mythic archetype for every victor's "requital," the feasting of Herakles among the gods. Pindar describes the scene thus at the end of Nemean 1:

> αὐτὸν μὰν ἐν εἰρήνᾳ τὸν ἅπαντα χρόνον ⟨ἐν⟩ σχερῷ
> ἡσυχίαν καμάτων μεγάλων ποινὰν λαχόντ' ἐξαίρετον
> ὀλβίοις ἐν δώμασι, δεξάμενον θαλερὰν Ἥβαν ἄκοιτιν καὶ γάμον
> δαίσαντα πὰρ Δὶ Κρονίδᾳ, σεμνὸν αἰνήσειν νόμον.
>
> (N. 1.69–72)

[He prophesied] that [Herakles] would praise the august ordinance [of Zeus] when, in peace for all time in succession, he had been allotted quiet as special recompense for great toils in the blessed houses, and he had received blooming Hebe as wife and feasted his marriage beside Zeus, son of Kronos.

We recall that in gift-exchange cultures, a legendary hero is often imagined as the first recipient of the most valued gifts from the gods and that each actual exchange then re-presents this original model.[14] As Slater argues, the scene of Herakles in bliss in Pindar's poem is the prototype for athletic victory in general and for Chromios' celebratory *kōmos* in particular.[15] Epinikion, like gift exchange, forges a temporal chain, a direct link to the past.

---

[13]Carey (1981.5) designates such moments of scripted spontaneity as the poet's "oral subterfuge."

[14]Mauss 1967.42–43 and 110–111 nn. 186, 187.

[15]Slater 1984.249–253. See also Gundert 1935.44 and 126 n. 208.

We should note, furthermore, what Herakles' ποινά consists of. Within the setting of the house, ὀλβίοις ἐν δώμασι, the three spheres of gift exchange cluster together: recompense (καμάτων μεγάλων ποι-νάν), the bride as gift (δεξάμενον θαλερὰν Ἥβαν ἄκοιτιν), and the hospitality of a shared table (δαίσαντα πὰρ Δὶ Κρονίδᾳ). Or rather, the recompense is itself bride and *xenia* within the houses of the highest god.[16] And Herakles, in exchange for his eternal condition of bliss, sounds his unending praise of Zeus's "august ordinance" (σεμνὸν αἰνή-σειν νόμον).[17] Gift exchange, with praise as one of its elements, is projected whole, as it were, from the present occasion to the mythic plane. This projection validates the rightness of the current celebration by analogy. Just as Herakles earned his *hēsychia* by aiding the gods in the gigantomachy (N.1.67–69), Chromios has earned his by his expenditure in contests and his struggles in war.[18] Thus the final lines put the celebrations of both Herakles and Chromios under the "august ordinance" of Zeus.

Other poems establish in other forms a chain of recompense linking up with the ancestors or with the divine plane. Within the victory catalog of Diagoras of Rhodes in Olympian 7, Pindar refers thus to the Rhodian epichoric games:

τόθι λύτρον συμφορᾶς οἰκτρᾶς γλυκὺ Τλαπολέμῳ
ἵσταται Τιρυνθίων ἀρχαγέτᾳ,
ὥσπερ θεῷ,
μήλων τε κνισάεσσα πομπὰ καὶ κρίσις ἀμφ᾽ ἀέθλοις. τῶν ἄνθεσι
    Διαγόρας
ἐστεφανώσατο δίς,

(O.7.77–81)

There sweet requital for pitiful misfortune is established for Tlepolemos, colonial leader of the Tirynthians, just as for a god—both a procession of sheep for sacrifice and the judgment over athletic prizes. With the blooms of these Diagoras was crowned twice.

---

[16]Gift-exchange terms from different spheres tend to cluster together when they appear, perhaps because of the totality of the system which Mauss stresses: even when it is only operating on the metaphorical level, the basic gift-exchange model tends to pervade and shape the poet's imagination.

[17]Accepting νόμον on the evidence of the scholia, rather than δόμον or γάμον, the readings offered by all the MSS. Γάμον is obviously taken from the end of the previous line, while δόμον is, as Farnell observes, "weak" after δώμασι in the line above (Farnell 1930.2.250).

[18]Slater 1984.257–264.

The games themselves, the κρίσις ἀμφ' ἀέθλοις, together with heroic honors, are conceived as the recompense of "pitiful misfortune" for Tlepolemos, the founder of Rhodes. Presumably, the "pitiful misfortune" refers to his forced flight to Rhodes after the murder of his kinsman Likymnios, which Pindar describes in the poem's second triad (O.7.20–33).[19] Thus, the celebration of the games, itself a repeated act of ritual recompense, becomes the setting for the *ponos* of the victor, which earns him in turn the requital of song.[20] Pindar emphasizes the connection, the cycle of *ponos* and *apoina* which links Tlepolemos and Diagoras, by his use of the verb ἐστεφανώσατο in line 81. The victor's crown recalls the poet's statement of purpose, weaving together the λύτρον of the hero with the ἄποινα of his descendant,

εὐθυμάχαν ὄφρα πελώριον ἄνδρα παρ' Ἀλφειῷ στεφανωσάμενον
αἰνέσω πυγμᾶς ἄποινα.

(O.7.15–16)

in order to praise a prodigious man crowned beside the river Alpheios, as recompense of boxing.

In this case, the heroization of Tlepolemos represents civic honor and recompense in which Diagoras participates by competing.[21] Here, as elsewhere, it is impossible to separate the levels of community drawn in by the poet's strategies. We should simply recognize that Pindar forges a vertical chain as a prop for the victor's horizontal community. By representing Diagoras' *ponos* as a compensatory offering to Rhodes's hero-founder, Tlepolemos, the poet implicates the entire community in

[19]As the scholia assume (Drachmann 1903.228–229). See also Gildersleeve 1890.190.

[20]Nagy (1986a.93–94, 1986b.73–77, and 1990.136–145) postulates this link between the commissioned victory ode and a chain of ritual recompenses. He points to the tradition of games established as recompense for the accidental death or murder of a mythical figure—Ino's son Melikertes at the Isthmus and Opheltes at Nemea (see Pausanias 1.44.7–8 and 2.1.3 for Melikertes, 2.15.2–3 and 8.48.2 for Opheltes). We should note that the games at Rhodes, at least as Pindar characterizes them, deviate from this model in one very important respect: they function not as recompense for the murdered Likymnios but to compensate his murderer for the misfortune of exile. Given this deviance, we should note also the scholiast's emphatic assertion that "Pindar lies here: the games were not in honor of Tlepolemos, but in honor of the Sun" (ἐψεύσατο δὲ ὁ Πίνδαρος· οὐ γὰρ Τληπολέμῳ, τῷ δὲ Ἡλίῳ τιθέασι τὸν ἀγῶνα [Drachmann 1903.229]). Is it possible that Pindar has reshaped local tradition in order to turn the games into a chain of recompenses linking the mythical founder of Rhodes with Diagoras, the city's glorious son?

[21]On the civic aspects of founder cult and its relevance to epinikion, see Dougherty-Glenn 1988.146–157.

his victory and underscores the victor's right to his own recompense in song.

But if the chain stretches through time, binding a man to his ancestors, it also links him to the gods as the givers of the current victory. In Pythian 5, immediately after asserting that Arkesilaos' ancestors take part in the celebration of his chariot victory as in a funeral libation, Pindar continues:

> τὸν ἐν ἀοιδᾷ νέων
> πρέπει χρυσάορα Φοῖβον ἀπύειν,
> ἔχοντα Πυθωνόθεν
> τὸ καλλίνικον λυτήριον δαπανᾶν
> μέλος χαρίεν.

(P. 5. 103–107)

It is fitting that [Arkesilaos] celebrate gold-sworded Apollo in the song of young men, since he has from Pytho the lovely *kallinikos* strain as atonement for his expenditures.

Here Arkesilaos is told that he owes honor in song to Apollo because he himself received the lovely *kallinikos* strain from Pytho as λυτήριον δαπανᾶν.[22] Song itself becomes the gift to be handed on—at least in subject matter—from the victor and his ancestors to the god as requital for his benefaction. Again, the spinning out of a chain of reciprocal gifts behind the victory reconciles the victor's community as the potlatch model may not. For instead of a single eclipsing act of expenditure, victory is seen from a wider perspective as only a link in a chain that ultimately extends to the founding heroes and the gods.

If the *apoina* model starts from the conceptualization of athletic competition as loss, the analogy of marriage is predicated on the notion of the victor's success as a treasure in a system of gift exchange. As *apoina* imagery concretizes the poet's *chreos*, marriage figures in contexts of *charis*, for marriage is the preeminent *charis* occasion, and as such, it serves as a compelling analogy for the victory celebration. Marriage offers the poet a model for his relation to the victor, while it subtly enforces a positive reception by the victor's aristocratic community.

---

[22]Note particularly the adjective χαρίεν, "having *charis*." This adjective is frequently used in Homer to describe gifts, sacrifices, or the recompense desired from sacrifice (e.g., *Iliad* 1.39, 8.203–204, 9.598–599; *Odyssey* 3.58, 8.167). So here, the adjective marks the *kallinikos* song as an element in a reciprocal exchange of gifts.

Furthermore, since marriage ensures the preservation of the wider community through the lawful procreation of children, it forges the same double community as penal recompense: it draws together both the aristocrats who participate in the exchange and the larger group that benefits from the arrangement.

Gift-exchange imagery drawn from the sphere of marriage is less common than the metaphorical use of *apoina* or *xenia*. Still, it does exist, exhibiting many of the same features as the other spheres. The appearance of the word *hedna* itself is extremely rare in Pindar, but we can account for this rarity partially by the narrowness of its meaning.[23] When Finley included *hedna* as one of three specialized terms for the most significant spheres of gift-exchange, he understood it as all the gifts given on both sides to accompany wooing and marriage, arguing that *hedna* and δῶρα refer to the same things in the Homeric poems.[24] But since that time, W. K. Lacey's analysis has superseded Finley's. Lacey argues from the Homeric evidence that *hedna* is a narrower technical term for marriage gifts different from the more general δῶρα. He reconstructs the schema:

> A father or other κύριος could be approached with δῶρα and offers of ἕδνα for his daughter; the δῶρα would be accepted from all the contestants, and on the basis of the offers made and of his own judgement he would select a son-in-law, whose offer of ἕδνα would be accepted, and Homeric society being what it was, this would normally be the largest offer. In due course the bride would be sent off with what ἕδνα her father thought fit (or had perhaps agreed to give) in the light of his own self-esteem and that in which he held his son-in-law to be. If the girl ceased to be a wife for cause other than her death or that of her husband there was liable to be a claim for the return of ἕδνα. Homeric society, however, with its code of gift-giving, also provided for δῶρα as well as ἕδνα by which the goodwill of the parties was manifested.[25]

Furthermore, we must recognize clearly what Finley seems unwilling

[23]See Slater, 1969a, s.v. ἕδνον. The word appears once in the singular ἕδνον (O.9.10) and once in the plural ἕδνα (P.3.94), in both contexts referring to actual gifts in mythic marriages.

[24]Finley 1953.

[25]Lacey 1966.60; cf. Morris 1986b.106–110. Finley's and Lacey's model accords well with Mauss's description of marriage in a gift-exchange culture: "Thurnwald has analysed too one of the facts which best illustrates this system of reciprocal gifts and the nature of the misnamed 'marriage by purchase.' In reality, this includes prestations from all sides, including the bride's family, and a wife is sent back if her relatives have not offered sufficient gifts in return" (Mauss 1967.30).

or unable to admit—that the bride is part of the gift exchange, that she is herself an object exchanged to establish a bond between houses.[26] As Jean-Pierre Vernant formulates it: "The framework is that of social interchange between the great noble families, with the exchange of women seen as a means of creating links of union or dependence, of acquiring prestige or confirming vassaldom. In this interchange the women play the role of precious objects; they can be compared to the *agalmata* which Louis Gernet has shown to have been so important to the social practice and thought of the Greeks during the archaic period."[27] Thus, we can accept Finley's discussion insofar as he recognizes that marriage and gifts within marriage form one specialized sphere of gift exchange, but we must widen the set of terms beyond the relatively specific *hedna* to all the gifts exchanged in and around marriage, including the bride.

It is true that forms of *hedna* never appear metaphorically for the relationship of the poet and the victor, except perhaps in the tantalizing fragment, γυ]ναικῶν ἐδνώσεται, on which the scholiast offers the gloss ἐδνώσατο· ἀντὶ τοῦ ὑμνήθη (Paean 4.4).[28] Still, the elaborate simile that opens Olympian 7 clearly sets up an analogy between the exchange of the bride and the relationship of poet to patron:

Φιάλαν ὡς εἴ τις ἀφνειᾶς ἀπὸ χειρὸς ἑλών
ἔνδον ἀμπέλου καχλάζοισαν δρόσῳ
δωρήσεται
νεανίᾳ γαμβρῷ προπίνων οἴκοθεν οἴκαδε, πάγχρυσον, κορυφὰν
κτεάνων,

[26]The most comprehensive anthropological treatment of the exchange of women in marriage as gift exchange is that of Lévi-Strauss 1969. He articulates very clearly that the bride is herself a gift within a system of gift exchange: "It would then be false to say that one exchanges or gives gifts at the same time that one exchanges or gives women. For the woman herself is nothing other than one of these gifts, the supreme gift among those that can only be obtained in the form of reciprocal gifts" (Lévi-Strauss 1969.65). In trying to demolish the "marriage-by-purchase" model, Finley seems to go too far in the opposite direction, never admitting that the bride is an object in the exchange system. Instead, he neatly sidesteps the question: "The reason for gift-giving in wooing was simply that gift-giving was a part of all important occasions. Marriage was, of course, a major occasion, and particularly so in the upper social circles in which Homeric heroes moved. There a marriage was, among other things, a political alliance; in fact, marriage and guest-friendship were the two fundamental devices for the establishment of alliances among the nobles and chieftains. And the exchange of gifts was their invariable expression of the conclusion of an alliance" (Finley 1955.238). What Finley says is true, but it should be said that the central gift that embodies the alliance between noble houses is the bride (on which, see also Vernant 1980.49–52 and Redfield 1982.186).

[27]Vernant 1980.49–50. See also Lacey 1966.55, Morris 1986b.113.

[28]See Slater 1969a on ἐδνόω and Wilamowitz 1922.474.

συμποσίου τε χάριν κᾶδός τε τιμάσαις ⟨ν⟩έον, ἐν δὲ φίλων
παρεόντων θῆκέ νιν ζαλωτὸν ὁμόφρονος εὐνᾶς·
καὶ ἐγὼ νέκταρ χυτόν, Μοισᾶν δόσιν, ἀεθλοφόροις
ἀνδράσιν πέμπων, γλυκὺν καρπὸν φρενός,
ἱλάσκομαι,
Ὀλυμπίᾳ Πυθοῖ τε νικώντεσσιν· ὁ δ' ὄλβιος, ὃν φᾶμαι κατέχωντ'
    ἀγαθαί·
ἄλλοτε δ' ἄλλον ἐποπτεύει Χάρις ζωθάλμιος ἀδυμελεῖ
θαμὰ μὲν φόρμιγγι παμφώνοισί τ' ἐν ἔντεσιν αὐλῶν.

(O.7.1–12)

As if someone, having taken from a rich hand a cup, foaming within with
the dew of the grape, all-golden peak of possessions, presents it to a
young bridegroom, toasting from house to house, thereby honoring the
grace of the symposium and his new relation-in-marriage. And thereby,
with friends present, he makes him an object of emulation on account of
his like-minded marriage [lit. bed]. In like manner, I propitiate men who
are victors, sending poured nectar, the gift of the Muses, sweet fruit of
mind, for those who have won at Olympia and Pytho. But he is blessed,
whom good reports surround; but at different times, Charis, who causes
life to bloom, gazes upon different men with the sweet-speaking phor-
minx and the full-voiced equipment of auloi.

There has been much critical discussion of this simile recently.[29] It
seems to be generally agreed that it represents not the marriage ceremony itself but the *engue*, the pledge between the bride's father and the
prospective bridegroom at which the bride was not actually present.[30]
Scholars have worried a great deal about the identities of τις and the
ἀφνειᾶς . . . χειρός, the representatives in the simile of Pindar and the
Muses, respectively. The most plausible solutions offered thus far are
those of Christopher Brown and Robert Stoddart. Brown suggests that
the "generous hand" from which the cup is given belongs to the groom's
prospective father-in-law and that τις is a herald or "some intermediary
figure who proposes the toast on behalf of the father of the bride."
Thus, in the second half of the simile, the Muses are parents to the song
and Pindar is fulfilling the traditional role of the poet as Μουσεῶν
θεράπων.[31] Stoddart argues that the simile represents a pre-Solonian

---

[29]See Lawall 1961, Young 1968.69–74, Braswell 1976, Verdenius 1976, Rubin 1980,
Stoddart 1990.50–57, Brown 1984, Verdenius 1987.40–88.
[30]See Braswell 1976.241 (esp. n. 27), Redfield 1982.186, Brown 1984.38–41, and
Stoddart 1990.57.
[31]Brown 1984.39–42, quotation from 39–40.

engue, in which the head of the bride's clan would preside at the ceremony; thus he is the ἀφνειᾶς . . . χειρός and the bride's father is τις:
"And the man who hands the chalice to the bride's father is one of his
wealthy relations; perhaps Pindar's aristocratic audience would have
seen in him the head of the clan, investing family property in a new
alliance." In terms of the simile, Stoddart then assigns the roles somewhat differently: "If we suppose that the Muses are the chiefs of Pindar's
γένος, the administrators of its wealth; that Pindar is the father or legal
guardian of the bride; and that the victor is the son-in-law, one question
remains: who is the bride whom Pindar entrusts to the victor and whom
the Muses dower with the potion of immortality (νέκταρ)? She is the
song itself—αἱ δὲ σοφαὶ Μοισᾶν θύγατρες ἀοιδαί (N.4.2–3)."[32]

What is significant about both these solutions is that they acknowledge Pindar's complete vagueness about these figures at the personal
level: the identity of both is defined only by their function, by their
relation to the house and the ceremony in which they participate. Much
more central is the bond between houses which the ceremony establishes, expressed by the emphatic οἴκοθεν οἴκαδε at the center of the
simile.[33] This point is sharpened in Pindar's simile by the notable
absence of the bride. If she were present, she would be, in the simile as
in Greek life, the center of attention. In her absence, we see with
particular clarity the lines of force, the bonds of *charis* and community
being forged between two men and the houses they represent. As James
Redfield observes, the Greek wedding is "both a transfer and a transformation. As a transfer, enacted in the *engue*, it belongs to the men. As a
transformation, it is the special responsibility of the women."[34]

But what relevance does this bond between houses have at the metaphorical level of the relationship of poet and patron? Or to put it in more
basic terms, why is marriage or betrothal an appropriate image for the
epinikian contract? The lowest common denominator of the two halves
of the simile—the basic likeness—is *charis*.[35] Though the poet sets up a
whole series of equivalences between tenor and vehicle, the only word

[32]Stoddart 1990.57, 58–59.

[33]As Vernant observes, the pre-Solonian *engue* "turns the union between a man and a
woman into a social action whose effect reaches beyond the two individuals involved to
seal, through them, a commitment between two domestic households, two 'houses'"
(Vernant 1980.45).

[34]Redfield 1982.188.

[35]As Gundert observes, "The innermost point of the comparison is *charis*" (Gundert
1935.127 n. 216, my translation). See also Schadewaldt 1928.275 n. 1 and Lawall 1961,
who emphasizes the theme of grace throughout the poem.

that is actually repeated in the first twelve lines is χάρις. W. J. Slater takes χάριν in line 5 as the preposition with the genitive, "for the sake of the symposium," but W. J. Verdenius notes that "the double τε seems to show that χάριν depends on τιμάσαις."[36] From the point of view of the meaning as well, it seems preferable to give to χάρις in this context its full weight because betrothal and marriage are occasions peculiarly imbued with *charis* from a Greek point of view. Or we could say in anthropological terms that betrothal and marriage are occasions for the exchange of top-rank gifts. Thus the father of the the bride or head of the clan bestows on the bridegroom a precious cup, "all-golden peak of possessions," thereby honoring simultaneously the *charis* of the occasion and his new relation. In like manner, on the special occasion of the celebration of an Olympic or Pythian victory (the poet is very specific), Χάρις herself for a brief moment "looks upon" the victor, shedding on him through song the same grace or glamour a bridegroom possesses.

But we can be even more specific about the similarity of the occasions and the *charis* involved. For marriage is an especially significant form of gift exchange, and this is what infuses the ceremony and its participants with *charis*. At the center is the bride, and the bride is a gift that, at least potentially, bestows immortality. According to Christopher Brown:

> What is relevant is that the marriage will make the groom immortal through children: in antiquity a good marriage meant good children. . . . A parallel for the proem of the Seventh Olympian is Ol. 10.86–96, where Pindar compares the *kleos* granted to the victor by the Muse with the birth of a longed-for heir to an old man. In the present passage we may take the argument a step further by seeing the cup as a pledge of the real gift, the bride, who represents the groom's hope of immortality. The epinician poem is also a pledge of the immortality which comes to the victor through the Muses.[37]

Furthermore, through the marriage simile, Pindar is implying a bond

[36]Slater 1969a, s.v. χάρις and (apparently) Gildersleeve 1890.185. Slater's interpretation is refuted by Verdenius 1987.45–46. See also Kirkwood 1982.100. I do not find the interpretation of Braswell 1976.236–239 (reading συμποσίῳ) convincing; see the comments of Verdenius 1976.244–245.

[37]Brown 1984.40–41. See also Young 1968.74. Compare with Brown's argument here Firth's observations on spheres of exchange among the Tikopia of New Zealand: "Apart from the three spheres of exchange mentioned a fourth may be recognized in cases where goods of unique quality are handed over. Such for instance was the transfer of women by the man who could not otherwise pay for his canoe. Transfers of land might be put into the same category. Women and land are given in satisfaction of unique obligations; they are alike in that their productive capacity is vast but incalcuable!" (Firth 1965.344).

between poet and patron which is that of relatives by marriage, κηδεσ-
ταί. And as Stoddart emphasizes, "Even in fourth-century Athens,
according to Demosthenes, it was the transfer of wealth from house to
house and not the mere cohabitation of two human beings that established the relationship (κῆδος) between their families."[38] We must take
this image and its implications quite seriously, following the lead of the
emphatic οἴκοθεν οἴκαδε.[39] In metaphorical terms, then, what are the
houses involved, what is the wealth transferred? The poet's "house"
seems to be a metaphor for his poetry itself, so that the wealth he
transfers from it to the victor consists of the "gems" of his poetic talent.
The wealth of the victor's house in this context—the "property" he
brings to the match—is his athletic achievement as the reification of his
hereditary aretē. The individual epinikion, then, is the "wedding" of the
wealth of these two houses in a single beautiful package, handed over to
the victor for the sake of ensuring his immortality.[40]

    Thus, the simile of the betrothal constructs the relationship of poet
and patron as that of aristocratic exchange partners, trading their culture's most precious gifts. But the simile also implicates its audience,
drawing them in and dictating their proper response by analogy. It is
significant in this respect that Stoddart finds in Olympian 7 a description of a pre-Solonian engue, for as Gernet observes, the engue is the
aristocratic ceremony par excellence.[41] Pindar can expect the aristocrats
in his audience to recognize the occasion: the simile speaks particularly
to them. Indeed, the victor's noble peers are involved in the simile as
witnesses to the betrothal, designated by the genitive absolute φίλων
παρεόντων in lines 5–6. In this context, ὁμόφρονος εὐνᾶς may evoke
the locus classicus for the theme of like-mindedness in marriage, Odysseus' parting wish to Nausikaa:

σοὶ δὲ θεοὶ τόσα δοῖεν ὅσα φρεσὶ σῇσι μενοινᾷς,
ἄνδρα τε καὶ οἶκον καὶ ὁμοφροσύνην ὀπάσειαν

[38]Stoddart 1990.51.
[39]See, for example, the tantalizing but unexplained statement of Rubin 1980.252: "By
implication, the connection between Pindar's 'house' and that of the victor is pledged and
sealed through the victory ode, the sweet fruit of Pindar's mind."
[40]A striking parallel comes from the tradition of Irish praise poetry. Carney notes that
it is a topos of such praise poetry (composed between the seventh and seventeenth
centuries A.D.) for the poet to refer to the prince whom he serves as his spouse, with
many passionate expressions of devotion (Carney 1985.112–140). The Irish metaphor
goes even farther than the Greek; Pindar represents himself and the victor as in-laws,
while in Irish, the patron and poet are husband and wife. This difference may reflect the
lifetime commitment of the Irish poet to a single patron.
[41]Gernet 1981b.284.

ἐσθλήν· οὐ μὲν γὰρ τοῦ γε κρεῖσσον καὶ ἄρειον,
ἢ ὅθ᾽ ὁμοφρονέοντε νοήμασιν οἶκον ἔχητον
ἀνὴρ ἠδὲ γυνή· πόλλ᾽ ἄλγεα δυσμενέεσσι,
χάρματα δ᾽ εὐμενέτῃσι·

(*Odyssey* 6.180–185)

May the gods grant you as much as you desire in your wits—may they bestow a husband and a home and noble like-mindedness. For there is nothing stronger or better, than when husband and wife hold a house, like-minded in their thoughts—many griefs for their enemies, but joys for their friends.

The Homeric echo implies the appropriate reaction; to his friends the victor's success, like a bridegroom's, should be a χάρμα, a source of joy.

But, it may be objected, the adjective ζαλωτός, used in this context to characterize the bridegroom, encodes a different response. For certain commentators have claimed that ζαλωτός represents a reflex of the theme of envy in epinikion, thereby introducing a negative element into the vignette of the *engue*.[42] But this interpretation collapses the distinction between ζῆλος and φθόνος, emulation and envy. A derivative of ζῆλος occurs only here in the epinikia, although Pindar repeatedly refers to φθόνος and μῶμος that greet the victor's achievement. Thus we must look elsewhere to determine the force of ζαλωτός. In the compendium of popular wisdom that makes up the second book of the *Rhetoric*, Aristotle devotes two chapters to envy and emulation. Emulation, he observes, wishes to possess honorable goods for itself, whereas envy begrudges such goods to those who actually possess them (*Rhet.* 1388a32–b). Therefore, emulation is a spur to virtue and achievement, whereas envy is a hostile, negative emotion. Emulation characterizes men who are reasonable (ἐπιεικεῖς), the young (νέοι), and the great-souled (μεγαλόψυχοι); in contrast, envy is a trait of the base (φαῦλοι) and the small-minded (μικρόψυχοι) (*Rhet.* 1387b22–88b2). Aristotle's distinctions are generally confirmed by the usage of archaic lyric, elegy, and Attic drama, where ζῆλος and ζηλωτός occur mainly in positive contexts, designating people and conditions that are "blessed."[43]

Thus ζαλωτός in Olympian 7 does not imply that the bridegroom (or

---

[42]Thummer 1968.1.80–81, Verdenius 1987.47.

[43]Cf. Archilochus 54 Tarditi (line 21); Theognis 455; Simonides 584 PMG; Aeschylus *Agamemnon* 939, *Persians* 710, 712, *Prometheus Bound* 330; Sophocles *Antigone* 1161, *OC* 943, *OT* 1526, *Electra* 1027, *Ajax* 552; Euripides *Andromache* 5, *Hecuba* 352, *Helen* 1435, *Medea* 243, 1035, *Orestes* 247, 542, 973, fr. 453.3 Nauck; Aristophanes, *Ach.* 1008, *Eccles.* 837, *Wasps* 451, 1450, *Thesmo.* 175, 1118, *Clouds* 463, 1210, *Peace* 860, 1038.

athlete) is envied by the family and friends who witness the occasion. Rather his φίλοι rejoice in his success, while they aspire to achieve the same. Ζαλωτός in Pindar is equivalent to Odysseus' assertion that "nothing is stronger or better" than ὁμοφροσύνη between husband and wife. Like a bridegroom who has made the ideal match, Diagoras has attained the most coveted prize of his class—the immortality that athletic victory and song alone can bestow. As Hermann Fränkel observes, ζαλωτόν in line 6, like ὄλβιος in line 10, is a version of the μακαρισμός.[44] The "calling blessed"—μάκαρ, ὄλβιος, or εὐδαίμων—is appropriate to both bridegroom and victorious athlete. Normally a spontaneous outcry, it is here scripted into the performance to emphasize the overlap between two top-rank occasions and to dictate a particular positive relationship between the protagonist of the celebration and its audience.

The same strategy informs the μακαρισμός at line 10, ὁ δ' ὄλβιος, ὅν φᾶμαι κατέχωντ' ἀγαθαί ("He is fortunate, whom good reports surround"). The formula ὁ δ' ὄλβιος in the context of the extended simile of betrothal must evoke the μακαρισμοί that were uttered for a bridegroom, the traditional substance of which was: "You are blessed *in your bride*" (like ζαλωτὸν ὁμόφρονος εὐνᾶς in the first half of the simile).[45] Transformed into epinikian terms, the blessing refers not specifically to the victory ode as a source of the victor's good fortune but rather to a more general good repute. These φᾶμαι . . . ἀγαθαί are not just the poet's words but the response of the surrounding community to the victor's success.[46] This is the reason for the adversative δέ in line 10: the poet sends the poem, but the victor's perfect happiness depends on the approval of the wider community. And yet the very terms in which the poet acknowledges the victor's dependence on the group program its approval, for they take the form of the blessing traditionally uttered by the witnesses. Again, the response of the audience is scripted by the poet. The last lines of the proem then offer the reason the audience should approve and accept the victor. As Verdenius notes, ἄλλοτε . . . ἄλλον in line 11 represents the common epinikian motif of vicissitude.[47] But the notion that Charis looks now on one, now on another, is

[44]Fränkel 1973.431 n. 12.

[45]Cf. Hesiod fr. 211.7–11 MW; Sappho fr. 112 LP; Euripides fr. 781.27–31 Nauck; Aristophanes *Peace* 1333–1334; Theocritus *Id.* 18.16–20. See Mangelsdorff 1913.6–7, 16, 25.

[46]Φάμα in Pindar designates not the poet's song but one's reputation in the community: cf. P.2.16, I.4.22, Δ.2.27.

[47]Verdenius 1987.50; see also Lawall 1961.37, 44–47.

also particularly appropriate in a marriage context. Each member of the community, the poet implies, has his moment at the center, irradiated by grace at the betrothal or the wedding ceremony. As the other aristocrats aspire to their own radiant moment (recall ζαλωτόν), they should allow the current victor his.

The simile that opens Olympian 7 represents the economy of praise as marriage exchange. Like marriage, the exchange of epinikian verse bestows immortality on the victor and evokes the joyful participation of his φίλοι. But the marriage model expands within epinikion, representing victory itself—its bestowal and its reception—as versions of marriage exchange. As with apoina, the expanding circle of marriages integrates and motivates victory within a network of reciprocal gift exchange, playing on the aristocracy's commitment to the system to extort its goodwill. Thus in Pythian 5 we find a conflation of athletic success with the ἀγωγή of a bride:

> φιλεῖν δὲ Κάρρωτον ἔξοχ᾽ ἑταίρων·
> ὃς οὐ τὰν Ἐπιμαθέος ἄγων
> ὀψινόου θυγατέρα Πρόφασιν Βαττιδᾶν
> ἀφίκετο δόμους θεμισκρεόντων·
> ἀλλ᾽ ἀρισθάρματον
> ὕδατι Κασταλίας ξενωθεὶς γέρας ἀμφέβαλε τεαῖσιν κόμαις,
>
> (P. 5.26–31)

And [remember] to love Karrhotos exceedingly of your companions, who did not come to the houses of the Battidai who rule by right, leading Excuse, the daughter of late-minded Afterthought. But hosted by the water of Kastalia, he has encircled your locks with the honor of the best chariot.

These lines addressed to Arkesilaos, king of Kyrene, bid him cherish his charioteer, Karrhotos, implying that he has led home not Excuse, daughter of Afterthought, but Victory as his bride. The king is urged to act the part of a φίλος for Karrhotos, receiving the bride Victory and installing her in the houses of the Battidai.[48] In lines 30–31 the poet abruptly shifts registers from the image of victory as bride to a com-

[48]According to the scholia, Arkesilaos was actually related to Karrhotos by marriage: Karrhotos was Arkesilaos' wife's brother. The scholia are uncomfortable with the elaborate praise of Karrhotos, observing that "the praise is more appropriate for a κηδεστής than for a charioteer" (Drachmann 1910.176). Their discomfort arises from their failure to comprehend the analogy between victory and marriage.

pressed metaphor of the charioteer's success as *xenia* (to which I shall return in the next chapter). Still, both spheres of gift-exchange imagery imply the same relationship between Karrhotos and Apollo: the god of Delphi has bestowed victory on Arkesilaos' charioteer. It is this special relationship that motivates Pindar's instructions to the king: honor Karrhotos since Apollo has honored him.

In the lines immediately following Pindar describes the charioteer's dedication of the victorious chariot in language that evokes both guest-gift and marriage exchange:

> ἀλλὰ κρέμαται
> ὁπόσα χεριαρᾶν
> τεκτόνων δαίδαλ' ἄγων
> Κρισαῖον λόφον
> ἄμειψεν ἐν κοιλόπεδον νάπος
> θεοῦ·
>
> (P. 5.34–39)

But they hang [there], however many wrought objects of dexterous craftsmen leading, he passed the Krisaian hill into the grove of the god, which lies in a hollow.

In return for the victory he leads home, Karrhotos leads the finely wrought work of craftsmen to the god's glen. Ἄγων in line 36 picks up the same participle from line 27, evoking the marriage context. At the same time, the phrase χεριαρᾶν τεκτόνων δαίδαλ' suggests the precious objects exchanged between guest and host.[49] Karrhotos reciprocates the *agalma* the god has bestowed—the victory crown—by dedicating the highly wrought chariot.

By deploying imagery drawn from two different spheres of gift exchange, Pindar represents the process of competition and victory as a chain of *charis*, originating with a benevolent deity and binding king, charioteer, and audience in a single joyful circuit. This network of reciprocal relations is revealed by the multiple referents of the gnome with which the poet closes this section:

> ἑκόντι τοίνυν πρέπει
> νόῳ τὸν εὐεργέταν ὑπαντιάσαι.
>
> (P. 5.43–44)

[49]In Homer, δαίδαλος is the standard epithet of *keimelia*, "the medium of aristocratic intercourse," as Gernet (1981a.113) observes. See *Iliad* 4.133–136, 5.60, 6.418, 8.195, 9.187, 13.331, 719, 14.179, 16.222, 17.448, 18.379, 390, 400, 479, 482, 612, 19.13, 19, 380, 22.314, *Odyssey* 1.131, 10.315, 367, 17.32, 19.227, 23.200.

It is fitting, then, to meet one's benefactor with willing mind.

The obligation to reciprocate one's benefactor applies equally to the charioteer's dedication (34–42), Arkesilaos' gratitude to the charioteer (26–32), and the king's debt to Apollo (23–25).[50]

Finally, Pindar turns to address the charioteer directly, reverting as he does so to marriage imagery, for the poet utters what is essentially a μακαρισμός for Karrhotos:

> Ἀλεξιβιάδα, σὲ δ' ἠύκομοι φλέγοντι Χάριτες.
> μακάριος, ὃς ἔχεις
> καὶ πεδὰ μέγαν κάματον
> λόγων φερτάτων
> μναμήι·
>
> (P.5.45–49)

O son of Alexibias [Karrhotos], you the lovely haired Graces inflame. Blessed [are you], who have even after great toil memorials consisting of the best words.

This blessing forges the final link in the chain of *charis*, for it situates the poem as the final reciprocal gift in the sequence. The Graces who inflame Karrhotos are simultaneously the patron deities of epinikion and of marriage. The poet discharges Arkesilaos' obligation to his charioteer by commemorating his achievement in song. Again, where we expect, "You are blessed in your bride," the poet substitutes "memorials consisting of the best words"—that is, the poem. Thus, Karrhotos' "bride" has modulated from victory itself to the poetic commemoration of victory which will ensure his immortality.

The same proliferation of the bonds of *charis* is evident in Pythian 9. As Anne Carson has shown, the imagery of Telesikrates' victorious return is that of a bridegroom's leading home his bride:[51]

> ἔνθα νικάσαις ἀνέφανε Κυράναν, ἅ νιν εὔφρων δέξεται
> καλλιγύναικι πάτρᾳ
> δόξαν ἱμερτὰν ἀγαγόντ' ἀπὸ Δελφῶν.
>
> (P.9.73–75)

Having won there, he proclaimed Kyrene, who will receive him gladly in his homeland, full of beautiful women, as he leads lovely glory from Delphi.

[50]Compare the discussion of Hubbard 1985.128 n. 78.
[51]Carson 1982.121–124. See also Robbins 1978.103 n. 38 and Köhnken 1985.74–76.

That δόξα is the bride reveals the emphasis of the metaphor, for the victor's reputation, like a wife, will guarantee him a kind of immortality. But this brief image, drawn from the wedding ἀγωγή, also includes the moment of reception.[52] The eponymous nymph Kyrene will receive him εὔφρων, "gladly," like the mother of the groom in the marriage ceremony. The easy confusion of city and nymph, so common in Pindar, has the effect here of casting the entire polis of Kyrene in the role of Telesikrates' nearest relatives. As in the case of apoina in Olympian 7, the marriage model is extended to embrace the entire civic community.

But in fact, this image of the bridal ἀγωγή can only be understood in the context of the entire poem, in which marriages—mythical, historical, and metaphorical—abound, setting up a complex network of relations among Apollo, the victor, and his homeland. The marriage of Apollo and Kyrene constitutes the central myth of the poem (ll. 5–70). The scholia inform us that Pindar took the romance of Apollo and the Thessalian nymph Kyrene from Hesiod's *Ehoiai*.[53] Various scholars have suggested, however, that the identification of the Thessalian nymph with the Libyan city is Pindar's innovation: Pythian 9 is at least the earliest version of the transferral to Libya extant.[54] If it is an innovation, it is Pindar's choice to represent the foundation of the city Kyrene as the *hieros gamos* of Apollo, god of colonists, and the eponymous nymph.

Indeed, the poet is emphatic, for he describes the marriage of Apollo and Kyrene three times in the course of the poem. On each occasion, their union is presented as an exchange, but an exchange of a different kind from that of Olympian 7. There, the bride was a gift transferred between men; in Pythian 9, the transfer takes place between Apollo and his huntress bride. Thus, the first time the marriage is described, the terms of the exchange are carefully balanced:

> τὰν ὁ χαιτάεις ἀνεμοσφαράγων ἐκ Παλίου κόλπων ποτὲ Λατοΐδας
> ἅρπασ', ἔνεικέ τε χρυσέῳ παρθένον ἀγροτέραν
> δίφρῳ, τόθι νιν πολυμήλου
> καὶ πολυκαρποτάτας θῆκε δέσποιναν χθονός

[52]Carson 1982.122.

[53]Drachmann 1910.221.

[54]For Libya as an innovation by Pindar or some intermediate source, see Lübbert 1881.6–7, Duchemin 1967.59, Köhnken 1985.102–103, and Dougherty-Glenn 1988. 191–211, 215. West (1985.86–87) thinks that Libya may have figured in the *Ehoiai* version, but he is not certain.

ρίζαν ἀπείρου τρίταν εὐήρατον θάλλοισαν οἰκεῖν.
ὑπέδεκτο δ᾽ ἀργυρόπεζ᾽ Ἀφροδίτα
Δάλιον ξεῖνον θεοδμάτων
ὀχέων ἐφαπτομένα χερὶ κούφᾳ·

(P.9.5–11)

Her the long-haired son of Leto once snatched from the hollows of
Pelion, where the wind echoes, and he bore the wild maiden in his golden
chariot. There he caused her, as mistress of a land rich in flocks and rich in
fruit, to inhabit the third lovely, blooming root of the world. And silver-
footed Aphrodite received the Delian stranger, laying hold of his god-
built chariot(s) with light hand.

Kyrene was a παρθένος, and now she will be δέσποινα. She was
ἀγρότερα, "more wild," and now she will be mistress of an οἶκος
(οἰκεῖν [8]) in a cultivated land (πολυμήλου καὶ πολυκαρποτάτας . . .
χθονός [6a–7]). She used to frequent the barren "hollows of Pelion,
where the wind echoes"; now she inhabits a "lovely, blooming" land. In
exchange for her virginity and for her former life, Apollo bestows on
her as her bridal portion the territory of Kyrene.[55] Indeed, so complete
is the identification of nymph and territory once the transfer is accomplished that in the context of what is conventionally the leading home of
the bride to the house of the groom, Apollo himself is referred to as "the
Delian stranger" (10).[56]

    The second time, the mythic marriage is described by Chiron, proph-
esying to Apollo:

ταύτᾳ πόσις ἵκεο βᾶσσαν
τάνδε, καὶ μέλλεις ὑπὲρ πόντου
Διὸς ἔξοχον ποτὶ κᾶπον ἐνεῖκαι·
ἔνθα νιν ἀρχέπολιν θήσεις, ἐπὶ λαὸν ἀγείραις
νασιώταν ὄχθον ἐς ἀμφίπεδον· νῦν δ᾽ εὐρυλείμων πότνιά σοι Λιβύα
δέξεται εὐκλέα νύμφαν δώμασιν ἐν χρυσέοις
πρόφρων· ἵνα οἱ χθονὸς αἶσαν
αὐτίκα συντελέθειν ἔννομον δωρήσεται,
οὔτε παγκάρπων φυτῶν νάποινον οὔτ᾽ ἀγνῶτα θηρῶν.

(P.9.51–58)

[55]On such oppositions, see Robbins 1978.97–100, Woodbury 1982.251–254, and
Carson 1982.124–128. Carson considers the marriage-victory analogy from the perspective of transformation; my analysis is intended to complement hers, by considering the
elements of transfer (to borrow the dichotomy developed by Redfield 1982.185–188) as
well.
[56]Carson. 1982.122.

As husband for this one you have come to this glen, and you are going to bear her over the sea to the special garden of Zeus. There you will make her the leader of cities, having gathered an island people to a hill encircled by plain. But now Mistress Libya with broad meadows will gladly receive the glorious bride in her golden houses. There she will immediately present her with a share of the land to be counted as her lawful possession, neither without reward of all kinds of fruits nor without experience of wild animals.

Here, though ξεῖνος, Apollo is clearly πόσις, and he carries Kyrene off to his father's place, Διὸς ἔξοχον ποτὶ κᾶπον. Chiron repeats the language of the poet's narration to describe Apollo's compensation to Kyrene. Pindar had said, τόθι νιν . . . θῆκε δέσποιναν χθονός; Chiron says, ἔνθα νιν ἀρχέπολιν θήσεις. And in addition to her lot as "leader of cities," Kyrene will receive from Libya, as πότνια δόμων, a grant of territory (notice δωρήσεται [57]). The description of Kyrene's portion of land picks up the poet's dual characterization from the earlier passage. Οὔτε παγκάρπων φυτῶν νάποινον corresponds to πολυκαρπωτάτας, while οὔτ' ἀγνῶτα θηρῶν replaces πολυμήλου, substituting wild animals for domesticated. Given the parallelism, the use of νάποινον in this context is striking. It is certainly a roundabout way of saying that Libya is a fertile land, but it does introduce the notion of compensation into the description of Kyrene's "lawful lot." The implication is that Kyrene is being "compensated" for the existence she has lost.[57] By transferring the Greek nymph Kyrene to Libya and making the region her bridal portion from the god, Pindar legitimates the colonists' claim to their territory. Again, the marriage model extends to the whole polis, in this case providing it with a foundation legend.[58]

The third and final narrative of the union of Apollo and Kyrene closes the mythic section of the ode:

> θαλάμῳ δὲ μίγεν
> ἐν πολυχρύσῳ Λιβύας· ἵνα καλλίσταν πόλιν
> ἀμφέπει κλεινάν τ' ἀέθλοις.

(P.9.68–70)

---

[57]Anne Carson points out to me that "ancient lexicographers sometimes refer to the gifts given to the bride at the wedding as *ta diaparthenia* and explain that they are compensation in exchange for the *parthenia* of the bride (e.g., Pollux 3.39)." (Private correspondence, spring 1987.)

[58]On the interconnection of marriage and colonial themes in P.9, see Dougherty-Glenn 1988.184–217.

And they were united in the golden bedchamber of Libya, where she possesses a city most beautiful and glorious in contests.

Πόλιν ἀμφέπει picks up ἀρχέπολιν (54), so that the ἵνα clause seems once more to characterize Kyrene's bridal portion. In exchange for the union in the chamber of Libya, Kyrene presides over a city. And like her portion of land in the first two passages, the city is doubly characterized: it is most beautiful and glorious in contests. Thus the poet uses this originary marriage to establish a special, preferential relationship between Delphi and Kyrene and thereby to motivate the victor's athletic success. Kyrene has been dowered with athletic victory down through the ages. The victor's success represents a direct link with that founding act of exchange.[59]

Indeed, in the lines immediately following, Pindar spins out the chain of marriage exchanges. As we have already noted, the victor leads home lovely glory like a bride from Delphi. But this is only half of a double marriage exchange. The preservation of Apollo's status as ξεῖνος in Libya makes possible a metaphorical exchange of brides in the context of Telesikrates' Pythian victory:

> καί νυν ἐν Πυθῶνί νιν ἀγαθέᾳ Καρνειάδα
> υἱὸς εὐθαλεῖ συνέμειξε τύχᾳ·
> ἔνθα νικάσαις ἀνέφανε Κυράναν, ἅ νιν εὔφρων δέξεται
> καλλιγύναικι πάτρᾳ
> δόξαν ἱμερτὰν ἀγαγόντ' ἀπὸ Δελφῶν.
>
> (P.9.71–75)

And now in holy Pytho the son of Karneiades has mixed her together with flourishing fortune. Having won there, he proclaimed Kyrene, who

---

[59]There is a striking parallel for the association of a divine dowry with a tradition of athletic success in N.1, where Pindar says of Sicily, "Sprinkle now a certain radiance on the island that the lord of Olympus, Zeus, gave to Persephone, and he nodded for her with his locks, to set upright rich Sicily as the best of the fertile land with the wealthy peaks of cities. And the son of Kronos bestowed a people in love with brazen war, armed horsemen, and frequently indeed mixed with the golden leaves of Olympic olives" (N.1.13–18). The scholia explain that Pindar is representing Sicily as Zeus's gift to Persephone on the occasion of her marriage to Hades. (The scholia specifically designate it as part of her ἀνακαλυπτήρια, the gifts given to the bride when she removes her veil.) Notice that Zeus's gifts, emphasized by the verbs ἔδωκεν, κατένευσεν, and ὤπασε, correspond almost exactly to the elements of Kyrene's "dowry" in P.9. In both contexts, the nymph or goddess is dowered with a fertile land, glorious cities, and a people successful in the highest contests. In N.1, as in P.9, this originary marriage gift serves to establish a preferential relationship between the site of the games and the victor's homeland, and thereby at least partially to account for the current victory.

will receive him gladly in his homeland, full of beautiful women, as he
leads lovely glory from Delphi.

The νιν in line 71 must refer to Kyrene, who is the subject of the verb
ἀμφέπει in line 70. Thus Pindar describes the victory as Telesikrates'
"mixing Kyrene with flourishing good fortune," as if he were her *kyrios*
and his athletic success reenacted her fruitful "mixing" with Apollo
(note especially μίγεν in line 68).[60] In exchange for thus reuniting
Kyrene with Apollo at Delphi, Telesikrates leads home the bridelike gift
bestowed on him by the god, δόξαν ἱμερτάν . . . ἀπὸ Δελφῶν.

It is interesting in this context to consider the observations of Claude
Lévi-Strauss on "dual organization," the system whereby two segments or moieties within a society habitually exchange brides: "From
a more general point of view, it will be sufficient to note here that a new
marriage renews all marriages concluded at other times, and at different
points in the social structure, so that each connexion rests upon all the
others and gives them, on its establishment, a recrudescence of activity."[61] Just so, Telesikrates' "marriage" to glory rests upon the originary marriage of Apollo and Kyrene, which is renewed at the moment
of victory. The poet seems to be mapping both colonization and athletic
victory as a continuum of marriage exchanges between Greece and
Libya.

The intermediate link in the chain of marriages set up by the poem is
that of Telesikrates' ancestor Alexidamos, described in the last triad. His
is simultaneously marriage by contest and marriage as gift exchange,
for he wins his bride in a race, but the poet uses the language of the
gift:[62]

> οὕτω δ᾽ ἐδίδου Λίβυς ἁρμόζων κόρᾳ
> νυμφίον ἄνδρα·
>
> (P.9.117–118)

And thus the Libyan was giving [her], fitting a bridegroom to his daughter.

---

[60]Pace Carson 1982.124. Carson would like to take συνέμειξε with εὐθαλεῖ . . . τύχᾳ,
so that Telesikrates "mingling with Victory" at 72 parallels Kyrene "mingling" with
Apollo at 69, but we cannot ignore the pronoun νιν. On συμμείγνυμι with accusative
and dative, see Slater 1969a and LSJ.

[61]Lévi-Strauss 1969.65.

[62]Finley (1953.234) lists marriage by contest as a separate form from gift exchange, but
the distinction does not appear so clear-cut here and in Olympian 9.

The poet emphasizes the bride's Libyan background in the narration of this episode (here, 105–106, 108, and 123). Since he has already kept Apollo as Greek ξεῖνος and associated Kyrene closely with Libya "in her golden houses," the ethnic emphasis here seems to make literal the exchange between Greece and Africa which the poem has mapped out, even as this episode literalizes the association of marriage with athletic victory.[63] The description of the marriage of Apollo and Kyrene implies a preferential relationship between the god of Delphi and all Kyrenean athletes. The "rousing up of the ancient glory" of Telesikrates' ancestors motivates his particular victory—on the literal level, by the family tradition of racing prowess; on the metaphorical level, by its participation in Greek-Libyan marriage exchange.[64]

The end of Pythian 9 combines marriage by contest with gift exchange to literalize the analogy between athletic victory and marriage. The same combination occurs in an allusive reference to Elis in Olympian 9:

> ἀλλὰ νῦν ἑκαταβόλων Μοισᾶν ἀπὸ τόξων
> Δία τε φοινικοστερόπαν σεμνόν τ᾽ ἐπίνειμαι
> ἀκρωτήριον Ἄλιδος
> τοιοῖσδε βέλεσσιν,
> τὸ δή ποτε Λυδὸς ἥρως Πέλοψ
> ἐξάρατο κάλλιστον ἕδνον Ἱπποδαμείας·
>
> (O.9.5–10)

But now from the bows of the far-shooting Muses, I sweep Zeus of the red thunderbolt and the august height of Elis with such darts, [Elis] which indeed once the Lydian hero Pelops won as most beautiful dowry of Hippodameia.

Ἐξάρατο suggests a contest in which the prize must be won, while ἕδνον evokes a gift-exchange model for marriage. Together they point us to Olympian 1, for there Pindar implicitly sets up Pelops' winning of

[63]We should note in this context that the fourth marriage in the poem—the marriage of the Danaids, which inspires the Libyan bride race—is also between African women and Greek men (Pindar tells us emphatically that the race took place in Argos, P.9.112). Indeed, Pythian 9 appears a veritable paean to exogamy, which we may understand as the poet's way of metaphorically glorifying Greek colonization and the participation of Greek colonists in the Panhellenic games (i.e., the ongoing exchange between mainland Greece and the rest of the Greek world). It is significant that what is essentially an issue of Greek politics can be subsumed to the model of marriage exchange.

[64]On the rationale behind the poem's final triad, see Köhnken 1985.103–109.

Hippodameia as a kind of etiological myth for the horse races at Olympia.[65] These associations are very suggestive for Gregory Nagy's notion about the foundation of the great games, which he believes were conceived in their origin and in each repetition as a chain of ritual *apoina*, whose last link is the relationship of victor and poet as manifested in the epinikion.[66] But in Olympian 9 and Olympian 1 we get the sense instead that the foundation of the games is being assimilated to the model of marriage.[67]

Perhaps we must take Nagy's theory a step further and postulate that the foundation and functioning of the games can be assimilated to any one of the three spheres of gift exchange. That is, *apoina*, marriage, and *xenia* are equivalent insofar as they are all gift-exchange models available to Pindar to conceptualize the victor's relationship to the games and the poet's relationship to the victor. The essential thing, then, is the fact of gift exchange rather than its form; it is the single system that connects the current victor to the gods and mythic foundation of the games and, in turn, the poet to the victor. In each case, the model of gift exchange expands to embrace every element of the epinikian world. We should not regard this cosmic expansion of gift exchange cynically as the poet's elaborate self-justification for the fact of payment. To do so would be to ignore the social dimension of the poet's program. For at the center of Pindar's poetics stands not the poet but the victor, confronting the heterogeneous community to which he seeks reentry. The construction of the epinikian world as gift exchange accomplishes this reintegration with one sector of the victor's community at least. For this representation is an affirmation of aristocratic ideology, but as such, it is a two-edged sword. On the one hand, Pindar's deployment of the metaphysics of gift exchange ratifies the terms of aristocratic self-definition; on the other hand, these same terms obligate the victor's fellow aristocrats to accept his success "with good grace."

[65]On the etiology of the Olympic chariot race, see Nagy 1986b.81–87.

[66]Nagy 1986a.93–94, 1986b.73–77, 1990.136–145.

[67]Especially since in Olympian 1 Pindar seems to be suppressing the version of the myth in which Pelops wins by sabotaging and killing Oinomaos with the help of his charioteer Myrtilos, and then killing Myrtilos himself—both crimes that would indeed require *apoina* (see Pausanias 5.1.7, 6.20.17, 8.14.10–12; and Apollodorus *Epitome* 2.6–9).

CHAPTER 6

Guest-Friends and
Guest-Gifts

Of the three spheres of gift exchange differentiated by technical terminology, *xenia* occurs most frequently in the epinikia as an image for the relationship of poet and victor. But unlike *apoina* and *hedna*, its metaphorical quality is obscured by its possible reality; biographical criticism takes literally Pindar's statement that he is a *xenos* of the victor's family, reconstructing a life full of travels and visits.[1] Hermann Fränkel and Hermann Gundert long ago recognized the fallacy of such biographical reconstruction. Fränkel suggested that Pindar's frequent claim to be the victor's *xenos* was merely an image, and Gundert observed that it must rarely have been the case that the personal connection was any older than the contract itself. Nevertheless, as Gundert went on to point out, we need not take the *xenia* relationship as an empty fiction; rather, the contractual obligation was patterned on "a particular form of social exchange, which counted as *xenia*."[2] More important than the reality of Pindar's visits in particular cases is the fact that he conceptualizes the relationship of poet and victor in general as one of *xenia*, of reciprocal hospitality and gift exchange. Thus in Nemean 7, the poet says ξεῖνός εἰμι (N.7.61), and he closes Isthmian 2 with the injunction to the chorus leader, "Impart these things, whenever you come to my customary *xenos*."

As Slater observes, the relationship of *xenia* has certain implications for the poet's act of praise, and this is the reason it is included in the

[1]For examples, see Wilamowitz 1922 and Bowra 1964.99–158.
[2]Fränkel 1930.10 n. 2, Gundert 1935.35–36. See also Maehler 1963.88, Fränkel 1973.432–433, and Crotty 1982.74.

epinikian "argument": "Pindar several times claims to be a *xenos* of the victor; . . . a *xenos* is under an obligation a) not to be envious of his *xenos* and b) to speak well of him. The argumentation is: *Xenia* excludes envy, I am a *xenos*, therefore I am not envious and consequently praise honestly."[3] The bond of *xenia* authenticates the poet's encomium, but it also participates in a precise social context. As the words of Xerxes quoted by Herodotus (7.237) suggest, long-distance bonds of *xenia* are the special province of the nobility, often at least implicitly opposed to the ideology of civic solidarity. Thus Pindar characterizes his bond with the victor as a peculiarly aristocratic one, and this characterization not only affirms the sincerity of the poet's words but implicates the aristocratic audience in the act of praise.

The coercive force of the *xenia* relationship on its aristocratic audience is perhaps clearest in the gnomic opening of Olympian 4. As if to motivate his utterance in general, Pindar observes,

> ξείνων δ' εὖ πρασσόντων
> ἔσαναν αὐτίκ' ἀγγελίαν ποτὶ γλυκεῖαν ἐσλοί·
>
> (O.4.4–5)

When their *xenoi* fare well, they immediately show joy at the happy message, those who are noble.

The language here is strikingly similar to Xerxes': ξεῖνος δὲ ξείνῳ εὖ πρήσσοντί ἐστι εὐμενέστατον πάντων ("A *xenos* is the most well disposed of all things to a *xenos* when he fares well" [Herodotus 7.237.3]). There is one notable difference between the two passages, however, for Pindar says explicitly what is only implied in Xerxes' words: it is the ἐσλοί, the noble, who feel such perfect sympathy with the fortunes of their *xenoi*. Indeed, the placement of ἐσλοί at the end of the gnome (and the end of the line) is emphatic; it almost constitutes a challenge to its audience. Those who are truly noble will prove themselves by the quality of their response to the victor's achievement.[4]

Furthermore, the aristocrats in the audience are implicated not merely by their investment in the ideology of *xenia* but by their own participation in the victory celebration. They are themselves recipients

---

[3]Slater 1979a.80. On the obligations of *xenoi*, see Herman 1987.116–161.

[4]Cf. N.1.24–25, which I translate, following Waring 1982, "To bear water against the soot of those who blame is the task allotted to the noble" (ἐσλούς). In this context, immediately after praise of Chromios' φιλοξενία, the general statement extends the obligation to praise to all those who consider themselves noble and who enjoy Chromios' hospitality. Thus the model of *xenia* expands and imposes itself compellingly on the poem's aristocratic audience.

of the victor's hospitality, so that the poet necessitates their kindly reception of the victory as well as his own praise by incorporating *xenia* into the epinikia. Thus on occasion Pindar incorporates the scene of celebration into the ode itself, setting an entire poem within the context of hospitality at the victor's house. Such a frame vividly marks the poem's performance as an occasion infused with *charis*, at which it is peculiarly appropriate for the guests to praise their generous host. In Olympian 1, for example, he sets the scene at "the rich blessed hearth of Hieron":

οἷα παίζομεν φίλαν
ἄνδρες ἀμφὶ θαμὰ τράπεζαν. ἀλλὰ Δωρίαν ἀπὸ φόρμιγγα πασσάλου
λάμβαν', εἴ τί τοι Πίσας τε καὶ Φερενίκου χάρις
νόον ὑπὸ γλυκυτάταις ἔθηκε φροντίσιν,

(O.1.16–19)

What sorts of things we men play frequently about the table of a friend. But take the Dorian lyre from its peg, if at all the grace of Pisa and Pherenikos has put your mind under the influence of the sweetest thoughts.

Here the poet is only one of a group of guests gathered to entertain each other around Hieron's hospitable table. In this context, the verb παίζομεν and the injunction to "take the Dorian lyre from its peg" offer examples of the scripted spontaneity we observed in Isthmian 8 and Olympian 7. The two verbs simulate the effect of a spontaneous out-pouring of praise inspired by the *charis* of the occasion. This response, which motivates the poem, also serves as a paradigm for all those who are enjoying the benefit of Hieron's hospitality.

Similarly, Nemean 9 begins with the poet's summons to the Muses to celebrate the *kōmos* at the house of Chromios, "where the doors flung wide are overwhelmed by guests" (ἔνθ' ἀναπεπταμέναι ξείνων νενίκανται θύραι [N.9.2]). The poem's end returns to the festivites with a scene of the arrival of the *kōmos* and the beginning of the symposium.[5] Into this vivid symposiastic setting, the poet integrates his celebratory song and the concrete emblems of Chromios' victory:

ἡσυχία δὲ φιλεῖ μὲν συμπόσιον· νεοθαλὴς δ' αὔξεται
μαλθακᾷ νικαφορία σὺν ἀοιδᾷ· θαρσαλέα δὲ παρὰ κρατῆρα φωνὰ
γίνεται.

[5]On the festive frame of the poem, see Carey 1981.110 and Crotty 1982.85. On the obligation the frame imposes on the entire audience, see Hubbard 1985.157.

ἐγκιρνάτω τίς νιν, γλυκὺν κώμου προφάταν,
ἀργυρέαισι δὲ νωμάτω φιάλαισι βιατάν
ἀμπέλου παῖδ᾽, ἅς ποθ᾽ ἵπποι κτησάμεναι Χρομίῳ πέμψαν
θεμιπλέκτοις ἀμᾶ
Λατοΐδα στεφάνοις ἐκ τᾶς ἱερᾶς Σικυῶνος.

(N.9.48–53)

Peace loves the symposium, but new-blooming victory is exalted with
gentle song. And the voice becomes bold beside the krater. Let some one
mix [it], the sweet spokesman of the *kōmos*, and let someone ply the
violent child of the grape in the silver cups, which once his horses, having
acquired for Chromios sent together with the crowns of the son of Leto,
woven in justice, from holy Sikyon.

Again the spontaneous enjoyment of the symposium by the guests who
throng Chromios' house seems to be scripted into the very performance
of the epinikion. Thus the indefinite third-person injunction ἐγκιρνάτω
τις, like τις . . . ἀνεγειρέτω κῶμον at the beginning of Isthmian 8,
implicates the poet's audience in the celebration, while the presence of
the silver cups, the prize from Sikyon, makes palpable the reason for the
festivities.[6]

As a kind of dense metaphorical ellipse for such sympotic celebration
accompanied by song, the poet sometimes focuses on the moment of
sharing the wine and pouring the libation. Thus Isthmian 6 begins with
an elaborate sympotic metaphor:

Θάλλοντος ἀνδρῶν ὡς ὅτε συμποσίου
δεύτερον κρατῆρα Μοισαίων μελέων
κίρναμεν Λάμπωνος εὐαέθλου γενεᾶς ὕπερ,

(I.6.1–3)

As when the symposium of men is blooming, we mix a second krater of
strains of the Muses for the sake of the family of Lampon, successful in
contests.

The poet goes on to compare this, his second ode for the sons of
Lampon, to the second libation offered at the symposium. The poet's

[6]Crotty 1982.85 compares ἐγκιρνάτω τις to the injunctions in Anacreon 396 PMG,
"Bring water, bring wine, boy, bring blooming crowns for us." But as I.6.3 and I.5.24–
25 suggest, to mix the wine is the task not of a slave but of one of the symposiasts. Thus
we may assume that ἐγκιρνάτω τις, like τις . . . ἀνεγειρέτω in I.8, is addressed to the
members of the audience. On such indefinite commands in general, see Slater 1969b.

use of the plural verb κίρναμεν, "we mix," is significant in this context. For it engages the entire sympotic group in the act of praise, just as every member of the symposium would participate in the prayers that accompanied the ritual libations to the gods.[7] As in the contexts of marriage and betrothal, the elaborate conceit of the poem dictates the proper response of the audience. And such coercion is even more effective here, where image and reality merge, for the libations of song are an image, but presumably the poem was actually performed at a celebratory symposium at the house of Lampon.

Thus, as with the imagistic spheres of *apoina* and *hedna*, one aspect of the poet's use of *xenia* imagery is its power to coerce the approval of the aristocratic group. But we should not limit our understanding of the *xenia* relation to its negative aspects—to the obligation not to envy it imposes on the poet and the aristocratic community alike. We might say we have considered the *chreos* of *xenia* but not its *charis*, for *xenia* is, like recompense and marriage, a top-rank occasion at which *agalmata* are exchanged between aristocratic peers. What are the implications of the poet's use of *xenia* as a model for his relationship with the victor, and what are the "gifts" exchanged?

The poet's representation of *xenia* draws in important respects on the Homeric model, for as always, Homer is the school for Greece, but especially for archaic aristocrats. That is to say, the invocation of the Homeric model is not merely a literary allusion but an ideological gesture common to the poet and his aristocratic group. As Lacey observes, "The importance of the *xenos* in the Homeric poems is particularly great, no doubt because of the aristocratic society they portray, and that society must be first considered, not least because of the fact that Homer was the basic educational medium in Greece, and hence the institutions and ideas of the society he portrayed cannot but have been influential in shaping Greek thought in a way in which the historical Mycenaean society did not."[8] According to the Homeric model of guest-friendship, poet and victor are aristocratic equals, long-distance *xenoi* who exchange hospitality and the treasures of their houses. In

---

[7]Slater (1969b.90) asserts that "there is no difference to be understood between first-person singular and plural, unless deliberately stated, in such expressions, so that we may confidently assume that φεύγομεν [at O.6.90] may refer to Pindar, the chorus, or both." I suggest that first-person plural verbs, especially those that occur at the beginning of poems, implicate the audience as well as the ἐγώ (the poet/chorus) in the act of praise, unless it is specifically designated as the ἐγώ alone. Cf. O.1.10, 16, O.6.1–3, P.6.3–4, N.9.1, I.8.6a–8.

[8]Lacey 1968.31–32.

these contexts, the bond of *xenia* is inevitably invoked to explain or motivate Pindar's song, for the poet conceptualizes the *xenia* relationship as entailing his poem, his praise of the victor, within a reciprocal exchange of goods and services.

Pindar's calm assumption of perfect equality with important victors has often disconcerted modern critics, for they have not appreciated the structure and ideology of aristocratic *xenia* which inform such passages. Thus, at the end of Olympian 1, Pindar returns to the hospitable scene that opens the poem but narrows the focus to victor and poet alone:

> εἴη σέ τε τοῦτον ὑψοῦ χρόνον πατεῖν,
> ἐμέ τε τοσσάδε νικαφόροις
> ὁμιλεῖν⁹ πρόφαντον σοφίᾳ καθ᾽ Ἕλλανας ἐόντα παντᾷ.
>
> (O.1.115–116)

May it be for you to tread aloft for this time, as for me to the same extent [lit. to this extent] to keep company with victors, being preeminent throughout Greece in all poetic skill.

The parallelism of language and syntax here is iconic for the reciprocal relationship of poet and patron, emphasized by the central τοσσάδε, which equalizes the gifts and responsibilities of the two. Indeed, these last lines make clear what each partner brings to the relationship—Hieron his success and the poet his *sophia*—as matching "gifts."

It is noteworthy that these are the same metaphoric "gifts" I postulated in the context of marriage imagery. Given the poem's frame of *xenia*, one image Pindar uses along the way takes on more concrete significance. Toward the end of the ode, the poet asserts,

> πέποιθα δὲ ξένον
> μή τιν᾽ ἀμφότερα καλῶν τε ἴδριν †ἅμα καὶ δύναμιν κυριώτερον
> τῶν γε νῦν κλυταῖσι δαιδαλωσέμεν ὕμνων πτυχαῖς.
>
> (O.1.103–105)

I am confident that I have garbed in the glorifying folds of songs no *xenos* who is both [more] skilled in beautiful things and at the same time more authoritative in power, of those now at any rate.

Here Pindar specifically refers to Hieron as his *xenos* and allots to himself and his patron nearly the same equivalent "gifts" as at the end of

⁹For ὁμιλεῖν in a sympotic context, cf. P.6.52–54.

the poem. Hieron is outstanding for his cultivation and kingly power, Pindar for his poetic artistry. In this context, Pindar's image of his song as an elaborately wrought robe in which he enfolds Hieron evokes the sumptuous garments often exchanged as guest gifts in the Homeric poems.[10]

The poet assumes the same equality with Thorax, prince of Thessaly, in Pythian 10, his earliest preserved ode. Though written in honor of the Thessalian Hippokleas, the poem was commissioned by Thorax. At the close of the poem, Pindar turns from a wish for greater victories for Hippokleas to the topic of his own relationship with Thorax:

> τὰ δ' εἰς ἐνιαυτὸν ἀτέκμαρτον προνοῆσαι.
> πέποιθα ξενίᾳ προσανέι Θώρακος, ὅσπερ ἐμὰν ποιπνύων χάριν
> τόδ' ἔζευξεν ἅρμα Πιερίδων τετράορον,
> φιλέων φιλέοντ', ἄγων ἄγοντα προφρόνως.
> πειρῶντι δὲ καὶ χρυσὸς ἐν βασάνῳ πρέπει
> καὶ νόος ὀρθός.
>
> (P. 10.63–68)

But it is impossible to know in advance the things to come in a year. But I trust to the soothing hospitality of Thorax, the very one who, bustling after my grace, yoked this four-horse chariot of the Pierides, as friend to friend, leading one who leads well-disposed. Gold also shines forth on the touchstone for the one testing it, and an upright mind.

Again the perfectly balanced clauses, φιλέων φιλέοντ', ἄγων ἄγοντα, express the equality and reciprocity that obtain between poet and patron. In this context, the composition of poetry is central to the *xenia* relationship, for what makes Thorax the poet's ξένος and φίλος is the fact that he "yoked this four-horse chariot of the Pierides"—that is, this poem. Furthermore, Pindar's assertion that he "trusts to the gentle hospitality of Thorax" must be understood in terms of the gnome that immediately precedes: "the things to come in a year" refer both to the victor's (presumed) wish to win at the Olympic games and the poet's own hope to celebrate that victory (note ἔλπομαι κτλ. [P. 10.55–58]). To say he trusts to his patron's ξενία in this context can only mean he counts on him for the future commission to which he alludes. Yet

[10]Cf. *Odyssey* 13.10–11, 14.320, 15.123–129, 24.276–279; and see Finley's discussion of such woven objects as one form of *keimelion* (Finley 1977.61, 64) and Block 1985 on the pattern of clothing exchange in the *Odyssey*.

Pindar frames this statement not as a business proposition but rather as an enduring bond of friendship between himself and Thorax.[11]

An understanding of the *xenia* whose product is the poem will help us in turn to fathom the odd expression ἐμᾶν ποιπνύων χάριν. Ποιπνύω seems a troubling verb to use of the nobleman Thorax: in Homer, it frequently refers to the "bustling" of servants or attendants (*Iliad* 1.600, 18.421, 24.475, *Odyssey* 3.430, 20.149). Scholars are clearly discomfited by its use here, recalling that Pindar was only about twenty and that this may have been his first commission. The attempt is made to palliate the oddness of the verb by understanding ἐμᾶν . . . χάριν as "for my sake": the young poet, we are told, is very grateful for the nobleman's attention.[12] I would contend, however, that Pindar nowhere uses χάριν as a preposition; all of Slater's examples have more force if we take χάρις as a substantive.[13] So here Pindar says "bustling after my grace, [he] yoked this four-horse chariot of the Pierides"—that is, Thorax exerted himself to establish a relationship of goodwill with Pindar. Like an attentive Homeric host, he speeds the poet on his way, preparing the chariot of the Muses to traverse its road of song.[14] What seems to us to be oddness or impropriety of expression is explicable within the ethos of gift exchange. Pindar emphasizes Thorax's eagerness to make his own obligation greater. Thus this poem, his countergift to Thorax, must be superlative. In addition, the poet implies that he is just as eager to return the compliment of service when another victory provides opportunity. As in the marriage contexts, *charis* is at the heart of the analogy. Because the poet's gift is given freely, out of goodwill, it will be a treasure like the precious objects exchanged between *xenoi*. Thorax's eagerness to elicit Pindar's goodwill marks their interaction as a top-rank occasion.

Finally, Pindar closes his meditation on *xenia* with the gnomic comparison of an upright mind to gold on the touchstone. As Gundert observes, this is a peculiarly aristocratic sentiment, familiar from many repetitions in the Theognidea.[15] Here, it marks both poet and patron as participants in the privileged circle of aristocratic guest-friendship. The quality of exchange partners, like that of their gifts, is the highest: they show themselves to be pure gold. At the same time, the gnome com-

---

[11]Thus Farnell 1930.2.220 takes these lines. See Kirkwood 1982.244 for a somewhat different interpretation.

[12]Thus LSJ ποιπνύω 1, Gildersleeve 1890.356, Slater 1969a.543, etc.

[13]Cf. O.7.5, P.2.70, P.3.95, P.11.12, and N.1.6. See Kirkwood 1982.100 and 244.

[14]Cf. *Odyssey* 3.475–480, 15.86–159.

[15]Gundert 1935.37, 123 n. 162. Cf. Theognis 117–128, 415–418, 449–452, 499–502; Bacchylides fr. 14.1–5 SM.

pletes the representation of perfect reciprocity, for it applies equally to
Pindar and Thorax. Applied to the poet's patron, it picks up πέποιθα
ξενίᾳ from line 63: Thorax has shown and will show his dependability
as a *xenos* by his continuing poetic commissions. Applied to Pindar
himself, the saying affirms the sincerity of his praise and the superlative
quality of his gift of song, while it implies a promise for the future.[16]

But we can perhaps chart the workings of epinikian *xenia* most
clearly in a couple of passages where the roles are reversed, where the
poet seems to act as host.[17] For the poet to host the victor within the
frame of the poem is problematic for any literal, biographical reading of
Pindar's *xenia* relations but conforms perfectly to the Homeric model of
reciprocal exchanges. Consider the first strophe of Nemean 4:

> Ἄριστος εὐφροσύνα πόνων κεκριμένων
> ἰατρός· αἱ δὲ σοφαί
> Μοισᾶν θύγατρες ἀοιδαὶ θέλξαν νιν ἁπτόμεναι.
> οὐδὲ θερμὸν ὕδωρ τόσον γε μαλθακὰ τεύχει
> γυῖα, τόσσον εὐλογία φόρμιγγι συνάορος.
> ῥῆμα δ' ἐργμάτων χρονιώτερον βιοτεύει,
> ὅ τι κε σὺν Χαρίτων τύχᾳ
> γλῶσσα φρενὸς ἐξέλοι βαθείας.

(N.4.1–8)

Festivity is the best doctor of toils that have reached their crisis, and
songs, wise daughters of the Muses, charm them, fastening onto them.[18]
Not even warm water makes limbs as soft as praise accompanied by the
lyre. But the report of deeds lives longer, whatever the tongue should
draw out of a deep mind with the favor of the Graces.

Here, a cluster of elements—εὐφροσύνα, song, a warm bath, and
enduring remembrance of actions—evokes the kind of hospitality displayed by Homer's princes. We find some of the same elements, in the
same order, in Telemachus' words to Mentes in the first book of the
Odyssey:

> ἀλλ' ἄγε νῦν ἐπίμεινον ἐπειγόμενός περ ὁδοῖο,
> ὄφρα λοεσσάμενός τε τεταρπόμενός τε φίλον κῆρ
> δῶρον ἔχων ἐπὶ νῆα κίῃς, χαίρων ἐνὶ θυμῷ,

[16]Compare the multiplicity of referents of the gnome at P.5.43–44.
[17]Compare Hubbard 1985.157–158.
[18]Like Slater 1969a, s.v. νιν (following Didymus), I take νιν to refer back to πόνων
rather than εὐφροσύνα.

τιμῆεν, μάλα καλόν, ὅ τοι κειμήλιον ἔσται
ἐξ ἐμεῦ, οἷα φίλοι ξεῖνοι ξείνοισι διδοῦσι.
(*Odyssey* 1.309–313)

But come now, remain, though you are eager for the road, in order that, having bathed and having satisfied your heart [with food and drink], you go to your ship bearing a gift, rejoicing in your spirit—an honorable gift, very beautiful, which will be a treasure for you from me, what sorts of things dear *xenoi* give to their *xenoi*.

Or again, within a context of feasting and *euphrosyne* among the Phaiakians, Alkinoos instructs Arete's maids in the proper treatment of the guest,

ἀμφὶ δὲ οἱ πυρὶ χαλκὸν ἰήνατε, θέρμετε δ' ὕδωρ,
ὄφρα λοεσσάμενός τε ἰδών τ' εὖ κείμενα πάντα
δῶρα, τά οἱ Φαίηκες ἀμύμονες ἐνθάδ' ἔνεικαν,
δαιτί τε τέρπηται καὶ ἀοιδῆς ὕμνον ἀκούων.
καὶ οἱ ἐγὼ τόδ' ἄλεισον ἐμὸν περικαλλὲς ὀπάσσω,
χρύσεον, ὄφρ' ἐμέθεν μεμνημένος ἤματα πάντα
σπένδῃ ἐνὶ μεγάρῳ Διί τ' ἄλλοισίν τε θεοῖσιν.
(*Odyssey* 8.426–432)

Warm a cauldron for him over the fire, and heat the water, in order that, having bathed and seen well laid out all the gifts that the peerless Phaiakians have borne here for him, he rejoice in the feast and hearing the strain of the song. And I shall give to him this goblet of mine, very beautiful, of gold, in order that he remember me every day when he pours libation to Zeus and the other gods in his own halls.

Here we find warm water for the bath, pleasure in the meal and in the accompanying song, but what Alkinoos adds to this cluster of elements is also relevant—a precious golden cup "in order that he remember me every day."

Looking back at the opening of Nemean 4, we can see that Pindar is playing the role of the Homeric host and that he is distinguishing two kinds of song as two forms of *xenia*. The first consists of the ἀοιδαί that accompany and foster *euphrosyne*, communal festivity, associated with the typical accouterments of a Homeric feast—pleasure, a warm bath, and the attendance of the singer. But the δέ of line 6 is truly adversative, setting in contrast to this ephemeral, soothing power of song in its sympotic setting the permanent gift of a ῥῆμα . . . χρονιώτερον that will preserve the memory of the victor's achievements.[19] Still, the *xenia* metaphor continues, for Pindar represents this enduring utterance as a kind of Homeric *keimelion*—a precious object drawn from the poet's "innermost chamber." Ἐξέλοι is a very concrete verb and the adjective βαθείας, juxtaposed to it, takes on more literal force.[20] Thus the poet offers as his guest-gift "whatever the tongue should draw out of a deep mind," like a Homeric host descending into his "fragrant inner chamber . . . where the treasures lie" (*Odyssey* 15.99–101).[21] And it is precisely in the context of drawing up a poetic treasure from the depths of his mind that Pindar seeks the aid of the Graces. Only with their attendance (σὺν Χαρίτων τύχᾳ) can he fashion an *agalma*, a truly enduring memorial of the victor's deeds.[22] We see here most clearly that *charis* is the quality of top-rank occasions which bestows on them and on the gifts exchanged their peculiar radiant value. We can see further the implications of the metaphorical *xenia* relationship: the poet himself has a metaphorical μυχός or θάλαμος from which he draws the treasures of his poetic *sophia* to hand on to the victor.

The poet also depicts himself as host in the *xenia* relationship at the end of Pythian 4.[23] In his closing plea to Arkesilaos for the reinstatement of Damophilos, Pindar offers us an image of that nobleman moving from *xenia* in Thebes to *euphrosyne* at home:

ἀλλ' εὔχεται οὐλομέναν νοῦσον διαντλήσαις ποτέ
οἶκον ἰδεῖν, ἐπ' Ἀπόλλωνός τε κράνᾳ συμποσίας ἐφέπων
θυμὸν ἐκδόσθαι πρὸς ἥβαν πολλάκις, ἔν τε σοφοῖς
δαιδαλέαν φόρμιγγα βαστάζων πολίταις ἡσυχίᾳ θιγέμεν,
μήτ' ὦν τινι πῆμα πορών, ἀπαθὴς δ' αὐτὸς πρὸς ἀστῶν·
καί κε μυθήσαιθ', ὁποίαν, Ἀρκεσίλα,
εὗρε παγὰν ἀμβροσίων ἐπέων, πρόσφατον Θήβᾳ ξενωθείς.

(P.4.293–299)

[19]On the distinction between the immediate pleasure of the *kōmos* and the lasting power of song, see Bundy 1962.2, 11, 22–23, and on this passage in particular, 2.

[20]For ἐξαιρέω, cf. O.1.26 (Klotho removing Pelops from the cauldron).

[21]For the motif of drawing one's most precious treasure from the μυχός or θάλαμος of the house, see *Odyssey* 8.438–439 and 15.99–108. In the latter passage the quality of the treasure as the innermost thing is doubly characterized: first Helen and Menelaus "go down into the fragrant θάλαμος . . . where the κειμήλια lie" (15.99–101), then Helen chooses the most beautiful robe, which "lay lowest [under] all the rest" (15.108). Compare *Iliad* 6.288–295, where Hecuba selects a robe to offer to Athena.

[22]The poet's dependence on the Graces in this context may account for the optative ἐξέλοι where we would expect the subjunctive, if Bury is correct in his claim that "the optative seems to express the event as more contingent" (Bury 1890.68).

[23]Compare Hubbard 1985.158.

But he prays at some time to see his home [again], having bilged out ruinous disease, and, devoting himself to symposia beside the spring of Apollo, to render his spirit on many occasions to youth, and, fastening onto the ornate lyre, to lay hold of peace amid his wise fellow citizens, furnishing no grief to anyone and himself suffering nothing at the hands of his fellow citizens. And he could tell, Arkesilaos, what sort of spring of immortal words he found when he was recently hosted at Thebes.

This double image of sympotic *euphrosyne* crystallizes around two springs, the κράνα of Apollo in Kyrene and Pindar's παγὰ ἀμβροσίων ἐπέων in Thebes. As in Nemean 4, the immediate healing power of sympotic celebration is associated with water (ἐπ᾽ Ἀπόλλωνός τε κράνᾳ συμποσίας ἐφέπων),[24] and in this context the poet's gift of the poem is simultaneously a refreshing spring for his guest and a permanent (immortal) guest-gift (notice the epithet of the poet's words, ἀμβροσίων). The ode itself is the poet's ξένιον to Damophilos, a precious gift that pleads his case to the king.

But as with *apoina* and *hedna*, the *xenia* relationship seems inevitably to expand beyond the narrow limits of a direct connection between poet and victor. Bonds of *xenia* proliferate to subsume the whole process of athletic competition, victory, and celebration. The poet represents all these phenomena as a chain of *charis* relations, in which the *xenia* or *philia* of poet and patron often participates as the last link. As with the other two spheres of gift exchange, the games themselves can be assimilated to *xenia*. This representation explains the victory in terms that force acceptance on the poet's aristocratic audience. Thus, on occasion, the poet invokes a long-standing bond of *xenia* between the victor's family and a god. In Nemean 10, for example, Pindar attributes Theaios' success to the gratitude of the Dioscuri for an ancestor's hospitality:

Κάστορος δ᾽ ἐλθόντος ἐπὶ ξενίαν πὰρ Παμφάη
καὶ κασιγνήτου Πολυδεύκεος, οὐ θαῦμα σφίσιν
ἐγγενὲς ἔμμεν ἀεθληταῖς ἀγαθοῖσιν· ἐπεί
εὐρυχόρου ταμίαι Σπάρτας ἀγώνων

[24]The element of healing is prominent here, as in N.4.1–8. There, *euphrosyne* is called "best doctor of toils"; here Damophilos wishes, "having bilged out ruinous disease," to enjoy *hēsychia* at home. Recall that Pindar designates the king ἰατὴρ ἐπικαιρότατος as he begins his plea for Damophilos (P.4.270). In Kyrene, Arkesilaos alone (like Alkinoos in *Odyssey* 8) can offer the healing powers of water and *euphrosyne* to the wanderer.

μοῖραν Ἑρμᾷ καὶ σὺν Ἡρακλεῖ διέποντι θάλειαν,
μάλα μὲν ἀνδρῶν δικαίων περικαδόμενοι. καὶ μὰν θεῶν πιστὸν γένος.

(N. 10.49–54)

But since Castor and his brother Polydeukes came for hospitality to the
house of Pamphaes, it is no wonder that it is inborn for them to be good
athletes. Since it is the stewards of spacious Sparta who, together with
Hermes and Herakles, arrange the blooming share of contests, taking
very good care of men who are just. And indeed, the race of the gods is
trusty.

In this context, Pindar's use of the word ταμίαι to characterize the
authority of the Dioscuri is interesting. While εὐρυχόρου ταμίαι Σπάρτας is a perfectly natural phrase taken quite literally as "stewards of the
city," its setting here seems to endow it with a metaphorical tinge as
well. Having just referred to the hospitality of Pamphaes, Pindar goes
on to describe Castor and Polydeukes as the ταμίαι who "arrange
the blooming share of contests" together with Hermes and Herakles.
Θάλειαν is, of course, a common Homeric epithet for the feast, and
μοῖραν is suitably ambiguous, since it refers both to one's "lot" and to a
portion of meat.[25] Thus these lines seem to carry a kind of afterimage of
the Dioscuri presiding at the games as at a banquet, allotting to each
participant his "portion" of success and glory. In this role, their favor to
Pamphaes' descendant becomes exact reciprocity in kind for the hospitality he showed them, justifying Pindar's final assertion that "the race
of the gods is trusty."[26]

Pindar suggests a similar kind of cause and effect in Olympian 6,
attributing Hagesias' victory to the favor of Hermes:

εἰ δ' ἐτύμως ὑπὸ Κυλλάνας ὄρος, Ἀγησία, μάτρωες ἄνδρες
ναιετάοντες ἐδώρησαν θεῶν κάρυκα λιταῖς θυσίαις
πολλὰ δὴ πολλαῖσιν Ἑρμᾶν εὐσεβέως, ὃς ἀγῶνας ἔχει μοῖράν τ'
    ἀέθλων,
Ἀρκαδίαν τ' εὐάνορα τιμᾷ· κεῖνος, ὦ παῖ Σωστράτου,
σὺν βαρυγδούπῳ πατρὶ κραίνει σέθεν εὐτυχίαν.

(O.6.77–81)

[25]For θαλεία as an epithet of the banquet, see Iliad 7.475, Odyssey 3.420, 8.76, 99,
Homeric Hymn to Hermes 480. Μοῖρα has the meaning "share," "cut of meat," more often
in the plural (Odyssey 3.40, 3.66, 8.470, 15.140, 19.423, 20.260, 280, Homeric Hymn to
Hermes 128), but also in the singular, as in Odyssey 17.335. See Svenbro 1976.22–25.
[26]Compare πιστόν here with πέποιθα ξενίᾳ at P.10.63 and πέποιθα δὲ ξένον at
O.1.103. In all three cases, the notion of trustworthiness is grounded in the xenia
relationship.

But if truly, O Hagesias, your maternal ancestors who dwelt under Mount Kyllene often reverently presented many sacrifices accompanied by prayers to Hermes, the herald of the gods, who holds games and the allotment of prizes and who honors Arkadia with its noble men—it is that one, O child of Sostratos, together with his loud-thundering father, who ordains your good fortune.

Here, the poet puts it conditionally: if Hagesias' maternal ancestors have indeed offered the proper "hospitality" to Hermes, it is he who has accomplished Hagesias' good fortune (together with his father Zeus, for it is an Olympic victory). Their hospitality is phrased in religious terms—they presented the herald of the gods with sacrifices and prayers—but the relationship of man and god is also a relationship of two houses. As the poet emphasizes, they are neighbors. This is the reason for specifying that Hagesias' family lives under Mount Kyllene, the traditional birthplace of Hermes (ὑπὸ Κυλλάνας ὄρος . . . ναιετάοντες).[27]

The poet proceeds almost immediately to extend the chain of hereditary relations to his own connection with the victor:

> ματρομάτωρ ἐμὰ Στυμφαλίς, εὐανθὴς Μετώπα,
> πλάξιππον ἃ Θήβαν ἔτικτεν, τᾶς ἐρατεινὸν ὕδωρ
> πίομαι, ἀνδράσιν αἰχματαῖσι πλέκων
> ποικίλον ὕμνον.

(O.6.84–87)

My mother's mother [was] Stymphalian, lovely blooming Metope, who bore horse-driving Thebe. Her lovely water I shall drink as I weave an embroidered hymn for warlike men.

Pindar identifies the Stymphalian nymph Metope as his grandmother, for she was the mother of Thebe, eponymous nymph of Thebes. Stymphalos was an Arkadian city adjacent to Mount Kyllene in the south, so that Pindar's identification establishes a bond of *philia* between himself and Hagesias' Arkadian ancestors. Just as the hereditary link with Hermes motivates the victory, the familial connection of poet and patron motivates the victory ode. And this concatenation of *charis* relations is reinforced by the persistent imagery of hospitality between neighbors: as Hagesias' maternal ancestors offered Hermes their sacrifices (θυσίαις), Pindar offers the victor's Arkadian family a hymn elab-

---

[27]For the association of Hermes with Mount Kyllene, see *Homeric Hymn to Hermes* 2, 387 and Allen, Halliday, and Sikes 1936.277–278.

orately plaited like a precious garment or wreath (πλέκων ποικίλον ὕμνον).[28]

When a traditional connection did not exist between the victor or his family and a particular divinity, the poet would invent one. Or rather, we should say, the model of human-divine *xenia* is extended into metaphor in such a way that the victory itself is conceptualized as an act of hospitality. Thus the patron divinity of the games "hosts" the athlete and bestows victory on him as a kind of guest-gift. Again, it is *charis* that forms the ground of the metaphor: to have won at the games is to have enjoyed the patron divinity's particular "favor." Thus victory presupposes divine *charis*, and the victor alone can be said to have been "hosted" by the god. This representation of victory as divine grace gives the victor's aristocratic peers no choice but to accept his success, if they care to maintain their allegiance to gift exchange.

This metaphorical usage is clear in Pythian 5, when Pindar, addressing the victor, Arkesilaos, says of the winning charioteer Karrhotos:

> ἀλλ᾽ ἀρισθάρματον
> ὕδατι Κασταλίας ξενωθεὶς γέρας ἀμφέβαλε τεαῖσιν κόμαις,
>
> (P.5.30–31)

But [Karrhotos], hosted by the water of Kastalia, crowned your locks with the honor of a chariot victory.

Here, as in Nemean 4 and Pythian 4, this metaphorical hospitality is analyzed into its two components, the pleasantness of the charioteer's stay at Delphi (again associated with spring waters) and the permanent guest-gift, the victory crown he bears home to Kyrene.[29] As we have seen, the image of *xenia* here forms part of a complex network of gift exchange which plays through the thirty-line section of the ode devoted

---

[28]Recall O.1.105, where the song is a garment exchanged between *xenoi*. Here as there, Pindar may be punning on the folk etymology of ὕμνος from ὑφαίνω; cf. Bacchylides 5.9–10 and the comments of Maehler 1982.2.90.

[29]Slater notes the connection of *xenia* and victory in these lines from Pythian 5 but takes ὕδατι Κασταλίας ξενωθείς quite literally: "To be victorious was to be . . . treated as a ξένος and awarded ξένια by the Delphians. The award of ξένια to celebrities can be illustrated by many inscriptions. Pausanias tells us that the victors at Olympia were honoured by a banquet in the prytaneum in the Altis, and it can be assumed that the Delphians honoured their victors as they did so many others with a banquet in the prytaneum also" (Slater 1979b.67). Here we may well have the origin of Pindar's metaphorical elaboration of *xenia* imagery for victory, but given the parallels with *apoina* and marriage imagery, I would not want to overvalue the literal interpretation of such passages.

to Arkesilaos' charioteer. Metaphors of marriage and *xenia* combine to link in a single chain of *charis* Apollo, Arkesilaos, Karrhotos, and the poet.

In Isthmian 1, Pindar assimilates the victory to a special case of *xenia*—the good relations that exist between neighbors. Herodotus, a Theban, has won an Isthmian victory and thus has enjoyed the particular favor of Poseidon. But the way in which the poet chooses to express the relationship of god and victor is significant:

> ἄμμι δ' ἔοικε Κρόνου σεισίχθον' υἱόν
> γείτον' ἀμειβομένοις εὐεργέταν
> ἁρμάτων ἱπποδρόμιον κελαδῆσαι,
>
> (I.1.52–54)

And it is fitting for us to celebrate in song the earthshaking son of Kronos, as recompense to a neighbor and horse-racing benefactor of chariots.

As with Hermes in Olympian 6, the poet emphasizes that the god is a "neighbor," thus setting the human-divine relationship into the model of the interaction of houses. By framing the relationship in these terms, Pindar implies that this interaction is necessary—for one cannot avoid one's neighbors—but can also be very positive (as it is here, since the poet describes Poseidon also as εὐεργέταν).[30] Poseidon is "neighbor" to Thebes insofar as he is worshiped at Onchestos in Boeotia (cf. I.1.32–33). Erich Thummer makes the important point that Poseidon of Onchestos is being invoked here as the bestower of an *Isthmian* victory. This is extraordinary practice for Pindar: it would be much more natural in context to invoke Poseidon as god of the Isthmus. We must conclude that the poet is specifically grounding Herodotus' victory in his γειτωνία with Poseidon.[31] Within this model of the human-divine

---

[30]Bundy 1962.70 refers to the "neighbor motive" in this passage but does not elaborate at all on the term. It is useful in this context to recall Hesiod's lines on neighbors (*Works & Days* 342–351; see West [1978.243–244] for interesting parallels). As these lines make clear, neighboring is, in a sense, the extreme case of *xenia*.

[31]Thummer 1968.2.31. The same anomaly (again in relation to a Theban victor) occurs in I.4.19–21: ὁ κινητὴρ δὲ γᾶς 'Ογχηστὸν οἰκέων / καὶ γέφυραν ποντιάδα πρὸ Κορίνθου τειχέων, / τόνδε πορὼν γενεᾷ θαυμαστὸν ὕμνον ("And the shaker of the earth, who resides at Onchestos and the bridge of the sea before the walls of Corinth, granting this marvelous hymn to the clan"). Here it appears that Poseidon is situated *first* in Onchestos to make his giving (πορών) of new glory in the form of song a result of his status as neighbor. Of course, the clearest example of the neighbor motif is N.7, where Pindar addresses his prayers for Sogenes' future success to Herakles *because* Herakles is the boy's neighbor (N.7.86–101). On N.7, see Rusten 1983.

relationship, the poem functions as a countergift for the god's hospitality: Pindar, acting on the victor's behalf, feels that it is his obligation (ἔοικε) to require (ἀμειβομένοις) the divine neighbor's benefaction with celebratory song (κελαδῆσαι). Once more, the relations of *xenia* and *philia* extend to the poet's involvement as well. Pindar reciprocates Poseidon's gift on behalf of Herodotus because, as he reminds us in the proem of the ode, he too is a dutiful son of Thebes (I.1.1–5).

Again, in Pythian 8, Pindar's thankful prayer to Apollo sets Aristomenes' athletic victories squarely within the frame of human-divine *xenia*:

> τὺ δ', Ἑκαταβόλε, πάνδοκον
> ναὸν εὐκλέα διανέμων
> Πυθῶνος ἐν γυάλοις,
> τὸ μὲν μέγιστον τόθι χαρμάτων
> ὤπασας, οἴκοι δὲ πρόσθεν ἁρπαλέαν δόσιν
> πενταεθλίου σὺν ἑορταῖς ὑμαῖς ἐπάγαγες·
>
> (P.8.61–66)

And you, O Farshooter, who govern the glorious all-welcoming temple in the hollows of Pytho, there, on the one hand, you bestowed the greatest of joys, but to [Aristomenes'] home before you led the coveted gift of the pentathlon together with your festivals.

The poet designates Aristomenes' successes as the gifts of Apollo (ὤπασας, δόσιν), bestowed either at the god's "house" (πάνδοκον ναόν) or at the victor's own (οἴκοι).[32] In this context, the use of the epithet πάνδοκον is surely not fortuitous: it emphasizes the god's generous "hospitality" and specifically recalls the lines describing the crowning of the victor:

> . . . Ἀπόλλωνος· ὃς εὐμενεῖ νόῳ
> Ξενάρκειον ἔδεκτο Κίρραθεν ἐστεφανωμένον
> υἱὸν ποίᾳ Παρνασσίδι Δωριεῖ τε κώμῳ.
>
> (P.8.18–20)

[32]Οἴκοι is an old locative, which, used here with a verb of motion (ἐπάγαγες), may express "place whither" or "limit of motion" (Smyth 1956.351). Such a construction reinforces the image of guest-gifts exchanged: Apollo bestows one such gift in his own home and sends another to the house of the victor. Or else we can understand οἴκοι as the "pregnant" use of the locative: "you brought it so as to be at home." Construed thus, the word emphasizes the character of the pentathlon victory as a permanent treasure to be stored away in the victor's house.

. . . of Apollo, who received Xenarkes' son crowned from Kirrha with Parnassian grass and Dorian *kōmos*.

Πάνδοκον picks up ἔδεκτο, and εὐμενεῖ νόῳ underscores the particular divine favor the victor enjoys. In these lines, athletic victory is concretized as the god's "kind reception" of the victor into his home, crowned "with Parnassian grass and Dorian *kōmos*." The zeugma of ἐστεφανωμένον, which refers to both the literal victory crown and the celebration thereof, corresponds to the yoking of victory and *xenia*, for reception and crowns are key elements in the acknowledgment of victory and in the gestures of hospitality. Apollo receives the victor as presiding divinity of the Pythian games and as host, while the victory crown merges with the garlands traditionally worn by komasts and symposiasts. In this way, these lines powerfully superimpose the ritual props and gestures of *xenia* and athletic victory, much as the end of Pythian 9 fuses marriage and victory in the scene of the *phyllobolia*.[33]

Once we recognize that athletic victory can be assimilated to the *xenia* of the victor by the presiding divinity of a place, we are better able to appreciate the metaphorical cast of Pindar's language in his prayers and victory catalogs. Consider, for example, the extended catalog in Isthmian 2:

> Ἰσθμίαν ἵπποισι νίκαν,
> τὰν Ξενοκράτει Ποσειδάων ὀπάσαις,
> Δωρίων αὐτῷ στεφάνωμα κόμᾳ
> πέμπεν ἀναδεῖσθαι σελίνων,
> εὐάρματον ἄνδρα γεραίρων, Ἀκραγαντίνων φάος.
> ἐν Κρίσᾳ δ᾽ εὐρυσθενὴς εἶδ᾽ Ἀπόλλων νιν πόρε τ᾽ ἀγλαΐαν
> καὶ τόθι κλειναῖς ⟨τ᾽⟩ Ἐρεχθειδᾶν χαρίτεσσιν ἀραρώς
> ταῖς λιπαραῖς ἐν Ἀθάναις, οὐκ ἐμέμφθη
> ῥυσίδιφρον χεῖρα πλαξίπποιο φωτός,
> τὰν Νικόμαχος κατὰ καιρὸν νεῖμ᾽ ἁπάσαις ἁνίαις·
> ὅν τε καὶ κάρυκες ὡρᾶν ἀνέγνον, σπονδοφόροι Κρονίδα
> Ζηνὸς Ἀλεῖοι, παθόντες πού τι φιλόξενον ἔργον·
> ἁδυπνόῳ τέ νιν ἀσπάζοντο φωνᾷ
> χρυσέας ἐν γούνασιν πίτνοντα Νίκας

___

[33]As Richard Kannicht has suggested to me, these lines may describe the actual crowning of the victor, coming from "the plain of Kirrha" (where the competition took place) into the temple of Apollo (where the crowning ceremony would occur). On the end of P.9, see Carson 1982.123–124. For the same constellation of crowned komasts seeking reception in a context of literal *xenia*, see Plato *Symposium* 212d2–213a1.

γαῖαν ἀνὰ σφετέραν, τὰν δὴ καλέοισιν Ὀλυμπίου Διός
ἄλσος· ἵν' ἀθανάτοις Αἰνησιδάμου
παῖδες ἐν τιμαῖς ἔμιχθεν.

(I.2.13–29)

an Isthmian victory with horses, which Poseidon bestowed on Xenokrates and sent a crown of Dorian celery to him to bind on his locks,
thereby honoring a man with splendid chariots, the light of the Akragan-
tines. And in Krisa, Apollo, broad in strength, looked on him and gave
him splendor, and there, in shining Athens, fitted with the glorious
graces of the Erechtheidai, he did not blame the chariot-preserving hand
of a horse-driving man, [the hand] which Nikomachos plied opportunely
with all the reins. Him the heralds of the seasons also acknowledged, the
Elean truce-bearers of Zeus, son of Kronos, having experienced, I suppose, some act of hospitality. And him they greeted with a voice breathing sweetness as he fell upon the knees of golden victory in their land,
which indeed [men] call the grove of Zeus. There, the children of
Ainesidamos have been mingled with immortal honors.

Here, the entire victory catalog is framed in terms of gifts bestowed or
exchanged by the gods or officials who preside at the sites of the games.
Poseidon, bestowing an Isthmian victory, sent Xenokrates a crown
(ὀπάσαις . . . πέμπεν . . . γεραίρων); in Krisa, Apollo saw him and
gave the splendor of victory (εἶδ' . . . πόρε τ' ἀγλαΐαν). Next he was
fitted with the glorious graces of the Erechtheidai in shining Athens.
These words, at the center of the victory catalog, designate Xenokrates'
Athenian triumph in terms so general that they embrace both athletic
success and *xenia*, revealing their common ground in *charis*.

Always the geographic marker stands in an emphatic position, conjuring up the image of Xenokrates (or his charioteer) progressing from
one glorious "host" to another. This imagery seems to generate in turn a
chain of *charis* through which relations of reciprocal goodwill extend
down from the divine benefactors to the human participants. Xenokrates, "fitted with . . . graces" in Athens, "did not blame" his charioteer
Nikomachos—that is, he honored or praised him.[34] As a relationship of
reciprocal goodwill exists between Xenokrates and his charioteer, so too
a similar relationship obtains between the charioteer and the κάρυκες
ὡρᾶν. Here again, scholars take ἀνέγνον and παθόντες πού τι φιλό-
ξενον ἔργον quite literally; L. R. Farnell, for example, explains that "the
κήρυκες ὡρῶν are the Elean officials who went round the various cities

---

[34]On such negative expressions of positive statements, see Race 1983.

announcing the dates of the coming Olympia and proclaiming 'the truce of God' (σπονδοφόροι). It is obvious that Nikomachos had entertained them hospitably at Athens and that they had afterwards recognized him when he was at Olympia as driver of Theron's chariot."[35] The consideration of the rest of this passage and other such passages, however, suggests that it would be more productive to try to assimilate these lines to the context of athletic victory. Farnell is probably right to understand the κάρυκες ὡρᾶν as the officials who proclaimed the truce, but surely in lines 25–27 these heralds are serving another function—proclaiming the victor at the games themselves. Thus lines 23–27 establish a *xenia* relationship behind the charioteer's victory. When the heralds were in his land, he hosted them; "in their land" (γαῖαν ἀνὰ σφετέραν), they do him the service of acknowledging his victory and proclaiming him gladly (ἀνέγνον . . . ἀδυπνόῳ τέ νιν ἀσπάζοντο φωνᾷ).[36] Furthermore, Pindar seems to be implying that Nikomachos' hospitality was the *cause* of his victory, for πού τι mark these words as the poet's speculation rather than known fact.[37] Within the system Pindar elaborates here, the Deinomenids' victories are earned by their maintenance of hospitable relations with the presiding divinities of the games, the "heralds of the seasons," and their own charioteer Nikomachos.

By this exploration of the poet's metaphoric uses of gift exchange, I hope to have exposed the social framework of epinikian *charis*. *Charis* appears as a central concept of gift-exchange ideology: it organizes the cosmos within the epinikia in accordance with an aristocratic world view. Within the syntax of aristocratic exchange, *charis* acts as social

[35]Farnell 1930.2.345.

[36]It must be noted that the athletic victory here is no longer Xenokrates', but his brother Theron's at Olympia (see Thummer 1968.2.44). Therefore, Nikomachos was also Theron's charioteer at Olympia, implying another link in the chain of *charis*, for Theron also owes gratitude to Nikomachos, whose achievements for both brothers are acknowledged and repaid by the prominence of his praise here.

[37]Thummer 1968.2.45 acknowledges that που marks the participial phrase as the poet's speculation. He then explains the function of the phrase: "The participial phrase is therefore on the one hand praise of Nikomachos, on the other hand grounds for ἀνέγνον, corresponding to the increasing demand for logical justification" (my translation). The weakness of Thummer's interpretation is that he does not explain why Pindar should choose to include the irrelevant detail of the heralds' "recognizing" Nikomachos in the first place. If, however, we take ἀνέγνον in this context as "recognized him as winner" (i.e., heralded his victory), this apparent irrelevancy disappears. (Compare with this use of ἀναγιγνώσκω Pindar's use of the simplex γιγνώσκω at O.7.83 and P.9.79. For an independent argument that ἀναγιγνώσκω refers to the victory announcement in Pindar, see Wasserstein 1982.)

glue, and its workings can be charted along what we may call syntagmatic and paradigmatic axes.[38]

By syntagmatic, I mean *charis* as that force which creates community,
which links the victor to the gods, his family, his aristocratic group, and
the poet. The poem is the product of this relationship between poet and
victor, but as Pindar emphasizes by his multiplication of connections,
this single link cannot be separated from a whole chain of *charis*. This
circuit of *charis* constrains the aristocratic group into peaceable coexist-
ence and acceptance of the victory.

By paradigmatic, I mean *charis* as the quality that infuses top-rank
occasions, bestowing on them their peculiar prestige. We can view this
aspect of *charis* as paradigmatic because it seems to be the source of the
poet's use of any other top-rank occasion as an analogy for the victory
celebration. These occasions are, so to speak, substitutions for a single
slot within the social system. And if we describe *charis* as the quality of
occasions on which *agalmata* are exchanged, epinikian *charis* reveals
another paradigmatic dimension: the use of the past for models and
parallels for the present occasion. We recall that the value of top-rank
gifts is peculiarly enhanced by their past history. This phenomenon has
implications for both the victory and the poem as the *agalmata* exchanged. Thus the foundation and history of the various games find a
prominent place within the epinika (e.g., O.1, O.3, O.7, O.10, P.12),
for they enhance the prestige of the current victory.[39] In like manner,
the current victory celebration is the appropriate occasion to recall all
the athletic successes of the victor's family. These "crowns" are the
treasured heirlooms of the house, brought out for display on this special
occasion. The materiality of the family's past victories is suggested by
Pindar's language at N.6.25–26:

> ἕτερον οὔ τινα οἶκον ἀπεφάνατο πυγμαχία ⟨πλεόνων⟩
> ταμίαν στεφάνων μυχῷ Ἑλλάδος ἁπάσας.

Boxing has proclaimed no other house as steward of more crowns in the
hollow of all Greece.

But the poet also has his heirlooms. He enhances the quality of his
gift, the poem, by incorporating into it the wisdom of past authorities,

---

[38]For the terms, see Saussure 1974.122–127.
[39]Note especially the material focus of O.3 and P.12—their obsession with concrete
objects with divine pedigrees which are associated with the games.

both mythical and poetic. Thus, in order to praise the victor, he invokes the Old Man of the Sea (P.9.93–96) or the *Works & Days* of Hesiod (I.6.66–69).[40] And just as the poem itself is concretized as an *agalma*, so too these paradigms of *sophia* become the poet's inherited treasures, precious objects passed on to the victor to honor his victory. No poem illustrates more vividly than Pythian 6 the association between poetry as an *agalma* and epinikion's peculiar use of the past. In the first strophe, Pindar introduces the image of a "treasure-house of hymns" built at Delphi:

> Πυθιόνικος ἔνθ' ὀλβίοισιν Ἐμμενίδαις
> ποταμίᾳ τ' Ἀκράγαντι καὶ μὰν Ξενοκράτει
> ἑτοῖμος ὕμνων θησαυρὸς ἐν πολυχρύσῳ
> Ἀπολλωνίᾳ τετείχισται νάπᾳ·

(P.6.5–9)

There a Pythian-victory treasure-house of hymns is built ready for the blessed Emmenidai and for rivery Akragas and indeed for Xenokrates in the grove of Apollo, rich in gold.

Implicit in these lines are the poet's *chreos* and the entire system of epinikian gift exchange I have been outlining, for the Emmenidai by their achievements have earned a treasure-house of hymns, but only the poet can build it for them. It is significant that at the very moment the poet forges this bond of *charis* with the victor's family, he represents the poem as a concrete *agalma* passed between them. This representation suggests the inextricability of the syntagmatic and paradigmatic axes of *charis*: they intersect in the festal occasion and in the poem.

The concrete imagery for song continues and indeed forms the frame for the central myth. Pindar says in praise of Thrasyboulos, the victor's son,

> σύ τοι σχεθών νιν ἐπὶ δεξιὰ χειρός, ὀρθὰν ἄγεις ἐφημοσύναν,
> τά ποτ' ἐν οὔρεσι φαντὶ μεγαλοσθενεῖ
> Φιλύρας υἱὸν ὀρφανιζομένῳ
> Πηλείδᾳ παραινεῖν· μάλιστα μὲν Κρονίδαν,
> βαρύοπα στεροπᾶν κεραυνῶν τε πρύτανιν,
> θεῶν σέβεσθαι· ταύτας δὲ μή ποτε τιμὰς
> ἀμείρειν γονέων βίον πεπρωμένον.
> ἔγεντο καὶ πρότερον Ἀντίλοχος βιατὰς νόημα τοῦτο φέρων,

(P.6.19–29)

---

[40]For other examples of the same phenomenon, see O.6.12–17, I.2.9–11, and Bacchylides 5.191–193.

By holding him [your father] on your right hand, you lead upright the
advice they say the son of Philyra once gave to Peleus' mighty son, when
he was deprived of his parents: Honor the son of Kronos, deep-voiced
lord of thunder and lightning, most of the gods, and never scant the fated
life of your parents of this honor. Formerly, there was also mighty
Antilochus bearing this thought.

The scholiast tells us that Pindar is drawing on the Χείρωνος Ὑποθῆ-
και, attributed in antiquity to Hesiod.[41] Thus the poet invokes the
mythical authority of Chiron and the poetic authority of Hesiod in
praise of Thrasyboulos. But the language in which Pindar frames his
quotation of *parainesis* is perhaps as important as the quotation itself, for
he treats it as a concrete object with a glorious pedigree, passed on to
Thrasyboulos himself at the moment of victory.[42] In the statement "you
lead upright the advice" of Chiron, ἄγεις is a very concrete word,
which suggests the victor's guiding home a crown or prize.[43] Pindar
uses the same concrete imagery of Antilochus, who formerly bore this
thought. Here τοῦτο specifically designates the precept of lines 23–27,
while φέρων makes "this thought" into a concrete object.[44] This pattern of imagery highlights the process of transmitting the verbal "treasure"—from Chiron to Achilles to Antilochus and now to Thrasyboulos. At least part of the point of the myth is the direct connection it
forges between the mythical past and the present occasion through this
"nugget" of *sophia*.[45]

[41]Drachmann 1910.196–197. For the implications of this use of *hypothekai* for Pythian
6, see Kurke 1990.

[42]Contra Wilamowitz 1922.138–139, it is a fair assumption from Pythian 6 that
Thrasyboulos drove the winning chariot for his father. Wilamowitz rejects this pos-
sibility because Nikomachos is named as Xenokrates' charioteer in Isthmian 2, but as
Farnell points out, there is a time gap of thirteen years or more between the two odes
(Farnell 1930.2.183).

[43]Cf. O.13.29, I.7.21–22, and P.8.38, λόγον φέρεις, on which Gildersleeve (1890.330)
comments, "As a prize."

[44]On τοῦτο marking a quotation, see Pelliccia 1987.41–46 and cf. I.6.67, Theognis 15–
18. On νόημα not just as thought but as the particular verbal formulation of an idea, see
LSJ s.v. νόημα 4, and cf. O.7.72; Parmenides fr. 8.34 DK; Dionysius of Halicarnassus
Letter to Ammaeus 2.24; Longinus 12.1.

[45]Maehler makes a similar suggestion for Bacchylides 5. Noting that the poem alludes
to a number of very famous episodes in epic—the simile comparing men to leaves,
Odysseus stringing his bow, Prometheus defying Zeus, the death of Hektor, and the
scene of Priam and Achilles mourning together—he goes on to suggest: "It is certain that
the educated listener knew all these passages; we can assume that he recognized them in
Bacchylides' adaptations and valued these 'quotations' as particular highlights. . . . [Such
an assumption] would cast an entirely new and surprising light on the introductory
words γνώσῃ μὲν . . . Μοισᾶν γλυκύδωρον ἄγαλμα . . . ὀρθῶς (3–6) ['You will
recognize aright this ornament, sweet gift of the Muses']" (Maehler 1982.118, my

The final link in this chain of transmission is implied in the imagery that frames the central myth. In the first strophe, the poet uses two images for his poetic activity: first plowing (1–4), then the construction of a treasure-house of hymns (5–9). In the poem's final strophe, Pindar says in praise of Thrasyboulos,

> ἄδικον οὔθ᾽ ὑπέροπλον ἥβαν δρέπων,
> σοφίαν δ᾽ ἐν μυχοῖσι Πιερίδων·
>
> (P.6.48–49)

Culling [no] unjust or insolent youth, but [culling] wisdom in the hollows of the Pierides.

Some critics have taken these lines to mean that Thrasyboulos was himself a poet, but I think that is to miss the point.[46] Rather, these lines pick up and complete the imagery for the poet's activity in the first strophe: in the secluded places of the Pierides, Thrasyboulos "culls" the wisdom the poet sowed.[47] Ἐν μυχοῖσι merges in a single rich phrase the two spheres of imagery, for μυχός is both the innermost chamber of a house, where the treasure is stored, and a natural secluded grove.[48] Thus Pythian 6 thematizes the transmission of a precious bit of wisdom through the mythical heroes of the past to the representative of the Emmenidai at the current victory celebration. And it expresses that theme through the recurring image of a concrete treasure.

Because it explicitly establishes the connection between its mythical background and the present occasion, Pythian 6 shows us with peculiar clarity the function of myth in the celebration. But we should not fail to apply this lesson to contexts in which the relation of past and present is only implicit. It is of course a commonplace to say that the myth in epinikion is in some way a paradigm for the victor or the celebration

---

translation). That the incorporation of traditional heroic tales (and even "quotations") is somehow linked with the poem's quality as an *agalma* is exactly what I am suggesting for Pythian 6.

[46]Thus, for example, Norwood 1945.156, 261 n. 40, Burton 1962.23.

[47]Though vegetal imagery informs both passages, there is a shift from one to the other. Plowing in the first strophe applies to the cultivation of grain (cf. N.6.32, N.10.26), while δρέπων and μυχοῖσι suggest a secluded grove of fruit or flowers (cf. O.9.27). Still, both images derive from the same sphere of vegetable cultivation, while the activities of poet and addressee are complementary. For the use of related but not identical imagery at the beginning and end of an epinikion, see Greengard 1980.81–89.

[48]See Slater 1969a and LSJ, s. v. μυχός. For the former meaning, see N.1.42; for the latter, O.3.26, O.10.33, P.8.79, P.10.8, N.10.42, and I.1.56.

itself.[49] What I would like to emphasize is the gift-exchange mentality that underlies such use of myth. That mentality, which concretizes the poem as an *agalma*, also links the present occasion to the mythic past to mark the *charis* of the celebration and increase the value of the gifts exchanged. Like the persistent construction of the epinikian world as one of gift exchange, this use of myth is ideologically loaded: it represents the appropriation of the past for aristocratic self-definition and affirmation.

[49]For examples, see Gundert 1935.58–61, Jaeger 1945.217–218, J. H. Finley 1955.40–41, Köhnken 1971.228–238, Young 1971.35–38, Rose 1974, Slater 1979b and 1984. It is interesting to note the language Jaeger chooses in his discussion of Pythian 6: "Thus the poet enlightens and glorifies every individual case of areta by a great example taken from the vast *treasure* of heroic paradeigmata, and constantly idealizes and recreates the immediate by transfusing it with the power of tradition" (Jaeger 1945.217–218, my italics).

PART III

PINDAR'S
POLITICAL
ECONOMY

CHAPTER 7

Adorning the City:
The Politics of *Megaloprepeia*

Yet once more we must expand the circle of the poet's audience and the victor's community, for Pindar's patrons lived neither in isolation nor in the spacious Homeric world of great independent households: they lived, rather, within the confines of a polis.[1] The civic community demanded different responses and to some extent even a different ideology from its aristocratic elite. As A. W. H. Adkins observes, "Homeric values are suited to a community organized primarily on a basis of scattered individual households. Its values stress the prowess of the individual, and justify in the individual at the least a considerable panache; and accordingly the Homeric hero requires free space in which to manoeuvre. . . . In a city more cooperation is required from heads of households than the implications of arete are likely to produce."[2] To what extent do Pindar's epinikia acknowledge and adapt themselves to the constraints of life in the polis? The traditional scholarly answer is not at all. Thus Werner Jaeger closes his discussion of Pindar with the observations,

> Pindar's work was to survive through the new world, led by Athens, which was fundamentally alien to him. . . . But the world to which Pindar's heart belonged, the world which he had glorified, was even then passing away. It almost seems to be a spiritual law of nature, that no great

---

[1]Only one of the forty-five epinikia was composed for a victor who was *not* a citizen of a polis: Pythian 10, for Hippokleas of Thessaly.

[2]Adkins 1960.75–76. On the development from competitive to cooperative virtues within the city-state, see Adkins 1960 and 1972 passim.

historical type of society has the strength to formulate its own ideal with deep and sure knowledge until the moment when its life is over: as if then its immortal soul were shaking itself free from its transitory mortal shape. Thus in its last agony the aristocratic culture of Greece produced Pindar, the dying Greek city-state, Plato and Demosthenes, and the mediaeval hierarchy of the Church, when it had passed its height, brought forth Dante.[3]

This passage and especially the last sentence reveal Jaeger's teleological assumptions. "The new world, led by Athens," is the democratic polis as the perfection and culmination of Greek development (and hence the foundation of Western culture).

A favorite topos of this genre of scholarship is the juxtaposition of Pindar, backward-looking Boeotian aristocrat, with his contemporary Aeschylus, Attic tragedian and Marathonomachos, who marches boldly forward in "the great clamorous stream of history."[4] For those scholars who prefer Aeschylus, Pindar is an outmoded reactionary, a relic of the past in his own time.[5] As for those who prefer Pindar, their only recourse is to remove him from the stream of history altogether. For these scholars, Pindar can be redeemed only by transposition to the world of eternal verities. Thus John Finley responds to the historical analysis of Eduard Meyer: "Through his conservative Theban background, but in large part certainly through his visionary temperament, Pindar is not interested in social change. His concern is for absolute being, a state which he feels men rise to in great moments and which alone sheds meaning on life. . . . Pindar's relevance . . . stands essentially outside of history and intellectual change, in the sense that response to the reposed shapes of life and feeling for momentary or lasting harmony in things are themselves apperceptions which defy change."[6]

The problems of this approach to Pindar are manifold. Much of it is inspired by the Athenocentrism of modern scholars, which merely replicates and endorses the bias of most of our ancient sources.[7] The

---

[3]Jaeger 1945.222.

[4]The phrase is Jaeger's (1945.220). For the comparison of Pindar and Aeschylus along these lines, see Meyer 1901.3.449–459, Jaeger 1945.221, J. H. Finley 1955, esp. 3–8, 283–288, M. I. Finley 1968.38–43. For a similar portrait of Pindar, without the contrast with Aeschylus, see Wilamowitz 1922.12, 89, 443–446, Bowra 1964.100–104.

[5]Thus Meyer 1901.3.452–455, Burton 1962, M. I. Finley 1968.42–43.

[6]J. H. Finley 1955.6–8. Compare Bowra 1964.158.

[7]Compare, for example, the comments of Wilamowitz (1922.12–13) and J. H. Finley (1955.4–7) on the Athenian and Boeotian "temperaments" with Thucydides' opposition of the restless intelligence of the Athenians and the stable conservatism of the Spartans (see especially Thucydides 1.68–78).

modern bias is exacerbated by the same teleological assumptions we observed in Jaeger's statement—a teleology both political and literary. Thus, not only is the democratic polis of Athens juxtaposed to the static oligarchy of Thebes, but the dying genre of choral lyric is confronted by its vigorous successor tragedy. According to the latter model, the evolution of the Greek spirit is perfectly reflected in the neat generic periodization of epic, lyric, and tragedy. Yet, as Glenn Most has pointed out, the apparent shift from epic to lyric is a historical accident rather than an evolutionary development, and Nagy has suggested that it is the professionalization of music rather than the advance of the the Greek *Geist* which shortened the life-span of choral lyric.[8]

Recent discussions are more moderate in their judgment of Pindar, but they are animated by similar preconceptions. Thus we read in Lacey's treatment of the family in classical Greece that "to Pindar in the early fifth century the family of the aristocrats for whom he wrote his epinician odes was still much more important than the city. . . . But even Pindar was conscious that these families lived in a city-state, and the political conditions of the city cannot be ignored."[9] We shall have cause to examine this "But even Pindar": how far is Pindar's attitude the mere grudging acknowledgment of the city's existence, as Lacey's words suggest? What effort (if any) does the poet make to integrate the household of his patrons into the polis, and the polis, in turn, into his poems? This will be the subject of our inquiry in this and the following two chapters.

There are many avenues available for exploring the relationship of the victor and his civic community in the poet's rhetoric.[10] Here, as in the last three chapters, I want to consider how the economy of praise is shaped by the dominant system of exchange. But how are we to characterize the dominant system of exchange within the polis? Here again, Pindar and his patrons inhabit a different world from that of Homeric gift exchange, although that system remains accessible to them. The household now operates within a money economy, as does the poet, who composes for a wage. This system too, then, necessarily shapes the poet's thinking and impinges on his work. And indeed, money and wealth figure prominently in the epinikia. Many modern critics, like their ancient counterparts, take all such references to money as proof of

[8]Most 1982.85–89, Nagy 1990.104–115, and see also Dover 1964.196–212.

[9]Lacey 1968.78. Thus also Crotty 1982.79–81, 121, implicitly, by referring to Pindar's audience as "the *koinōnia* of good men."

[10]For example, Pindar's equivocations as to the connections between athletic victory and cult honors deserve analysis from the perspective of civic ideology.

the poet's venality.[11] As Leonard Woodbury emphasizes, however, Pindar does not value money for its own sake:

> Pay and profit are seen to be more dangerous and are more markedly depreciated than naked wealth. But all are on the same footing in finding their value in serving the ends to which Pindar and his society have given their approval. He is consistent in praising the conspicuous use of wealth for these ends and in slighting its mere acquisition and accumulation. This is important, because both ancient scholiasts and modern commentators have found fault with his attitude, in the belief that his praise is given to wealth for its own sake and that his exhortations to spend conceal an unsatisfied greed for money. Such an opinion cannot withstand an unprejudiced reading of his own works.[12]

Pindar's concern in the epinikia is not with money per se but with its proper use. Those critics who find open advertisements for pay in the poet's references to money are reading the epinikia with completely anachronistic assumptions. Neither Pindar nor his patrons experienced "economic life" as we know it. Rather, the attitudes Woodbury describes are characteristic of what Karl Polanyi calls an embedded economy. Polanyi points out that the self-regulating market of the nineteenth century is a historical anomaly, the extreme case of a disembedded economy:

> The disembedded economy of the nineteenth century stood apart from the rest of society, more especially from the political and governmental system. In a market economy the production and distribution of material goods in principle is carried on through a self-regulating system of price-making markets. It is governed by laws of its own, the so-called laws of supply and demand, and motivated by fear of hunger and hope of gain. No blood-tie, legal compulsion, religious obligation, fealty, or magic creates the sociological situations which make individuals partake in economic life, but specifically economic institutions such as private enterprise and the wage system.[13]

Modern economists make a grave mistake, Polanyi argues, when they retroject the model of the market economy and its laws onto earlier societies, for in these earlier societies (including that of ancient Greece at least to the age of Aristotle), "the elements of the economy are . . .

[11]M. I. Finley 1968, Gzella 1969–1970a and b, Svenbro 1976.162–193.
[12]Woodbury 1968.539.
[13]Polanyi 1968.81–82.

embedded in non-economic institutions, the economic process itself being instituted through kinship, marriage, age-groups, secret societies, totemic associations, and public solemnities. The term 'economic life' would here have no obvious meaning." Instead of attempting to analyze the ancient economy in itself and for itself, Polanyi insists, we must engage in "institutional analysis" of "the maze of social relations in which the economy was embedded."[14] In the last part we considered gift exchange within the epinikia as a system embedded in and representative of aristocratic ideology. The three chapters in this part will attempt an institutional analysis of those aspects of the economy reflected in the epinikia which appear to be embedded specifically in the polis system.

Let us begin with a passage from Xenophon's *Oeconomicus*, in which the aristocracy, the polis, and money all intersect. In the course of his dialogue with Socrates, Ischomachos, Xenophon's ideal gentleman farmer, expresses a desire for "wealth increasing well" (πλούτου καλῶς αὐξομένου *Oec.* 11.8). When Socrates expresses surprise at his wish for wealth, with all its attendant worries, Ischomachos explains:

ἡδὺ γάρ μοι δοκεῖ, ὦ Σώκρατες, καὶ θεοὺς μεγαλείως τιμᾶν καὶ φίλους, ἄν τινος δέωνται, ἐπωφελεῖν καὶ τὴν πόλιν μηδὲν ⟨τὸ⟩ κατ' ἐμὲ χρήμασιν ἀκόσμητον εἶναι. (*Oec.* 11.9)

For it seems sweet to me, O Socrates, to honor the gods greatly, and to assist my friends if they need anything, and [it seems sweet] that the city lack for nothing by way of adornment if I can help it.

Ischomachos serves as Xenophon's model in a treatise devoted to the ins and outs of οἰκονομία, estate management, and demonstrates for us precisely what the καλὸς κἀγαθός, the Athenian gentleman, desires from his οἰκία. He wants money (πλοῦτος) saved up in excess of his needs (περιποιεῖν), for the specific purpose of "adorning the city" (τὴν πόλιν κοσμεῖν).

But what exactly does adorning the city entail? The two speakers are referring briefly to the virtue known as *megaloprepeia*, the lavish public expenditure of wealth by those who can afford it. In the frame dialogue of the *Oeconomicus*, between Socrates and the wealthy Kritoboulos, Socrates offers us a detailed inventory of *megaloprepeia*. Explaining to Kritoboulos why even three times his present wealth would not suffice

[14]Polanyi 1968.84, 120.

him, Socrates lists all the expenditures expected of his rich interlocutor by the city:

Ὅτι πρῶτον μὲν ὁρῶ σοι ἀνάγκην οὖσαν θύειν πολλά τε καὶ μεγάλα, ἢ οὔτε θεοὺς οὔτε ἀνθρώπους οἶμαί σε ἂν ἀνασχέσθαι. ἔπειτα ξένους προσήκει σοι πολλοὺς δέχεσθαι, καὶ τούτους μεγαλοπρεπῶς. ἔπειτα δὲ πολίτας δειπνίζειν καὶ εὖ ποιεῖν, ἢ ἔρημον συμμάχων εἶναι. ἔτι δὲ καὶ τὴν πόλιν αἰσθάνομαι τὰ μὲν ἤδη σοι προστάττουσαν μεγάλα τελεῖν, ἱπποτροφίας τε καὶ χορηγίας καὶ γυμνασιαρχίας καὶ προστατείας, ἂν δὲ δὴ πόλεμος γένηται, οἶδ' ὅτι καὶ τριηραρχίας [μισθοὺς] καὶ εἰσφορὰς τοσαύτας σοι προστάξουσιν ὅσας σὺ οὐ ῥᾳδίως ὑποίσεις. ὅπου δ' ἂν ἐνδεῶς δόξῃς τι τούτων ποιεῖν, οἶδ' ὅτι σε τιμωρήσονται Ἀθηναῖοι οὐδὲν ἧττον ἢ εἰ τὰ αὑτῶν λάβοιεν κλέπτοντα. (Oec. 2.5–7)

First because I see that it is necessary for you to offer many and great sacrifices, or I think that neither gods nor men would put up with you. Then it's your duty to receive many foreigners as guests, and these lavishly. Then also [you must] feast and benefit the citizens, or be bereft of allies. Still, in addition to that, I perceive the polis commanding you to spend a great deal of money in some ways already, on the raising of horses and the production of choruses and superintending the *palaistra* and accepting presidencies. But in the event of war, I know that they will demand of you trierarchies and property taxes so high that you will not easily bear them. And wherever you seem to do any of these things inadequately, I know that the Athenians will punish you no less than if they had caught you stealing their own property.

Socrates is emphasizing the element of compulsion here to justify his claim that Kritoboulos' wealth makes him pitiable, but behind that emphasis, the outlines of the rich man's obligations are accurate enough. He is expected to sacrifice abundantly and to entertain foreigners and citizens lavishly (μεγαλοπρεπῶς). In addition, the city orders him to raise horses, produce choruses, and act as gymnasiarch in peacetime; to serve as trierarch and pay additional levies in the event of war.[15] The *eisphora*, trierarchy, *choregia*, and gymnasiarchy are all new developments of the polis system—expenditures that directly benefit the civic community. But in the sacrifices, acts of hospitality, and raising of

---

[15]It is perhaps significant that the most prominent of his peacetime liturgies—the one Socrates thinks to mention first—is the raising of horses. We shall find again and again that this form of expenditure seems to have particular prestige, especially in political contexts.

horses, we can still trace the origins of *megaloprepeia* in the system of aristocratic gift exchange. Indeed, such lists make clear that the elements of *megaloprepeia* are much older than the polis or a money economy, that they go back to the prestige expenditure of the Homeric heroes (and even before) and have analogues in such systems as potlatch all over the world. *Megaloprepeia*, then, represents the civic appropriation of aristocratic competitive expenditure, transforming private gift exchange into the public adornment of the city.[16] This passage makes it abundantly clear that *megaloprepeia* is by nature a political concern: the polis expects (if it does not compel) such public expenditure as the service of its wealthy citizens.[17]

Aristotle, in his definition and discussion of the "virtue" of *megaloprepeia* in the *Nichomachean Ethics*, offers a very similar list of obligations:[18]

ἔστι δὲ τῶν δαπανημάτων οἷα λέγομεν τὰ τίμια, οἷον τὰ περὶ θεούς, ἀναθήματα καὶ κατασκευαὶ καὶ θυσίαι, ὁμοίως δὲ καὶ περὶ πᾶν τὸ δαιμόνιον, καὶ ὅσα πρὸς τὸ κοινὸν εὐφιλοτίμητά ἐστιν, οἷον εἴ που χορηγεῖν οἴονται δεῖν λαμπρῶς ἢ τριηραρχεῖν ἢ καὶ ἑστιᾶν τὴν πόλιν. . . . τῶν δὲ ἰδίων ὅσα εἰσάπαξ γίνεται, οἷον γάμος καὶ εἴ τι τοιοῦτον, καὶ εἰ περί τι ἡ πᾶσα πόλις σπουδάζει ἢ οἱ ἐν ἀξιώματι, καὶ περὶ ξένων δὲ ὑποδοχὰς καὶ ἀποστολάς, καὶ δωρεὰς καὶ ἀντιδωρεάς. (*Nich. Ethics* 1122b19–23a4)

They are expenditures of the sort we call honorable, for example, those concerning the gods, dedications and equipment and sacrifices, and likewise concerning the entire divine sphere, and however many things are proper objects of ambition in the public sphere, for example, if they think

[16]As Gernet observes, "It is the relic of the nobility's *mores* which helps explain the city's 'liturgies' and their twofold quality of obligation and generosity" (Gernet 1981b.285). The question of when and how the city appropriated this much older form of lavish public expenditure for its own purposes is an intriguing one, though beyond the scope of this study. Sally Humphreys observes: "By a process which we are not yet able to trace clearly, the competition for power and prestige among the Greek nobility, from about the seventh century onward, moved away from the display of wealth at home and attraction of a personal following to displays of munificence in the city center and contests for political office and political support independent of personal ties" (Humphreys 1978.69).

[17]See Finley 1975.151–152.

[18]I put "virtue" in quotation marks, here and throughout the chapter, to avoid prejudging the issue. That is to say, within the polis, *megaloprepeia* is an ambiguous term (as we shall see): there is a particular ideological position that endorses it as a virtue. Thus Woodbury refers to *megaloprepeia* as "the characteristically aristocratic disposition" or as "the quasi-virtue of magnificence" (Woodbury 1968.538).

it is necessary to produce a chorus splendidly or man a trireme or even to host the city. . . . But of private expenditures, however many occur only once, like marriage and if there is any [other] such thing, and if there is anything for which the entire city is eagerly striving, or [at least] those of rank, both concerning the receptions and dispatching of guests, and gifts and countergifts.

Again, many of the objects of expenditure Aristotle lists—sacrifice, marriage, reception of *xenoi*, and the general "gifts and countergifts" (δωρεὰς καὶ ἀντιδωρεάς)—look familiar from the consideration of gift exchange. Yet, the ideology behind such lavish expenditure has changed. It is no longer the private preserve of aristocrats, used to establish special bonds of *charis* between noble households and to define the aristocracy in opposition to the polis. Instead, Aristotle's definition underscores the political character of this "virtue": notice especially "however many things are proper objects of ambition in the public sphere" (καὶ ὅσα πρὸς τὸ κοινὸν εὐφιλοτίμητά ἐστιν) and "if there is anything for which the entire city is eagerly striving" (καὶ εἰ περί τι πᾶσα ἡ πόλις σπουδάζει). Indeed, Aristotle concludes his list with the general observation, "The *megaloprepēs* spends not for himself but for the community" (οὐ γὰρ εἰς ἑαυτὸν δαπανηρὸς ὁ μεγαλοπρεπὴς ἀλλ' εἰς τὰ κοινά [*Nich. Ethics* 1123a4–5]).

As we have observed, athletic victory hovers between two divergent models of gift exchange in the late archaic and classical periods. On the one hand, I have argued, Pindar can represent athletic victory within the closed circuit of aristocratic gift exchange. On the other hand, victory at the games can be located within the public sphere of *megaloprepeia*, as a common benefaction bestowed on the city by the victor. Clear evidence for the latter perception is the custom, attested in Athens and elsewhere, of feasting athletic victors at public expense at the prytaneum or civic hearth, for this honor was conferred only on those who were considered benefactors (εὐεργέτεις) of the city.[19] In the context of gift exchange, I suggested that the poet's choice to represent victory as private aristocratic exchange was ideologically loaded and directed primarily at the aristocrats in his audience. An analogous argument applies to the poet's representation of athletic victory within the public domain: it is reasonable to assume that such representation is intended to appeal to the wider civic community.

But before we can explore the extent of Pindar's participation in the

[19]See Xenophanes fr. 2 DK, Plato *Apology* 36d.

civic appropriation of gift exchange, we must develop a dossier on the public "virtue" of *megaloprepeia*—its nature, its advantages and disadvantages, and its ideology.[20] Unfortunately for our purposes, almost all the prose sources available on the subject are by Athenian authors or about Athens. Still, we know that the system of liturgies obtained in other Greek cities, and therefore it may be permissible to use the Attic evidence with some caution.[21] The ultimate test of the validity of this method is the pertinence of the prose evidence to the reading of Pindar.

Thucydides provides useful testimony on the political nature of *megaloprepeia* in the speech he puts in the mouth of Alcibiades at the beginning of Book 6. There, the confrontation of Nicias and Alcibiades over the leadership of the Sicilian expedition turns into a veritable dialogue on *megaloprepeia* when Nicias asserts that Alcibiades' only qualification for generalship is his enormous expenditure on horse breeding (Thucydides 6.12). Alcibiades begins his speech of self-justification with a long discourse on the place of *megaloprepeia* in the polis:

ὧν γὰρ πέρι ἐπιβόητός εἰμι, τοῖς μὲν προγόνοις μου καὶ ἐμοὶ δόξαν φέρει ταῦτα, τῇ δὲ πατρίδι καὶ ὠφελίαν. οἱ γὰρ Ἕλληνες καὶ ὑπὲρ δύναμιν μείζω ἡμῶν τὴν πόλιν ἐνόμισαν τῷ ἐμῷ διαπρεπεῖ τῆς Ὀλυμπίαζε θεωρίας, πρότερον ἐλπίζοντες αὐτὴν καταπεπολεμῆσθαι, διότι ἅρματα μὲν ἑπτὰ καθῆκα, ὅσα οὐδεὶς πω ἰδιώτης πρότερον, ἐνίκησα δὲ καὶ δεύτερος καὶ τέταρτος ἐγενόμην καὶ τἆλλα ἀξίως τῆς νίκης παρεσκευασάμην. νόμῳ μὲν γὰρ τιμὴ τὰ τοιαῦτα, ἐκ δὲ τοῦ δρωμένου καὶ δύναμις ἅμα ὑπονοεῖται. (Thucydides 6.16.1–3)

For concerning the things for which I am most abused, these things bear glory to my ancestors and to me, and benefit to my homeland. For the Greeks believed our city to be greater even beyond her power by the splendor of my attendance at the Olympic games, though before they were expecting her to be all warred out, because I entered seven chariots (a number no private citizen has ever entered before) and I came in first,

[20]This is not to imply that the topic has not been explored; there is much interesting discussion by historians, but it has rarely been applied to the reading of Pindar. On *megaloprepeia* and the related topics of liturgies and *philotimia*, see Lewis 1960, Adkins 1960.202–205, 211–214, Adkins 1972.121–125, Stein 1965, Connor 1971.18–22, Finley 1975.150–154, Finley 1983.24–49, Humphreys 1978.69–70, Gernet 1981b.282–287, Davies 1967, Davies 1971.xvii–xxxi, Davies 1981, Lauffer 1974, Whitehead 1983, Ober 1989.199–247.
[21]Lauffer 1974.147, Finley 1983.32, 36.

second, and fourth, and I arranged the rest worthily of the victory. For by custom such things are a source of honor, and at the same time, from the thing done power is conjectured.

Alcibiades' first words hearken back to an older aristocratic ethos. The *megaloprepēs* confers glory (δόξαν) not only on himself but on his entire family (τοῖς μὲν προγόνοις μου). Indeed, Alcibiades asserts that what he has done redounds *first* to the glory of his ancestors, but he immediately modulates from the aristocratic household to the city: his tremendous displays of wealth, he claims, also benefit his homeland. For this moment at least, the interests of the two spheres converge.

Yet, where we might expect Alcibiades to go on to speak of trierarchies or productions of choruses, he turns instead to the splendor of his embassy to Olympia, where he entered seven chariots and came in first, second, and fourth. Here *hippotrophia* takes the first place in a catalogue of *megaloprepeia*, preeminent among expenditures in a highly politically charged context. Alcibiades argues that such ostentation leads the other Greeks to assume greater power for the city of Athens (δύναμιν μείζω), when they had hoped that she was "all warred out" (καταπεπολεμῆσθαι). Thus, in the view of Alcibiades at least, such lavish display by an individual serves an important part in Athens' foreign policy.

These are the advantages the polis derives from *megaloprepeia*, but what of the individual benefactor? The words δόξα, κῦδος and τιμή are all used to characterize the reward for such generosity. For example, Gorgias is credited with the pithy quip that Kimon "possessed money in order to use it, and used it in order to be honored" (τὰ χρήματα κτᾶσθαι μὲν ὡς χρῷτο, χρῆσθαι δὲ ὡς τιμῷτο [Plutarch *Life of Kimon* 10]).[22] But we should not fail to recognize concrete political advantages in these abstract "honors."[23] That the *megaloprepēs* wins a more sympathetic hearing in the assembly and even an edge toward elected office is clear from Nicias' bitter words against Alcibiades:

εἴ τέ τις ἄρχειν ἄσμενος αἱρεθεὶς παραινεῖ ὑμῖν ἐκπλεῖν, τὸ ἑαυτοῦ μόνον σκοπῶν, ἄλλως τε καὶ νεώτερος ὢν ἔτι ἐς τὸ ἄρχειν, ὅπως θαυμασθῇ μὲν ἀπὸ τῆς ἱπποτροφίας, διὰ δὲ πολυτέλειαν καὶ

[22]Colace (1978.741) cites the Gorgian quip as a parallel for Pindar's attitude toward wealth, but she treats it as a development of the pre-Socratics rather than a conception current at the time which both authors were expressing.

[23]On this aspect of *megaloprepeia*, see the interesting discussion in Connor 1971.18–22; see also Finley 1983.32–49, Ober 1989.226–244.

ὠφεληθῇ τι ἐκ τῆς ἀρχῆς, μηδὲ τούτῳ ἐμπαράσχητε τῷ τῆς πόλεως
κινδύνῳ ἰδίᾳ ἐλλαμπρύνεσθαι, νομίσατε δὲ τοὺς τοιούτους τὰ μὲν
δημόσια ἀδικεῖν, τὰ δὲ ἴδια ἀναλοῦν, καὶ τὸ πρᾶγμα μέγα εἶναι καὶ
μὴ οἷον νεωτέρῳ βουλεύσασθαί τε καὶ ὀξέως μεταχειρίσαι. (Thucydides 6.12.2)

And if anyone, glad that he has been elected to lead, advises you to sail
out, considering only his own affairs, both in other respects and still
being too young to lead, in order that he be marveled at for the raising of
horses and, on account of the great expense, in order that he be benefited
in some way from the command—do not give this man the power to
distinguish himself in private at the risk of the city. But consider that such
men wrong the common concerns and squander their own resources, and
that the matter is great and not the sort to be advised on and adminstered
by one who is too young.

Nicias obviously feels a great need to counteract Alcibiades' persua-
sive power and, at least by implication, seems to attribute it and his
election to generalship in large measure to his being admired for horse
breeding (θαυμασθῇ μὲν ἀπὸ τῆς ἱπποτροφίας). Nicias tries hard to
relegate Alcibiades' conspicuous expenditures to the sphere of private
interest and to contrast them with true public service (τὸ ἑαυτοῦ μόνον
σκοπῶν; ἰδίᾳ ἐλλαμπρύνεσθαι; τὰ μὲν δημόσια ἀδικεῖν, τὰ δὲ ἴδια
ἀναλοῦν).[24] Yet Nicias is fighting an uphill battle. For, as J. K. Davies
observes, from the first quarter of the sixth century to the end of the
fifth, chariot racing was a preferred object of massive expenditure
because it carried with it political influence. As Davies puts it, "For
Alcibiades, as for Alkmeon . . . and Kallias . . . the point was not so
much athletic prowess as magnificence and display: the former might
well carry with it personal honours . . . and was attainable even by
poorer men, but only the latter could provide the base of a really viable
claim for political position." Indeed, Davies suggests that the explosion
of opportunities for chariot competitions in the first third of the sixth
century was a "response to pressure" from politically ambitious aristocrats throughout the Greek world.[25]

[24]For a similar attempt to strip such lavish expenditure of its political clout, see
Lykourgos *Against Leokrates* 139, 140; for a theoretical formulation of the problem, see
Aristotle *Pol.* 1309a17, F88, 89 Rose.

[25]Davies 1981.99, 103–105. Davies suggests that chariot racing "in intention and
probably in effect" was a replacement for political influence based on cult power and that
it was replaced in its turn around 400 B.C. by rhetorical and administrative skills (Davies
105–115).

Furthermore, though he did not keep horses, Nicias himself was no stranger to what Connor calls "the politics of largess."[26] According to Plutarch:

Περικλῆς μὲν οὖν ἀπό τε ἀρετῆς ἀληθινῆς καὶ λόγου δυνάμεως τὴν πόλιν ἄγων οὐδενὸς ἐδεῖτο σχηματισμοῦ πρὸς τὸν ὄχλον οὐδὲ πιθανό-τητος, Νικίας δὲ τούτοις μὲν λειπόμενος, οὐσίᾳ δὲ προέχων, ἀπ' αὐτῆς ἐδημαγώγει. . . . χορηγίαις ἀνελάμβανε καὶ γυμνασιαρχίαις ἑτέραις τε τοιαύταις φιλοτιμίαις τὸν δῆμον, ὑπερβαλλόμενος πολυτε-λείᾳ καὶ χάριτι τοὺς πρὸ ἑαυτοῦ καὶ καθ' ἑαυτὸν ἅπαντας. (Plutarch Life of Nicias 3.1–3)

Pericles then led the city from true virtue and power of speech, and he never needed any pretense toward the mob or trick of persuasiveness. But Nicias, who lacked these qualities but was preeminent in property, was a leader of the demos from that. . . . He used to win the demos by means of his *choregiai* and gymnasiarchies and other such honorific activities, surpassing all his predecessors and contemporaries in his expenditure and appeal to *charis*.[27]

Nicias was a "leader of the demos" from his wealth: in this context, the exchange of material benefactions for political favors could not be more explicit. And the word Plutarch uses to designate the goodwill earned by Nicias' generosity is *charis*. In the "gratitude" of the Athenian people we see again the transferral to the public domain of an element of gift exchange—in this case, the *charis* that binds together aristocratic exchange partners. Davies sees the use of *charis* in this passage as a remnant of a much older system, in which "*charis* was nothing less than the primary basis both of election to office and of preponderant political influence."[28]

But as Davies observes, by the fourth century it is rare to find *charis* mentioned in contexts of election and influence in the assembly. Rather, the sphere of *charis* is the lawcourt, where the individual could expect to derive direct benefit from public displays of generosity. The influence of public expenditure is clear from a number of speeches of the Attic orators, in which, no matter what the charge, the defendant devotes a good deal of time to cataloging exactly how much he has spent in public liturgies and appealing for acquittal on the grounds of these benefac-

[26]Connor 1971.18–22.
[27]I follow Davies 1981.97 in translating χάριτι "appeal to *charis*."
[28]Davies 1981.96. See also Finley 1983.39–49.

life and [the magnitude] of his ambition apparent in all his actions in
everything with which he was concerned, became his enemies, suspect-
ing him of desiring tyranny.

As Thucydides' narrative unfolds, it is impossible to say if this suspicion
is justified, since Alcibiades is relieved of his command and the city
"tripped up" without him.[33] Still, it was a suspicion that shadowed
Alcibiades through his career, so that, real or not, we must acknowledge that the association of *megaloprepeia* and tyranny was compelling
for the Greeks.

The other link the Greeks perceived between ostentatious expenditure and tyranny was not so much one of intent as of necessary result. In
this scheme, the *megaloprepēs* is a kind of spending addict who is finally
compelled to seek the status of a tyrant to provide himself with sufficient resources.[34] We can see the germ of this notion also in Thucydides'
discussion of Alcibiades' motives. In this instance, he is seeking not
tyranny but command in the ruinous Sicilian expedition to augment his
flagging fortune. But the pattern of one man's advocating and leading a
project that has disastrous consequences for the city, out of motives of
private gain, is exactly that of the incipient tyrant to the Greek mind.
Indeed, what Thucydides implies in the case of Alcibiades, Plato turns
into a theoretical model for the declension of forms of government. In
Books 8 and 9 of the *Republic*, Socrates considers the progressive degen-
eration of forms of government in order to understand the same process
of corruption within the individual soul. In his scheme, the ideal city
turns first into a timocracy, then an oligarchy, then a radical democracy,
then a tyranny. Money and expenditure occupy a prominent place in the
processes by which these last two forms of government appear. First, in
Plato's account, the oligarchic man becomes a [radical] democrat by
ousting stinginess (φειδωλία) in favor of all kinds of freedom and
excess:

Τούτων δέ γέ που κενώσαντες καὶ καθήραντες τὴν τοῦ κατεχομένου
τε ὑπ' αὐτῶν καὶ τελουμένου ψυχὴν μεγάλοισι τέλεσι, τὸ μετὰ

[33]On the exact significance of Thucydides' verbs καθεῖλεν and ἔσφηλαν, see
Gomme, Andrewes, and Dover 1970.4.242–245.
[34]Admittedly, the source of his addiction is not monetary; rather, it is a desire to
preserve his ἀξίωμα, honor or standing with his fellow citizens, so that the same "vice"
could be called φιλοτιμία. Yet a significant strand emphatically connects tyranny with
the spending of money, and this we can trace by focusing on *megaloprepeia*. On *philotimia*,
see Whitehead 1983.

τοῦτο ἤδη ὕβριν καὶ ἀναρχίαν καὶ ἀσωτίαν καὶ ἀναίδειαν λαμπρὰς
μετὰ πολλοῦ χοροῦ κατάγουσιν ἐστεφανωμένας, ἐγκωμιάζοντες καὶ
ὑποκοριζόμενοι, ὕβριν μὲν εὐπαιδευσίαν καλοῦντες, ἀναρχίαν δὲ
ἐλευθερίαν, ἀσωτίαν δὲ μεγαλοπρέπειαν, ἀναίδειαν δὲ ἀνδρείαν. . . .
Ζῇ δὴ οἶμαι μετὰ ταῦτα ὁ τοιοῦτος οὐδὲν μᾶλλον εἰς ἀναγκαίους ἢ
μὴ ἀναγκαίους ἡδονὰς ἀναλίσκων καὶ χρήματα καὶ πόνους καὶ
διατριβάς. (Republic 560d8–561a8)

Having emptied [him] of these things and pulled down the soul of the one
restrained and ruled by them with great rites, after this they lead in
arrogance and lawlessness and wastefulness and shamelessness, magnifi-
cent with crowns and a great chorus. They celebrate the kōmos and speak
fair words, calling arrogance good education, lawlessness freedom,
wastefulness *megaloprepeia*, and shamelessness courage. . . . Such a man, I
think, lives after this squandering his money and efforts and free time for
the satisfaction of unnecessary as much as necessary pleasures.

Lavish and indiscriminate expenditure is the hallmark of such a regime,
and that which impels it inexorably toward tyranny. "The race of idle
and extravagant men" (τὸ τῶν ἀργῶν τε καὶ δαπανηρῶν ἀνδρῶν
γένος, [Republic 564b4–5]) become its leaders, and one of them eventually makes himself tyrant in the course of a struggle with those whose
money he wants to support his habit of expenditure (Republic 566a2–7).

We can see the connection of *megaloprepeia* and tyranny from another
angle if we turn from the theories of Plato to the anecdotes of Herodotus. Beginning his narrative of the establishment of Alkmeonid leadership in the Thracian Chersonese, Herodotus introduces his characters
thus:

ἐν δὲ τῇσι Ἀθήνῃσι τηνικαῦτα εἶχε μὲν τὸ πᾶν κράτος Πεισίστρατος,
ἀτὰρ ἐδυνάστευέ γε καὶ Μιλτιάδης ὁ Κυψέλου, ἐὼν οἰκίης τεθριπποτρόφου, τὰ μὲν ἀνέκαθεν ἀπ᾽ Αἰακοῦ τε καὶ Αἰγίνης γεγονώς. (Herodotus 6.35.1)

And in Athens at that time Pisistratus held all power, but Miltiades the
son of Kypselos was also influential, being of a household that kept four-
horse chariots and descended originally from Aiakos and Aigina.

We can if we wish take the phrase ἐὼν οἰκίης τεθριπποτρόφου as a
shorthand measure of the degree of wealth of the Alkmeonidai, as the
translator Aubrey de Sélincourt does. He expands Herodotus' terse
characterization to a whole sentence: "Miltiades belonged to a family

whose fortune was great enough to allow them to enter a four-horse chariot for the Games."[35] But this is not what Herodotus says: for him the association of horse breeding with political power seems more immediate, more direct. And indeed, another installment of the Alkmeonid story later in Book 6 suggests that not only Herodotus but the Pisistratids themselves considered expenditure on horse breeding and on Olympic victories *politically* significant. Herodotus tells the story of Kimon, brother of the Miltiades just mentioned and father of the Miltiades who commanded at Marathon:

τὸν πατέρα Κίμωνα τὸν Στησαγόρεω κατέλαβε φυγεῖν ἐξ Ἀθηνέων Πεισίστρατον τὸν Ἱπποκράτεος. καὶ αὐτῷ φεύγοντι Ὀλυμπιάδα ἀνελέσθαι τεθρίππῳ συνέβη, καὶ ταύτην μὲν τὴν νίκην ἀνελόμενόν μιν τὠυτὸ ἐξενείκασθαι τῷ ὁμομητρίῳ ἀδελφεῷ Μιλτιάδῃ. μετὰ δὲ τῇ ὑστέρῃ Ὀλυμπιάδι τῇσι αὐτῇσι ἵπποισι νικῶν παραδιδοῖ Πεισιστράτῳ ἀνακηρυχθῆναι, καὶ τὴν νίκην παρεὶς τούτῳ κατῆλθε ἐπὶ τὰ ἑωυτοῦ ὑπόσπονδος. καί μιν ἀνελόμενον τῇσι αὐτῇσι ἵπποισι ἄλλην Ὀλυμπιάδα κατέλαβε ἀποθανεῖν ὑπὸ τῶν Πεισιστράτου παίδων, οὐκέτι περιεόντος αὐτοῦ Πεισιστράτου. (Herodotus 6.103.1–3)

It befell his father, Kimon the son of Stesagoras, to flee Pisistratus the son of Hippokrates as an exile from Athens. And it happened that he won an Olympic chariot victory while in exile (and by this victory he carried off the same honor as his half brother Miltiades). But after this, when he won at the next Olympiad with the same mares, he hands it over to Pisistratus to be heralded, and by handing the victory over to this one, he returned home on his own terms. And it befell him, when he had carried off another Olympic victory with the same horses to die at the hands of the sons of Pisistratus (Pisistratus himself was no longer around).

This narrative reveals the political clout of an Olympic chariot victory, if an exile can obtain his return by "handing it over" to the ruling tyrant of his country. Indeed, this detail makes the juxtaposition of events in the last sentence all the more intriguing. "And it befell him, when he had carried off [yet] another Olympic victory with the same horses to die at the hands of the sons of Pisistratus," Herodotus tells us

[35]De Sélincourt 1972.399. Notice also the language Aristotle uses to describe the wealth of Kimon the son of Miltiades: ὁ γὰρ Κίμων, ἅτε τυραννικὴν ἔχων οὐσίαν ("For Kimon, since he had tyrant-scale property" [Aristotle *Ath. Pol.* 27.3]), and the claim of Theopompus that Kimon's fabled generosity was an imitation of Pisistratus (Theopompus *FGrH* 2 F89; see Connor 1968.30–36 for discussion).

in an even tone. Is there a connection implied in the minds of the tyrants or of the historian? It almost seems that Kimon was perceived as a threat, as a rival aspirant to Pisistratus' power, *because* he had won three Olympic chariot victories.[36]

If *megaloprepeia* is perceived as the path to tyranny, the converse is also a Greek commonplace: the tyrant is the perfect, the most complete *megaloprepēs*.[37] He is, first, because he can afford it. As Aristotle observes, "The one who spends beyond his means is 'profligate.' Therefore we do not call tyrants profligates, for it does not seem to be easy for them to spend beyond their means for gifts and expenses" (Aristotle *Nich. Ethics* 1120b24–27).[38] But perhaps more compellingly to the Greek imagination, the tyrant embodies all that is excessive, overreaching the limitations of normal humanity.[39] In the work of Herodotus, who is the first to use μεγαλοπρεπής/είη in extant Greek, five of the seven occurrences of these words refer to the deeds of kings and tyrants.[40] In an act of typically tyrannical ostentation, for example, Kleisthenes of Sikyon hosted thirteen suitors for his daughter's hand for an entire year, while he decided who the best man was:

ὅσον γὰρ κατεῖχε χρόνον αὐτούς, τοῦτον πάντα ἐποίεε καὶ ἅμα ἐξεί-
νιζε μεγαλοπρεπέως. (Herodotus 6.128.1–2)

[36]For a similar interpretation of this passage, see Raschke 1988.40.

[37]It may be that there is a significant connection here: that the tyrants were, in a sense, the "inventors" of *megaloprepeia*. Gernet (1981b.286–287), citing the evidence collected by Ure (1962), suggests that the tyrants achieved their prominence because they knew how to manipulate the new money economy. Farenga's consideration of the early tyrants is also suggestive on this point. What he calls their "public thesaurization"—their conspicuous dedications at the great Panhellenic centers—is their invention of a new mode of *public* magnificence (Farenga 1985.42–46; see also Morris 1986a.9–13). Farenga argues further that Kleisthenes of Sikyon blurred the boundaries of public and private space, soliciting suitors for his daughter at the Olympic games and then turning his house into a public space (with *palaistra*, racecourse, etc.) to entertain them for a year (Farenga 1985.47–48). In both instances it seems that the tyrants are the men who realize the value of lavish public displays of wealth. Other evidence that might be adduced is the public building programs typical of the tyrants.

[38]These comments actually appear in Aristotle's discussion of *eleutheria*, but Aristotle recognizes *eleutheria* and *megaloprepeia* as kindred "virtues," both "concerning money." *Megaloprepeia* differs from *eleutheria* in that it is concerned only with the expenditure of money and in the magnitude of the expenditure involved (*Nich. Ethics* 1122a18–22). Thus *megaloprepeia* could be described as *eleutheria* on a grand scale.

[39]For discussion of this phenomenon, see Gernet 1981a.128, 1981b.289–301, Vernant 1982.

[40]Twice the great kings of Persia (6.22, 7.57); once the Macedonian king (5.18); twice Greek tyrants (3.125, 6.128). The other two occurrences refer to the "magnificence" of Persian names (1.139) and of a Kyzikian festival for the Mother of the Gods (4.76).

Since, for as long as he kept them, for all this time he was doing this and at the same time hosting them magnificently.

And Polykrates, perhaps the most flamboyant of Greek tyrants, earns the following epitaph from the historian:

ἀπικόμενος δὲ ἐς τὴν Μαγνησίην ὁ Πολυκράτης διεφθάρη κακῶς, οὔτε ἑωυτοῦ ἀξίως οὔτε τῶν ἑωυτοῦ φρονημάτων· ὅτι γὰρ μὴ οἱ Συρηκοσίων γενόμενοι τύραννοι, οὐδὲ εἷς τῶν ἄλλων Ἑλληνικῶν τυράννων ἄξιός ἐστι Πολυκράτεϊ μεγαλοπρεπείην συμβληθῆναι. (Herodotus 3.125.2)

And having reached Magnesia, Polykrates perished wretchedly, in a way that was worthy neither of himself nor of his aspirations. For the fact is that aside from those who became tyrants of the Syracusans, no one of the rest of the Greek tyrants deserves to be compared to Polykrates in *megaloprepeia.*

Thus Herodotus, Thucydides, and Plato reveal a whole series of connections between *megaloprepeia* and tyranny. These associations suggest that from the point of view of the city, *megaloprepeia* can be perceived as a prelude to tyranny. On the other hand, from the point of view of the individual, lavish expenditure has the disadvantage of inevitably generating envy on the part of one's fellow citizens. This is such a commonplace for the Greeks that Alcibiades can say blandly in his defense of *megaloprepeia*:

καὶ ὅσα αὖ ἐν τῇ πόλει χορηγίαις ἢ ἄλλῳ τῳ λαμπρύνομαι, τοῖς μὲν ἀστοῖς φθονεῖται φύσει, πρὸς δὲ τοὺς ξένους καὶ αὕτη ἰσχὺς φαίνεται. . . . οἶδα δὲ τοὺς τοιούτους, καὶ ὅσοι ἔν τινος λαμπρότητι προέσχον, ἐν μὲν τῷ καθ' αὑτοὺς βίῳ λυπηροὺς ὄντας, τοῖς ὁμοίοις μὲν μάλιστα, ἔπειτα δὲ καὶ τοῖς ἄλλοις ξυνόντας, τῶν δὲ ἔπειτα ἀνθρώπων προσποίησίν τε ξυγγενείας τισὶ καὶ μὴ οὖσαν καταλιπόντας, καὶ ἧς ἂν ὦσι πατρίδος, ταύτῃ αὔχησιν ὡς οὐ περὶ ἀλλοτρίων οὐδ' ἁμαρτόντων, ἀλλ' ὡς περὶ σφετέρων τε καὶ καλὰ πραξάντων. (Thucydides 6.16.3–6)

And however many things I have done within the city, by the production of choruses or by any other means, to distinguish myself, these things are naturally a source of envy to my fellow citizens, but they also make a show of strength for strangers. . . . And I know that such men, however many are preeminent in splendor for anything, are grievous in their own lifetime, most of all to their peers, but then also when they have dealings with the rest. But [I know that] such men leave behind to some of future generations the claim of relationship (even where it does not exist), and whatever country they belong to, in this they leave behind an exalted reputation—not as if they are strangers or men who have done wrong but rather as natives and men who have accomplished noble things.

The citizen who makes himself conspicuous (λαμπρύνομαι; λαμπρό-τητι) by his expenditures is *by nature* envied by his fellow citizens: he can count on being "grievous" (λυπηροὺς ὄντας) to his contemporaries, though future generations will be proud to claim him as their own.[41] Alcibiades is registering not so much shock as resignation at this state of affairs, for it is completely natural (φύσει) for his fellow citizens to respond thus.

As I have said, this outline of the ideology of *megaloprepeia* is drawn almost exclusively from the Athenian situation. It is proper to ask, therefore, whether these findings, based on the rather exceptional polis of Athens, can be applied to Pindar's commissions throughout Greece. The answer is to be found in the Pindaric corpus itself. A careful reading of the epinikia will show not only that Pindar is familiar with the concept of *megaloprepeia* but also that defusing the political tensions it involves is an essential part of his program.

First, what does Pindar say explicitly of the "virtue" of *megaloprepeia*? As Woodbury observes, "The idea [of magnificence] does not find expression in a single word in Pindar (note, however, the Κροίσου φιλόφρων ἀρετά of Pyth. 1.94) but is diffused almost everywhere in the odes."[42] It is true that the word *megaloprepeia* itself never appears, but we should not fail to see a veritable unpacking of the term in one of the most familiar passages of Pindar, the opening of Olympian 1:

> Ἄριστον μὲν ὕδωρ, ὁ δὲ χρυσὸς αἰθόμενον πῦρ
> ἅτε διαπρέπει νυκτὶ μεγάνορος ἔξοχα πλούτου·
> εἰ δ' ἄεθλα γαρύεν
> ἔλδεαι, φίλον ἦτορ. . . .

> (O.1.1–4)

[41]Compare Aristotle's list of those things that excite *phthonos* (*Rhetoric* 1387b25–88a19).
[42]Woodbury 1968.538 n.17. The nonappearance of the word in Pindar may be a matter of style, for *megaloprepeia* occurs only in prose, except for one appearance in Aristophanes (*Birds* 1125).

Water is best, but gold, like fire blazing in the night, is conspicuous most
of wealth that makes a man great. But if you wish to sing of prizes, dear
heart. . . .

Together, διαπρέπει and μεγάνορος offer us the constituent elements
of the compound, endorsing *megaloprepeia* in the most prominent position of the poem. And Pindar's abrupt simile, αἰθόμενον πῦρ ἅτε
διαπρέπει, has special relevance in this context: we have seen from
Alcibiades' words in Thucydides, for example, that the language of illumination belongs to the sphere of *megaloprepeia* (recall τῷ ἐμῷ διαπρεπεῖ τῆς Ὀλυμπίαζε θεωρίας; λαμπρύνομαι; λαμπρότητι). So
here, gold is "like fire" most especially when it is being used to "make a
man great," or in prosaic terms, "illustrious" (λαμπρός) or "visible"
(φανερός).[43] We should also note as part of the "aura" of *megaloprepeia*,
how easy and natural the transition is from wealth to athletic prizes (2–
3). "Gold" and "prizes" are not completely unrelated forms of "the
best" in different spheres: in a sense, Pindar is simply moving from the
general (expenditure of wealth) to the particular (expenditure on horse
breeding leading to prizes).[44]

Again, the opening of Pythian 5 is an emphatic endorsement of
megaloprepeia:

[43]I take μεγάνωρ here to be a factitive bahuvrihi, as Jochem Schindler has described
the class (Seminar, Harvard University, October 25, 1986; see also Williger 1928.18–19).
Thus I would translate, giving due weight to both elements of the compound, "wealth
which makes a man great" (thus also Colace 1978.744 n. 19; for a different treatment, see
Gerber 1982.13–14). A good parallel for this meaning in Pindar is fr. 109 SM; there the
poet contrasts μεγαλάνορος Ἡσυχίας / τὸ φαιδρὸν φάος with στάσιν . . . πενίας
δότειραν, ἐχθρὰν κουροτρόφον. In contrast to civic strife, which is a "hateful nurse of
young men," Ἡσυχία "makes men great." Another good parallel is P.8.2, where
Ἡσυχία is invoked as ὦ μεγιστόπολι. Here, commentators routinely translate "she
who makes cities greatest" (e.g., Farnell 1930.2.192–193, Slater 1969a, s.v. μεγιστό-
πολις).

For the same association of gold, expenditure, and light imagery as the ruling metaphor in Bacchylides' Third Ode, see Carson 1984.111–119. For λαμπρός and φανερός,
see Herodotus, Thucydides, Lysias, Isocrates, Demosthenes, etc., and Davies 1981.98–
99.

[44]The link is reinforced by the shared light imagery of these two terms (see Gerber
1982.4, 18–19). Carson (1984.116–119) observes that two priamels of Bacchylides
"pivot" on their penultimate term (specifically through the connection of wealth and
euphrosyne) and cites Olympian 1 as a parallel for such pivoting. What I am proposing for
Olympian 1 is a slight modification of her thesis: that the pivoting starts between the
second and third elements of the priamel, that gold and the light it produces lead us
thematically to the light of the games. This interpretation would make the function of
χρυσός in Pindar's priamel even closer to that which Carson proposes for Bacchylides 3

'Ο πλοῦτος εὐρυσθενής,
ὅταν τις ἀρετᾷ κεκραμένον καθαρᾷ
βροτήσιος ἀνὴρ πότμου παραδόντος αὐτὸν ἀνάγῃ
πολύφιλον ἐπέταν.

(P. 5. 1–4)

Wealth is broad in strength, whenever any mortal man leads it forth
mixed with pure virtue, when fate has bestowed it, as an attendant that
makes many friends.

Indeed, we may wish to go so far as to understand ἀρετά in this context
as *megaloprepeia* itself (like the φιλόφρων ἀρετά of Croesus in Pythian
1), though Pindar's language, as often, seems deliberately vague.[45]
Then these lines would mean approximately, "Wealth is broad in
strength, when a man possesses it mixed with the proper sense of how
to use it." In Olympian 2 the poet says:

ὁ μὰν πλοῦτος ἀρεταῖς δεδαιδαλμένος φέρει τῶν τε καὶ τῶν
καιρὸν βαθεῖαν ὑπέχων μέριμναν †ἀγροτέραν,
ἀστὴρ ἀρίζηλος, ἐτυμώτατον
ἀνδρὶ φέγγος·

(O. 2. 53–56)

Wealth laced with virtues bears the opportunity of these things and those,
supporting profound, ambitious concern. It is a conspicuous star, truest
light for a man.

"Wealth laced with virtues" (πλοῦτος ἀρεταῖς δεδαιδαλμένος) reminds
us of wealth mixed with pure *aretē* ([πλοῦτον] ἀρετᾷ κεκραμένον
καθαρᾷ) in Pythian 5. And though the corruption in line 54 obscures
the poet's meaning, his final words are clear enough. As in the prose

---

(Carson 1984.111–119). For the gleam of gold (as Duchemin [1955.224–228] and
Bresson [1979.73–84] point out) links it with the imperishable natural world of water,
while the simile of "fire blazing in the night" implies that gold must be spent to give forth
light, carrying us forward to the even more vivid light of the Olympic games. Whereas
Bacchylides pivots on the ambiguity of gold as imperishable element and as source of
euphrosyne, Pindar bases his ambiguity on a prior expenditure—that required to obtain
the victory itself. Thus I cannot agree with Krischer (1974.90), who sees an antithesis
between material and ethical values in the second and third terms of the priamel. I believe
we cannot make this distinction, because the "ethical" use of gold is already implied in
the second term.
[45]At P.1.94, Gildersleeve notes, "ἀρετά: 'Generosity,' as often" (Gildersleeve
1890.252).

sources, the proper use of wealth illuminates: it is a star, far conspicuous, the "truest light for a man."

In other contexts, the poet tells us more specifically what he considers proper expenditure, and his list agrees nicely with those of Xenophon and Aristotle. In Isthmian 2, for example, praising the "sweet disposition" (ὀργά . . . γλυκεῖα) of Xenokrates, the poet says:[46]

> αἰδοῖος μὲν ἦν ἀστοῖς ὁμιλεῖν,
> ἱπποτροφίας τε νομίζων ἐν Πανελλάνων νόμῳ·
> καὶ θεῶν δαῖτας προσέπτυκτο πάσας· οὐδέ ποτε ξενίαν
> οὖρος ἐμπνεύσαις ὑπέστειλ᾽ ἱστίον ἀμφὶ τράπεζαν·
>
> (I.2.37–40)

He was respectful in keeping company with his fellow citizens, even practicing *hippotrophia* according to the custom of all the Greeks. And he welcomed warmly all the feasts of the gods, and never did a favoring breeze blowing cause him to reef the sail [of his generosity] about a hospitable table.

But the single form of expenditure Pindar seems to endorse most and most emphatically is, not surprisingly, the keeping of horses. In Nemean 9, he says in praise of the citizens of Aitna:

> ἐντί τοι φίλιπποί τ᾽ αὐτόθι καὶ κτεάνων ψυχὰς ἔχοντες κρέσσονας
> ἄνδρες.
>
> (N.9.32–33)

There are in this place men who are lovers of horses and who have souls superior to their possessions.[47]

In Isthmian 4 he praises the Kleonymidai:

[46]It is tempting to understand ὀργά . . . γλυκεῖα here, like ἀρετά in certain contexts, as referring to the "disposition" or "temperament" of generosity or munificence, especially since εὐανθεῖ . . . ἐν ὀργᾷ appears in Pythian 1 in what is clearly a *megaloprepeia* context: "And you are steward of many, and many are the trusty witnesses for both. If indeed you love always to hear a sweet hearing, holding fast in this blooming temper [εὐανθεῖ δ᾽ ἐν ὀργᾷ παρμένων], do not toil too much over expenditures" (P.1.88–90). On this sense of ὀργά, see Woodbury 1981.247–248 (discussing I.1.41, I.6.14 and P.1.89).

[47]As a parallel for κτεάνων ψυχὰς ἔχοντες κρέσσονας as a formula for praising munificence see P.8.88–92.

οὐδὲ παναγυρίων ξυνᾶν ἀπεῖχον
καμπύλον δίφρον, Πανελλάνεσσι δ' ἐριζόμενοι δαπάνᾳ χαῖρον ἵππων.
(I.4.28–29)

They have never kept their curved chariot from the common assemblies,
but vying with all the Greeks, they rejoiced in expenditure on horses.

Just as Alcibiades claims that lavish public expenditure bears "glory
to my ancestors and to me" (τοῖς μὲν προγόνοις μου καὶ ἐμοὶ δόξαν
φέρει), Pindar confidently assures his patrons that willing *dapanē* will
bring them *doxa*:

> ἴστε μὰν Κλεωνύμου
> δόξαν παλαιὰν ἄρμασιν·
> καὶ ματρόθε Λαβδακίδαισιν σύννομοι
> πλούτου διέστειχον τετραοριᾶν πόνοις.
>
> (I.3.15–17b)

Know that the glory of Kleonymos with chariots is ancient. And [those
men] related to the Labdakids on their mother's side walked in the ways
of wealth with the toils of four-horse teams.

Indeed, in this context it seems that Pindar's confidence has a more
concrete foundation than Alcibiades', for as the poet tells us, his own
poetry bestows this enduring *doxa*. Thus, in Pythian 1 he admonishes
Hieron,

> εἴπερ τι φιλεῖς ἀκοὰν ἁδεῖαν αἰεὶ κλύειν, μὴ κάμνε λίαν δαπάναις·
>
> . . . . .
>
> ὀπιθόμβροτον αὔχημα δόξας
> οἶον ἀποιχομένων ἀνδρῶν δίαιταν μανύει
> καὶ λογίοις καὶ ἀοιδοῖς. οὐ φθίνει Κροίσου φιλόφρων ἀρετά.
>
> (P.1.90–94)

If indeed you love always to hear a sweet hearing [i.e., to be well spoken
of], do not toil too much over expenditures. . . . only the acclaim of men
to come, consisting of glory, reveals the way of life of men who have
passed away, by means of both chroniclers and poets. The kindly generosity of Croesus does not waste away.

Pindar's αὔχημα δόξας, a boast "consisting of glory," recalls the αὔχησις Alcibiades claims the munificent earn among later generations, and

Pindar is explicit in telling us that that αὔχημα is conferred by "chroniclers and poets."

In his explicit statements about wealth, its attributes, and its use, Pindar appears to occupy the same world of discourse as the prose authors we have considered. But Pindar's poems are not just the means of ensuring remembrance of *megaloprepeia*: they are themselves the products or objects of this "virtue." And as such, they correspond in many ways to Aristotle's description of the proper objects of expenditure. The philosopher tells us:

οὐ γὰρ εἰς ἑαυτὸν δαπανηρὸς ὁ μεγαλοπρεπὴς ἀλλ᾽ εἰς τὰ κοινά, τὰ δὲ δῶρα τοῖς ἀναθήμασιν ἔχει τι ὅμοιον. μεγαλοπρεποῦς δὲ καὶ οἶκον κατασκευάσασθαι πρεπόντως τῷ πλούτῳ (κόσμος γάρ τις καὶ οὗτος), καὶ περὶ ταῦτα μᾶλλον δαπανᾶν ὅσα πολυχρόνια τῶν ἔργων (κάλλιστα γὰρ ταῦτα), καὶ ἐν ἑκάστοις τὸ πρέπον· οὐ γὰρ ταὐτὰ ἁρμόζει θεοῖς καὶ ἀνθρώποις, οὐδ᾽ ἐν ἱερῷ καὶ τάφῳ. (*Nich. Ethics* 1123a4–10)

For the *megaloprepēs* spends not for himself but for the community, and his gifts have something like to dedications. And it is characteristic of the *megaloprepēs* also to equip his house as befits his wealth (for this also is an ornament) and to spend more concerning these things, however many works are long lasting (for these are most beautiful), and [to spend] in each thing what is fitting. For the same things are not suited to men and gods, or in a temple and a tomb.

The proper objects of munificence are long lasting (πολυχρόνια) and public (εἰς τὰ κοινά). We find Pindar laying claim to these same characteristics for his poetry. Thus, as Aristotle specifies πολυχρόνια, Pindar tells us explicitly that what makes poetry such a suitable object of expenditure is its enduring quality:

εἰ δέ μοι πλοῦτον θεὸς ἁβρὸν ὀρέξαι,
ἐλπίδ᾽ ἔχω κλέος εὑρέσθαι κεν ὑψηλὸν πρόσω.
Νέστορα καὶ Λύκιον Σαρπηδόν᾽, ἀνθρώπων φάτις,
ἐξ ἐπέων κελαδεννῶν, τέκτονες οἷα σοφοὶ
ἅρμοσαν, γινώσκομεν· ἁ δ᾽ ἀρετὰ κλειναῖς ἀοιδαῖς
χρόνια τελέθει· παύροις δὲ πράξασθ᾽ εὐμαρές.

(P.3.110–115)

But if god offer me luxurious wealth, I expect that I would find lofty *kleos* beyond. Nestor and Lykian Sarpedon, proverbial among men, we know from sounding words, what sort skilled craftsmen [of song] have fitted together. For achievement turns out to be enduring through songs that make glorious: but to accomplish [this] is easy for few men.

Pindar speaks here in the first person, but the message to and about his patrons is clear.[48] If one has money, the best use one can make of it is to invest in κλειναῖς ἀοιδαῖς, which endure forever and so make the memory of one's aretē endure (χρονία τελέθει).

If we look more closely at Aristotle's description, we discover that he alludes to certain concrete objects that combine the qualities of being long lasting and public. These objects are referred to in general terms in the words ὅσα πολυχρόνια τῶν ἔργων, where τῶν ἔργων must mean primarily "works of art" or "public works." And indeed, Aristotle has already mentioned a specific class of such "works." In the context of the public character of *megaloprepeia*, he offers us an unexpected analogy: "and its gifts have something like to *anathemata*." The salient characteristics of *anathemata* for this context seem to be that they are concrete monuments, publicly dedicated and displayed for all time. But I must emphasize the metaphorical nature of the philosopher's statement. He does not say, though he could, that *anathemata* are an example of *megaloprepeia*. Instead, it is as if this conjunction of qualities (their enduring character and their public purpose) forces even the prosaic Aristotle to resort to the simile of the concrete. This same conjunction of qualities leads Pindar to use the same concrete imagery for his poems. Thus in Isthmian 1 he sets out to praise the Theban victor Herodotus with the words, ἀλλ' ἐγὼ Ἡροδότῳ τεύχων τὸ μὲν ἅρματι τεθρίππῳ γέρας ("But I, building for Herodotus an honor for the four-horse chariot" [I.1.14]). The use of the concrete verb τεύχων here is not fortuitous, for the poet picks up the imagery with the theme again later in the same ode:

> ἐπεὶ κούφα δόσις ἀνδρὶ σοφῷ
> ἀντὶ μόχθων παντοδαπῶν ἔπος εἰπόντ' ἀγαθὸν ξυνὸν ὀρθῶσαι καλόν.
>
> (I.1.45–46)

Since it is a light gift for a skilled man in exchange for all sorts of toils, by saying a good word, to set up a common ornament.

Ὀρθῶσαι καλόν conjures up the concrete image of erecting a stele or an *anathema*, while ξυνόν asserts that the poem is an ornament for the entire state. The scholia exactly capture the flavor of the metaphor in ξυνὸν

---

[48]On the "generalized first person" and its uses in Pindar, see Young 1968.12.

ὀρθῶσαι καλόν, when they gloss, κόσμος γάρ ἐστι καὶ τῶν ἄλλων πολιτῶν τὸ περὶ ἕνα γινόμενον ἐγκώμιον ("The encomium that occurs for the sake of one man is an ornament also for the rest of the citizens").⁴⁹

Again, the opening of Pythian 6 incorporates exactly these two elements in the image of the θησαυρός of hymns:

> Πυθιόνικος ἔνθ᾽ ὀλβίοισιν Ἐμμενίδαις
> ποταμίᾳ τ᾽ Ἀκράγαντι καὶ μὰν Ξενοκράτει
> ἑτοῖμος ὕμνων θησαυρὸς ἐν πολυχρύσῳ
> Ἀπολλωνίᾳ τετείχισται νάπᾳ·
>
> (P.6.5–9)

There a Pythian-victory treasure-house of hymns is built ready for the blessed Emmenidai and rivery Akragas, and indeed for Xenokrates in the grove of Apollo, rich in gold.

Pindar seems to choose this image partly for the enduring power of the concrete monument, for he goes on emphatically:

> τὸν οὔτε χειμέριος ὄμβρος, ἐπακτὸς ἐλθὼν ἐριβρόμου νεφέλας
> στρατὸς ἀμείλιχος, οὔτ᾽ ἄνεμος ἐς μυχοὺς
> ἁλὸς ἄξοισι παμφόρῳ χεράδει
> τυπτόμενον.
>
> (P.6.10–14)

Neither wintry rain, a harsh foreign army of loud-roaring cloud advancing, nor wind will carry it, struck with debris that carries all with it, into the depths of the sea.

But a *thesauros* is not just any building: it was one of the most lavish and conspicuous *anathemata* that could be dedicated at the great Panhellenic cult centers.⁵⁰ In the earliest period of their construction, the

⁴⁹Drachmann 1926.207. The final appearance of concrete architectural imagery in the poem is worth noting. Very near the close of the poem, at the end of the victory catalog, Pindar prays for Herodotus' future success: "May it be for him, raised up on the glorious wings of the tuneful Pierides, in future to fence his hand [φράξαι χεῖρα] with shoots from Pytho and picked out ones from the Olympic games, building honor for seven-gated Thebes [τιμὰν ἑπταπύλοις Θήβαισι τεύχοντ᾽]" (I.1.64–67). Inspired by the poet's song of praise, the victor will "fence his hand" with wreaths, "building honor for seven-gated Thebes." Here used for the victor, not the poet, the architectural imagery indicates that Herodotus' continued *ponos* and *dapanē* should create an enduring monument to adorn his city.

⁵⁰On *thesauroi* as *anathemata*, see Dyer 1905.303–308. He cites the inscription of the

thesauroi were the dedications of tyrants and δυνάσται, though, as time went on, they came to be considered the common property of the demos.[51] Thus, for example, Pausanias tells us that the "treasury of the Sikyonians" was built by the tyrant Myron to commemorate an Olympic chariot victory, and Plutarch that the "treasury of the Akanthians," dedicated at Delphi to celebrate their victory over the Athenians, was inscribed, Βράσιδας καὶ ᾿Ακάνθιοι ἀπ᾿ ᾿Αθηναίων.[52] It is certainly significant that Pindar uses almost exactly the same formula in Pythian 6: the treasure-house "is built ready" for the Emmenidai, the ruling house, and the city of Akragas, and finally for Xenokrates, the actual victor. The family of the patron and his entire polis share in the glory conferred by the poem as monument.

In Nemean 8, Pindar is equally explicit about his poem as an *anathema* dedicated publicly for the common good, though at the expense of an individual patron:

> ἱκέτας Αἰακοῦ σεμνῶν γονάτων πόλιός θ᾿ ὑπὲρ φίλας
> ἀστῶν θ᾿ ὑπὲρ τῶνδ᾿ ἅπτομαι φέρων
> Λυδίαν μίτραν καναχηδὰ πεποικιλμέναν,
> Δείνιος δισσῶν σταδίων καὶ πατρὸς Μέγα Νεμεαῖον ἄγαλμα.
>
> (N.8.13–16)

As a suppliant on behalf of this dear city and these citizens, I fasten onto the august knees of Aiakos bearing a variegated, sounding Lydian headband as a Nemean adornment of the double furlong courses of Deinis and his father Megas.[53]

Historical critics have claimed that Pindar's plea here on behalf of the city of Aigina and her citizens reflects the island's dire political situation at the time, but surely the poet's emphasis on the common advantage in his dedication of a "sounding Lydian headband" is exactly what we should expect in such a *megaloprepeia/anathema* context.[54] And if we had

---

Andrians' "house" at Delos—οἶκος ὃν ἀνέθησαν οἱ ῎Ανδριοι ("the 'house' which the Andrians dedicated"); on the equivalence of θησαυρός, οἶκος, and ναός used of these structures, see Dyer 1905.301, 305).

[51]See Herodotus 1.14, Strabo 9.3.4 and Dyer 1905.308–311.

[52]Pausanias 6.19; Plutarch, *Life of Lysander* 1.1.

[53]For fillets or headbands used as dedications, see Hock 1905.10.

[54]For the historical interpretation, see, for example, Bury: "It was written in the day of [Aigina's] humiliation; and the death of Megas gave Pindar an opportunity for introducing some mournful Lydian measures, which might at the same time convey his sympathy to the island in her distress. The allusions to the political situation could scarcely be clearer than they are without becoming more than allusive" (Bury 1890.145).

any doubts that it *is* an *anathema* context, Pindar reinforces the point by the use of the word ἄγαλμα, whose implications J. B. Bury draws out: "Ἄγαλμα suggests that the ode will serve as a statue for Deinis and a sepulchral stele for Megas."[55] Even if we do not wish to go as far as Bury (since it is only in the later fifth century that ἄγαλμα comes to have the specialized meaning "statue, portrait"), we should recognize the strong association of the word with gifts to the gods and *anathemata*.[56]

Pythian 7 offers us perhaps the most elaborate example of this metaphor, when Pindar rousingly "lays the foundation course of songs" for the *genos* of the victor:

> Κάλλιστον αἱ μεγαλοπόλιες Ἀθᾶναι
> προοίμιον Ἀλκμανιδᾶν εὐρυσθενεῖ
> γενεᾷ κρηπῖδ᾽ ἀοιδᾶν ἵπποισι βαλέσθαι.

(P.7.1–4)

The great city of Athens is the most beautiful prelude to cast down as foundation course of songs for the clan of the Alkmeonidai, broad in strength, for their horses.

Here, their membership in the Athenian polis is itself part of the monument of praise the poet constructs for the Alkmeonidai. But the glorious reputation of Athens—what makes it the most beautiful κρηπίς of songs—depends, in turn, on the *megaloprepeia* of the Alkmeonidai, for Pindar goes on to say:

> πάσαισι γὰρ πολίεσι λόγος ὁμιλεῖ
> Ἐρεχθέος ἀστῶν, Ἄπολλον, οἳ τεόν
> δόμον Πυθῶνι δίᾳ θαητὸν ἔτευξαν.

(P.7.9–11)

For the reputation of the citizens of Erechtheus keeps company with all cities—[those] who made wondrous your home in shining Pytho, O Apollo.

As we know from Herodotus (5.62), it was the Alkmeonidai who built Apollo a wondrous temple at Delphi, but Pindar gives the credit here to

---

[55]Bury 1890.152–153. See also N.8.44–48, where the poet says he will set up a λίθον Μοισαῖον for Megas and Deinis.

[56]See LSJ ἄγαλμα, definitions 4 and 5 for the later specialized meanings, and 2 for the association with *anathemata*. See also Gernet 1981a, esp. 115, 117–118, 142–143.

the entire polis, using the general phrase "citizens of Erechtheus." Thus, this poem subtly encodes that model of reciprocal advantage between the *oikos* and the polis which is the ideal of *megaloprepeia*, and encodes it specifically through the imagery of a built monument.[57]

The point deserves to be emphasized. In these contexts at least, it appears that the ethos of *megaloprepeia* generates the imagery of concrete *agalmata* and *anathemata* as a means of expressing simultaneously the enduring quality and communal scope of Pindar's poetry. We can now suggest the reason for the particular kenning for poets Pindar chooses at the end of Pythian 3. In what is clearly a *megaloprepeia* context (note πλοῦτον at 110), he calls them τέκτονες . . . σοφοί, "wise carpenters [of song]" (113). It is true that this is a traditional designation for poets, but Pindar is still opting to use it in this context, thereby adapting the traditional image to a new civic setting.[58]

The collocation of *megaloprepeia* with concrete imagery which transforms the poet into a craftsman is suggestive, in turn, for what Jesper Svenbro calls "the materiality of poetic discourse." By this phrase, Svenbro designates Pindar's frequent images of building and other forms of "making" to characterize his own activity. Following Stanisław Gzella, Svenbro assumes that the focus of this imagery of *poiesis* is the relation of poet and victor.[59] As a result, he concludes that wherever the poet refers to himself as τέκτων, he is underscoring the contractual nature of his work and reminding the victor to pay him.[60] But this is to

[57]For a striking parallel for this use of the imagery of the monument, consider the remarks of Ober 1989.243–244 on the function of monuments in the political and forensic speeches of the Attic orators: "The choregic monument served as a metaphor for the ideal relationship among honor, wealth, and the state. . . . The *chorēgos* who had financed the chorus awarded the first prize was himself awarded a tripod and granted the right to set up (at his own expense) a monument incorporating his prize. The monument was a permanent record of his achievement and his generosity to the people, to which he could later refer with justifiable pride, in court and elsewhere. The rich man thus competed with other rich men in giving to the demos; the *chorēgos* who had given the most to the demos was allowed to make a public display. The masses, even though they had a deciding role in the authorization of the monument, were nonetheless impressed by the man who had built it, and they paid him due honor."

[58]Already in epic we find the language of building or crafting associated with intellectual activity in general and song in particular (e.g. *Iliad* 10.19, *Odyssey* 12.183, 17.385, 24.197, *Homeric Hymn to Aphrodite* [2].20; see Fränkel 1925.4–5). Comparative evidence (mainly from Vedic Sanskrit and Old Avestan) suggests that the image of the poet as craftsman may be of Indo-European antiquity (see Durante 1968b.261–290 and Schmitt 1967.14, 297–298).

[59]Gzella 1969–1970b and 1971, Svenbro 1976.186–212.

[60]Svenbro 1976.185–193, esp. 192.

apply the assumptions of market economics completely anachronisti-cally to an embedded economy.

We have observed two models of exchange available to the poet and used by him to describe the various systems of relations of which his poem is a part. Both of these models are founded on the institutions and assumptions of an embedded economy, but each addresses a different sector of the social world. The poet employs the model of gift exchange for the connection between himself and the victor when he wants to fit it into a whole network of aristocratic relations which converge on athletic competition and victory. Within this model, the poet stands as the victor's equal, composing the poem out of the feeling of *chreos* or *charis* which exists between them. Money and pay have no place in this system.

The second model is that of *megaloprepeia*. Within this model money plays an important part, and the poet often depicts himself as a crafts-man fashioning a precious object to the victor's specifications but for the common good. Given all we know about Greek attitudes toward labor, we are much mistaken if we try to claim that the poet glorifies or promotes *himself* by using the image of the τέκτων. For, as M. M. Austin and Pierre Vidal-Naquet remind us, in the embedded economy of classical antiquity, "while the work of the artisan was admired, he was neglected or down-graded as a person."[61] Furthermore, as Jean-Pierre Vernant observes, "the ability of the artisan takes second place to the demands of the user": "When considering a product, the ancient Greeks were less concerned with the process of manufacture, the ποίησις, than with the use to which the article was to be put, the χρῆσις. And, for each piece of work, it is this χρῆσις that defines the εἶδος that the worker embodies in matter. In effect, the manufactured object, like living creatures, is subject to final causes. Its perfection lies in its adaptation to the need for which it has been produced."[62] It is time that these concepts, so familiar within the context of ancient economics and technology, were applied to Pindar's imagery of craftsmanship. We must displace the poet as the focus of this imagery and shift our atten-tion to the "users" of his craft, the patron who commissions the poem and the audience for which it is commissioned. The frame of *mega-loprepeia* suggests that the imagery of craftsmanship is primarily di-rected at a civic audience. The purpose of this imagery is to glorify not the poet but the product of his craft, the *poem*, and thereby to enhance

[61]Austin and Vidal-Naquet 1977.12 (and see their source reading no. 11, pp. 177–178).
[62]Vernant 1983.260–261.

the status of the victor who commissioned it within his community. At the center of this system of images is the confrontation of the poet's aristocratic patron and his fellow citizens. Pindar's attempt to reconcile them suggests that the poet is much more conscious of the polis and much more concerned to adapt epinikion to civic ideology than his critics have allowed.

CHAPTER 8

Envy and Tyranny:
The Rhetoric of *Megaloprepeia*

In the imagery of dedications, as in his explicit statements about wealth, Pindar appears to be participating in the civic discourse of munificence. But what of the specifically political tensions I detected in the "virtue" of *megaloprepeia*? Are these reflected and addressed in the rhetoric of epinikian poetry? Indeed, in Pindar's odes, as in political life, the workings of *megaloprepeia* are not entirely free from tensions. The problems associated with it in the work of Thucydides and other ancient sources are also apparent in the epinikia composed for private citizens: from the point of view of the individual, munificence evokes the envy of his fellow citizens; from the point of view of the city, it breeds the suspicion of tyrannical aspirations. And since it is the poet's purpose to reintegrate the victor into his community, such tensions must be defused. Epinikion deploys a double rhetorical strategy for dealing with the problems of *megaloprepeia*: inclusion of the city and rejection on the part of the individual of any kind of overreaching or excessive ambition.

That the victor's fellow citizens feel *phthonos* at his good fortune is an epinikian commonplace.[1] To cite just one example, consider Pythian 7. The architectural imagery that opens the poem seems to be built on the ideal of *megaloprepeia* as a system mutually advantageous to the *oikos* and the polis. Yet this ideal modulates into unpleasant political reality within

---

[1]For *phthonos* of the victor's fellow citizens, see I.2.43, P.7.19; for *phthonos* in myth, O.1.47, P.11.29; and in general, O.6.74, P.1.85, P.2.90, N.4.39, N.8.21. On the topic, see Bundy 1962.40, Thummer 1968.1.80–81, and Stoneman 1976.191–192.

the compass of this short ode, for the poet concludes the victory catalog
with the words,

> νέᾳ δ' εὐπραγίᾳ χαίρω τι· τὸ δ' ἄχνυμαι,
> φθόνον ἀμειβόμενον τὰ καλὰ ἔργα.
>
> (P.7.18–19)

I rejoice at their new success, but I am grieved at the envy that requites
their noble works.

'Αμειβόμενον here suggests that we are dealing with the same reciprocal relationship of *genos* and polis with which the poem began. But in
this context, the polis reciprocates the "noble works" of the Alkmeonidai with envy.

The poet's strategy to allay the envy of the victor's fellow citizens is to
include them emphatically, both in the poem as paradigm of *megaloprepeia* and in the victory itself. Only once is this strategy completely
explicit, in the surprisingly defensive words that close Olympian 7,
where the poet prays to Zeus,

> μὴ κρύπτε κοινόν
> σπέρμ' ἀπὸ Καλλιάνακτος· 'Ερατιδᾶν τοι σὺν χαρίτεσσιν ἔχει
> θαλίας καὶ πόλις· ἐν δὲ μιᾷ μοίρᾳ χρόνου
> ἄλλοτ' ἀλλοῖαι διαιθύσσοισιν αὖραι.
>
> (O.7.92–95)

Do not hide the common seed from Kallianax: to be sure, the city also has
festivities together with the epinikian celebration of the Eratidai. But in
one share of time, different blasts shift rapidly at different moments.

Kallianax is probably a relatively recent ancestor of Diagoras, and the
Eratidai are his clan.[2] Thus, lines 93–94 mean that together with the
epinikian celebration of the family (σὺν χαρίτεσσιν), the city *also* has
festivities.[3] Καὶ πόλις already bothered the scholiasts, who say, "The
conjunction is superfluous" (ὁ δὲ σύνδεσμος περιττεύει).[4] But the καὶ
is hardly superfluous: it is the poet's brief but revealing acknowledgment of the tensions or hostilities likely to exist between the aristocratic
household and the polis.

[2]Farnell 1930.2.57.
[3]For this meaning of χάριτες, already mentioned, see Gundert 1935.30–45, Slater
1969a, χάρις, 1.b.β.
[4]Drachmann 1903.235

More commonly, this strategy is more covert. The inclusion of the city in the commemorative ode takes the form of "praise of the victor's homeland," as Thummer categorizes it.[5] Such praise abounds in the epinikia, because it affirms the public or common nature of the patron's commission. Thus the poem itself, that monument to the victor's *megaloprepeia*, is also an "ornament" (a κόσμος, κοσμεῖν [N.6.46]) or a "common light" (κοινὸν φέγγος [N.4.12–13]) for the entire city.[6]

The opening of Olympian 13, for example, moves through expanding circles of inclusion, implying that the celebration of the victorious house of the Oligaithidai must necessarily entail glorification of their city:[7]

> Τρισολυμπιονίκαν
> ἐπαινέων οἶκον ἥμερον ἀστοῖς,
> ξένοισι δὲ θεράποντα, γνώσομαι
> τὰν ὀλβίαν Κόρινθον, Ἰσθμίου
> πρόθυρον Ποτειδᾶνος, ἀγλαόκουρον·
>
> (O.13.1–5)

By praising a house with three Olympic victories, gentle to its fellow citizens and ministering to strangers, I shall come to know blessed Corinth, the portal of Isthmian Poseidon, [a city] splendid with young men.[8]

And indeed, Pindar proceeds from the relative ἐν τᾷ (6) to fill the entire first triad with praises of Corinth. He then returns to the topic after the first victory catalog:

> ἐγὼ δὲ ἴδιος ἐν κοινῷ σταλείς
> μῆτίν τε γαρύων παλαιγόνων
> πόλεμόν τ’ ἐν ἡρωίαις ἀρεταῖσιν
> οὐ ψεύσομ’ ἀμφὶ Κορίνθῳ.
>
> (O.13.49–52)

As a private citizen dispatched in a common [cause], I shall not lie about Corinth when I celebrate the cunning of those born long ago and war with the achievements of heroes.

[5]For examples, see Thummer 1968.1.55–65. As with "praise of the victor's family," Thummer makes no attempt to explain *why* praise of the victor's homeland should figure so prominently in the epinikian program: he merely catalogs all the appearances of such praise.

[6]For other examples of the poem designated as a good for the whole city in common, see O.10.11, O.13.49 (κοινός), and I.1.46 (ξυνός).

[7]See Wilamowitz 1922.371.

[8]Wasserstein 1982 reads θεράποντ’ ἀγγνώσομαι: "I shall herald" blessed Corinth, rather than "I shall come to know."

Pindar's metaphor here is drawn from the sphere of *megaloprepeia*. Acting on behalf of his patron, the poet performs a kind of *theōria*, providing a lavishly decorated vessel of songs to carry the city's praises to Panhellenic prominence.[9] Appropriately enough, these words mark the introduction to the myth of Bellerophon's taming Pegasos, a long elaboration of one of the *city's* glories.[10]

The inclusion of the city through the incorporation of its myths is a strategy the poet employs frequently. Thus, the elaborate priamel opening of Isthmian 7 recalls the mythic highlights of Thebes in order to imply that Strepsiades' victory is merely the most recent of the city's "local glories" (καλῶν ἐπιχωρίων [I.7.2]), and thus in the Aiginetan odes, Pindar frequently glorifies the island through its mythical heroes, the Aiakidai.[11] In Pythian 8, for example, he says:

> ἔπεσε δ' οὐ Χαρίτων ἑκάς
> ἁ δικαιόπολις ἀρεταῖς
> κλειναῖσιν Αἰακιδᾶν
> θιγοῖσα νᾶσος·
>
> (P.8.21–24)

[This] island with just city has fallen not far from the Graces in laying hold of the glorious achievements of the Aiakidai.

The implication of Pindar's words is that it is the Aiakidai's "glorious achievements" that have brought the island of Aigina near the Graces— that is, to epinikian celebration. Or again, in Isthmian 5 the poet asserts:

> τὸ δ' ἐμόν,
> οὐκ ἄτερ Αἰακιδᾶν, κέαρ ὕμνων γεύεται·
> σὺν Χάρισιν δ' ἔμολον Λάμπωνος υἱοῖς
> τάνδ' ἐς εὔνομον πόλιν.
>
> (I.5.19–22)

As for me, my heart never tastes of songs without the Aiakidai. But together with the Graces I have come to this well-ordered city for the sons of Lampon.

---

[9]On the *architheōria* as a form of *megaloprepeia*, see Aristotle *Nich. Ethics* 1122a25 and Thucydides 6.16 (and see as a parallel P.2.62 εὐανθέα . . . στόλον). Various interpretations of this image are offered by Mezger 1880.454, Fennell 1893.131, Bowra 1964.360, and Peron 1974.36–37.

[10]Indeed, Pindar has prepared for this myth in lines 16–17 and 20.

[11]On the opening of Isthmian 7, see Bundy 1962.6, Young 1971.18, Krischer 1974.82, and Race 1982.ix. Compare the priamel opening of Nemean 10, which makes the victory one of Argos' glories.

Through praise of the Aiakidai, the sons of Lampon and their city seem to be irradiated equally by the "Graces" the poet brings with him.[12]

Isthmian 5 also shows us a subtle movement through myth to communal praise. Later in the ode, in response to a series of rhetorical questions about the heroes' great deeds (39–42; cf. opening of I.7), Pindar tells us:

> τοῖσιν Αἴγιναν προφέρει στόμα πάτραν,
> διαπρεπέα νᾶσον· τετείχισται δὲ πάλαι
> πύργος ὑψηλαῖς ἀρεταῖς ἀναβαίνειν.
>
> (I.5.43–45)

[Those] for whom the mouth proclaims Aigina their homeland, [that] illustrious island. Long since a tower was built to be scaled by their lofty achievements.[13]

Then, through their common homeland, the poet modulates from praise of the Aiakidai to praise of the Aiginetan sailors who fought at Salamis:

> καὶ νῦν ἐν Ἄρει μαρτυρῆσαι κεν πόλις Αἴαντος ὀρθωθεῖσα ναύταις
> ἐν πολυφθόρῳ Σαλαμὶς Διὸς ὄμβρῳ
> ἀναρίθμων ἀνδρῶν χαλαζάεντι φόνῳ.
>
> (I.5.48–50)

And now in war, Salamis, the city of Ajax, will bear witness, since it was set upright by sailors in the much-destructive rain of Zeus, with the slaughter of countless men, thick as hail.

Finally, still under the topic of their common homeland, the poet shifts to praise of the victor's family, praise that takes an interesting form:

> μαρνάσθω {δέ} τις ἔρδων
> ἀμφ' ἀέθλοισιν γενεὰν Κλεονίκου

---

[12]See on this passage the discussion of Bundy 1962.56 n. 51.

[13]The language of this passage, especially διαπρεπέα and τετείχισται . . . πύργος ὑψηλαῖς ἀρεταῖς, strikingly echoes the language we have observed in megaloprepeia contexts. In this context it almost seems that megaloprepeia provides the metaphor through which Pindar praises the Aiakidai, and this impression is reinforced by the poet's use of economic imagery for the heroes earlier in the ode: "And in fact, those of the heroes who were good warriors profited in report [λόγον ἐκέρδαναν]" (I.5.25–26). The Aiakidai, by their lavish "expenditure" of heroic deeds, have built a tower for their city, while they themselves have "profited" by an enduring λόγος. Thus, it appears that the system works both ways: the victor's megaloprepeia can be assimilated to the city's mythic glories (as in Olympian 13 and Isthmian 7), or the achievements of the city's heroes can be assimilated to megaloprepeia.

ἐκμαθών· οὔτοι τετύφλωται μακρός
μόχθος ἀνδρῶν οὐδ' ὁπόσαι δαπάναι
ἐλπίδ' ἔκνιξαν ὄπιν.

(I.5.54–58)

Let someone strive for accomplishment in contests, once he is fully acquainted with the line of Kleonikos. To be sure [they] do not lie in obscurity—the long toil of men and however many expenditures sting the regard with hope.

Although the corruption of line 58 makes Pindar's meaning here somewhat obscure, the general sense of lines 56–58 is clear: toil and expenditures pay off in the end.[14] But rather than simply praise the family's willingness to suffer and to spend, the poet holds them up as a paradigm of civic virtue, like the Aiakidai or the men who fought at Salamis. In this context, the τις of line 54 is surely a fellow citizen, who is encouraged to admire and emulate the μόχθος and δαπάναι of the clan of Kleonikos rather than envy their success. Athletic victory is completely assimilated to the great deeds of the past which redound to the city's glory. And the proof of the family's achievement is this commemorative ode, itself the product and evidence of their expenditures.

In other odes, Pindar succeeds in merging the *oikos* and the polis through the narration of foundation myths. By their very nature, foundation myths are political myths, which transform an entire polis into a single family descended from a common mythic ancestor. Their purpose is to unify a city and to evoke for it the loyalty and services due one's family, so it is significant that Pindar chooses such myths as centerpieces in certain odes.[15] And the rhetoric with which he introduces these myths contributes to their unifying effect. In Olympian 7, for example, the poet tells us that he is going to "hymn [Rhodes], the marine child of Aphrodite, in order to praise Diagoras and his father, Damagetos, pleasing to justice" (13–17). Then he glides smoothly into the myth with the words,

[14]Both MSS offer ἐλπίδων and a singular verb (ἔκνιξ' B, ἔκνιζ' D, ἔκνισ' Sch.). Since ὁπόσαι δαπάναι appears to be the subject, a plural verb is preferable, and for the sake of the meaning, the dative ἐλπίδ(ι) seems better than the genitive plural. I am still uncomfortable with the use and meaning of κνίζω here. But see the discussion of Thummer 1968.2.95–96.

[15]See the discussion of Dougherty-Glenn 1988 on the relevance of foundation myths and colonial themes for Pindar's epinikian project.

ἐθελήσω τοῖσιν ἐξ ἀρχᾶς ἀπὸ Τλαπολέμου
ξυνὸν ἀγγέλλων διορθῶσαι λόγον,
Ἡρακλέος
εὐρυσθενεῖ γέννᾳ.

(O.7.20–23)

I wish, announcing [it] for them from the beginning, from Tlepolemos,
to correct the common account for the mighty race of Herakles.

Τοῖσιν in line 20 refers to Diagoras and his father, but through the
ξυνὸν . . . λόγον of line 21 they are imperceptibly merged with the
entire city in the appositional Ἡρακλέος / εὐρυσθενεῖ γέννᾳ.[16] The
myth ultimately goes all the way back to the divine ancestors Helios and
Rhodes, in a scene that replicates the opening simile and thereby transforms all Rhodes's "children" into a single symbolic *oikos* (69–76).[17]

Olympian 9 shows us the same strategies at work. Pindar begins the
ode with the "ready-made" Ἀρχιλόχου μέλος which is sung for every
victor at the moment of victory. This sufficed, he says, for the immediate celebration, but now for the full-blown festivities in the victor's
homeland, a more elaborate, personally "tailored" song is required.
And its subject will be not the generic Herakles of the Archilochus strain
but "praise of glorious Opus and her son" (14).[18] By the time we get to
the words, "Bear your tongue to the city of Protogeneia" (φέροις δὲ
Πρωτογενείας ἄστει γλῶσσαν [O.9.41]), it has been made abundantly
clear that this poem is a special object of the victor's *megaloprepeia*,
personally commissioned and tailored to his specifications. And at the
center of this elaborate *kosmos* are the foundation myths of the city of
Opus: first Pyrrha and Deukalion, the primeval parents of the Opuntian
nobility (42–56), then the union of Zeus with the daughter of Opus to
produce the eponymous king of the land (57–79). Both these myths
simultaneously glorify the city and "her son," the victor.[19]

[16]Thummer (1968.1.57) notes the close connection between the naming of the father
and son and the mythic praise of the city (though he does not mention the rhetorical glide
it contains). With the dative τοῖσι, compare υἱοῖς (I.5.21), and see Bundy 1962.56 n. 51
on its significance.

[17]Note especially ξυνόν in this context, emphasizing the communal service Pindar's
ode performs. The adjective points to the city simultaneously as civic whole *and* as
audience, thus enacting its inclusion in the performance of the poem.

[18]On O.9.14–21, see Simpson 1969b.113–124. If Simpson is correct in his suggestion
that Archilochus' poem contained the Herakles myth that Pindar rejects in Triad B', the
movement from Herakles to Opus is doubled within the ode.

[19]The final example of a poem that contains a foundation myth is Pythian 9, but it will
be considered later in a slightly different context.

202 Pindar's Political Economy

Thus far, we have considered contexts in which the poet sedulously includes the victor's city in the poem and in the glory it confers. But he is also concerned to convince the polis that it had a share in the victory itself, for that good fortune is also a locus of *phthonos*. Again, we find these tensions revealed only once, when the poet observes:

αἰεὶ δ' ἀμφ' ἀρεταῖσι πόνος δαπάνα τε μάρναται πρὸς ἔργον
κινδύνῳ κεκαλυμμένον· εὖ δὲ τυχόντες σοφοὶ καὶ πολίταις ἔδοξαν
ἔμμεν.

(O. 5. 15–16)

Always over achievements toil and expenditure strive toward a deed obscured by risk. But those who succeed seem to be wise even to their fellow citizens.

These seem surprising lines to encounter in an epinikian context, for the καί suggests that one's fellow citizens will only finally, grudgingly approve of toil and money successfully spent.[20]

Generally though, if such tensions exist in the community, the poet does not reveal them. Instead, his is a picture of complete harmony, between the individual and his family and between the family and the polis. The announcement of victory in Isthmian 3 provides an excellent example of this rhetoric of harmony, for it manages to include the individual, his city, and his ancestors in the event:

ἔστι δὲ καὶ διδύμων ἀέθλων Μελίσσῳ
μοῖρα πρὸς εὐφροσύναν τρέψαι γλυκεῖαν
ἦτορ, ἐν βάσσαισιν Ἰσθμοῦ δεξαμένῳ στεφάνους, τὰ δὲ κοίλᾳ
   λέοντος
ἐν βαθυστέρνου νάπᾳ κάρυξε Θήβαν
ἱπποδρομίᾳ κρατέων· ἀνδρῶν δ' ἀρετάν
σύμφυτον οὐ κατελέγχει.
ἴστε μὰν Κλεωνύμου
δόξαν παλαιὰν ἅρμασιν·

(I. 3. 9–16)

There is a share also of double prizes for Melissos, to turn his heart to sweet festivity, since he received crowns in the glens of the Isthmus and he heralded Thebes in the hollow valley of the deep-breasted lion when

---

[20]Because of the oddness in tone, Stoddart 1990. 24 takes this to be a Pindaric "joke" on the topos of the envy of one's fellow citizens.

he won in horse racing. And he does not shame the inborn quality of men. Know that the glory of Kleonymos with chariots is ancient.

Of Melissos' "double prizes," he seems to take the first, the Isthmian, for himself and to allot the second to his city: at Nemea "he heralded Thebes." And both these victories prove him a true son of his family, whose "inborn *aretē*" he has not shamed. The city is neatly slotted in between the victor and his ancestors.

It is, however, rare to find all three—victor, city and family—mentioned in the announcement of victory. The poet generally focuses either on the victor and his family or on the individual and the polis. In this context it is the latter collocation that interests us, for it is there that we see the poet smoothing out the political tensions inherent in athletic success. This he does by telling us emphatically that the victory is a source of honor or glory for the city. Thus, in Nemean 5 the victory announcement runs,

Λάμπωνος υἱὸς Πυθέας εὐρυσθενής
νίκη Νεμείοις παγκρατίου στέφανον,

. . . . .

ἐκ δὲ Κρόνου καὶ Ζηνὸς ἥρωας αἰχματὰς φυτευθέντας καὶ ἀπὸ
χρυσεᾶν Νηρηΐδων
Αἰακίδας ἐγέραιρεν ματρόπολίν τε, φίλαν ξένων ἄρουραν·

(N.5.4–5, 7–8)

Pytheas son of Lampon, broad in strength, won the crown for the pancration at the Nemean games . . . and he honored the hero spearmen planted from Kronos and from Zeus, and from the golden Nereids, the Aiakidai, and his mother-city, land dear to strangers.

Pytheas won the crown at Nemea, and thereby honored (ἐγέραιρεν) the city and her heroes.

Pindar suggests the nature of this honor in the much fuller statement that opens Olympian 5:

Ὑψηλᾶν ἀρετᾶν καὶ στεφάνων ἄωτον γλυκύν
τῶν Οὐλυμπίᾳ, Ὠκεανοῦ θύγατερ, καρδίᾳ γελανεῖ
ἀκαμαντόποδός τ' ἀπήνας δέκευ Ψαύμιός τε δῶρα·
ὃς τὰν σὰν πόλιν αὔξων, Καμάρινα, λαοτρόφον,
βωμοὺς ἓξ διδύμους ἐγέραρεν ἑορταῖς θεῶν μεγίσταις
ὑπὸ βουθυσίαις ἀέθλων τε πεμπαμέροις ἀμίλλαις,

204   Pindar's Political Economy

ἵπποις ἡμιόνοις τε μοναμπυκίᾳ τε. τὶν δὲ κῦδος ἁβρόν
νικάσας ἀνέθηκε, καὶ ὃν πατέρ᾽ Ἄκρων᾽ ἐκάρυξε καὶ τὰν νέοικον
ἕδραν.

(O.5.1–8)

Daughter of Ocean, receive with laughing heart the sweet peak of highest
achievements and of crowns from Olympia, the gifts of the untiring-
footed chariot and of Psaumis. Exalting your city, which nurtures the
people, O Kamarina, he honored the twelve altars at the greatest festivals
of the gods with sacrifices and the five-day competitions of contests, with
horses and mules and single-horse racing. And having won, he dedicated
to you luxurious *kudos*, and he heralded his father, Akron, and his new-
founded seat.

"Exalting [αὔξων] your city, . . . Kamarina, he honored the twelve
altars at the greatest festivals of the gods" by sacrifices of cattle and by
competitions for prizes.[21] The message could not be clearer: Psaumis
has displayed the public virtue of *megaloprepeia* by spending on sacrifices
and horse (and mule) racing. Not only has he spent, but he has won, and
his victory is also phrased in terms of public service: "he heralded his
father, Akron, and his new-founded seat."

Striking throughout this passage is the concrete imagery it employs
in the context of *megaloprepeia*. First Kamarina is asked to "receive"
graciously the "sweet peak" of lofty achievements and crowns as the
gifts of the chariot and of Psaumis (1–3). Then the strophe ends with the
imagery of the concrete in the phrase "he dedicated to you the luxurious
kudos" that he won (τὶν δὲ κῦδος ἁβρὸν νικάσας ἀνέθηκε). Τίν refers
to Kamarina: the victor has "dedicated" to her "luxurious *kudos*," and
this is surely the foremost of his gifts. What the victor offers and what
the city receives frame the triad, equating his *kudos* with the proferred
crown. Again we encounter the language of *anathemata* in a *megaloprepeia* context, along with the adjective ἁβρός, an appropriate word
to describe the "luxurious prestige" bought by munificence.

The explicit language of dedication used with *kudos* in Olympian 5 is
suggestive for a series of similar passages in other poems. In Olympian
4, it is said of the same Psaumis,

Οὐλυμπιονίκαν
δέξαι Χαρίτων θ᾽ ἕκατι τόνδε κῶμον

[21]Compare with αὔξων Thucydides' use of αὔχησις in a *megaloprepeia* context
(Thucydides 6.16.5).

χρονιώτατον φάος εὐρυσθενέων ἀρετᾶν. Ψαύμιος γὰρ ἵκει
ὀχέων, ὃς ἐλαίᾳ στεφανωθεὶς Πισάτιδι κῦδος ὄρσαι
σπεύδει Καμαρίνᾳ.

(O.4.8–12)

[O Zeus,] receive this Olympic victory *kōmos* by the grace of the Charites, longest-lasting light of mighty achievements. For it comes for the
chariot(s) of Psaumis, who, crowned with Pisatan olive, is eager to rouse
kudos for Kamarina.

At the opening of Pythian 12, Pindar prays to Akragas, the victor's city,

ἵλαος ἀθανάτων ἀνδρῶν τε σὺν εὐμενίᾳ
δέξαι στεφάνωμα τόδ' ἐκ Πυθῶνος εὐδόξῳ Μίδᾳ
αὐτόν τε νιν Ἑλλάδα νικάσαντα τέχνᾳ,

(P.12.4–6)

[O mistress Akragas,] gracious toward immortals and with kindness
toward men, receive this crown from Pytho for glorious Midas and
receive him himself, [the man] who has beaten Greece in his craft,

And finally, in Isthmian 1, Pindar says he will celebrate the Isthmus,

ἐπεὶ στεφάνους
ἐξ ὤπασεν Κάδμου στρατῷ ἐξ ἀέθλων,
καλλίνικον πατρίδι κῦδος.

(I.1.10–12)

Since it bestowed six crowns from contests on the people of Kadmos,
victorious *kudos* for the homeland.

These passages reveal a persistent linking of the victor's crowns with
kudos for the city (στεφανωθεὶς . . . κῦδος [O.4], στεφάνους . . .
καλλίνικον πατρίδι κῦδος [I.1], perhaps στεφάνωμα . . . εὐδόξῳ
[P.12]). Olympian 5 and Pythian 12 both ask the city to "receive" the
victor's crown graciously, and Olympian 5 tells us also that the victor
"dedicates" his *kudos*. The link between crown and *kudos* is very suggestive when we recall Emile Benveniste's analysis of *kudos* in Homer.
Benveniste insists that *kudos* is not simply a synonym for *kleos*; it
designates rather a magical, talismanic force that guarantees victory:
"The gift of *kûdos* ensures the triumph of the man who receives it: in
combat the holder of *kûdos* is invariably victorious. Here we see the

fundamental character of *kûdos*: it acts as *a talisman of supremacy*. We use the term talisman advisedly, for the bestowal of *kûdos* by the god procures an instantaneous and irresistible advantage, rather like a magic power, and the god grants it now to one and now to another at his good will and always in order to give the advantage at a decisive moment of a combat or some competitive activity." Benveniste goes on to observe that "the expression is often accompanied by a dative indicating the beneficiary [either the king or the whole community]: 'carry off the *kûdos* for someone.' "[22]

We may regard epinikian *kudos* as the civic adaptation of its Homeric precursor. The athlete, like the Homeric hero, is endowed by the gods with *kudos* that ensures his victory. This talismanic force lingers with the victor, haloing him with dangerous power. The civic community replaces the Homeric sovereign as the beneficiary of the victor's *kudos*, which, when shared with the city, contributes to its supremacy. If this is so, the association of the victor's crown, *kudos*, and dedication suggests a sharing of talismanic power through the public dedication of the crown. We know that the athletic victor sometimes dedicated his crown on his return to his native city.[23] And Pindar emphatically links that dedication with the acquisition of *kudos* for the polis. Nor is this association limited to Pindar: Louis Robert has collected a whole series of agonistic inscriptions that use the expression στεφανοῦν τὴν πόλιν ("to crown the city") to describe the victor's achievement, and he notes at least one case in which the verb στεφανόω is replaced by κυδαίνω:

> τοιγὰρ κυδαίνω γενέτην ἐμὸν Εἰρηναῖον
> καὶ πάτρην Ἔφεσον στέμμασιν ἀθανάτοις.

Accordingly I bestow *kudos* upon my father Eirenaios and my homeland Ephesus with immortal garlands.[24]

---

[22]Benveniste 1973.348, 351, and in general 346–356. On the concept of *kudos* in Homer, see also Steinkopf 1937.23–27 and Fränkel 1973.80 with n. 14.

[23]See Stengel 1920.210–211, Blech 1982.114, Slater 1984.245 with n. 24. For the practice, cf. N.8.13–16 (Λυδίαν μίτραν as a dedication to Aiakos), N.5.50–54 (accepting the manuscripts' φέρειν rather than Wilamowitz' φέρε), O.9.110–112 (the victor crowns the altar of Ajax Oiliades "at his festival").

[24]Ebert 1972. no. 76B.9–10 (= *I. Olympia* 225.17–18, dated A.D. 49); see Robert 1967.17–27, esp. 25. On the semantics of κυδαίνω, see Benveniste 1973.354; for the expression, cf. O.10.66 and P.1.31. For the same collocation of the crown and *kudos* for the father, see O.14.22–24. This is not necessarily to claim that the magical quality of *kudos* was still felt in A.D. 49, simply that the formulas and collocations of such inscriptions were established when *kudos* was still a living concept and became traditional within the genre.

Here as in Pindar, the bestowal of *kudos* is linked with the victor's crown (designated by the elevated στέμμασιν ἀθανάτοις). I suggest that these linguistic collocations, in Pindar and in the inscriptions, reflect ritual practice: the victor dedicated his crown, and that public dedication symbolically represented the sharing of his talismanic power with the whole civic community.[25] If this is the case, the ritual gesture is very significant, for it explicitly makes the victory into a civic triumph. And the poet, by evoking this ritual act in his language, emphasizes at the opening of the poem the common or public nature of the event he celebrates.

In what seems to be a further metaphorical extension of the same ritual, the poet makes the returning victor himself into the artifact, an ornament for his city:

> ὀφείλει δ᾽ ἔτι, πατρίαν
> εἴπερ καθ᾽ ὁδόν νιν εὐθυπομπός
> αἰὼν ταῖς μεγάλαις δέδωκε κόσμον Ἀθάναις,
>
> (N.2.6–8)

but it is still owed, since a life that guides him straight along the ancestral road has given him as an ornament to great Athens.[26]

And in Pythian 9, Telesikrates is himself the crown the city is to receive:[27]

> Ἐθέλω χαλκάσπιδα Πυθιονίκαν
> σὺν βαθυζώνοισιν ἀγγέλλων

[25]That this sharing is not completely unproblematic is suggested by the cases in which rejected victors become cult heroes (see Fontenrose 1968, Bohringer 1979, Crotty 1982.122–138). In these terms, we may characterize victors who become heroes as those who do not accomplish the normal sharing of *kudos* with the city. For, as Bohringer (1979) observes, the weakness of Fontenrose 1968 is that Fontenrose's typology obscures rather than clarifies why some victors become heroes and others do not. Bohringer suggests that we focus instead on the needs of the individual poleis, where, he observes, victors become heroes under conditions of civic crisis. I would translate Bohringer's interpretation into an economics of *kudos*: originally rejected, these rogue victors retain the charisma of victory for themselves. In these cases, we see the dangerous side of *kudos* when it is not properly channeled and controlled. Only later, under conditions of great danger to the city, does the polis attempt to appropriate the *kudos* of the rejected victor by making him into a cult hero.

[26]Notice the parallel usage of *kudos* in Homer, where Nestor, Agamemnon, and Odysseus are called the "*kudos* of the Achaians" (*Iliad* 9.673, 10.87, 544, 555, 11.511, 14.42, *Odyssey* 3.79, 202, 12.184). On this expression, see Benveniste 1973.353.

[27]Thus I do not accept the interpretation of Nisetich 1975.63–64 (following Gildersleeve 1890.339), that στεφάνωμα is *appositio ad sententiam*, designating the whole process of announcement and celebratory song as a crown.

Τελεσικράτη Χαρίτεσσι γεγωνεῖν
ὄλβιον ἄνδρα διωξίππου στεφάνωμα Κυράνας·

(P.9.1–4)

I wish, heralding the bronze-shielded Pythian victor Telesikrates together
with the deep-girdled Graces, to sing of [this] fortunate man, crown of
Kyrene.

The poet's intent in all these passages is to make the entire polis feel
that it participates in the victory won. And within the same poems,
Pindar reaps the benefits for the victor of these acts of inclusion. Thus
the closing injunction of Nemean 2 is directed to Timodemos' fellow
citizens, urging them to give him a proper festive reception: Διὸς
ἀγῶνι. τόν, ὦ πολῖται, κωμάξατε Τιμοδήμῳ σὺν εὐκλέι νόστῳ ("Celebrate Zeus, O citizens, in the kōmos together with the glorious return
for Timodemos" [N.2.24]). In Pythian 9, the poet conjures directly
with the possibility of hostility in a civic context, pleading on the
victor's behalf:

οὕνεκεν, εἰ φίλος ἀστῶν, εἴ τις ἀντάεις, τό γ' ἐν ξυνῷ πεπονναμένον εὖ
μὴ λόγον βλάπτων ἁλίοιο γέροντος κρυπτέτω·
κεῖνος αἰνεῖν καὶ τὸν ἐχθρόν
παντὶ θυμῷ σύν τε δίκᾳ καλὰ ῥέζοντ' ἔννεπεν.

(P.9.93–96)

Therefore, whether someone of the citizens is a friend or an enemy, let
him not hide the thing well suffered in the common interest, thereby
harming the saying of the Old Man of the Sea. That one said to praise
even one's enemy with all one's spirit and with justice, when he has
accomplished noble things.

The project of the entire poem has been, in a sense, to convince Telesikrates' ἀστοί, his fellow citizens, that his victory is a "thing well suffered in the common interest" (ἐν ξυνῷ is important in this context).[28]

---

[28]For this reason I take πόλιν τάνδ(ε) in line 91 to refer to Kyrene, not Thebes (with
Fennell 1893.256, Bundy 1962.21 n. 48, 23 n. 53, Burton 1962.53–54, Fränkel 1973.444,
Miller 1981.140; contra Wilamowitz 1922.265, Farnell 1930.2.201, Rose 1931.159,
Bowra 1964.143–144, and Peron 1976.71–72). The poet designates three of Telesikrates'
victories by saying "I have glorified this (his) city three times." I believe this is the only
way to explain the connective οὕνεκεν in line 93, for Pindar has just represented
Telesikrates' victories as a "common good" for his city and now says, "Therefore abide
by the saying of the Old Man of the Sea."

Asserting these things here, the poet goes on to say that even the victor's enemy within the city (for that is the implication of εἴ τις ἀντάεις, according to the extent of τὸ ξυνόν), should praise him wholeheartedly for his "noble deeds." And finally in Isthmian 1 the poet asserts:

ὃς δ' ἀμφ' ἀέθλοις ἢ πολεμίζων ἄρηται κῦδος ἁβρόν,
εὐαγορηθεὶς κέρδος ὕψιστον δέκεται, πολιατᾶν καὶ ξένων γλώσσας
    ἄωτον.

(I. 1. 50–51)

But whoever wins luxurious *kudos* in contests or in war, by being well spoken of he receives the highest profit, the peak of the tongue of citizens and strangers.

Linking contests with war implies that such a man wins *kudos* on behalf of his city, since no one wars for himself. Whoever wins such *kudos* shares it to gain universal good repute. The city "receives" the *kudos* (O.5.3, O.5.7, P.12.5) and the individual "receives" praise from everyone, but first and foremost from his fellow citizens. As in Pythian 9, the generalizing condition here indicates to the victor's fellow citizens the proper response to his achievement represented as a common good.[29]

Pindar's rhetoric serves the individual's interests by defusing the *phthonos* of his fellow citizens, but the poet is also very conscious of the city's point of view—of its distrust of *megaloprepeia* as an avenue to tyranny. The other side of the poet's project to reintegrate his patron is his attempt to allay the city's fears by insisting that the victor will not aim too high. This is the concrete political context that often underlies Pindar's denunciations of *koros* and *hybris*; the rejection of these qualities almost inevitably occurs in contexts that treat *megaloprepeia* within a civic frame. On occasion, the poet justifies his praise of the victor in positive terms:

ἐπεί νιν αἰνέω, μάλα μὲν τροφαῖς ἑτοῖμον ἵππων,
χαίροντά τε ξενίαις πανδόκοις,
καὶ πρὸς Ἡσυχίαν φιλόπολιν καθαρᾷ γνώμᾳ τετραμμένον.

(O.4.14–16)

[May the god be kind to his future prayers,] since I praise him as one very

---

[29]I shall return to the implications of the imagery of profit in these lines in Chapter 9.

ready [to spend] on *hippotrophiai* and rejoicing in acts of hospitality which receive all, and turned toward city-loving Hēsychia with pure intent.

The first two lines praise his activity in two typical spheres of *megaloprepeia*, horse breeding and *xenia*; then the third line immediately asserts that he aims at nothing dangerous to the city by this munificence. Rather, he is "turned toward city-loving Hēsychia with pure intent." Hēsychia in this context, as her epithet makes clear, represents harmonious peace among the citizens, as the opposite of *stasis*, and this is the ideal to which, the poet tells us, Psaumis is devoted.[30] We should pay particular attention to τετραμμένον, with the imagery of turning or curbing one's own interests which it implies, for such concrete images of restraint repeatedly recur in similar contexts.

Pindar can express the same sentiment in terms of the *koros* or *hybris* the victor avoids. Thus he generalizes at the opening of Isthmian 3:

> Εἴ τις ἀνδρῶν εὐτυχήσαις ἢ σὺν εὐδόξοις ἀέθλοις
> ἢ σθένει πλούτου κατέχει φρασὶν αἰανῆ κόρον,
> ἄξιος εὐλογίαις ἀστῶν μεμίχθαι.
>
> (I.3.1–3)

> If a man who is fortunate either in glorious athletic contests or by strength of wealth restrains dread ambition in his wits, he deserves to be mixed with the praises of his fellow citizens.

"Glorious athletic contests" (εὐδόξοις ἀέθλοις) and "strength of wealth" (σθένει πλούτου) characterize, respectively, the specific and general categories of the victor's *megaloprepeia*, whereas κατέχει φρασὶν αἰανῆ κόρον seems almost an apotropaic reflex to protect his success from the suspicion of tyrannical aspirations. Again the language of restraint is prominent: he bridles insolence within his wits.[31] The last

[30]It may be for very similar reasons that Pindar invokes Hēsychia at the opening of Pythian 8: as "daughter of Justice who makes cities greatest," she is asked to "receive the Pythian victory honor for Aristomenes." Her reception of the victor home denotes in a single ritual gesture his proper reintegration in his polis. On *hēsychia* in Pindar, see Burton 1962.175–176, Slater 1981, and Dickie 1984.

[31]The use of ἔχω compounds to describe bridling or restraint goes back at least to Hesiod, who says of the silver race, ὕβριν γὰρ ἀτάσθαλον οὐκ ἐδύναντο / ἀλλήλων ἀπέχειν ("For they were unable to keep reckless *hybris* away from each other" [*Works & Days* 134–135]). It is no accident that the nearest parallels for this use of κατέχω come from the elegies of Solon in which he warns the citizens against the prospect of tyranny (fr. 4W.9 and fr. 9W.5). The use of κατέχω in contexts of civic restraint is continued by Thucydides at 2.65.8 and 8.86.5 (of an orator restraining the people of democratic Athens; see Edmunds and Martin 1977.191).

line finally makes clear the audience to whom these remarks are addressed: the ἀστοί, the victor's fellow citizens, who are admonished to praise the victor for his combination of munificence and self-restraint.

At the end of Olympian 7 Pindar prays to Zeus for the victor and his house within their city, and justifies his wishes for them thus:

δίδοι τέ οἱ αἰδοίαν χάριν
καὶ ποτ᾽ ἀστῶν καὶ ποτὶ ξείνων. ἐπεὶ ὕβριος ἐχθρὰν ὁδόν
εὐθυπορεῖ,

(O.7.89–91)

And grant to him reverent grace both from citizens and strangers. Since he goes straight along the road hateful to *hybris*.

The reason the victor deserves "reverent grace" (αἰδοία χάρις) from his fellow citizens as well as strangers is that he "goes straight along the road hateful to *hybris*." "From citizens and strangers" is, as Bundy recognized, a universalizing doublet. Yet it seems significant that the victor's fellow citizens figure first in Pindar's division of the world, especially conjoined with the mention of αἰδοία χάρις. This phrase may remind us of the request for the *charis* of one's fellow citizens by the defendant in the lawcourts in the context of *megaloprepeia*. This coincidence of themes suggests that the rejection of *hybris* occurs here in an essentially political context.[32]

Again in Isthmian 4 the poet tells us "the Kleonymidai have always bloomed with achievements":

τοὶ μὲν ὦν Θήβαισι τιμάεντες ἀρχᾶθεν λέγονται
πρόξενοί τ᾽ ἀμφικτιόνων κελαδεννᾶς τ᾽ ὀρφανοί
ὕβριος·

(I.4.7–9)

It is said that they were honored from the beginning in Thebes, as *proxenoi* of the dwellers-around and bereft of sounding *hybris*.

They have been "honored from the beginning in Thebes"—that is, they are an old aristocratic family with a great deal of prestige in their city. Their status derives at least partly from their activities as *proxenoi* of the

[32]On universalizing doublets, see Bundy 1962.24–26 and, on this passage in particular, 67. Stoddart 1990.18 also takes this to be a political passage. On forensic *charis*, see Davies 1981.93–97 and Ober 1989.226–233, 241–247. The phrase also has old associations with αἰδώς in contexts of public speaking within a community (see Martin 1984.45 n. 35 on *Odyssey* 8.169–175 and *Theogony* 79–93).

neighboring peoples, a typical forum for aristocratic munificence. But the poet goes on immediately to assure us that they would never take advantage of their prestige in Thebes to reach too high: they are also "bereft of sounding *hybris*."

The clear implications of such contexts can, in turn, clarify passages in which the poet's language is more elliptical. In Isthmian 5 Pindar says,

> σὺν Χάρισιν δ' ἔμολον Λάμπωνος υἱοῖς
> τάνδ' ἐς εὔνομον πόλιν. εἰ δὲ τέτραπται
> θεοδότων ἔργων κέλευθον ἂν καθαράν,
> μὴ φθόνει κόμπον τὸν ἐοικότ' ἀοιδᾷ
> κιρνάμεν ἀντὶ πόνων.

(I.5.21–25)

Together with the Graces I have come to this well-ordered city for the sons of Lampon. And if a man is turned along the pure road of god-given deeds, do not begrudge to mix a fitting boast in song in exchange for toils.

"If a man is turned along the pure road of god-given deeds" signifies more in this context than mere athletic success. Pindar's language here seems to be generated by εὔνομον πόλιν ("this well-ordered city").[33] This phrase sets the discourse within a political context and colors the generalizing εἰ clause that follows. Thus we recognize τέτραπται and καθαράν as the language of civic self-restraint (cf. O.4.16); the protasis refers, then, to the man who combines success with the proper (anti-hybristic) attitude within the polis. This allusion to civic virtue, in turn, makes more pointed the poet's admonition μὴ φθόνει ("Do not begrudge to mix," but also absolutely, "Do not envy"). In the apodosis, Pindar urges himself to praise without envy in order to act as a model of behavior for the victor's fellow citizens.

A near parallel that supports this reading is Nemean 11.13–17:

> εἰ δέ τις ὄλβον ἔχων μορφᾷ παραμεύσεται ἄλλους,
> ἔν τ' ἀέθλοισιν ἀριστεύων ἐπέδειξεν βίαν,
> θνατὰ μεμνάσθω περιστέλλων μέλη,
> καὶ τελευτὰν ἀπάντων γᾶν ἐπιεσσόμενος.
> ἐν λόγοις δ' ἀστῶν ἀγαθοῖσιν ἐπαινεῖσθαι χρεών,

[33]Εὔνομος in this context seems to be a highly charged political catchphrase. Cf. Solon fr. 4W.32–39 on εὐνομία.

If a man who has prosperity surpasses others in form and has shown his
might by winning in contests, let him remember that he clothes mortal
limbs and that he will wear earth as his last of all garments. But he ought
to be praised in the good words of his fellow citizens.

Here we have first the generalizing εἰ clause describing the victor's areas
of superiority; then the poet frames his denunciation of *hybris* as an
admonition to "remember that he clothes mortal limbs." At this point
line 17 makes clear Pindar's implied audience: if Aristagoras demonstrates such excellence with the proper attitude, he deserves to be
praised by his *fellow citizens*.

In the final praise of Lampon which closes Isthmian 6, Pindar offers
us a fuller version of all the same themes, in a perfect picture of the
uneasy cooperation of *oikos* and polis in the "virtue" of *megaloprepeia*.
He begins with the entire family:

τόν τε Θεμιστίου ὀρθώσαντες οἶκον τάνδε πόλιν
θεοφιλῆ ναίοισι· Λάμπων δὲ μελέταν
ἔργοις ὀπάζων Ἡσιόδου μάλα τιμᾷ τοῦτ᾽ ἔπος,
υἱοῖσί τε φράζων παραινεῖ,
ξυνὸν ἄστει κόσμον ἑῷ προσάγων·
καὶ ξένων εὐεργεσίαις ἀγαπᾶται,
μέτρα μὲν γνώμᾳ διώκων, μέτρα δὲ καὶ κατέχων·
γλῶσσα δ᾽ οὐκ ἔξω φρενῶν· φαίης κέ νιν ἄνδρ᾽ ἐν ἀεθληταῖσιν ἔμμεν
Ναξίαν πέτραις ἐν ἄλλαις χαλκοδάμαντ᾽ ἀκόναν.

(I.6.65–73)

And having set upright the house of Themistios, they inhabit this city
dear to the gods. And Lampon, bestowing attention on his works, very
much honors this word of Hesiod and, declaring [it] to his sons, gives
them advice, thereby leading forth a common ornament for his city. And
he is loved for his benefactions to strangers, pursuing measured things in
his intent and restraining [others] so that they are measured. And his
tongue does not outrun his mind—as a man among athletes, you would
call him a Naxian whetstone, which masters bronze among other stones.

The juxtaposition of οἶκον and τάνδε πόλιν in line 65 is significant: the
poet wants to imply by the collocation that the interests of *oikos* and
polis converge in the actions of the sons of Lampon. Once he has
mentioned the city, Pindar proceeds with an essentially political discourse on the positive and negative aspects of aristocratic munificence.
We recognize that *megaloprepeia* is the theme already at line 69, where

Lampon "leads forth a common ornament (ξυνὸν . . . κόσμον) for his city." Here again, the theme of munificence generates the concrete imagery of *anathemata*.[34] The poet goes on to mention two typical objects of aristocratic expenditure: the hosting of foreigners (70) and the support of his sons' athletic activities (72–73). But set right in the middle of this positive catalog of *megaloprepeia*, as if generated by it as a reflex, is a rejection of excessive ambition (71–72). Lampon, the poet assures us, pursues "measured things in his intent" and restrains "others so that they are measured." Κατέχων recalls the language of curbing or restraint in a similar context in Isthmian 3.

All these passages show us denunciations of *hybris* or *koros* in contexts that situate the victor's *megaloprepeia* within a civic frame. But none of them makes explicit the nature of the political excess the poet rejects so vehemently: what right have we, then, to read the fear of tyranny into such passages? Pythian 11 gives us a clear answer, for it is a poem largely devoted to the rejection of the tyrant's lot. In this ode, Pindar has thematized the rejection of tyranny to the extent that it governs the choice of the myth—the disastrous doings of the house of Atreus. As D. C. Young observes in his essay on Pythian 11, "We may now understand why Pindar took such pains to use this myth, despite its being formally somewhat inconvenient. Far from being irrelevant, the myth perfectly and vividly describes with concrete examples the anxious, λυπηρός life which offers brilliant and frightening foil for the moderate, pleasurable life attributed to Thrasydaios and commended in vv. 50b–58. The relevance of the myth, then . . . is precisely what has caused such consternation: there is nothing in the myth which pertains to Thrasydaios or to his kind. That is the point." Young goes on to assert, quite rightly, "If we are to understand Pythian 11, we must understand why the topos [of the rejection of tyranny] is applied to Thrasydaios, how the treatment of the topos relates to the poem as a whole, and why, indeed, the topos assumes such importance that it apparently even dictates the choice of the myth."[35]

It is in answering these questions that Young's interpretation falls short, for he fails to take account of *megaloprepeia* as an element in the system. Instead, as a shortcut in the argument, he quotes the wish of Euripides' Hippolytus to be "first at the great games, second in the city" (*Hippolytus* 1016–1017), and points to this as the ultimate connection of

[34]Note the emphatic ξυνόν, as in the phrase ξυνὸν ὀρθῶσαι καλόν (used of the poet) at I.1.46.
[35]Young 1968.17.

thought generating the use of the topos in Pythian 11.[36] But from our perspective, it is clear that athletic victory and tyranny form a natural contrast because the former is the product of *megaloprepeia*, the latter its frequently suspected goal. In this sense, the myth is not as irrelevant to Thrasydaios as Young would have it: the suspicion of tyrannical aspirations is rather the specter that haunts the athletic successes of his family until it is resolutely exorcised by the poet. Thus, it is the mention of the three victories of Thrasydaios' house which sets off the myth (11–14), and thus, as Young observes,[37] the "central, pivoting point of the myth" is the gnomic cluster

> κακολόγοι δὲ πολῖται.
> ἴσχει τε γὰρ ὄλβος οὐ μείονα φθόνον·
> ὁ δὲ χαμηλὰ πνέων ἄφαντον βρέμει.
>
> (P.11.28–30)

But the citizens speak evilly, for prosperity brings with it the same degree of envy [lit. no less envy], but the one with lowly aspirations roars in obscurity.

The moral lesson—that the lot of tyrants is not really enviable—could not be clearer.[38]

Further, as Young cogently argues, Pindar takes up the same theme again in the first-person statements of lines 50b–58, which, like the myth itself, seem to be directly inspired by the mention of the family's successes in lines 43–50. It is noteworthy that although the current victor is a runner, chariot racing seems to be the traditional family sport (P.11.46–48). Given the association of *hippotrophia* with tyranny, it is tempting to suggest that it is partly this family pastime that inspires Pindar's extensive rejection of tyranny in this poem. However that may be, at the end of the victory catalog Pindar speaks in the "generalized first person," defined by Young as the "well-known Pindaric use of ἐγώ whereby general commendations, often applicable to everyone but

[36]Young 1968.17–22.
[37]Young 1968.4.
[38]Thus, I cannot agree with Slater that this gnomic cluster represents "a whole series of mental stepping stones" with "practically nothing to do with the rest of the myth, and nothing at all to do with the main point of the myth" (Slater 1979b.66). Slater makes this claim because he finds the *Grundgedanke* of Pythian 11 (and the connection of the myth to the victor) in *xenia* (note the repeated ξένου [16] and ξένον [34] at the beginning and end of the myth [Slater 1979b.66–68]). Slater's point is well taken. *Xenia* is an element here, but it is not the only element, for it does not account at all for lines 50–58.

usually specifically applicable to the victor, are cast in statements made
in the first person singular."³⁹ This generalized first-person statement
deserves our close attention, for it combines in a single context all the
themes we have been tracing:

> θεόθεν ἐραίμαν καλῶν,
> δυνατὰ μαιόμενος ἐν ἁλικίᾳ.
> τῶν γὰρ ἀνὰ πόλιν εὑρίσκων τὰ μέσα μακροτέρῳ
> ⟨σὺν⟩ ὄλβῳ τεθαλότα, μέμφομ᾽ αἶσαν τυραννίδων·
> ξυναῖσι δ᾽ ἀμφ᾽ ἀρεταῖς τέταμαι· φθονεροὶ δ᾽ ἀμύνονται
> ⟨-⟩ εἴ τις ἄκρον ἑλὼν ἡσυχᾷ τε νεμόμενος αἰνὰν ὕβριν
> ἀπέφυγεν, μέλανος ⟨δ᾽⟩ ἂν ἐσχατιὰν
> καλλίονα θανάτου ⟨στείχοι⟩ γλυκυτάτᾳ γενεᾷ
> εὐώνυμον κτεάνων κρατίσταν χάριν πορών·

(P. 11.50–58)⁴⁰

May I desire noble things from the gods, striving for things that are
possible for my age. For finding that the middle position of those in the
city blooms with longer prosperity, I blame the lot of tyrannies. And I am
strained over common achievements, and the envious are fended off [. . .]
if a man who has taken the highest peak [of achievement], dwelling in
peace, flees dread *hybris*. And he would go to a better end of black death,
since he has granted to his sweetest offspring the grace of a good name as
the best of possessions.

The first two lines are a general statement of human limitation, focused
by the phrase ἀνὰ πόλιν specifically on the civic sphere. Within the city,
the generalized "I," "finding that the middle position . . . blooms with
longer prosperity," rejects the lot of tyranny.⁴¹ This is a clear message to
the victor's fellow citizens about his attitude: the family has no designs
on rule within the city, despite its conspicuous expenditure on horse
racing and athletics in general.

³⁹Young 1968.12, and see also 15 and 17, and Young 1971.10–11.
⁴⁰The text is mainly that of the eighth edition of the Teubner (ed. B. Snell and H. Maehler), but with slight changes in punctuation: no period after ἀμύνονται, and no conjecture offered to provide an extra syllable in line 55. My reading of these lines mainly agrees with Young 1968.9–16 and 21, though in considering the theme of *megaloprepeia*, I suggest some divergent interpretations.
⁴¹Connor's observation that in archaic Greek literature, tyranny is viewed negatively from the point of view of the city and its citizens but often positively from the point of view of the tyrant (Connor 1977.98–104) is significant for this context, for it supports the claim that Pindar's rhetoric in such passages is aimed at the civic community and the victor's integration therein. It is this civic context throughout Pythian 11 which probably explains the Solonian echoes J. K. Newman detects in the ode (Newman 1982.189–195).

The poet continues, "I am strained over common achievements," setting up a contrast to the tyrannical aspirations he has just rejected. In this context, ξυναῖσι δ' ἀμφ' ἀρεταῖς τέταμαι must be a positive reference to *megaloprepeia*. The use of the perfect medio-passive of τείνω, "I am strained," together with ξυναῖσι, recalls other *megaloprepeia* contexts in which the poet emphasizes effort by the city or on its behalf. As we saw in Olympian 4, Psaumis is described as "eager to rouse *kudos* for Kamarina" (κῦδος ὄρσαι σπεύδει Καμαρίνᾳ [O.4.12]), whereas in Nemean 5 the poet declares, "I rejoice because the entire city is striving for noble things" (χαίρω δ' ὅτι ἐσλοῖσι μάρναται πέρι πᾶσα πόλις [N.5.47]). We should also recall the language Aristotle uses to define the proper objects of expenditure: "everything for which the entire city is zealously striving, or [at least] those citizens of stature" (καὶ εἰ περί τι ἡ πᾶσα πόλις σπουδάζει ἢ οἱ ἐν ἀξιώματι [*Nich. Ethics* 1123a1–2]). These semantic parallels suggest that ξυναὶ ἀρεταί represent the effort and conspicuous expenditures members of the aristocratic elite are expected to make on behalf of the city.[42] By opting for such "common achievements" in the generalized first person, the poet commends the victor's lifestyle and implies that his victory benefits the whole city.

Of the last four lines Young observes: "The passage obviously recounts the fruits of the life recommended in the preceding verses. Jealousy is held at bay, if a man obtains the summit (ἄκρον ἑλών is definitely, though not exclusively, a description of athletic victory) but conducts himself peaceably (the noun, ἡσυχία, is the opposite of στάσις, the tool of the prospective tyrant and constant fear of the successful one) and avoids ὕβρις; he may then bequeath to his children the finest of κτέανα, a famous but good (not infamous, like that of the tyrant) name."[43] Like Young, I take φθονεροὶ δ' ἀμύνονται as one

---

[42]On this phrase I must diverge from Young's interpretation (1968.16), which explains line 54: "Similarly, *Ion* 625f. ought to solve the problem of ξυναῖσι ἀρεταῖς (Py. 11,54), as δημότης recalls ξυναῖσι and shows that those who reject the extreme political position, monarchy, may present, as a corollary, their conformity and devotion to the public good, through mere common citizenship." But "mere common citizenship" seems inadequate to explain the strong language of ξυναῖσι δ' ἀμφ' ἀρεταῖς τέταμαι. Bundy is closer to the mark when he takes this whole passage as the "liberality motif" and glosses ξυναὶ ἀρεταί as εὐεργεσίαι (Bundy 1962.86 with n. 117, on which see Young 1968.14 n. 3; recall the close connection of liberality with *megaloprepeia*). Bundy's interpretation falls short, however, in ignoring the political aspect of the topos, for he glosses αἶσαν τυραννίδων merely as πλουτεῖν. Combining the interpretations of Bundy and Young very closely approximates the reading I am suggesting—understanding *megaloprepeia* and the political tensions inherent in it as the shaping theme in these lines.
[43]Young 1968.21.

apodosis of the generalizing εἰ clause that follows. Although this interpretation requires the very rare passive use of ἀμύνονται, I think that the parallel passages—Isthmian 3.1–3, Isthmian 5.21–25, and (with slight variation) Nemean 11.13–17—militate for this reading.[44] Just as in these three examples, Pythian 11 has a generalizing εἰ clause whose substance is "If a man wins athletic victories *and* shows self-restraint within the polis"; it also has an apodosis that banishes the envy of the victor's fellow citizens under such conditions. All four passages occur in contexts where *megaloprepeia* is one of the elements under consideration, though only in Pythian 11 is this theme explicitly combined with that of tyranny. Yet it is significant for our understanding of all these passages that in this context, tyranny is implicitly equated with αἰνὴ ὕβρις and opposed to ἡσυχᾷ . . . νεμόμενος. This association suggests that the rejection of tyranny also informs Olympian 4.16 ('Ησυχίαν φιλόπολιν . . . τετραμμένον), Isthmian 3.2 (κατέχει φρασὶν αἰανῆ κόρον), Olympian 7.90 (ὕβριος ἐχθρὰν ὁδὸν εὐθυπορεῖ), and Isthmian 4.8–9 (ὀρφανοὶ / ὕβριος). In all these contexts, then, *koros*, *hybris*, and *hēsychia* participate in a specifically political discourse. Much has been written about Pindar's profound religiosity and his keen sense of human limitations when confronted with the divine, transfiguring moment of victory. All this may be true, but the citation of the many passages in which the poet decries *hybris* does not demonstrate it, for in the epinikia *hybris* is not a religious sin but a political one.[45]

Thus Pindar's epinikia accommodate strategies of civic inclusion and the rejection of tyranny which assist the reintegration of the victor who is a private citizen. But what of tyrants and dynasts? If the contention is true that Pindar's rhetoric takes account of the victor's political status, we would expect a different set of strategies in victory odes written for monarchs, for as I observed in surveying *megaloprepeia*, if the private citizen's munificence lays him open to suspicions of tyrannical aims, the

[44]Jurenka 1893.20 notes only one other occurrence of ἀμύνομαι used as a passive, in Plato *Laws* 845c3. Gildersleeve (1890.363), Thummer (1957.112), Slater (1969a, s.v. ἀμύνω), and Peron (1986.15–16), along with Young, take it as passive (though Gildersleeve and Thummer read a somewhat different text).

[45]For the traditional view of *hybris* in Pindar, see Bowra 1964.80–82 and Dickie 1984. For other political uses of *hybris*, see O.13.10, P.1.72, P.4.112, P.8.12. The same claim might also be made of those passages in which Pindar enjoins the victor, "Do not seek to become a god" (O.5.24, I.5.14), since these occur in the vicinity of explicitly political statements (and cf. N.11.13–17). For complementary discussions of the nature of *hybris* in other Greek authors, see MacDowell 1976, Fisher 1976 and 1979, Ober 1989.208–212.

converse is also true: the king or tyrant is considered the consummate *megaloprepēs*. This common Greek assumption does indeed find its reflection in the rhetoric of epinikion, where there is a marked difference in tone and content in the poems addressed to rulers. No limits are placed on their expenditure and the boasts it engenders. For example, in Pythian 2 Pindar declares proudly:

> εἰ δέ τις
> ἤδη κτεάτεσσί τε καὶ περὶ τιμᾷ λέγει
> ἕτερόν τιν' ἀν' Ἑλλάδα τῶν πάροιθε γενέσθαι ὑπέρτερον,
> χαύνᾳ πραπίδι παλαιμονεῖ κενεά.
>
> (P.2.58–61)

If anyone claims that any other man throughout Greece of those before is superior in possessions and in honor, he wrestles empty things with an idle thought.

Pindar's unqualified boast is paralleled by the language of Bacchylides 3, written for the same monarch:

> ὅσοι ⟨γε⟩ μὲν Ἑλλάδ' ἔχουσιν, οὔτις,
> ὦ μεγαίνητε Ἱέρων, θελήσει
> φάμεν σέο πλείονα χρυσὸν
> Λοξίᾳ πέμψαι βροτῶν.
>
> (Bacch. 3.63–66)

However many men hold Greece, no one of mortals, O greatly praised Hieron, will wish to say that he has sent more gold to Loxias than you have.

Some earlier lines make the connection between monarchy and munificence even clearer:

> ἆ τρισευδαίμων ἀνήρ,
> ὃς παρὰ Ζηνὸς λαχὼν
> πλείσταρχον Ἑλλάνων γέρας
> οἶδε πυργωθέντα πλοῦτον μὴ μελαμ-
> φαρέϊ κρύπτειν σκότῳ.
> βρύει μὲν ἱερὰ βουθύτοις ἑορταῖς,
> βρύουσι φιλοξενίας ἀγυιαί·
> λάμπει δ' ὑπὸ μαρμαρυγαῖς ὁ χρυσός,
>
> (Bacch. 3.10–17)

Ah, the thrice-blessed man, who has been allotted from Zeus the honor of ruling the most people of the Greeks—he knows not to hide his towered wealth in black-cloaked darkness. The temples teem with bull-sacrificing festivals, the streets teem with acts of hospitality, and gold shines with flashings.

In Pindar's poems for tyrants, no attempt is made to defuse the *phthonos* their success awakens; that they will be envied is taken for granted. In such odes, the enviers are mocked rather than mollified. Thus, again in Pythian 2, Pindar observes,

χρὴ δὲ πρὸς θεὸν οὐκ ἐρίζειν,
ὃς ἀνέχει τοτὲ μὲν τὰ κείνων, τότ' αὖθ' ἑτέροις ἔδωκεν μέγα κῦδος.
  ἀλλ' οὐδὲ ταῦτα νόον
ἰαίνει φθονερῶν· στάθμας δέ τινος ἑλκόμενοι
περισσᾶς ἐνέπαξαν ἕλκος ὀδυναρὸν ἑᾷ πρόσθε καρδίᾳ,
πρὶν ὅσα φροντίδι μητίονται τυχεῖν.

(P.2.88–92)

But a man must not fight against the god, who sometimes supports the affairs of one group of men and, at other times in turn, bestows great *kudos* on others. But not even these things cheer the mind of the envious, but by plucking at a very long plumbline, they fix a grievous wound in their own heart, before they achieve what they have plotted in their wits.[46]

If there is danger of *koros* in such contexts, it is not the tyrant's danger but the poet's: the laudator fears that his praises will cause satiety in his audience long before he approximates the tyrant's virtues. Thus at the end of Olympian 2:

αὐδάσομαι ἐνόρκιον λόγον ἀλαθεῖ νόῳ,
τεκεῖν μή τιν' ἑκατόν γε ἐτέων πόλιν φίλοις ἄνδρα μᾶλλον
εὐεργέταν πραπίσιν ἀφθονέστερόν τε χέρα
Θήρωνος. ἀλλ' αἶνον ἐπέβα κόρος
οὐ δίκᾳ συναντόμενος, ἀλλὰ μάργων ὑπ' ἀνδρῶν
τὸ λαλαγῆσαι θέλον κρυφὸν τιθέμεν ἐσλῶν καλοῖς
ἔργοις· ἐπεὶ ψάμμος ἀριθμὸν περιπέφευγεν,
καὶ κεῖνος ὅσα χάρματ' ἄλλοις ἔθηκεν,
τίς ἂν φράσαι δύναιτο;

(O.2.92–100)

[46]In translating these lines, I follow the interpretation of Most 1987.571–584, including his restoration of the MSS' τινος for Snell and Maehler's τινες.

I shall declare a word under oath with true thought—that for a hundred years the city has produced no man more beneficent in spirit and more generous in hand than Theron. But satiety that does not meet with justice mounts upon praise, while babbling by intemperate men wishes to conceal the good deeds of noble men. Just as sand escapes number, so also however many joys that man has made for others—who could tell?

Fear of *koros* in the aesthetic realm dictates the limit of Pindar's poem. Theron's kindnesses, like the sands of the sea, remain unnumbered, and the poem ends with the aporetic query, Who could tell them? The same is true in Pythian 1, where the poet admonishes himself:

καιρὸν εἰ φθέγξαιο, πολλῶν πείρατα συντανύσαις
ἐν βραχεῖ, μείων ἕπεται μῶμος ἀνθρώπων· ἀπὸ γὰρ κόρος ἀμβλύνει
αἰανὴς ταχείας ἐλπίδας,
ἀστῶν δ' ἀκοὰ κρύφιον θυμὸν βαρύνει μάλιστ' ἐσλοῖσιν ἐπ'
    ἀλλοτρίοις.
ἀλλ' ὅμως, κρέσσον γὰρ οἰκτιρμοῦ φθόνος,
μὴ παρίει καλά.

(P.1.81–86)

If you should speak opportunely, drawing together the limits of many things in a short compass, less blame of men attends. For dread *koros* blunts swift hopes and the saying of the citizens burdens a hidden spirit, most of all for other men's goods. But still, since envy is better than pity, do not pass by noble things.

Here, the poet wishes to "speak καιρός, drawing together the limits of many things in a short compass," in order to avoid the censure that arises from satiety in his audience. In the end, though, he resigns himself to the muttering of the citizens over another man's goods and accepts *phthonos* as a necessary evil attendant on the tyrant's success. In the admonition to Hieron with which he closes, the poet recommends just the opposite behavior from his own: the poet must limit his praise to avoid *koros*, but the tyrant is urged to go all out in his pursuit of *kala* and his expenditures (86–94). Pindar's reason for this directive—that "envy is better than pity"—is a sentiment frequently excerpted to illustrate the values of the poet and his aristocratic audience, but in fact, it would be unimaginable in a poem commissioned by a private citizen.[47]

[47]See, for example, Adkins 1972.77. On the other hand, Fränkel 1968.67–68 n. 3 sees in Pindar's phrase the fixed political jargon of the tyrants, for the very same sentiment (in very similar words) occurs in Herodotus' tale of Periander and his son Lykophron.

The difference in rhetorical strategies used for private citizens and tyrants may help in turn to solve a problem of chronology. There has been much scholarly debate about the relative dating of Isthmian 2, a poem commissioned for Xenokrates, whose brother, Theron, was tyrant of Akragas. Was the poem composed before or after the death of Theron and the fall of the Emmenidai in 472? The traditional scholarly position was that the poem postdated the family's fall from power both because Theron never appears in the ode and because Pindar was taken to be "hint[ing] at political difficulties facing the surviving Emmenidai" in his remarks about envy in lines 43–44.[48] More recently, the traditional dating has been challenged on the grounds that the mention of *phthonos* is a conventional epinikian topos, not a reference to the current political situation. Those who reject the old dating prefer to locate the poem's composition sometime between 476 (the date of Theron's Olympic victory) and 472 (the date of Theron's death).[49]

The revisionists are right to insist that *phthonos* is an epinikian topos, but, as we have seen, the topos takes one form in poems for private individuals and another in those for tyrants. Furthermore, Isthmian 2 contains other topoi that vary in form based on the status of the patron and his family. What is odd about the poem is that it seems to combine the rhetoric generally used for private individuals with that for tyrants. This anomalous mixture of styles suggests that the family has undergone a change in status and that Pindar is adapting his panoply of topoi to accommodate a unique situation.[50]

Yet Pindar's use of different registers is just the opposite of what we might expect. First, the poet praises the virtues of the victor Xenokrates, now dead:

> μακρὰ δισκήσαις ἀκοντίσσαιμι τοσοῦθ', ὅσον ὀργάν
> Ξεινοκράτης ὑπὲρ ἀνθρώπων γλυκεῖαν

Encouraging his son to take over the tyranny, Periander tells him, σὺ δὲ μαθὼν ὅσῳ φθονέεσθαι κρέσσον ἐστὶ ἢ οἰκτίρεσθαι ("But you have learned by how much it is better to be envied than pitied" [Herodotus 3.52.5]). See also Fränkel 1973.460.

[48]Wilamowitz 1922.310–311, Norwood 1945.152, and Bowra 1964.124–125, 410 date Isthmian 2 after the fall of the Emmenidai. Woodbury (1968.527–528 with n. 2, from which the quotation is taken) presents the arguments on both sides.

[49]Von der Mühll 1964.170, followed by Pavese 1966.103–104 and Nisetich 1977a.146.

[50]Nisetich (1977a) also finds in I.2 the adaptation of conventional topoi to a unique situation, which he takes to be the death of the patron between the commission and the performance of the ode. But this interpretation does not account for the specifically political anomalies of lines 35–40 and 43–45. For further discussion of I.2, see Chapter 10.

ἔσχεν. αἰδοῖος μὲν ἦν ἀστοῖς ὁμιλεῖν,
ἱπποτροφίας τε νομίζων ἐν Πανελλάνων νόμῳ·
καὶ θεῶν δαῖτας προσέπτυκτο πάσας· οὐδέ ποτε ξενίαν
οὖρος ἐμπνεύσαις ὑπέστειλ᾿ ἱστίον ἀμφὶ τράπεζαν·

(I.2.35–40)

By throwing a long way I would cast the javelin as far as Xenokrates held his sweet temperament beyond [other] men. He was respectful in keeping company with his fellow citizens, even practicing *hippotrophia* according to the custom of all the Greeks. And he welcomed warmly all the feasts of the gods, and never did a favoring breeze blowing cause him to reef the sail [of his generosity] about a hospitable table.

These lines portray Xenokrates as a model private citizen, respectful to his fellow citizens. The use of αἰδοῖος in this context recalls the prayer for civic harmony at the close of Olympian 7: δίδοι τέ οἱ αἰδοίαν χάριν καὶ ποτ᾿ ἀστῶν ("And grant to him respectful grace from his fellow citizens" [O.7.90]). As Maurice Bowra recognized, Isthmian 2.37 is "a defence against any imputation that [Xenokrates] may have shared the tyrannical tendencies of his family."[51] Xenokrates also engaged in *hippotrophia* "according to the custom of all the Greeks" (but not beyond it), and spread an unstintingly generous table.

Pindar proceeds almost immediately to admonish Thrasyboulos, the victor's son:

μή νυν, ὅτι φθονεραὶ θνατῶν φρένας ἀμφικρέμανται ἐλπίδες,
μήτ᾿ ἀρετάν ποτε σιγάτω πατρῴαν,
μηδὲ τούσδ᾿ ὕμνους·

(I.2.43–45)

Do not now, because envious hopes hang round the wits of mortals, ever keep silent your father's achievement [or, your hereditary *aretē*] or these hymns.

Here again the poet inverts the usual rhetoric, for his response to envy in these lines is close to the tone of his advice to tyrants. In poems for private individuals the poet generally makes an effort to defuse the envy

[51]Bowra 1964.125. Contrast the diction of this passage with the praises of tyrants at O.1.10–17, 103–108, O.2.6–8, 92–95, and P.3.71. All these passages emphasize the tyrant's uniqueness—his extremities of achievement and expenditure—and his power over "the citizens" tempered by virtue. Αἰδοῖος in contrast characterizes not hierarchical relations but the reciprocal respect of equals.

of the victor's fellow citizens. In other passages if he does not mollify envy, the poet simply acknowledges its existence with pained resignation.[52] But nowhere else does Pindar admonish a private citizen to *flout* the envy of his fellows: such advice is reserved for tyrants. Yet what Thrasyboulos is not supposed to veil in silence is not his own *aretē* but his father's. Thus both modes of rhetoric ultimately focus on Xenokrates, in such a way that Pindar foregrounds the model of the ideal citizen and his dutiful son. The fact of tyranny slips discreetly into the gap between these two modes of rhetoric, leaving behind only Xenokrates' civic virtue and his son's courageous effort to commemorate it.

Epinikion, at least in Pindar's hands, turns out to be a tool finely calibrated for registering and accommodating the particular status of the victor within his civic community. For victors who are *idiōtai*, the poet subtly and skillfully includes the whole community both in the victory itself and in the poem that commemorates it. He also ministers to the concerns of the victor's fellow citizens, assuring them that athletic victory is not a stepping-stone to political domination for the victor and his family. Conversely, for those victors who are tyrants, the poet applies a rhetoric of extremes which suits the preeminent position and gestures of his patrons. Thus we might note that the "superlative vaunt," which "assert[s] the superiority of the subject over all others," occurs most frequently in the epinikia composed for tyrants.[53] The superlative vaunt is emblematic of the tyrants' own self-presentation. They wish to be perceived as more than mortal men, unique in power and wealth, and the poet presents them as such, adapting his political rhetoric to their pretensions.

[52]For the pose of pained resignation, see O.6.74, P.7 19, and N.8.21.
[53]For the term "superlative vaunt" and the definition, see Race 1987.138–139 with nn. 23 and 24. Of the six passages Race cites from Pindar (O.1.104, O.2.93–94, O.13.31, P.1.49, P.2.60, N.6.25), four come from odes for tyrants, one designates a house (rather than an individual) as "steward of more crowns [than any other house] in Greece," and the last describes a private victor who won the Olympic pentathlon and the stadion in a single day, "what no mortal before had yet attained." It is noteworthy that the superlative vaunts for private individuals describe unique athletic achievements, while those for tyrants designate the unequaled power, generosity, or wealth of the subject (cf. Herodotus' epitaph for Polykrates, 3.125.2).

CHAPTER 9

Visible and
Invisible Property

We have considered at some length Pindar's strategies for reintegrating different classes of victors into their communities. Yet, in spite of all the poet's rhetoric, there remain tremendous disincentives built into the system of *megaloprepeia* for private citizens. Besides those problems which Pindar himself addresses, of *phthonos* and the suspicion of tyranny, there are others: the feeling of compulsion Xenophon's Socrates evokes and the basic economic damage wrought by *megaloprepeia*. These are the problems that lead Xenophon's Socrates to tell the fabulously wealthy Kritoboulos that he pities him for his poverty, implying that Kritoboulos will be bled dry of his entire estate by the city and then resented for his inability to perform further liturgies (*Oec.* 2.1–8).

Given these disincentives, it is clear that some wealthy citizens of the polis opted out of the system of *megaloprepeia* altogether.[1] This could be done, quite simply, by making one's "visible property" "invisible." Visible property (φανερὰ οὐσία) and its opposite, invisible property (ἀφανὴς οὐσία), are very slippery terms, as Moses Finley observes: "The significant point is that it was always concrete factual considerations, not juristic principles or broad economic categories, that determined the distinctions drawn and the language used in a given situation. That is why the Greeks could so frequently talk of 'visible' and 'invisible' property, a distinction that was very fluid and by no means always

---

[1] I do not refer here to those who remained within the system but took legal measures to challenge a particular liturgy (though they offer additional proof for some of the problems inherent in the system). For the legal procedures of *skepsis* and *antidosis* involved, see MacDowell 1978.162–164.

equivalent to real property and personal property or to frozen and liquid assets. 'Visible' and 'invisible' are to be understood quite literally."[2] Φανερὰ οὐσία is that property which a man is known to possess, on the basis of which he can be assessed for liturgies. Invisible property is just the opposite—hidden or secret wealth that cannot be assessed, which puts its owner outside of the clear status hierarchy on which the system of liturgies depends.

As Finley notes, the most common context for the discussion of visible and invisible property in the speeches of the Attic orators is the assessment of liturgies: "Thus, in the catalogue of crimes and misdeeds that the orator Aeschines drew up against Timarchos, one, charged to his opponent's father, was that he had deliberately sold some of his holdings, thereby rendering that portion of his wealth invisible and escaping liturgies. With variations, this accusation appears over and over in the orators, and there is good reason to believe that it was not always mere libel."[3] On two occasions the orator Isaeus says quite explicitly that the motive for "making one's property invisible" is the avoidance of the liturgies the polis would otherwise require. Thus, in the eleventh speech of Isaeus, the speaker declares:

καταλογίζεται τοίνυν ὡς ἐγὼ τρεῖς κλήρους εἰληφὼς καὶ πολλῶν χρημάτων εὐπορῶν ἀφανίζω τὴν οὐσίαν, ἵν᾽ ὡς ἐλάχισθ᾽ ὑμεῖς αὐτῶν ἀπολαύητε. (Isaeus 11.47)

[My opponent] alleges that having gotten three inheritances and being well-off with much money, I make my property invisible in order that you enjoy the least possible benefit from these things.

The nature of the benefits the speaker alludes to is spelled out in another passage, where the claimant to an inheritance justifies his adoptive father's will. This man adopted him and left him all his property, he claims, because he knew him to be a man who would use that wealth honorably:

οὐδ᾽ αὖ ἀφιλότιμον, ὃς τὰ ὄντα ἀφανιεῖν ἔμελλον ὥσπερ οὗτοι τὰ τοῦ κλήρου πεποιήκασιν, ἀλλὰ βουλησόμενον καὶ τριηραρχεῖν καὶ πολε-

---

[2]Finley 1952.54. See also Gernet 1981b.343–348, Gabrielson 1986.
[3]Finley 1952.54–55. Most of our evidence for invisible property comes from the fourth-century Attic orators, but as Gabrielson (1986.104–105) observes, jokes about making one's property invisible in Old Comedy suggest that the practice was also well known to fifth-century audiences (cf. Aristophanes *Frogs* 1065–1068, *Eccles.* 601–603).

μεῖν καὶ χορηγεῖν καὶ πάνθ' ὑμῖν τὰ προσταττομένα ποιεῖν, ὥσπερ
κἀκεῖνος. (Isaeus 7.35.3)[4]

[He knew me] to be a man not unambitious in public service, not the sort
who would make his property invisible, just as these have done with their
allotment. But he knew that I would willingly act as trierarch and participate in war and produce choruses and do for you all the things commanded, just as he had done.

As a tool to help us understand the implications of visible and invisible property, I would once again invoke Karl Polanyi's categories of
embedded and disembedded economies. This distinction explains
Finley's assertion that visible and invisible property are not "broad
economic categories" but "concrete factual considerations," for these
are the terms developed by an embedded economy to describe property
in the only relevant manner—according to its use and the status it
creates. Indeed, in the term *invisible property* we can see an embedded
economy trying to put a name to the process of its own *disembedding*, for
invisible property is the product of those who privilege pure economic
considerations over the social and political embedding of property.
Thus the motive of such men is strictly economic and the result of
making their property invisible is that they are themselves disembedded
from the social fabric of their community. As Sally Humphreys observes,

Transactions in the *oikos* sphere were part of a lasting pattern of social
relationships—kinship, affinity, friendship. Market transactions were
contractual and ephemeral. Frequent use was made of the distinction
between "visible" and "invisible" property. Visible property—especially
real property—was related to openly acknowledged social position and
commitments. Its owner's wealth and status could easily be assessed, he
could not evade tax obligations, his kin knew what they could expect
from him. With "invisible" property in cash and loans a man could
conceal his wealth and evade social obligations: it was difficult to "place"
him socially.[5]

This process of disembedding is a great threat to the precariously
poised system of *megaloprepeia*, as wealthy men opt out by making their

[4]Ἀφανιεῖν is Cobet's conjecture for the MSS ἀφιέναι. For other passages that refer to
making one's property invisible to avoid the performance of liturgies, see Isocrates
18.48, 60, Demosthenes 28.3–4, 7–8, 45.66, Isaeus 5.43–44, 7.40–41, Dinarchos 1.70.
[5]Humphreys 1983.10.

wealth invisible. The city depends for its economic survival on the willingness of its rich citizens to make their property visible and to contribute. Their willing participation in the system was essential, since, as Gabrielson argues, "it was virtually impossible to obtain a picture of a man's economic standing that was more or less accurate": in the end the accounting of property devolved upon the owner.[6] By the very nature of his enterprise, the epinikian poet is a defender of the embedded economy, an advocate of visible wealth, for without athletic competition and poetic commissions, there is no place for choral poetry. Hence the interests of the choral poet and the city converge on this point.

In this chapter we shall consider the rhetoric and imagery the poet uses to convince a sometimes recalcitrant aristocracy to continue its visible expenditure within the civic sphere. We have seen passages in which Pindar polemicizes, explicitly praising those who have "souls superior to wealth or possessions" (P.8.92, N.9.32–33) and explicitly admonishing, "Do not be deceived by [the prospect of] gains" (P.1.90–94, cf. N.7.17–19). But the poet has another strategy, at once more pervasive and more devious, for combating the obsession with wealth for its own sake: he takes over the elements of a disembedded economy—cash, profit, wage, and interest—and transforms them into metaphors for the highest rewards offered by the embedded economy. That is to say, he seems to make an enemy language serve his own purposes, encoding an implicit argument in his imagery. Leonard Woodbury recognizes this strategy, when he contrasts Pindar's use of wealth imagery with his treatment of literal profit in the odes: "By contrast, pay ($\mu\iota\sigma\theta\acute{o}\varsigma$) and profit ($\kappa\acute{\epsilon}\rho\delta o\varsigma$) are regarded more coolly. The highest pay or profit, in fact, is not any form of wealth, but fame (Nem.7.63 and Isth.1.50–52), and the pay that the poet expects for praise of Salamis is the $\chi\acute{\alpha}\rho\iota\varsigma$ of the Athenians (Pyth.1.75–77). When *not so transformed*, profit is a recurrent danger to other values."[7] We can see this strategy with particular clarity if we simply consider all Pindar's uses of *kerdos*.[8] Wherever the term is used literally, profit is presented as evil and corrupting (P.1.92, P.3.54, P.4.140, N.7.18, N.9.33, and N.11.47), whereas wherever it appears as a metaphor, it has a positive value (I.1.51 and I.5.27). *Never* does *kerdos* refer to the poet: in Pindar's metaphorical scheme, it is the victor who "profits" by being well spoken of.

---

[6]Gabrielson 1986.110, and see 110–113.
[7]Woodbury 1968.539, my italics.
[8]Ibid.

This last point is crucial and frequently overlooked. There are still critics who argue for Pindar's venality on the basis of a number of the passages we shall consider.[9] To do so is to misunderstand these passages and the poet's whole enterprise. It is quite clear that in these contexts money, pay, and profit are images, and images specifically directed to the poet's audience. The critics who take these passages as the self-advertising of a poet who sells his wares in the market make a fundamental mistake.[10] Pindar may speak the language of a disembedded economy, but he does so only in the service of its opposite—to convince those elements of the aristocracy whose enthusiasm is flagging that money in itself cannot bestow society's most desirable rewards.[11] Furthermore, we must see this polemic within the context of the polis, since the expenditures the poet advocates are those the city also regards as useful.

On one occasion, Pindar explicitly contrasts visible and invisible wealth:

οὐκ ἔραμαι πολὺν ἐν μεγάρῳ πλοῦτον κατακρύψαις ἔχειν,
ἀλλ᾽ ἐόντων εὖ τε παθεῖν καὶ ἀκοῦσαι φίλοις ἐξαρκέων.

(N. 1.31–32)

I do not long to keep much wealth in my hall, having hidden it away, but [instead] to enjoy what I possess and to be well spoken of while satisfying my friends.

Here, as in Pythian 11, Pindar uses the generalized first person to advocate a mode of behavior to his audience.[12] What the poet rejects here is not wealth itself (for that is desired in the words ἐόντων εὖ . . . παθεῖν), but making one's wealth invisible.[13] He would not hide great wealth within his house if he had it. This assertion leads naturally into

[9]Gzella 1969–1970a, 1969–1970b, and 1971 and Svenbro 1976.173–213.
[10]Gzella 1971.
[11]It may be that Pindar's patrons do not need such encouragement (though he gives it to them anyway at P.1.90–94, N.7.12–20, and I.1.64–67); nevertheless, it may be assumed from his ongoing polemic that Pindar perceives some portion of his audience as less committed to the manifestations of *megaloprepeia*.
[12]Contra Gzella (1971.197), who takes these lines to be a hint from the poet to his patron that he wants more money. Cf. P.3.110–111, where a similar sentiment is expressed again in the generalized first person, and see the discussion of Hubbard 1985.145–146.
[13]On the construction with the genitive ἐόντων, see Bury 1890.18–19, and LSJ πάσχω III.b, and cf. Theognis 1009.

his final wish via the bridge of *megaloprepeia*: given a sufficiency of wealth, he would spend his money in such a way that he would earn a good reputation, assisting his *philoi*.[14]

In another passage, the poet offers us his reason for preferring a good reputation to all else. The citizen who achieves great things and avoids *hybris*, he says,

$$\mu\acute{\epsilon}\lambda\alpha\nu o\varsigma\ \{\delta'\}\ \mathring{\alpha}\nu\ \mathring{\epsilon}\sigma\chi\alpha\tau\iota\grave{\alpha}\nu$$
$$\kappa\alpha\lambda\lambda\acute{\iota}o\nu\alpha\ \theta\alpha\nu\acute{\alpha}\tau o\upsilon\ \langle\sigma\tau\epsilon\acute{\iota}\chi o\iota\rangle\ \gamma\lambda\upsilon\kappa\upsilon\tau\acute{\alpha}\tau\alpha\ \gamma\epsilon\nu\epsilon\mathring{\alpha}$$
$$\epsilon\mathring{\upsilon}\acute{\omega}\nu\upsilon\mu o\nu\ \kappa\tau\epsilon\acute{\alpha}\nu\omega\nu\ \kappa\rho\alpha\tau\acute{\iota}\sigma\tau\alpha\nu\ \chi\acute{\alpha}\rho\iota\nu\ \pi o\rho\acute{\omega}\nu\cdot$$

(P.11.56–58)

would go to a better end of black death, since he has granted to his sweetest offspring the grace of a good name as the best of possessions.

"The grace of a good name" is the best possession to bequeath to one's children. We saw in Chapter 2 how this passage participates in the system of symbolic capital—the acquisition and transmission of glory within the individual house. We are now in a better position to appreciate the civic frame of Pindar's statement, for as we observed in Chapter 8, the protasis of this apodosis combines athletic success with the renunciation of tyranny. In the phrase εὐώνυμον κτεάνων κρατίσταν χάριν, Pindar encapsulates a whole polemic in the paradoxical juxtaposition of χάριν and κτεάνων.[15] For these two words represent the two poles of embedded and disembedded economy: at one end, the purely material concern for what one possesses; at the other end, a concern only with the effects of the use of wealth within a social and political framework. By assimilating *charis* to a possession in imagery the poet ultimately achieves the opposite: he subsumes all property to the service of a higher goal, the attainment of a state of "grace" in one's community. Pindar thereby affirms the commonality of interest of *oikos* and polis within an embedded economy.

The same use of economic imagery to endorse "noneconomic" goals shapes Pindar's language in Isthmian 5:

---

[14]Compare the words of Ischomachos in Xenophon's *Oeconomicus*: ἡδὺ γάρ μοι δοκεῖ . . . φίλους . . . ἐπωφελεῖν ("for it seems sweet to me to assist my friends" [*Oec.* 11.9]).

[15]Stoddart observes that the Attic orators "speak . . . often of inheritances of glory" (Stoddart 1990.20–21). This coincidence of imagery is no accident, since the orators, like Pindar, had a vested interest in promoting *megaloprepeia* among the wealthy citizens. Thus both rhetorical forms resort to the same appropriation of economic images for noneconomic achievements.

δύο δέ τοι ζωᾶς ἄωτον μοῦνα ποιμαίνοντι τὸν ἄλπνιστον, εὐανθεῖ
σὺν ὄλβῳ
εἴ τις εὖ πάσχων λόγον ἐσλὸν ἀκούῃ.

(I. 5. 12–13)

Two things alone shepherd the sweetest bloom of life, if a man faring well
with flourishing prosperity hear a noble word.

The two elements of the good life are exactly those Pindar cites at
N. 1. 32—the enjoyment of prosperity and a good reputation. In this
context, ποιμαίνοντι seems to offer us a concrete economic image for
anchoring material success within the proper social forms. It is noteworthy that the image is drawn from the sphere of farming, the most
embedded of economic pursuits and the only honorable occupation for
a Greek gentleman.[16]

The impression that ποιμαίνοντι represents an economic image is
confirmed by certain significant echoes in the lines that follow:

τὶν δ᾽ ἐν Ἰσθμῷ διπλόα θάλλοισ᾽ ἀρετά,
Φυλακίδα κεῖται, Νεμέᾳ δὲ καὶ ἀμφοῖν
Πυθέᾳ τε, παγκρατίου.

(I. 5. 17–19)

But for you, Phylakides, at the Isthmus double blooming achievement is
deposited, and at Nemea for both, for you and Pytheas, from the pancration.

Lines 12–13 offered a general scheme for human happiness; lines 17–19
elucidate why Phylakides and his brother Pytheas are particularly
blessed. In this context, διπλόα picks up δύο and θάλλοισ(α) corresponds to εὐανθεῖ. Thus the double achievement at the Isthmus and
Nemea represents both blooming prosperity and a good reputation.

---

[16]On the special status of farming, see Vernant 1976.67–74, 1983.248–270. Note the
use of ποιμήν in the context of literal wealth at O. 10.88. Concrete economic imagery is
associated with this topos again at O. 5.23–24, in lines that echo Isthmian 5 very closely:
ὑγίεντα δ᾽ εἴ τις ὄλβον ἄρδει, / ἐξαρκέων κτεάτεσσι καὶ εὐλογίαν προστιθείς, μὴ
ματεύσῃ θεὸς γενέσθαι (O. 5.23–24) ("But if someone waters healthy prosperity, being
generous with his possessions and adding good repute, let him not seek to become a
god" [O. 5.23–24]). Here the imagery is of tending a crop (ἄρδει) rather than of animal
husbandry (ποιμαίνοντι), but the concrete economic nature of the image is reinforced by
προστιθείς in its context: if, being satisfied with his possessions, he also adds εὐλογία.
The linking καί makes the literal possessions and a good reputation part of the same set,
while προστιθείς concretizes εὐλογία as the summit of a man's wealth.

The verb κεῖται then offers a very concrete economic image of valuables "deposited" at the two Panhellenic shrines. The banking image inherent in κεῖται is enhanced by the fact that the Panhellenic centers were most often the sites for such deposits because of their accessibility and prestige.[17] Yet the economic imagery in κεῖται is paradoxical, since money saved and stored away is exactly what this family of victors has foregone, instead spending lavishly on training, competing, and celebrating their victories. The treasure they have stored away, the poet implies, is much more valuable—a permanent store of arete and remembrance at the two Panhellenic centers.

The final appearance of economic imagery in Isthmian 5 applies the same metaphorical system to the family's mythic forerunners, the Aiakidai. Of them Pindar says:

> καὶ γὰρ ἡρώων ἀγαθοὶ πολεμισταί
> λόγον ἐκέρδαναν·
>
> (I.5.26–27)

For also of the heroes the good warriors profited in account.[18]

To assert the traditional glory of the aristocratic heroes par excellence, the poet has chosen a remarkably bold economic image. Rather than shun the whole notion of kerdos and the disembedded economics it represents, Pindar subsumes it completely to the values of epinikion: just as the victories of Pytheas and Phylakides are money in the bank for them, the eternal glory of the Aiakidai is a "profit" that continues to accrue.

All the passages considered thus far employ economic imagery in contexts that clearly refer to the victor and his family. But there are

---

[17]See LSJ, s.v. κεῖμαι III for a number of good examples of the meaning "to be deposited." On the use of the Panhellenic centers for such deposits, see Laum 1924.Column 71. Reading Φυλακίδα κεῖται, I accept the consensus of the MSS against Φυλακίδ᾽ ἄγκειται, Maas's conjecture from the scholia printed in the Snell-Maehler text. It is true that the scholia paraphrase these lines twice with ἀνάκειται, so that Maas's conjecture may be correct. If this is the case, the verb still has the concrete sense of "to be deposited, to be stored up" (see Slater 1969a on the two other appearances of ἀνάκειται in the epinikia), but it may also have the overtones of religious dedication (see LSJ ἀνάκειμαι I). Though these two meanings are clearly distinct in the case of literal deposits or dedications, in the realm of metaphor the two senses may blend and enhance each other. The glorious achievements of the brothers are simultaneously kleos in the bank for them and a devout dedication to the gods who preside over the shrines and contests.

[18]On ἐκέρδαναν see Bundy 1962.64 with n. 75.

other passages replete with economic terms, which can be taken to refer to the poet, passages that some scholars interpret as explicit references to the poet's contract and payment by the victor. These passages deserve particular attention, for they constitute a large part of the indictment against Pindar as venal poet. One such passage is the opening of Olympian 10:

Τὸν Ὀλυμπιονίκαν ἀνάγνωτέ μοι
Ἀρχεστράτου παῖδα, πόθι φρενός
ἐμᾶς γέγραπται· γλυκὺ γὰρ αὐτῷ μέλος ὀφείλων ἐπιλέλαθ'· ὦ
    Μοῖσ', ἀλλὰ σὺ καὶ θυγάτηρ
Ἀλάθεια Διός, ὀρθᾷ χερί
ἐρύκετον ψευδέων
ἐνιπὰν ἀλιτόξενον.
ἔκαθεν γὰρ ἐπελθὼν ὁ μέλλων χρόνος
ἐμὸν καταίσχυνε βαθὺ χρέος.
ὅμως δὲ λῦσαι δυνατὸς ὀξεῖαν ἐπιμομφὰν τόκος †θνατῶν· νῦν ψᾶφον
    ἑλισσομέναν
ὁπᾷ κῦμα κατακλύσσει ῥέον,
ὁπᾷ τε κοινὸν λόγον
φίλαν τείσομεν ἐς χάριν.

(O. 10. 1–12)

Read out for me the Olympic-victor child of Archestatos, from where it is written on my soul. For owing him a sweet strain, I forgot. But, O Muse, you and Truth, daughter of Zeus, fend off with upright hand the reproach that I have deceived a guest-friend with lies. For the future time coming up from far away has shamed my deep debt. But still interest (of mortals?) can loose sharp blame. Now, as the flowing swell engulfs the pebble/counter and whirls it away, so we shall pay the common account to dear *charis*.

Jesper Svenbro, for example, takes Pindar's mention of *chreos* in line 8 as a reference to the poet's contractual obligation, which he has for a time forgotten.[19] The weakness of this interpretation is that Pindar's language here actually inverts the terms of the contract: the poet appears to be paying the victor when he offers him interest (τόκος) to compensate for his lateness. Once we realize the inversion of the terms, we must conclude that what we have is not economic fact but economic metaphor. Ὀφείλων, χρέος, and τόκος are but three of many metaphorical

[19]Svenbro 1976.179.

terms in the passage. One of the meanings of ψᾶφος is a "counting pebble," for example; λόγος here can mean "account"; and τείσομεν means "we shall pay."[20] Indeed, the image underlying this whole passage appears to be that of two businessmen who have made a contract. One reads in his account book and realizes that his "payment" is overdue; so he sends it along with "interest" to the other.[21] Thus Pindar constructs his elaborate opening image from the sphere of disembedded economics.

But the poet skillfully undercuts his own image in lines 9–12. The τόκος he offers turns suddenly into a great sea wave which sweeps away (κατακλύσσει) the accounting pebble. The power and force of Pindar's poetry cannot be quantified and reduced to accounting—the business image is inadequate. The poet repeats the point with understated irony in lines 11–12: like the engulfing wave, "we shall pay the common account to dear *charis*." The relation of *charis* to *logos* here is that of the engulfing wave to the pebble, and that is precisely the relation of the embedded economy subsuming the narrowly economic concern with accounting. As we have seen, *charis* more than any other word in Pindar signifies the multiple embedding of poet and patron in the fabric of their society. So here, as the final word in Pindar's elaborate business image, *charis* completely undercuts the values of the world that image evokes.

And if this were not enough to make the point, consider the development of Olympian 10 as a whole. Toward the end of the ode, Pindar offers another image of the poem as τόκος that bestows *charis*:

ἀλλ᾽ ὧτε παῖς ἐξ ἀλόχου πατρί
ποθεινὸς ἵκοντι νεότατος τὸ πάλιν ἤδη, μάλα δέ οἱ θερμαίνει
    φιλότατι νόον·
ἐπεὶ πλοῦτος ὁ λαχὼν ποιμένα
ἐπακτὸν ἀλλότριον
θνᾴσκοντι στυγερώτατος·
καὶ ὅταν καλὰ {μὲν} ἔρξαις ἀοιδᾶς ἄτερ,
Ἀγησίδαμ᾽, εἰς Ἀίδα σταθμόν
ἀνὴρ ἵκηται, κενεὰ πνεύσαις ἔπορε μόχθῳ βραχύ τι τερπνόν. τὶν δ᾽
    ἁδυεπής τε λύρα
γλυκύς τ᾽ αὐλὸς ἀναπάσσει χάριν·

(O. 10.86–94)

[20]For the monetary image contained in ψᾶφος, see LSJ ψῆφος II.1, Gildersleeve 1890.215 and Norwood 1945.111–112.

[21]This is presumably the point of the imagery of reading and writing (ἀνάγνωτε and γέγραπται), which appears only here in Pindar. The poet has an internal account book in which the credits and debits of his business of praise are accurately inscribed. Thus also Norwood 1945.112, Nassen 1975.221 and Kromer 1976.423–425.

But as a child, long desired, from his wife for a father who has already come to the opposite of youth, very much warms his mind with affection (since wealth allotted to a foreign shepherd is most hateful to the one who is dying); just so, whenever a man comes to the dwelling of Hades, having accomplished noble things without song, Hagesidamos, having breathed empty things, he has given [only] brief pleasure to his toil. But upon you the sweet-speaking lyre and the sweet aulos sprinkle grace.

The "interest" in a pure economic relation has become the "child" born to an old man, a source of joy because he will inherit the old man's property and preserve his memory with funeral offerings ($\chi\acute{\alpha}\rho\iota\nu$).[22] The values of property embedded in its social frame have completely eclipsed those of business economics. The poet has constructed a subtle polemic in imagery, guiding his listeners from the seduction of invisible wealth to the glories of noble expenditure.[23]

Isthmian 1 offers us another passage that some critics have taken as the poet's self-justification for charging a fee. Thus Svenbro observes of Isthmian I.1.47–49: "Specifically, the choral poet had no choice: like every worker, he depended on the remuneration from his labor. Pindar himself defines this condition in irreducible terms: 'For their different labors, men love to receive each his remuneration (*misthos*): the shepherd, the field laborer, the fowler, and also the one whom the sea nurtures; each makes an effort to avert from his belly pernicious hunger.'"[24] But again, if we look at these lines in context, the message appears somewhat different:

εἰ δ' ἀρετᾷ κατάκειται πᾶσαν ὀργάν,
ἀμφότερον δαπάναις τε καὶ πόνοις,
χρή νιν εὑρόντεσσιν ἀγάνορα κόμπον
μὴ φθονεραῖσι φέρειν
γνώμαις. ἐπεὶ κούφα δόσις ἀνδρὶ σοφῷ
ἀντὶ μόχθων παντοδαπῶν ἔπος εἰπόντ' ἀγαθὸν ξυνὸν ὀρθῶσαι
καλόν.
μισθὸς γὰρ ἄλλοις ἄλλος ἐπ' ἔργμασιν ἀνθρώποις γλυκύς,
μηλοβότᾳ τ' ἀρότᾳ τ' ὀρνιχολόχῳ τε καὶ ὃν πόντος τράφει.
γαστρὶ δὲ πᾶς τις ἀμύνων λιμὸν αἰανῆ τέταται·

[22]See Stoddart 1990. 5–14.

[23]For a similar treatment of the thematic development in Olympian 10, see Kromer 1976. The strategy of Isthmian 2 is very similar, though it has a somewhat different starting point. In order to give Isthmian 2 the attention it deserves, I have reserved consideration of it for a separate chapter.

[24]Svenbro 1976.173–174, my translation.

ὃς δ' ἀμφ' ἀέθλοις ἢ πολεμίζων ἄρηται κῦδος ἁβρόν,
εὐαγορηθεὶς κέρδος ὕψιστον δέκεται, πολιατᾶν καὶ ξένων γλώσσας
ἄωτον.

(I.1.41–51)

But if a man expends himself for achievement in every impulse, both
with expenditures and toils, it is fitting to bear a lordly boast for those
who find it with ungrudging purpose. Since it is a light gift for a skilled
man in exchange for all sorts of toils, by saying a good word, to set up a
common ornament. For different wages are sweet for the different works
of men, for the shepherd and the plowman and the fowler and the man
whom the sea nourishes. And everyone strains to fend off dread hunger
from his belly. But whoever in contests or war wins luxurious *kudos*, by
being well spoken of he receives the highest profit, the peak of the tongue
of citizens and strangers.

The generalizing εἰ clause that opens this section points to the victor as a
type, and does so in economic imagery. For κατάκειται here is used as
the passive of κατατίθημι, "to pay down." Renehan translates these
lines, "And if a man is expended on virtue in every impulse—in both
respects, both with respect to costs and to labors—it is necessary to
bring, with ungrudging thoughts, lavish praise to those who have found
it [sc. ἀρετά]."[25] The victor "expends" himself utterly on achievement,
and as recompense the poet offers him ungrudging praises.[26] The poet's

[25]Renehan's argument is a model of philological lucidity, well worth quoting at length:
"As κεῖμαι is used as a passive of τίθημι in all its meanings, so too does κατάκειμαι
serve as a passive of κατατίθημι. κατατίθημι very frequently means 'put down as
payment,' 'pay down' (LSJ s.v. κατατίθημι I.3.a); Pindar so uses it metaphorically,
Nemean 7.75–76: νικῶντί γε χάριν . . . οὐ τραχύς εἰμι καταθέμεν. In our passage
κατάκειται = 'is paid out to' (or historically more correctly, perhaps, with middle force
'pays himself out to'); the image is pointed up by δαπάναις, used here in a literal sense,
and possibly is continued in κόμπον . . . φέρειν. See LSJ s.v. φέρω A.IV.2" (Renehan
1969a.111). See also Woodbury 1981.245–247. I am less convinced by Schmidt's attempt
to interpret κατάκειται as a transitive middle perfect, on the basis of parallels from
papyri of the second century B.C. Although he claims to have found fifth-century
examples of this phenomenon for compounds of κεῖται, he offers only a single example
that is truly middle and transitive (Herodotus 1.171.4), but in this instance the verb is
implicitly reflexive. See Schmidt 1975.36–39.
[26]This image of expending "himself" disturbs Schmidt, who objects, "It is unusual
that in this case, grammatically the 'payer' is himself payed out (or pays himself out) and
not what he puts in. Rather, what he puts in, according to Renehan, is supposed to
appear first in the accusative of respect . . . and then in the dative of respect" (Schmidt
1975.37, my translation). But this is precisely the core of epinikian economics: it is not
merely money that is at issue but the willing expenditure of all one has and is for victory.
For this all-embracing sense of "expenditure" in the context of epinikion, see Carson
1984.

praise "in exchange for all sorts of toils" becomes a dedication, "a common ornament" set up to commemorate the victory (45–46).

The γάρ of line 47 picks up the ἐπεί clause with its image of the poem as dedication. Thus lines 47–48 set out to explain *why* song is the proper "wage" for victors. As in the opening of Olympian 10, the terms of the actual contract are inverted in such a way that the poet is portrayed as paying the victor. Thus I cannot accept Svenbro's claim that lines 47–49 refer to the *poet's* need for remuneration (μισθός). Just the opposite: they refer to poetry as the remuneration of the victor's literal and figurative expenditure.[27]

We must look carefully at line 49 as well. Out of context, Svenbro takes it as the poet's apology for the needs of his own belly, very similar to Odysseus' words at *Odyssey* 7.208–221. But this is to misunderstand completely the function of this line in the priamel of lines 47–51. In lines 47–48 the poet sets up what appears to be an analogical priamel: "as pay is sweet to workmen," we expect to hear, "so praise is sweet to victors." But instead, line 49 transforms an analogical priamel into an antithetical one. Contrasted to all the lowly occupations whose only goal is to fend starvation from the belly, the winning of *kudos* in war or contests is raised to a higher level.[28] That elevation is perfectly captured in the adjective that modifies *kudos*—ἁβρόν—which designates *kudos* as a "luxury item," far beyond the aspirations of those struggling to escape starvation. Together with the heightened contrast between subsistence labor and luxurious *kudos*, the poet has introduced a contrast between those who work only for themselves and those who achieve on behalf of the community.[29] This civic achievement is represented in opposition to μισθός, but in the imagery of a disembedded economy, which places it in the same semantic field. By the last line of the priamel, the universal praise the victor deserves is no longer merely a wage; it is supreme profit. Thus the priamel contravenes our expectations and thereby

[27]Note that the poet moves from literal to figurative expenditure between lines 42 and 46. In line 42, he mentions δαπάναις as well as πόνοις, but in line 46 he refers only to μόχθων παντοδαπῶν. This development makes for a closer analogy between the victor and the wage earners of lines 47–48, likening the victor's efforts to the "works" of men (note ἐπ' ἔργμασιν [47]).

[28]For the classification of priamels as analogical or antithetical, see Krischer 1974.81–91. Though Race 1982.5–7 rejects these categories, they are useful for analyzing the expectations generated by the priamel and seeing how it changes course at line 49. According to Race's own analysis, μισθός and κέρδος ὕψιστον are merely equivalent terms (Race 1982.11–15). On the dynamics of the priamel in Isthmian 1, see Bundy 1962.66 and Fränkel 1973.490–491 n. 8.

[29]Notice that the verb Pindar uses to describe the desperate struggle against starvation, τέταται, occurs elsewhere to characterize proper civic striving (P.11.54).

simultaneously rejects economic life and appropriates its language to endorse civic service and expenditure.

In fact, this passage as a whole is permeated with money imagery that inverts the actual terms of the contract between poet and patron. The use of imagery drawn from the sphere of disembedded economics (particularly μισθός and κέρδος) has nothing to do with the poet and his fee. Rather this imagery is directed at the poet's audience: it takes up their concern with profit in order to convince them that the "highest profit" is to be praised by citizens and strangers.

The poet reiterates the message of κέρδος ὕψιστον in the final lines of the poem, again employing economic imagery to sharpen his point:

> εἰ δέ τις ἔνδον νέμει πλοῦτον κρυφαῖον,
> ἄλλοισι δ' ἐμπίπτων γελᾷ, ψυχὰν Ἀίδᾳ τελέων οὐ φράζεται δόξας
> ἄνευθεν.
>
> (I. 1.67–68)

> But if a man plies his wealth within so that it is hidden, and smiles when he meets with untoward circumstances, he does not realize that he pays his soul to Hades without repute.[30]

As Elroy Bundy sees clearly, these lines set up a "negative foil" for the victor, contrasting point for point with the praiseworthy model the poet offered at lines 41–46 and 50–51.[31] Thus both sections begin with a generalizing conditional clause; ἔνδον νέμει πλοῦτον κρυφαῖον then contrasts with willing expenditure, ἀμφότερον δαπάναις τε καὶ πόνοις. Continuity of imagery supports the formal pattern. Whereas the model for the victor is the man who expends himself utterly on achievement and so wins the highest profit by being well spoken of, the miserly man "pays his soul to Hades" (τελέων). He too expends himself, as all men must, but uselessly, wastefully. The emphatic last words, δόξας ἄνευθεν ("without repute"), stand in contrast to the victor's ultimate "profit"—γλώσσας ἄωτον ("the peak of the tongue"). Indeed, these two phrases of exactly the same shape occupy the same metrical position as the closing words of the last two triads. The poet shows us

---

[30]Contra Bundy (1962.84 n. 113) and Thummer (1968.2.34), I do not believe that ἔνδον νέμει means simply ἔχει; rather, I take the phrase to be a pointed oxymoron that underscores the impossibility of using wealth properly when it is hoarded at home (for this interpretation of νέμει, see Bury 1892.25). In translating ἄλλοισι δ' ἐμπίπτων γελᾷ, I follow the interpretation of Most 1988.

[31]Bundy 1962.83–85.

with ruthless clarity the final result of opting out of the system. To choose invisible wealth over visible wealth and *megaloprepeia* is to consign *oneself* to eternal invisibility.

There may be a double pun in Ἀΐδᾳ which underscores the point. The popular etymology of the common psilotic form Ἀΐδης was "the unseen" or "invisible one."[32] I believe that Pindar is playing on this meaning here (and throughout the epinikia). The miser disappears into the invisibility of the Underworld, so that he is for all eternity "hidden," like the money he hoarded in life. But Hades is also Ploutōn, as πλοῦτον and the metaphoric τελέων must remind us. In the case of the miserly man, the poet implies, the only one who "profits" is that master of invisible wealth, Hades himself.[33]

Yet again, close consideration of Pindar's language has revealed a poet whose rhetoric and imagery are well adapted for the conditions of life in the polis. Indeed, Pindar's paradoxical use of economic imagery does not even represent the interests of the aristocracy to the city. Instead this imagery inverts the poet's usual role of mediator, insofar as it promotes the interests of the city to the aristocracy. For the poet and the city both depend on the willing expenditure of those who can afford it in the public sphere. And the poet confronts the prospect of the economic and social disembedding of the wealthy in his audience by a bold appropriation of the discourse of money and profit in the service of civic ideology.

[32]See Cornutus *De natura deorum* 5.14; Mazon 1928.141 n. 1 (in a note on *Aspis* 224–227); Gernet 1981b.130.

[33]See Cornutus *De natura deorum* 5.15. For an example of the same wordplay on the name of Hades, see Sophocles *OT* 29–30 (in reference to the plague): ὑφ᾽ οὗ κενοῦται δῶμα Καδμεῖον· μέλας δ᾽ / Ἅιδης στεναγμοῖς καὶ γόοις πλουτίζεται ("By it the Kadmeian house is emptied, but black Hades is rich with groaning and lamentation").

CHAPTER 10

Isthmian 2: The Recuperation of *Megaloprepeia*

We have seen how the house asserts its integrity through space and time, drawing its descendants back from the ends of the earth to honor their ancestors; how houses interact ceremoniously with each other, exchanging recompenses, brides, and guest-gifts; how the house makes its uneasy settlement with the polis, turning a new economic system to a new virtue. Finally, we have seen how the poet deploys these real social systems to reinsert the victor into the expanding circles of his community—into the life of his family, the privilege of the aristocracy, and the precarious balance of the polis. But in order to observe the function of these metaphorical systems whole, we have fragmented and dismembered the individual odes. It is time to invert the process, to recombine the models we have extracted to make sense of whole poems. Indeed, this is the proof of the validity of the models—if, through them, the poems are transformed, accessible to our understanding, where before they were obscure. This is not to say that any single system explains all of Pindar; the epinikia are far too complex to reduce to a single key or set of keys. Thus, I claim no interpretive monopoly for the models laid out here. They simply offer a few systems among many to elucidate the complexities of these highly wrought poems.

The purpose of this chapter, then, is to apply the models developed to the analysis of an individual poem. I offer only a sample of such readings, focusing on Isthmian 2, a poem whose interpretation is central to any account of Pindar's economics. The proem of Isthmian 2 has often been read biographically as a reference to Simonides' *philokerdeia* or to a

240

special relationship between Pindar and Thrasyboulos.[1] I would like to offer an interpretation of Isthmian 2 which, though it locates the poem in history, does not depend on the reconstruction of personal details about the poet or the addressee. We shall find that this complex ode makes more sense when considered in the light of its audience, the victor's needs, and the poet's polemics.

The opening of Isthmian 2 has long baffled critics:

Οἱ μὲν πάλαι, ὦ Θρασύβουλε, φῶτες, οἳ χρυσαμπύκων
ἐς δίφρον Μοισᾶν ἔβαινον κλυτᾷ φόρμιγγι συναντόμενοι,
ῥίμφα παιδείους ἐτόξευον μελιγάρυας ὕμνους,
ὅστις ἐὼν καλὸς εἶχεν Ἀφροδίτας
εὐθρόνου μνάστειραν ἀδίσταν ὀπώραν.
ἁ Μοῖσα γὰρ οὐ φιλοκερδής πω τότ' ἦν οὐδ' ἐργάτις·
οὐδ' ἐπέρναντο γλυκεῖαι μελιφθόγγου ποτὶ Τερψιχόρας
ἀργυρωθεῖσαι πρόσωπα μαλθακόφωνοι ἀοιδαί.
νῦν δ' ἐφίητι ⟨τὸ⟩ τὠργεῖον φυλάξαι
ῥῆμ' ἀλαθείας ⟨˘ ˉ⟩ ἄγχιστα βαῖνον,
'χρήματα χρήματ' ἀνήρ' ὃς φᾶ κτεάνων θ' ἅμα λειφθεὶς καὶ φίλων.
ἐσσὶ γὰρ ὦν σοφός· οὐκ ἄγνωτ' ἀείδω. . . .

(I.2.1–12)

Those men long ago, O Thrasyboulos, who used to mount the chariot of the gold-frontleted Muses, meeting with a glorifying lyre, used lightly to fire off songs to boys, if there was anyone who, being handsome, had the sweetest late-summer summons to beautiful-throned Aphrodite. For not yet then was the Muse avaricious or a working girl, nor yet were sweet, gentle-voiced songs sold with faces painted silver by sweet-speaking Terpsichore. But now she bids us guard the saying of the Argive as going nearest the . . . of truth, "Money, money is the man," he said when he was deprived at once of his fortune and his friends. For you are wise: not unknown the things I sing. . . .

In spite of two excellent recent analyses, the proem remains problematic.[2] Leonard Woodbury suggests that the proem describes a "change in the condition of poetry," from the spontaneous monody of Alcaeus, Ibycus, and Anacreon to elaborate choral lyric composed on commis-

[1]For the reference to Simonides, see scholia (Drachmann 1926.214), Bury 1892.33–34, Wilamowitz 1922.312–314; for a personal relationship between Pindar and Thrasyboulos, see scholia, Norwood 1945.152–158, Bowra 1964.124–126, 162, 355–356.
[2]Woodbury 1968 and Nisetich 1977a, who give a good summary of earlier scholarship.

sion. The ultimate point of this contrast is praise of Thrasyboulos' *megaloprepeia*, for the new condition of poetry makes it a vehicle for demonstrating the patron's magnificence.[3] Although it makes an important contribution to the understanding of Isthmian 2, Woodbury's interpretation is open to two objections. First, his reading of the proem does not account for the prominence of erotic themes—the παι-δείους . . . ὕμνους of the opening lines. As Frank J. Nisetich observes, if the poet is simply making a distinction of genre, he could just as easily have alluded to the nonerotic poems of the monodists.[4]

Second, Woodbury asserts that "the contrast between the ancient poets and the mercenary Muse does not aim at approval of the former nor at reproof of the latter. Its purpose is to demonstrate the increased capabilities and achievements of wealth properly used, and so to praise the public use that Thrasybulus has made of his own wealth by commissioning and producing the present ode."[5] Yet it is very hard not to read Pindar's description of the modern "mercenary Muse" as a condemnation. Michael Simpson, following Wilamowitz, reminds us that both ἐργάτις (6) and ἐπέρναντο (7) evoke the image of prostitutes (πόρναι). Simpson goes on to analyze the negative elements in Pindar's portrait point by point:

> In contrast to this view of poetry there is "modern" poetry, described as the product of the harlot Muse, with individual poems offered for sale as painted prostitutes by Terpsichore. Each figure in the contrast enriches the other, brings new meaning from it. Whereas good poetry is a spontaneous response to *natural* beauty . . . , bad poetry possesses an *artificial, cosmetic* prettiness . . . in order to make it appealing to those who are unable to inspire poetry but must, rather, pay for poems "made up" to offer them a kind of satisfaction in return for money. . . . The chariot-bow metaphor, moreover, embodies an aristocratic concept of poetry in contrast to the falsely pretty poetry of a commercialized age. Finally, by associating gold (χρυσαμπύκων, 1) with good poetry and silver (ἀργυ-ρωθεῖσαι, 8) with bad poetry, Pindar reinforces the contrast, using these metals to express a qualitative difference, as his fellow Boeotian, Hesiod, did to distinguish a superior from an inferior age (*Works and Days* 109ff.).[6]

---

[3]Woodbury 1968. 533–542. Pavese (1966) offers a similar interpretation, although he does not see any distinction between οἱ μὲν πάλαι and νῦν δ' ἐφίητι.
[4]Nisetich 1977a. 138.
[5]Woodbury 1968. 540.
[6]Simpson 1969a. 471–472. Cf. Wilamowitz 1922. 311.

Woodbury's interpretation does not account for the extreme negativity of Pindar's portrayal of his own Muse in the proem. Other critics have attempted to solve this problem by taking the proem as a scathing allusion to Simonides. Surely, they reason, Pindar cannot be referring to his own poetry. Yet there is nothing in the poem to suggest that Pindar is not referring to choral lyric as he also composes it. On the contrary, the language is very similar to that of Pythian 11, where he is clearly addressing his own Muse:

> Μοῖσα, τὸ δὲ τεόν, εἰ μισθοῖο συνέθευ παρέχειν
> φωνὰν ὑπάργυρον, ἄλλοτ᾽ ἄλλᾳ {χρὴ} ταρασσέμεν
> ἢ πατρὶ Πυθονίκῳ
> τό γέ νυν ἢ Θρασυδάῳ,
>
> (P.11.41–44)

But, Muse, it is your task, if you have contracted to furnish your voice silvered for a wage, to set [it] in motion at different times in different ways, either for the Pythian-victor father or now, at any rate, for Thrasydaios.

In his analysis Nisetich accounts for love but not money as a theme of the proem. He argues that the poem's anomalies derive from the odd circumstances of its composition: the victor, Xenokrates, who commissioned the ode is dead, and Pindar is left addressing the epinikion to his son Thrasyboulos. Hence Pindar cannot compliment the poem's addressee with the conventional praises of the victor but must find other means. As Nisetich reconstructs the situation:

> Pindar cannot write Thrasyboulos an epinician ode, but he finds himself in the position of addressing one to him. He therefore tries to put Thrasyboulos in a favorable light, a light that victory itself cannot shed upon him. What occurs to him is the light of beauty. The old poets who addressed their lovers without more ado come to his mind because he also would address Thrasyboulos without more ado. This implies that Thrasyboulos, if he had lived then, would have been the subject of erotic songs, and that Pindar would have written them in his honor.[7]

This is a subtle analysis of the first five lines of the proem, but Nisetich's explanation of the contrasting modern Muse is less satisfactory. Nise-

---

[7]Nisetich 1977a.140.

tich implies that Pindar breaks off from his praise of Thrasyboulos with the plea that he is constrained by the commission he received to compose an epinikion for Xenokrates.[8] But under the circumstances, for Pindar to suggest such a constraint on his choice of work would be quite tactless, especially since it would imply a divergence of interest between father and son. But as the poet tells us in Pythian 1, χάρμα δ᾽ οὐκ ἀλλότριον νικαφορία πατέρος ("The victory of a father is no foreign joy" [P.1.59]). Surely Thrasyboulos would rejoice in the celebration of his father's victory, and Pindar would not feel obliged to apologize to him for the "constraint" of his commission.

Furthermore, although Nisetich acknowledges the strongly negative cast to Pindar's depiction of his own Muse, he does not explain it adequately: "It is, at first, hard to imagine how the epinician Muse, whom Pindar depicts as a public woman (6–8), can be an improvement on the spontaneous Muse of the old erotic poets. But it is even harder to imagine why Pindar would introduce her as an inferior when she dominates the ode. Pindar's critical attitude toward her ought to be taken ironically, as others have realized. In the proem Pindar ironically overstresses one aspect of her public nature, namely that she works for hire." He goes on: "The irony in the beginning is due in part to Pindar's tactfulness; he is, after all, praising his own poem, so he puts that praise in the form of a compliment to Thrasyboulos: Thrasyboulos' appreciation of the ode emerges against the background of an ironical depreciation of it."[9] But "ironical depreciation" of his own poetry is not necessary to compliment Thrasyboulos, and seems very uncharacteristic of Pindar. Furthermore, this explanation does not account for the focus of Pindar's "irony"—why should he choose to highlight the issue of money and payment for poetry?

Thus, it seems, problems remain. First, what is the relationship of love and money in the proem? It is not enough to say with Nisetich, "It is instead a contrast between poetry that has nothing to do with money and poetry that has a great deal to do with it."[10] There must be some significant link between the "then" and the "now" for Pindar's contrast to be meaningful. Second, no one has yet adequately accounted for Pindar's scathing portrayal of the "mercenary Muse" and where she fits in the logic of the poem.

[8]This I take to be the force of Nisetich's argument that χρήματα χρήματ᾽ ἀνήρ refers to the *poet* (Nisetich 1977a.140).
[9]Nisetich 1977a.141, 150.
[10]Nisetich 1977a.139.

I will address the second question first, for the answer will eventually lead back to the first query. Woodbury made an important observation when he identified the older poets as Alcaeus, Ibycus, and Anacreon; he noticed that Pindar effectively quotes two of the three in the proem. In addition to χρήματα χρήματ᾽ ἀνήρ, which the scholia attribute in abbreviated form to Alcaeus (Drachmann 1926.215), Woodbury notes that Pindar's description of the modern Muse is "an almost baroque development" of a line of Anacreon quoted by the scholia, οὐδ᾽ ἀργυρῆ κω τότ᾽ ἔλαμπε Πειθώ ("Never yet has Persuasion shone silver" [fr. 384 PMG]).[11] Woodbury concludes, "It could not be plainer that Pindar, in contrasting the predicament of the contemporary Muse with the easy habits of his predecessors, is turning the words of the latter to the description of the former."[12] Indeed, we may go a step farther. It appears that Pindar's description of the modern Muse is drawn *from the point of view of* the older poets, as his echoes of their words make clear. It is this older generation of poets which distrusted money and disapproved of poetry for pay. Here in the proem, Pindar allows the older poets (οἱ μὲν πάλαι) to have their say about the present condition of poetry.

But if the proem expresses the negative viewpoint of the older poets, the ode as it proceeds systematically revises that vision, redeeming the "mercenary Muse." That is to say, in the course of the poem, Pindar shifts his ground from an extremely negative view of money to a view that appropriates the money economy and validates expenditure in the service of the epinikian ideal. This is, I believe, the solution to Nisetich's objection: "If we grant that Woodbury is right about the proem, we should remember that Pindar devotes no less than ten lines toward the end of the ode (33–42) to the praise of Thrasyboulos and Xenocrates for openness to celebration and noble hospitality, both of which imply praiseworthy use of wealth. The praise at the end is straightforward and easily recognizable as a standard epinician topic. Why does Pindar, in an extremely allusive, indeed elliptical, manner bestow the same praise on Thrasyboulos at the start of the ode?"[13] The topic is repeated because there is a development in Pindar's position through the course of the ode. It is not so much that the "praise of wealth" at the beginning of the

[11]Woodbury 1968.533 (see Drachmann 1926.215). Drachmann prefers the reading of the MSS (Πυθώ) to Boeckh's emendation, Πειθώ. Yet, if we read Πυθώ, the scholiast's statement that Anacreon says something similar becomes quite obscure.

[12]Woodbury 1968.533.

[13]Nisetich 1977a.137–138.

246 Pindar's Political Economy

poem is "elliptical," as that the whole poem is an ellipse, turning back on itself and on the issue of money.

We can chart the stages of the poem's "argument," for the poet has clearly articulated them through the repetition of language and imagery. Pindar introduces two images in the opening lines of the proem to characterize the activity of the older poets: they "mounted the chariot of the . . . Muses" (ἐς δίφρον Μοισᾶν ἔβαινον) and shot their hymns like arrows at beautiful boys (ἐτόξευον).[14] The image of poetic marksmanship that aims at the object of praise may recur within the first triad, when Pindar says of the modern Muse:

νῦν δ᾽ ἐφίητι ⟨τὸ⟩ τὠργείου φυλάξαι
ῥῆμ᾽ ἀλαθείας ⟨˘ ˉ⟩ ἄγχιστα βαῖνον,
'χρήματα χρήματ᾽ ἀνήρ' ὃς φᾶ κτεάνων θ᾽ ἅμα λειφθεὶς καὶ φίλων.

(I.2.9–11)

But now she bids us guard the saying of the Argive as going nearest the . . . of truth, "Money, money is the man," he said when he was deprived at once of his fortune and his friends.

Βαῖνον here picks up ἔβαινον in line 2, and these lines may also include the image of shooting at a target: ἄγχιστα particularly suggests the notion of aim and accuracy.[15] Thus in the bitter words of the Argive, money as the essential quality of a man replaces beautiful boys as the target of poetic darts, articulating the first step in the process of the poem.[16]

Then, at the beginning of the final triad, both images of poetic

[14]On the conjunction of these images and their significance, see Simpson 1969a. Simpson notes the occurrence of the two images together in the proem of Isthmian 2 and concludes that Pindar is thereby marking the older poetry as "good" in contrast to the new poetry (Simpson 1969a.471). But the recurrence of the same imagery in Isthmian 2 for the new poetry suggests that we cannot simply equate old with good or new with bad.

[15]The presence of the image here depends on the word missing from line 10. As yet there is no satisfactory proposal. Turyn prints ὁδῶν, the conjecture of Hermann based on P.3.103. I am not completely comfortable with this suggestion (although it fits into the patterns of imagery I am tracing), because it seems that by its nature the "road of truth" should be singular (as in Pythian 3) rather than plural.

[16]Nisetich 1977a.140 takes ἀνήρ here to refer to the poet, who is constrained by his commission to write an epinikion. But I believe the coherence of the imagery militates against this interpretation. The ἀνήρ here replaces boys as the target of the poet's dart, and whereas their essential qualities were beauty and youth, the man's salient characteristic (indeed, his essence in Alcaeus' cynical words) is money. Thus the concern throughout, pointed by the imagery of shooting at a target, is with the *subject* of poetry.

activity—charioteering and marksmanship—recur to glorify the content and concerns of the new poetry:

> οὐ γὰρ πάγος οὐδὲ προσάντης ἁ κέλευθος γίνεται,
> εἴ τις εὐδόξων ἐς ἀνδρῶν ἄγοι τιμὰς Ἑλικωνιάδων.
> μακρὰ δισκήσαις ἀκοντίσσαιμι τοσοῦθ', ὅσον ὀργάν
> Ξεινοκράτης ὑπὲρ ἀνθρώπων γλυκεῖαν
> ἔσχεν. αἰδοῖος μὲν ἦν ἀστοῖς ὁμιλεῖν,
> ἱπποτροφίας τε νομίζων ἐν Πανελλάνων νόμῳ·
> καὶ θεῶν δαῖτας προσέπτυκτο πάσας· οὐδέ ποτε ξενίαν
> οὖρος ἐμπνεύσαις ὑπέστειλ' ἱστίον ἀμφὶ τράπεζαν·

(I.2.33–40)

For the road is not uphill or steep if someone should lead the honors of the Helikonian [Muses] to [the house] of glorious men. By throwing a long way I would cast the javelin as far as Xenokrates held his sweet temperament beyond [other] men. He was respectful in keeping company with his fellow citizens, even practicing *hippotrophia* according to the custom of all the Greeks. And he welcomed warmly all the feasts of the gods, and never did a favoring breeze blowing cause him to reef the sail [of his generosity] about a hospitable table.

The constellation of images mirrors that of the proem, for κέλευθος is specifically a carriage road, and οὐ γὰρ πάγος οὐδὲ προσάντης transfers to the new poetry the notion of ease expressed by ῥίμφα in line 3.[17] Throwing the javelin here replaces shooting arrows, but the basic imagery of poetic missiles is the same.[18] The metaphors which, in Simpson's terms, had expressed the accuracy and nobility of the old poetry are here transferred wholesale to the new poetry, aiming at the praise of wealth and its proper use rather than the praise of beauty.[19]

What has caused this turnaround, which is clearly marked by the poet's images for poetry? The answer must lie in the poem's second triad, situated as it is between the proem's denunciation of money and

[17]On the semantics of κέλευθος, see Becker 1937.7–14 and compare O.6.23, O.7.52, I.4.1, I.6.22. The parallel between ῥίμφα and οὐ γὰρ πάγος κτλ. was pointed out to me by Anne Carson.

[18]Or perhaps we should say the shift in imagery allows for a slight difference in emphasis: the idea behind the image of shooting arrows seems to be accuracy in hitting the target/topic (see Simpson 1969a), while Pindar's explicit conceit in the javelin image is one of extent. The poet strives to match the extent of Xenokrates' magnificence in his own poetic "cast" (thus, the topos of "praise to match" is mapped spatially). For a similar variation within the same field of imagery framing the poem, compare P.6.

[19]Simpson 1969a.470–471.

the lengthy praise of Xenokrates' magnificence which fills the strophe
and antistrophe of the third triad. The bulk of the second triad, the
center of the poem, is filled by a catalog of the victories of Xenokrates
and his brother, Theron. And whereas "the saying of the Argive" had
expressed very negatively that a man is nothing but his property in the
eyes of the world, the victory catalog shows us the positive side of
wealth consciously and properly employed. Implied in this catalog is
praise of Xenokrates for his expenditure on chariot racing (εὐάρματον
ἄνδρα γεραίρων [17]), on xenia to men and gods, and on celebration
and commemorative song (κώμων . . . ἐρατῶν . . . μελικόμπων ἀοιδᾶν
[31–32]).[20] Nisetich has rightly emphasized the importance of this last,
μελικόμπων ἀοιδᾶν, for in Pindar's scheme it is commemorative song
that guarantees "immortal honors to the children of Ainesidamos."[21]
But we should not fail to recognize that immortality appears here
climactically, as the result of a whole series of wise and willing expenditures culminating in the commissioning of celebratory song.

This positive reevaluation of the force of χρήματα χρήματ' ἀνήρ is
signaled in turn by the verbal echo οὐκ ἄγνωτ' (12) / οὐκ ἀγνῶτες (30),
which frames the victory catalog. Having first quoted the "saying of the
Argive," Pindar goes on,

ἐσσὶ γὰρ ὦν σοφός· οὐκ ἄγνωτ' ἀείδω
'Ισθμίαν ἵπποισι νίκαν,
τὰν Ξενοκράτει Ποσειδάων ὀπάσαις,
Δωρίων αὐτῷ στεφάνωμα κόμᾳ
πέμπεν ἀναδεῖσθαι σελίνων,

(I.2.12–16)

For you are wise: not unknown the Isthmian victory with horses which I
sing, the one Poseidon bestowed on Xenokrates, sending him a crown of
Dorian celery to bind on his hair.

The γάρ of line 12 marks an ellipse: "Money is the man . . . [I need say
no more; you'll understand], for you are wise: not unknown the Isth-

---

[20]In this context, the rest of line 17, 'Ακραγαντίνων φάος, alerts us to the implicit
theme of megaloprepeia. In his conspicuous expenditure on chariot racing, Xenokrates
illuminates his city. Recall that in Chapter 6, I argued that Pindar casts the entire victory
catalog within the frame of xenia, both human and divine.
[21]Nisetich 1977a.144. Nisetich underscores the significance of καὶ γάρ at line 30:
Pindar explicitly says that the children of Ainesidamos are mixed with immortal honors
because their houses are not ignorant of kōmoi and songs.

mian victory."[22] The ellipse and the use of σοφός tell Thrasyboulos riddlingly that he understands about the nature and uses of wealth; then the οὐκ ἄγνωτ' that immediately follows picks up σοφός and gives him a clue to the solution. For implied in οὐκ ἄγνωτ' . . . ἵπποισι νίκαν are all the expenditures that lead to immortality—horse racing, *xenia*, and celebratory song. The poet mentions horses explicitly, and οὐκ ἄγνωτ', as many scholars have noted, points to the poetic commemoration of victory.[23] Finally, the exchange of guest-gifts is suggested by the language of lines 14–16, especially ὀπάσαις and πέμπεν. But what is only implicit at the end of the first triad is elaborated throughout the victory catalog of the second, so that when Pindar repeats οὐκ ἀγνῶτες he is signaling the "solution" to the "riddle" of χρήματα χρήματ' ἀνήρ.[24] Money *is* the man, but this has become a positive fact, for knowing how to *use* one's wealth opens up the possibility of immortal honors. We might say in Polanyi's terms: the original force of Alcaeus' words is that the economy has become disembedded, that money by itself is taking over and breaking down the proper social categories. Pindar's strategy is to reembed wealth, to ground it completely in its uses in society. Once this is done, money no longer has to be a negative thing: it is, rather, a powerful tool to win prestige in socially acceptable forms.

Furthermore, the shift from a negative to a positive view of wealth is paralleled by the semantic shift undergone by the single word ἀγνώς. In its first appearance the adjective has a passive meaning—"not unknown" the victory I sing—just as the man in the Argive saying appears as the passive victim of his own wealth. By the end of the second triad,

---

[22]On the use of γάρ to mark an ellipse, see Denniston 1959.60–62 and Nisetich 1977a.142 with n. 49. On the meaning of ἄγνωτ' here see Woodbury 1968.541 n. 24 and Thummer 1968.2.42.

[23]See, for example, Pavese 1966.111, Nisetich 1977a.142, and Thummer 1968.2.42. Nisetich offers a subtle and somewhat different analysis of these lines.

[24]It may be that the time lag between posing the riddle and offering its solution (or rather, having the solution arise out of the process of the poem) is a characteristic element of the *ainos* form. Consider Hesiod's riddle of the hawk and the nightingale (*Works & Days* 202–212), which gets its solution only 70 lines later when the poet asserts: τόνδε γὰρ ἀνθρώποισι νόμον διέταξε Κρονίων, / ἰχθύσι μὲν καὶ θηρσὶ καὶ οἰωνοῖς πετεηνοῖς / ἔσθειν ἀλλήλους, ἐπεὶ οὐ δίκη ἐστὶ μετ' αὐτοῖς / ("For the son of Kronos ordained this as the law for men, for fish and wild animals and winged birds to eat each other, since there is no justice among them" [276–278]). And as Hesiod plays on the understanding of the kings (νῦν δ' αἶνον βασιλεῦσ' ἐρέω, φρονέουσι καὶ αὐτοῖς [*Works & Days* 202]), so Pindar emphasizes the aspect of knowledge or understanding with the repeated οὐκ ἄγνως. On Hesiod's riddle and the emergence of its solution from the process of the poem, see Nagy 1982.58–59; on the importance of an understanding audience for the *ainos* form, see Nagy 1979.239–240.

its meaning has become active: "Your houses are not ignorant/not inexperienced of *kōmoi* and sweet-boasting songs." Here οὐκ ἀγνῶτες represents the active, informed choice of the man who knows how to deploy his wealth to attain a kind of immortality.[25]

The positive view of wealth created by the second triad is ratified by the third in its expansive praise of Xenokrates. It is noteworthy that Pindar here explicitly praises Xenokrates for exactly those uses of wealth which are implied in the victory catalog: horse racing (38) and hospitality to men and gods (39–42). In addition, the final crucial expenditure of the victory catalog—the commissioning of celebratory song—is implied in the poet's injunction to Thrasyboulos:

> μήτ᾽ ἀρετάν ποτε σιγάτω πατρῴαν,
> μηδὲ τούσδ᾽ ὕμνους· ἐπεί τοι
> οὐκ ἐλινύσοντας αὐτοὺς ἐργασάμαν.
>
> (I.2.44–46)

Never keep silent your paternal *aretē* or these songs, since I did not fashion them to stand idle.

His father's *aretē*, which Thrasyboulos is enjoined not to bury in silence, is preserved specifically in Pindar's song, so that μήτ᾽ ἀρετάν . . . πατρῴαν, μηδὲ τούσδ᾽ ὕμνους is a kind of hendiadys.[26] Xenokrates' achievements, it is implied, have a better chance of enduring fame because he thought to commission Pindar's poem.

Having made this point, the poet picks up and completely inverts the opening image of the mercenary Muse. "Do not keep silent these hymns, since I did not fashion them to stand idle." The negative ἐργά-τις of the proem has become the positive ἐργασάμαν; the fact that these songs "work for their living," disseminating the patron's glory, is now

---

[25]It may be that the repetition of μελι- compounds for song also articulates the stages of the poem's development. First the παιδείους . . . ὕμνους of the older poets are described as μελιγάρυας (3), then the "gentle-voiced songs" are sold by μελιφθόγ-γου . . . Τερψιχόρας (7). Finally, at the climactic point at the end of the second triad, Pindar tells Thrasyboulos that his house "is not ignorant of μελικόμπων ἀοιδᾶν" (32). The second element of the compound epithet here is significant; rather than just speak sweetly, as the first two classes of song do, these songs "boast," and their boasting is what gains "immortal honors" for their patrons. We should note that, contra LSJ, the noun κόμπος is always positive in Pindar—and, in fact, always refers to his own celebratory song glorifying the victory (N.8.49, I.1.43, I.5.24; cf. P.10.4).

[26]This is not to reject the important observation of Nisetich 1977a.147 that these lines refer to both Pindar's song and Thrasyboulos' behavior as memorials of "paternal ἀρετή," playing on the double meaning of πατρῴαν.

their chief recommendation.[27] It is worth noting in this context the striking verbal parallels between Isthmian 2.44–46 and Nemean 5.1–2:

Οὐκ ἀνδριαντοποιός εἰμ᾽, ὥστ᾽ ἐλινύσοντα ἐργάζεσθαι ἀγάλματ᾽
ἐπ᾽ αὐτᾶς βαθμίδος
ἑσταότ᾽·

I am not a maker of statues to fashion images that stand idle upon their bases.

In Nemean 5, Pindar uses the language of the *tektōn* to assert the superiority of poetry: the chorus members performing his ode are not immobile statues but moving, breathing ones.[28] Insofar as these lines from Isthmian 2 partake of the image of the poet as *tektōn*, they underscore the theme of *megaloprepeia* and point to the relationship between the poet's patron and his community. For the "work" that Pindar's poems do is that of dedications, "works" erected to commemorate exceptional achievement in the public sphere. Like a dedication, the poem glorifies not its maker but the man who commissioned it for his service to the polis.

Finally, the last two lines of the poem shift from the *tektōn* model to that of gift exchange, transforming Pindar's relationship with Thrasyboulos into one of *xenia*:

ταῦτα, Νικάσιππ᾽, ἀπόνειμον, ὅταν
ξεῖνον ἐμὸν ἠθαῖον ἔλθῃς.

(I.2.47–48)

These things, O Nikasippos, apportion, whenever you come to my customary guest-friend.[29]

Commentators have taken the aptly named Nikasippos to be the chorus leader to whom Pindar entrusts the production and performance of his poem.[30] Thus the poet assimilates the performance of the ode to one

[27]Simpson finds in lines 45–46 a confirmation of the negative view of the new poetry, because he associates ἐλινύσοντας with the idling of prostitutes "waiting for customers" (Simpson 1969a.472–473). But surely the clear verbal echo ἐργάτις / ἐργασάμαν is more telling for the point of these lines.

[28]For the parallel between I.2.44–46 and N.5.1–2, see Svenbro 1976.190 and Race 1987.154–155.

[29]On the meaning of ἠθαῖον, see Watkins 1989.786–788.

[30]Thus, for example, Farnell 1930.2.346. Thummer (1968.2.54) and Race (1987.155 n. 68) are more cautious.

form of generosity for which Xenokrates has just been so lavishly praised. By this shift of models, Pindar completes the redemption of the mercenary Muse: instead of a prostitute, she has become an honored guest in Thrasyboulos' house.

But we must finally ask why Pindar should choose to construct his poem this way; why start out with the older poets' negative view of his "mercenary Muse"? On our way to answering this question, we may also perhaps find the answer to our first question—what connects love and money in the proem? Woodbury sees the proem as describing a change in the condition of poetry, and Nisetich emphasizes the public nature of Pindar's Muse.[31] We need only add that both kinds of poetry are inseparable from their social context. That is to say, the proem contrasts the conditions of poetry because it opposes two aristocratic value systems through the kinds of poetry they engender. That of the older poets is organized around small, private groups of aristocratic *hetairoi* in symposia.[32] In this context the poets performed solo, apparently spontaneously. The songs they performed were an endorsement of aristocratic values, social *paideia* in an erotic frame. This is the social significance of the παίδειοι ὕμνοι to which Pindar alludes.[33]

The aristocracy for which the older poets spoke was also rabidly opposed to money and the monetary economy. Alcaeus expresses his distrust of money not only in the words Pindar quotes, χρήματ' ἀνήρ, but also in the longer fragment 69 LP:

> Ζεῦ πάτερ, Λύδοι μὲν ἐπα[σχάλαντες
> συμφόραισι δισχελίοις στά[τηρας
> ἄμμ' ἔδωκαν, αἴ κε δυνάμεθ' ἴρ[αν
> ἐς πόλιν ἔλθην,
>
> οὐ πάθοντες οὐδάμα πῶσλον οὐ[δ' ἔ]ην
> οὐδὲ γινώσκοντες· ὁ δ' ὡς ἀλώπα[ξ
> ποικ[ι]λόφρων εὐμάρεα προλέξα[ις
> ἤλπ[ε]το λάσην.

[31] Woodbury 1968. 532–537, Nisetich 1977a. 141.

[32] See Rösler 1980. 26–77, Gernet 1981b. 284.

[33] Welcker (1834. 222–234), Von der Mühll (1964. 168–172), and Lasserre (1974. 17–20) have observed that these παίδειοι ὕμνοι are themselves a conventional form whose purpose is praise of aristocratic young men within their social group. As such, these poems affirm and transmit the aristocratic values of the group in which they are performed. It should be said that Pindar wrote such poems as well (indeed, fr. 124ab SM is a scolion or encomium addressed to Thrasyboulos). Of these poems, fr. 123 SM (to Theoxenos of Tenedos) seems to be a παίδειος ὕμνος in Welcker's sense. For Pindar's work in this genre, see van Groningen 1960.

Zeus Father, the Lydians, distressed by their misfortune, have given us
two thousand staters if we can go to the holy city, not having experienced
anything, not even one noble thing, or knowing us at all. But that one,
crafty-minded like a fox, hoped to escape notice, predicting an easy
outcome.

Unfortunately, we know nothing about the political situation behind
these lines.[34] Still, the poet's tone in describing the Lydians seems
amazed and even a little alarmed. The four negatives in lines 5–6 direct
us to the source of the poet's anxiety. In a premonetary culture, wealth
and the exchange of wealth are the prerogatives of the nobility, and
valuables travel in the well-worn channels of gift exchange. It is fundamental to the system that no exchange occur between strangers, at least
strangers known to be of a different social class. But here that system is
erased. The Lydians have not experienced any noble thing from us (οὐ
παθόντες)—that is, there is no preexistent gift-exchange framework.
Nor do they know anything about us (οὐδὲ γινώσκοντες): nor are there
grounds for current gift exchange in a mutual recognition of the other's
quality. The crucial word is ἔσλον (in the form που ἔσλον, so πῶσλον)
in line 5. Coinage threatens the distinction of nobility because anyone
can have money and anyone can give money to anyone else. Money is
exchanged between strangers.

This is the central danger of money for Alcaeus: it confers power and
status without guaranteeing the quality of its owner, and thus it undermines the power monopoly of the aristocratic elite.[35] Theognis, who
shares Alcaeus' hostility and distrust toward money, takes it even a step
farther. Because they honor wealth, the noble intermarry with the base

---

[34]For various possible scenarios, see Page 1955.230–233, Bowra 1961.140–142, Kirkwood 1974.61–62, Burnett 1983.163–166, and Tarditi 1984.

[35]Gernet (1981b.286–287) makes the same observation: "In Attica at least, money
proceeds originally from the nobility. . . . Still it is money that proves fatal to the nobility.
For the use of money allows and even legitimates losses of equilibrium in society.
Eunomia, according to its etymology (*nomos*), means precisely 'equilibrium.' In the
ancient state, one can say only that the *gene*—the recipients of local privileges and the
sacra associated with the earth—have some connection with 'demes' (often of the same
name). But at the end of the sixth century B.C. the *gene* are strangely dispersed throughout Attica. The locales are all confused, there is no real plan, and one can aspire to the
unlimited role of the *prostates*, or 'patron'; some put themselves up as 'patron of the
people.' However, the *prostates tou demou* is the tyrant, and what made the phenomenon
of tyranny possible was a new kind of economy that both perpetuated and distorted old
values. . . . On the other hand, the nobility is of necessity compromised by the progress
of an abstract economy that favors no particular individual. 'Money makes the man' says
a proverb dating from a period of crisis."

and taint the purity of their blood. Thus money undermines not merely the rule of the aristocrats but their very existence:

> χρήματα μὲν τιμῶσι· καὶ ἐκ κακοῦ ἐσθλὸς ἔγημε
> καὶ κακὸς ἐξ ἀγαθοῦ· πλοῦτος ἔμειξε γένος.
> οὕτω μὴ θαύμαζε γένος, Πολυπαΐδη, ἀστῶν
> μαυροῦσθαι· σὺν γὰρ μίσγεται ἐσθλὰ κακοῖς.

> (Theognis 189–192)

They honor money. A noble man marries the daughter of a base man, and a base man the daughter of a good man. Wealth has mixed the race. Thus do not marvel, O Polypaides, that the race of citizens has become obscure, for noble things are mixed with base.[36]

Sometimes their fear of money and the erotic setting of the old *paideia* intersect in the words of these aristocratic poets. Money, they fear, will buy eros and corrupt the aristocratic system by which *paideia* is accomplished through *paiderastia*.[37] This may well be the point of Anacreon's ironic quip, οὐδ' ἀργυρῆ κω τότ' ἔλαμπε Πειθώ. Thus Maurice Bowra interprets the fragment at any rate: "This must surely come from an amatory context, since Peitho is in some sense a divinity of love, and what counts is the adjective ἀργυρέη. Goddesses like Aphrodite may be called 'golden,' but Anacreon is thinking of a lower kind of love and calls it silver to indicate that it is for hire."[38]

The system Pindar espouses, in contrast, is an aristocratic code integrated into the polis. The poet starts out describing his art in more conservative aristocratic terms (adapting the words of the poet spokesmen of an earlier age), but the process of the poem turns the negative depiction of the mercenary Muse on its head. Pindar's ode validates in turn a new aristocratic ethos, which depends on embracing the money economy. This ethos, with its new virtue *megaloprepeia*, appears to be the invention of tyrants taken over by the polis to strike an uneasy peace with the aristocracy. The poetry of *megaloprepeia* contrasts with that of the older monodists in significant ways; as Nisetich observes, the new Muse is public, depending for her performance on choruses of cit-

---

[36]Theognis frequently contrasts money or the desire for money with aristocratic ἀρετή. See Theognis 83–86, 149–150, 173–174, 315–322, 463–464, 523–526, 683–684, 699–718, 751–752, 1061–1062, 1117–1118. On Theognis 189–192, see Nagy 1985.54–55.

[37]On the link between *paideia* and *paiderastia* in the old (aristocratic) education, see Havelock 1952.100–108, Marrou 1956.26–35, Dover 1978.202, Lewis 1985.197–222, Kurke 1990.

[38]Bowra 1961.296.

izens.[39] Given this performance setting, the poet must compose not merely for a small aristocratic elite but for the whole community. Moreover, the poetry of *megaloprepeia* differs from the older poetry in its attitude to money. Rather than denounce the money economy, the new public poetry appropriates it for the nobility as a means to power and prestige.

What finally links the new poetry to the old (in Pindar's proem as in the historical context) is its paideutic function. At first, poetry for hire, viewed through the hostile lens of the older ethos, seems to threaten the corruption of the aristocracy and its established modes of *paideia*. Thus, in the erotic terms of the old *paideia*, the new poetry is prostitution. But Isthmian 2 transforms that image of the modern Muse and thus embodies a new *paideia*, reeducating the nobility for its place in the new polis. Scholars have often noted the paideutic function of Pindar's epinikia, but they have tended to construe that *paideia* too narrowly, both in its intended audience and in its techniques.[40] Werner Jaeger, for example, begins his section "Pindar, the Voice of Aristocracy" with the assertion, "When we turn from Theognis to Pindar, we leave the fierce struggles of the nobility in Megara and elsewhere to defend its place in society, and mount to the summit of the calm, proud, inviolate life of early Greek aristocracy. At this height we can forget the problems and conflicts of Theognis' world, and be content to marvel at the power and beauty of that noble and distant ideal."[41] Jaeger here echoes the traditional view of Pindar as the backward-looking Boeotian aristocrat, serene in his outmoded views and oblivious to the upheavals of fifth-century Greece.[42] But Isthmian 2 shows us a very different poet, grappling with the position of the aristocracy in the polis by means that seem quite modern. Pindar accomplishes his public *paideia* by a kind of dialectic, guiding his audience from a traditional negative view of wealth to a positive reevaluation. And far from being oblivious to new developments, the poet consciously and masterfully appropriates them in the service of epinikian ideology. Furthermore, these techniques—of dialectic and appropriation—seem well suited to the condition of his patron and the historical circumstances.

Indeed, Pindar's educative effort serves a very practical function—the

---

[39]Nisetich 1977a.141.

[40]Jaeger 1945.205–222, J. H. Finley 1955.16–17, 25, Fränkel 1973.488–496, Rose 1974.149–155.

[41]Jaeger 1945.205.

[42]For this traditional view, see Meyer 1901.3.445–455, Wilamowitz 1922.12–13, 55–57, 445–446, J. H. Finley 1955.4–22, Burton 1962.192–193, Lacey 1968.78.

integration of the victor into the aristocracy and the polis.[43] In this case, such integration may have been a delicate operation. If it is true that Isthmian 2 was composed after the fall of the Emmenidai, Thrasyboulos occupies an anomalous position. Though the victory the ode celebrates was won while he and his father were members of a ruling house, he is now merely a private citizen, a member of the aristocracy. Thus, suddenly, the magnificence, the lavish public displays so characteristic of tyrants (of which the poem itself is an example), must be fitted into an aristocratic code. Just as historically the Greek aristocracy appropriates *megaloprepeia* from the tyrants, so also the poet enacts the same appropriation as a means of integrating his patron into the circle of aristocrats. The poet guides his aristocratic listeners step by step from complete antipathy to a money economy to a willing utilization of it, so that by the end they can meet Thrasyboulos on common ground—the public space of the poem and of *megaloprepeia*.

Thus Pindar is partly animated by a modernizing impulse. Ironically, that impulse takes the form of assimilating the new system of *megaloprepeia* to the older ideology of gift exchange in order to make it palatable to the aristocrats in the audience. As we have seen, the logic of the victory catalog is that of a chain of human-divine *xenia*, while the praise of Xenokrates in the third triad combines the rhetoric of *megaloprepeia* (37–38) with the representation of his generous participation in the system of gift exchange (39–40). Finally, the last four lines of the poem conflate *megaloprepeia* and gift exchange by representing the poet as *tektōn* and *xenos* in rapid succession. Faced with two competing ideologies, Pindar simply combines them to appeal at once to Thrasyboulos' civic community and to the aristocratic group to which he seeks entry with his new status.

---

[43]Rose 1974.149–155 clearly recognizes the interconnection of Pindar's *paideia* and his goal of integrating the victor into his aristocratic circle.

Epinikion as
Communal Drama

Let us return to the categories of genre and poetics as defined in the Introduction. I suggested there that we must conceptualize genre in terms of performance and poetics in terms of social function. We are now in a position to identify the basic building blocks of the genre of epinikion and to state with more precision the social functions it fulfills through performance. Finally, we can address the central question raised by public poetry in the archaic period: how do socially embedded forms cope with cultural change? To conclude, I would like to consider these questions in the light of a sociological poetics of Pindar.

Once we correlate genre with performance, we have at our disposal a great deal of recent work that attempts to decode the symbolic value of public rituals and ceremonials.[1] This discussion might usefully be applied to Pindar, since the extant texts of the odes are essentially scripts for public ceremonies. Thus we might conceptualize the workings of epinikion within the community in terms of a model recently proposed by W. R. Connor. Connor suggests that we must read archaic Greek ritual and ceremonial as forms of negotiation and communication between leader and people. As one example, Connor considers Herodotus' story of Pisistratus' restoration to power in the 550s B.C.[2] The historian tells us that this was done by the "ruse" of dressing a large woman named Phye as Athena and having her escort Pisistratus into the city in a chariot (Herodotus 1.60). Connor proposes that we interpret this ceremonial not as pure manipulation but as a "communal drama":

---

[1]For samples of such discussion, see Geertz 1973 and 1983, Trexler 1973, Muir 1981, MacCormack 1981, Price 1984, Darnton 1985, Connor 1987.

[2]Connor 1987.42–47.

As one looks more closely at the procession of Pisistratus and Phye it appears constantly richer and more evocative of underlying cultural patterns and more eloquent as an expression of the closeness between Pisistratus and the residents of Attica at this point in his career. The leader seems not to stand at a great distance from the attitudes and the behaviour of his fellow countrymen. Rather both appear to be linked by shared patterns of thought and united in a communal drama. The citizens are not naive bumpkins taken in by the leader's manipulation, but participants in a theatricality whose rules and roles they understand and enjoy. These are alert, even sophisticated, actors in a ritual drama affirming the establishment of a new civic order, and a renewed rapport among people, leader and protecting divinity.[3]

The "shared drama" of public ceremonial provides an analogue for the Pindaric ode in its performance context. Within the space of epinikion, the poet negotiates with the community on behalf of the returning victor. To ease the victor's acceptance by various segments of the audience, the poet dramatizes shared representations, portraying the victor as ideal citizen and ideal aristocrat. The audience, well trained to "read" the poet's symbolic message, also plays its part in the "communal drama," signaling approval by its participation in the festivities.[4]

As performance, epinikion was a relative newcomer to the public space of ceremonial.[5] Indeed, it is worth noting in this context Connor's suggestion about Solon's use of civic ritual. "Felix Jacoby," he writes, "long ago showed how much attention Solon paid to festivals and civic ritual and how important they were to his political reforms. Part of their rationale may have been to provide a civic alternative to the lavish aristocratic displays at funerals and on other occasions. Festivals such as the Genesia may thus reflect a similar tendency to that of sixth century sumptuary legislation—a curtailing of the political advantage enjoyed by those who could make a lavish display of their wealth and status."[6] It may be that the impetus behind epinikian performance represents a kind

---

[3]Connor 1987.46.

[4]Like Connor, I would like to emphasize the theatrical and mimetic aspects of the odes as ceremonial. For an anthropological theory of ritual dramas, see Turner 1974, and for a different perspective on the continuity of Attic tragedy with earlier forms of poetry, see Herington 1985.

[5]Recall that the earliest datable epinikion was composed around 520 B.C. and that ancient tradition credited Simonides with the invention of epinikion. Pindar's oldest poem, securely dated to 498 B.C., was thus composed only twenty or so years after the genre's inception.

[6]Connor 1987.49.

of counterrevolution on the part of the aristocracy. Constrained by sumptuary legislation, the aristocracy uses epinikion as a new outlet for prestige displays, a sort of ceremonial in competition with the newly bolstered civic rituals.[7]

But as a newcomer, the victory ode needed to validate itself to its diverse audience in order to be able to perform its social function. Scholars have recognized that epinikion was a fairly recent development when Pindar was composing, and they have devoted some attention to particular elements taken over from older poetic forms.[8] But such archaeology of epinikion has been almost completely confined to "literary" borrowings. Here, I have attempted to excavate the cultural stock of symbolic vocabulary on which Pindar drew to appeal to different segments of his audience. Part of this stock consists of a series of collective representations that inform the poetry: the loop of *nostos* as the proper shape of achievement, the association of achievement itself with new birth for the house, and the conception of wealth publicly spent as a source of illumination. The texture of epinikion as ceremonial also includes the incorporation of a whole set of ritual acts, objects, and gestures. Within the space of the poem, Pindar evokes funeral libations, marriage ceremonies, the giving of recompense, the offering of hospitality, and the solemn dedication of crowns and *agalmata*. Both metaphors and ritual mimesis cause this newcomer genre to resonate with its audience's most deeply felt cultural models, and so make its message of reintegration compelling. Paradoxically, Pindar's greatest innovation is his self-conscious traditionality. His confident deployment of traditional patterns in the service of a new genre makes him a master practitioner of this type of poetry.[9]

Collective metaphors and rituals form the building blocks of this poetry composed for performance. By these means, the poem enacts the reintegration of the victor into his heterogeneous community. But

[7]In support of this thesis, I would note that one sphere of imagery within the epinikia, that of ancestor cult and funeral libations, is a mode of aristocratic display that is specifically legislated against in the sixth century. Thus its inclusion in the epinikia can be seen as a way of smuggling this form of aristocratic display back into the public sphere.

[8]For discussions of various literary borrowings in Pindar's epinikia, see Bundy 1962.44–47 and 1972 on hymnic elements; Lasserre 1974 on erotic elements; Young 1971 on echoes of funerary inscriptions; Race 1982 on priamels.

[9]Cf. Connor 1987.50 on the strategies of archaic politicians: "A traditional festival form . . . is reshaped to fulfil a further function—arranging and displaying a new ordering of the civic body. The leader, like a tragic poet or actor, adapts familiar material to a new setting and structure."

the poet's use of traditional patterns is not simply a means of validating the genre and reinstating the status quo. As with many other public performances, epinikion not only plays on shared values but also attempts to influence them in turn.[10] Thus Pindar is also engaged in a kind of *paideia* as part of his negotiation with his audience. At times, he seems to be attempting to modify and modernize the behavior and attitudes of a reluctant aristocracy. For this educative effort, the poet employs two complementary strategies. On the one hand, he endorses new modes of behavior by representing them in traditional forms, as in Isthmian 2, where he assimilates *megaloprepeia* to the model of *xenia*. On the other hand, Pindar appropriates new concepts in the service of traditional values, as in his use of the language of disembedded economics to promote an embedded economy. These two strategies are a response to two different kinds of resistance by aristocrats: one group disdains money economics; the other group values money too highly. The risk is the same—that both groups will absent themselves from the public life of the polis. Pindar's *paideia* is an attempt to draw the aristocracy into this public space as the condition of its survival in a new era.

With the confrontation of the aristocracy and the polis, I come to my third point. The recontextualization of Pindar suggests that socially embedded poetry adapts by transforming traditional models and subsuming new phenomena to traditional forms. But how does such poetry accommodate social upheaval? I have attempted to answer by focusing on the different models the poet invokes to appeal to different segments of his audience. For the uneasy balance of different interest groups in the audience—the individual house, the Panhellenic aristocracy, and the city—is itself the result of profound historical developments in this period. Pindar's era was heir to the crisis of the aristocracy, the last flowering of tyranny, the rise of the democratic polis, and the shift from a premonetary to a money economy. Such social turbulence demands sophisticated poetic strategies. Pindar responds with a densely layered text that simultaneously evokes many different, even competing, symbolic systems and ideologies. Within a single poem, the poet can represent himself as a servant of the house of the victor, an aristocratic guest-friend, and a craftsman fashioning a public dedication on behalf of the victor. Both poet and victor are thus implicated in three competing systems of exchange, but all three are held in balance within the frame of the ode.

[10]For this reciprocal process, see the discussions of Gentili 1988.55–56, Greenblatt 1988.1–20, and Desan 1989.68–71.

In this proliferation of models, the poet is exploiting what Pierre Bourdieu calls "the logic of practice," operative in the rituals and organization of traditional societies:

> Symbolic systems owe their *practical coherence*, that is, their regularities, and also their irregularities and even incoherences (both equally *necessary* because inscribed in the logic of their genesis and functioning) to the fact that they are the products of practices which cannot perform their practical functions except insofar as they bring into play, in their practical state, principles which are not only coherent—i.e. capable of engendering intrinsically coherent practices compatible with the objective conditions—but also practical, in the sense of convenient, i.e. immediately mastered and manageable because obeying a "poor" and economical logic.

As Bourdieu emphasizes, incoherences and indeterminacies are necessary to the system in order to fulfill the variety of social functions required. Thus, for example, he observes that the anthropologist's attempt to construct a single complete calendar from the partial versions of many informants totalizes but also distorts the fluidity of the system in practice: "The establishment of a single series thus creates *ex nihilo* a whole host of relations (of simultaneity, succession, or symmetry, for example) between terms and guide-marks of different levels, which, being produced and used in different situations, are never brought face to face in practice and are thus compatible practically even when logically contradictory."[11] Such a logic of practice is applicable to all traditional societies, but a fortiori to traditional societies in flux. Pindar is a master of practical logic, responding to the growing heterogeneity of his audience by deploying a mutliplicity of models.

The corollary of this layering of models is that the reference of individual passages in the odes is frequently overdetermined. Accordingly, we must read them again and again through the lens of different conceptual models (thus for example, I have considered more than once the "treasure-house of hymns" in Pythian 6 or the generalized first-person prayer of Pythian 11.55–58). The first rule of Pindaric poetics is always have everything all ways. As Thomas Hubbard observes, this makes for a text that is profoundly open: "Webs of connotation, implication, and association branch out indefinitely in every direction; it remains for generations of future critics to chart their way through this

---

[11]Bourdieu 1977.109, 107, and see 96–158.

ever more complex hermeneutic labyrinth."[12] This portrait of Pindar may seem to have a great deal in common with the ambiguities and indeterminacies of poststructuralist literary theory. Yet in the end, the multivalence of the poetic signifier has less to do with deconstructive models than with the social construction of meaning. The openness of Pindar's text is akin to what Victor Turner describes as the openness of culture itself: "Coherent wholes may exist (but these tend to be lodged in individual heads, sometimes in those of obsessionals and paranoiacs), but human social groups tend to find their openness to the future in the variety of their metaphors for what may be the good life and in the contest of their paradigms."[13] In Pindar's odes we can observe in miniature the contest of paradigms of the late archaic period, always mediated by the poet himself. Indeed, much of the notorious difficulty of Pindar's poetry is attributable to the constant flux, overlap, and shift of the symbolic systems that inform his language and imagery. The text shimmers with multiple patterns of meaning which operate simultaneously, each pointing to a different segment of the poet's social world.

[12]Hubbard 1985.164. I wholeheartedly agree with Hubbard's call for a nonreductionist reading of Pindar, but I would situate the play of meaning which Hubbard locates in the Pindaric mind instead in the negotiation between the poet and his social context. Thus I would add a historical perspective to Hubbard's structural analysis.

[13]Turner 1974.14. Cf. Levine 1985.1–43.

Bibliography

Adkins, A. W. H. 1960. *Merit and Responsibility: A Study in Greek Values*. Oxford.
———. 1972. *Moral Values and Political Behaviour in Ancient Greece*. London.
Alexiou, M. 1974. *The Ritual Lament in Greek Tradition*. Cambridge.
Allen, T. W., W. R. Halliday, and E. E. Sikes, eds. 1936. *The Homeric Hymns*. Oxford.
Anderson, J. K. 1961. *Ancient Greek Horsemanship*. Berkeley, Calif.
Andrewes, A. 1956. *The Greek Tyrants*. London.
Austin, M. M., and P. Vidal-Naquet. 1977. *Economic and Social History of Ancient Greece: An Introduction*. Berkeley, Calif.
Bakhtin, M. M. 1986. *Speech Genres and Other Late Essays*. Trans. V. McGee. Ed. C. Emerson and M. Holquist. Austin, Tex.
Becker, O. 1937. *Das Bild des Weges und verwandte Vorstellungen im frühgriechischen Denken*. Hermes Einzelschriften, 4. Berlin.
Benveniste, E. 1948–1949. "Don et échange dans le vocabulaire indo-européen." *Problèmes de linguistique générale*. Vol. 1. Paris.
———. 1973. *Indo-European Language and Society*. Trans. E. Palmer. London.
Bernard, M. 1963. *Pindars Denken in Bilder*. Pfullingen.
Berve, H. 1967. *Die Tyrannis bei den Griechen*. 2 vols. Munich.
Bieler, L. 1970. "Σκιᾶς ὄναρ ἄνθρωπος." In *Pindaros und Bacchylides*. Wege der Forschung, 134. Ed. W. M. Calder III and J. Stern. Darmstadt.
Blech, M. 1982. *Studien zum Kranz bei den Griechen*. Berlin.
Block, E. 1985. "Clothing Makes the Man: A Pattern in the *Odyssey*." *TAPA* 115:1–11.
Boedeker, D. 1984. *Descent from Heaven: Images of Dew in Greek Poetry and Religion*. Chico, Calif.
Bohringer, F. 1979. "Cultes d'athlètes en Grèce classique: Propos politiques, discours mythiques." *REA* 81:5–18.
Bornemann, L. 1884. "Über die Aegiden, von denen angeblich Pindar stammte." *Philologus* 43:79–85.

Bourdieu, P. 1970. "The Berber House, or The World Reversed." *Social Science Information* 9:151–170.

———. 1977. *Outline of a Theory of Practice*. Trans. R. Nice. Cambridge.

Bowra, C. M. 1961. *Greek Lyric Poetry*. Oxford.

———. 1964. *Pindar*. Oxford.

Braswell, B. K. 1976. "Notes on the Prooemium to Pindar's Seventh Olympian Ode." *Mnemosyne* 4th ser., no. 29:233–242.

Bresson, A. 1979. *Mythe et contradiction: Analyse de la VIIe Olympique de Pindare*. Paris.

Brown, C. 1984. "The Bridegroom and the Athlete: The Proem to Pindar's Seventh Olympian." In *Greek Poetry and Philosophy: Studies in Honour of Leonard Woodbury*. Ed. D. E. Gerber. Chico, Calif.

Bundy, E. L. 1962. "Studia Pindarica I and II." *University of California Publications in Classical Philology* 18:1–34 and 35–92 (= *Studia Pindarica*. Berkeley 1986).

———. 1972. "The 'Quarrel between Kallimachos and Apollonios.' Part I: The Epilogue of Kallimachos's *Hymn to Apollo*." *CSCA* 5:39–94.

Burckhardt, J. 1952. *Griechische Kulturgeschichte*. 3 vols. Stuttgart.

Burkert, W. 1985. *Greek Religion*. Cambridge, Mass.

Burnett, A. P. 1983. *Three Archaic Poets: Archilochus, Alcaeus, Sappho*. Cambridge, Mass.

———. 1989. "Performing Pindar's Odes." *CP* 84:283–293.

Burton, R. W. B. 1962. *Pindar's Pythian Odes: Essays in Interpretation*. Oxford.

Bury, J. B., ed. 1890. *The Nemean Odes of Pindar*. London (= Amsterdam 1965).

———, ed. 1892. *The Isthmian Odes of Pindar*. London.

Campbell, D. A., ed. 1967. *Greek Lyric Poetry: A Selection*. London.

Campbell, J. K. 1964. *Honour, Family, and Patronage: A Study of Institutions and Moral Values in a Greek Mountain Community*. Oxford.

Carey, C. 1980. "Three Myths in Pindar: N.4, O.9, N.3." *Eranos* 78:143–162.

———. 1981. *A Commentary on Five Odes of Pindar: Pythian 2, Pythian 9, Nemean 1, Nemean 7, Isthmian 8*. New York.

———. 1989a. "The Performance of the Victory Ode." *AJP* 110:545–565.

———. 1989b. "Prosopographica Pindarica." *CQ* 39:1–9.

Carne-Ross, D. S. 1985. *Pindar*. New Haven, Conn.

Carney, J. 1985. *Medieval Irish Lyrics with the Irish Bardic Poet*. Mountrath Portlaoise, Ireland.

Carson, A. 1982. "Wedding at Noon in Pindar's Ninth Pythian." *GRBS* 23:121–128.

———. 1984. "The Burners: A Reading of Bacchylides' Third Epinician Ode." *Phoenix* 38:111–120.

———. 1986. "'Echo with No Door on Her Mouth': A Notional Refraction through Sophokles, Plato, and Defoe." *Stanford Literary Review* 3:247–261.

Cartledge, P. 1982. "Sparta and Samos: A Special Relationship?" *CQ* 32:243–265.

Chantraine, P. 1968–1980. *Dictionnaire étymologique de la langue grecque*. 4 vols. Paris.

Citron, A. 1965. *Semantische Untersuchung zu σπένδεσθαι-σπένδειν-εὔχεσθαι*. Winterthur.

Colace, P. 1978. "Considerazioni sul concetto di 'πλοῦτος' in Pindaro." In *Studi in onore di Anthos Ardizzoni*. Ed. E. Livrea and G. A. Privitera. Vol. 2. Rome.

Cole, A. T. 1987. "1 + 1 = 3: Studies in Pindar's Arithmetic." *AJP* 108:553–568.

Connor, W. R. 1968. *Theopompus and Fifth-Century Athens*. Cambridge, Mass.

———. 1971. *The New Politicians of Fifth-Century Athens*. Princeton, N.J.

———. 1977. "*Tyrannis Polis*." In *Ancient and Modern: Essays in Honor of Gerald F. Else*. Ed. J. H. D'Arms. Ann Arbor, Mich.

———. 1985. "The Razing of the House in Greek Society." *TAPA* 115:79–102.

———. 1987. "Tribes, Festivals, and Processions; Civic Ceremonial and Political Manipulation in Archaic Greece." *JHS* 107:40–50.

Crotty, K. 1982. *Song and Action: The Victory Odes of Pindar*. Baltimore.

Darnton, R. 1985. "A Bourgeois Puts His World in Order: The City as a Text." In *The Great Cat Massacre and Other Episodes in French Cultural History*. New York.

Davies, J. K. 1967. "Demosthenes on Liturgies: A Note." *JHS* 87:33–40.

———. 1971. *Athenian Propertied Families, 600–300 B.C.* Oxford.

———. 1981. *Wealth and the Power of Wealth in Classical Athens*. New York.

Denniston, J. D. 1959. *The Greek Particles*. 2d ed. Oxford.

Desan, S. 1989. "Crowds, Community, and Ritual in the Work of E. P. Thompson and Natalie Davis." In *The New Cultural History*. Ed. L. Hunt. Berkeley, Calif.

De Sélincourt, A., trans. 1972. *Herodotus: The Histories*. Revised by A. R. Burn. New York.

Detienne, M., ed. 1988. *Les savoirs de l'écriture en Grèce ancienne*. Lille.

Dickie, M. W. 1976. "On the Meaning of Ἐφήμερος" *ICS* 1:7–14.

———. 1984. "*Hēsychia* and *Hybris* in Pindar." In *Greek Poetry and Philosophy: Studies in Honour of Leonard Woodbury*. Ed. D. E. Gerber. Chico, Calif.

Diels, H., and W. Kranz, ed. 1951–1952. *Die Fragmente der Vorsokratiker*. 6th ed. 3 vols. Zurich.

Donlan, W. 1980. *The Aristocratic Ideal in Ancient Greece*. Lawrence, Kans.

Dornseiff, F. 1921. *Pindars Stil*. Berlin.

Dougherty-Glenn, C. 1988. "Apollo, Κτίσις, and Pindar: Literary Representations of Archaic City Foundations." Ph.D. diss., Princeton University.

Dover, K. J. 1964. "The Poetry of Archilochos." In *Archiloque*. Fondation Hardt pour l'étude de l'antiquité classique, Entrétiens 10. Geneva.

———. 1978. *Greek Homosexuality*. Cambridge, Mass.

Drachmann, A. B., ed. 1903. *Scholia Vetera in Pindari Carmina*. Vol. 1. *Scholia in Olympionicas*. Leipzig.

———. 1910. *Scholia Vetera in Pindari Carmina*. Vol. 2. *Scholia in Pythionicas*. Leipzig.

———. 1926. *Scholia Vetera in Pindari Carmina*. Vol. 3. *Scholia in Nemeonicas et Isthmionicas-Epimetrum-Indices*. Leipzig.

Duchemin, J. 1955. *Pindare: Poète et prophète*. Paris.

———. 1967. *Pindare, Pythiques (III, IX, IV, V)*. Paris.

Durante, M. 1968a. "Epea pteroenta. Die Rede als 'Weg' in griechischen und vedischen Bildern." In *Indogermanische Dichtersprache*. Wege der Forschung, Band 165. Ed. R. Schmitt. Darmstadt.

———. 1968b. "Untersuchungen zur Vorgeschichte der griechischen Dichtersprache. Die terminologie für das dichterische Schaffen." In *Indogermanische Dichtersprache*. Wege der Forschung, Band 165. Ed. R. Schmitt. Darmstadt.

Dyer, L. 1905. "Olympian Treasuries and Treasuries in General." *JHS* 25:294–319.

Ebert, J. 1972. *Griechische Epigramme auf Sieger an gymnischen und hippischen Agonen*. Abhandlungen der sächsischen Akademie der Wissenschaften zu Leipzig. Philologisch-historische Klasse 63.2. Berlin.

Edmunds, L., and R. Martin. 1977. "Thucydides 2.65.8: Ἐλευθέρως." *HSCP* 81:187–193.

Eernstman, J. P. A. 1932. Οἰκεῖος, Ἑταῖρος, Ἐπιτήδειος, Φίλος: *Bijdrage to de Kennis van de Terminologie der Vriendschap bij de Grieken*. Groningen.

Else, G. 1957. "The Origin of Τραγῳδία." *Hermes* 85:17–46.

Erbse, H. 1969. "Pindars dritte nemeische Ode." *Hermes* 97:272–291.

Euben, J. P., ed. 1986. *Greek Tragedy and Political Theory*. Berkeley, Calif.

Evans-Pritchard, E. E. 1940. *The Nuer*. Oxford.

———. 1951. *Kinship and Marriage among the Nuer*. Oxford.

Farenga, V. 1985. "La tirannide greca e la strategia numismatica." In *Mondo classico: Percorsi possibili*. Ravenna.

Farnell, L. R. 1921. *Greek Hero Cults and Ideas of Immortality*. Oxford.

—, ed. 1930. *The Works of Pindar*. 3 vols. London.

Fennell, C. A. M., ed. 1893. *Pindar: The Olympian and Pythian Odes*. Cambridge.

Figueira, T. J. 1981. *Aegina: Society and Politics*. New York.

Finley, J. H. 1955. *Pindar and Aeschylus*. Martin Classical Lectures, 14. Cambridge, Mass.

Finley, M. I. 1952. *Studies in Land and Credit in Ancient Athens, 500–200 B.C.* New Brunswick, N.J. (=Arno Reprint, 1973).

———. 1953. "Marriage, Sale, and Gift in the Homeric World." In *Economy and Society in Ancient Greece*. New York.

———. 1968. *Aspects of Antiquity: Discoveries and Controversies*. New York.

———. 1975. *The Ancient Economy*. London.

———. 1977. *The World of Odysseus*. Rev. ed. New York.

———. 1983. *Politics in the Ancient World*. Cambridge.

Firth, R. 1965. *Primitive Polynesian Economy*. London.

Fisher, N. R. E. 1976. "*Hybris* and Dishonour: I." *Greece & Rome* 2d ser., 23:177–193.

———. 1979. "*Hybris* and Dishonour: II." *Greece & Rome* 2d ser., 26:32–47.

Fitzgerald, W. 1987. *Agonistic Poetry: The Pindaric Mode in Pindar, Horace, Hölderlin, and the English Ode*. Berkeley, Calif.

Floyd, E. D. 1965. "The Performance of Pindar, Pythian 8.55–70." *GRBS* 6:187–200.

Fogelmark, S. 1972. *Studies in Pindar with Particular Reference to Paean VI and Nemean VII*. Lund.

Fontenrose, J. 1968. "The Hero as Athlete." *CSCA* 1:73–104.

Forssman, B. 1966. *Untersuchungen zur Sprache Pindars*. Klassisch-Philologische Studien, 33. Wiesbaden.

Fraenkel, E., ed. 1950. *Aeschylus: Agamemnon*. 3 vols. Oxford.

Frame, D. 1978. *The Myth of Return in Early Greek Epic.* New Haven, Conn.

Fränkel, H. 1925. "Griechische Wörter." *Glotta* 14:1–13.

———. 1930. Review of W. Schadewaldt, *Der Aufbau des pindarischen Epinikion.* In *Gnomon* 30:1–20.

———. 1946. "Man's 'Ephemeros' Nature according to Pindar and Others." *TAPA* 77:131–145.

———. 1961. "Schrullen in den Scholien zu Pindars Nemeen 7 und Olympien 3." *Hermes* 89:385–397.

———. 1968. *Wege und Formen frügriechischen Denkens.* 3d ed. Munich.

———. 1973. *Early Greek Poetry and Philosophy.* Trans. M. Hadas and J. Willis. New York.

Friis Johansen, H., and E. W. Whittle, eds. 1980. *Aeschylus: The Suppliants.* 3 vols. Copenhagen.

Frisk, H. 1960–1972. *Griechisches etymologisches Wörterbuch.* 3 vols. Heidelberg.

Fustel de Coulanges, N. D. 1980. *The Ancient City.* Baltimore.

Gabrielson, V. 1986. "Φανερά and Ἀφανὴς Οὐσία in Classical Athens." *Classica et Mediaevalia* 37:99–114.

Garvie, A. F., ed. 1986. *Aeschylus: Choephori.* Oxford.

Geertz, C. 1973. *The Interpretation of Cultures.* New York.

———. 1983. *Local Knowledge: Further Essays in Interpretive Anthropology.* New York.

Gelzer, T. 1985. "Μοῦσα αὐθιγενής: Bemerkungen zu einem Typ pindarischer und bacchylideischer Epinikien." *MH* 42:95–120.

Gentili, B. 1988. *Poetry and Its Public in Ancient Greece from Homer to the Fifth Century.* Trans. A. T. Cole. Baltimore.

Gerber, D. E. 1982. *Pindar's Olympian 1: A Commentary.* Toronto.

Gernet, L. 1981a. "'Value' in Greek Myth." In *Myth, Religion, and Society.* Trans. R. L. Gordon. Cambridge.

———. 1981b. *The Anthropology of Ancient Greece.* Trans. J. Hamilton and B. Nagy. Baltimore.

Giannini, P. 1982. "'Qualcuno' e 'nessuno' in Pindar, Pyth. 8.95." *QUCC* 40:69–76.

Gildersleeve, B. L., ed. 1890. *The Olympian and Pythian Odes.* 2d ed. New York.

Glotz, G. 1904. *La solidarité de la famille dans le droit criminel en Grèce.* Paris.

———. 1929. *The Greek City and Its Institutions.* London.

Goldhill, S. 1986. *Reading Greek Tragedy.* Cambridge.

———. 1987. "The Great Dionysia and Civic Ideology." *JHS* 107:58–76.

Gomme, A. W., A. Andrewes, and K. J. Dover. 1970. *A Historical Commentary on Thucydides., Vol. IV (Books VI 25–VII).* Oxford.

Greenblatt, S. 1988. *Shakespearean Negotiations: The Circulation of Social Energy in Renaissance England.* Berkeley, Calif.

Greengard, C. 1980. *The Structure of Pindar's Epinician Odes.* Amsterdam.

Gregory, C. A. 1982. *Gifts and Commodities.* London.

Gundert, H. 1935. *Pindar und sein Dichterberuf.* Frankfurt.

Gzella, S. 1969–1970a. "The Competition among the Greek Choral Poets." *Eos* 58, fasc. 1:19–32.

——. 1969–1970b. "Self-Publicity and Polemics in Greek Choral Lyrics." *Eos* 58, fasc. 2:171–179.

——. 1971. "Problem of the Fee in Greek Choral Lyric." *Eos* 59, fasc. 2:189–202.

Hamilton, R. 1974. *Epinikion: General Form in the Odes of Pindar*. The Hague.

Havelock, E. A. 1952. "Why Was Socrates Tried?" In *Studies in Honour of Gilbert Norwood*. Ed. M. E. White. Toronto.

——. 1963. *Preface to Plato*. Cambridge, Mass.

Heath, M. 1988. "Receiving the Κῶμος: The Context and Performance of Epinician." *AJP* 109:180–195.

Herington, J. 1985. *Poetry into Drama: Early Tragedy and the Greek Poetic Tradition*. Berkeley, Calif.

Herman, G. 1987. *Ritualised Friendship and the Greek City*. Cambridge.

Herzfeld, M. 1985. *The Poetics of Manhood: Contest and Identity in a Cretan Mountain Village*. Princeton, N.J.

Hewitt, J. W. 1927. "The Terminology of 'Gratitude' in Greek." *CP* 22:142–161.

Hock, G. 1905. "Griechische Weihgebraüche." Inaugural diss., University of Munich.

Hoekstra, A. 1950. "Hésiode, *Les travaux et les jours*, 405–407, 317–319, 21–24." *Mnemosyne* 4th ser., no. 3:89–114.

How, W. W., and J. Wells. *A Commentary on Herodotus*. 2 vols. Oxford.

Hubbard, T. K. 1983. "Pindaric *Harmonia* : Pythian 8.67–9." *Mnemosyne* 4th ser., no. 36:286–292.

——. 1985. *The Pindaric Mind: A Study of Logical Structures in Early Greek Poetry*. Mnemosyne Supplement 85. Leiden.

Huizinga, J. 1950. *Homo Ludens*. Boston.

Humphreys, S. C. 1978. *Anthropology and the Greeks*. London.

——. 1983. *The Family, Women, and Death: Comparative Studies*. London.

Illig, L. 1932. *Zur Form der pindarischen Erzählung: Interpretationen und Untersuchungen*. Berlin.

Instone, S. 1986. Review of D. C. Young, *The Olympic Myth of Greek Amateur Athletics*. In *JHS* 106:238–239.

Irigoin, J. 1952. *Histoire du texte de Pindare*. Paris.

Jacoby, Felix. 1923–1958. *Die Fragmente der griechischen Historiker*. Berlin and Leiden.

Jaeger, W. 1945. *Paideia: The Ideals of Greek Culture*. Vol. I. Oxford.

Jebb, R. C., ed. 1894. *Sophocles: The Plays and Fragments. Part 6: The Electra*. Cambridge.

Jones, J. 1962. *On Aristotle and Greek Tragedy*. Stanford, Calif.

Jurenka, H. 1893. "Novae lectiones pindaricae." *WS* 15:1–34.

Kirkwood, G. M. 1974. *Early Greek Monody: The History of a Poetic Type*. Ithaca, N.Y.

——. 1975. "Nemean 7 and the Theme of Vicissitude in Pindar." In *Poetry and Poetics from Ancient Greece to the Renaissance: Studies in Honor of James Hutton*. Ithaca, N.Y.

——, ed. 1982. *Selections from Pindar*. Chico, Calif.

——. 1984. "Blame and Envy in the Pindaric Epinician." In *Greek Poetry and Philosophy: Studies in Honour of Leonard Woodbury*. Ed. D. E. Gerber. Chico, Calif.

Köhnken, A. 1970. "Hieron und Deinomenes in Pindars erstem pythischen Gedicht." *Hermes* 98:1–13.

——. 1971. *Die Funktion des Mythos bei Pindar*. Berlin.

——. 1974. "Pindar as Innovator: Poseidon Hippios and the Relevance of the Pelops Story in Olympian 1." *CQ* 24:199–206.

——. 1985. " 'Meilichos Orga': Liebesthematik und aktueller Sieg in der neunten pythischen Ode Pindars." In *Pindare*. Fondation Hardt pour l'étude de l'antiquité classique, Entrétiens 31. Geneva.

Kraay, C. M. 1976. *Archaic and Classical Greek Coins*. Berkeley, Calif.

Krischer, T. 1965. "Pindars Rhapsodengedicht (zu Nem. 2)." *WS* 78:32–39.

——. 1974. "Die logischen Formen der Priamel." *Grazer Beiträge* 2:79–91.

Kroll, J. H., and N. M. Waggoner. 1984. "Dating the Earliest Coins of Athens, Corinth, and Aegina." *AJA* 88:325–340.

Kromer, G. 1976. "The Value of Time in Pindar's Olympian 10." *Hermes* 104:420–436.

Kurke, L. 1989. "Καπηλεία and Deceit: Theognis 59–60." *AJP* 110:535–544.

——. 1990. "Pindar's Sixth Pythian and the Tradition of Advice Poetry." *TAPA* 120:85–107.

Kurtz, D. C., and J. Boardman. 1971. *Greek Burial Customs*. London.

Kyle, D. G. 1985. Review of D. C. Young, *The Olympic Myth of Greek Amateur Athletics*. In *Echos du Monde Classique/Classical Views* 29 (=n.s. 4):134–144.

Lacey, W. K. 1966. "Homeric Ἕδνα and Penelope's Κύριος." *JHS* 86:55–68.

——. 1968. *The Family in Classical Greece*. Ithaca, N.Y..

Lasserre, F. 1974. "Ornements érotiques dans la poésie lyrique archaïque." In *Serta Turyniana: Studies in Greek Literature and Palaeography in Honor of Alexander Turyn*. Ed. J. H. Heller and J. K. Newman. Urbana, Ill.

Latacz, J. 1966. *Zum Wortfeld "Freude" in der Sprache Homers*. Heidelberg.

Lattimore, R. 1976. *The Odes of Pindar*. 2d ed. Chicago.

Lauffer, S. 1974. "Die Liturgien in der Krisenperiode Athens: Das Problem von Finanzsystem und Demokratie." In *Hellenische Poleis: Krise—Wandlung—Wirkung*. Ed. E. C. Welskopf. Vol. 1. Berlin.

Laum, B. 1924. "Banken." In *Real-Encyclopädie* , Supplement, 4.

Lawall, G. 1961. "The Cup, the Rose, and the Winds in Pindar's Seventh Olympian." *Rivista di Filologia e di Istruzione Classica* 39:33–47.

Lee, H. M. 1978. "The 'Historical' Bundy and Encomiastic Relevance in Pindar." *CW* 72:65–70.

Lefkowitz, M. 1963. "Τῶ Καὶ Ἐγώ: The First Person in Pindar." *HSCP* 67:177–253.

——. 1975. "The Influential Fictions in the Scholia to Pythian 8." *CP* 70:173–185.

——. 1977. "Pindar's Pythian 8." *CJ* 72:209–221.

——. 1980. "Autobiographical Fiction in Pindar." *HSCP* 84:29–49.

——. 1984. "The Poet as Athlete." *Studi Italiani di Filologia Classica* 3d ser., 2:5–12.

——. 1985. "Pindar's Pythian V." In *Pindare*. Fondation Hardt pour l'étude de l'antiquité classique, Entretiens 31. Geneva.

——. 1988. "Who Sang Pindar's Victory Odes?" *AJP* 109:1–11.

Levine, D. N. 1985. *The Flight from Ambiguity: Essays in Social and Cultural Theory.* Chicago.

Lévi-Strauss, C. 1969. *The Elementary Structures of Kinship.* Trans. J. H. Bell, J. R. von Sturmer, and R. Needham. Boston.

Lewis, J. M. 1985. "Eros and the Polis in Theognis Book II." In *Theognis of Megara: Poetry and the Polis.* Ed. T. J. Figueira and G. Nagy. Baltimore.

Lewis, N. 1960. "*Leitourgia* and Related Terms." *GRBS* 3:175–184.

Liddell, H. G., R. Scott, and H. S. Jones. 1940. *A Greek-English Lexicon.* 9th ed. Oxford.

Lloyd-Jones, H. 1973. "Modern Interpretation of Pindar." *JHS* 93:109–137.

Lobel, E., and D. Page. 1955. *Poetarum lesbiorum fragmenta.* Oxford.

Loraux, N. 1981. *Les enfants d' Athéna: Idées athéniennes sur la citoyenneté et la division des sexes.* Paris.

Lowenstam, S. 1979. "The Meaning of IE **dhal-*." *TAPA* 109:125–135.

Lübbert, E. 1881. "De Pindari studiis hesiodeis et homericis dissertio." Inaugural diss., University of Bonn.

MacCormack, S. 1981. *Art and Ceremony in Late Antiquity.* Berkeley, Calif.

MacDowell, D. M. 1976. "*Hybris* in Athens." *Greece & Rome* 2d ser., 23:14–31.

——. 1978. *The Law in Classical Athens.* Ithaca, N.Y.

Macleod, C. 1983. *Collected Essays.* Oxford.

McNeal, R. A. 1978. "Structure and Metaphor in Pindar's Fourth Isthmian." *QUCC* 28:135–156.

Maehler, H. 1963. *Die Auffassung des Dichterberufs im frühen Griechentum bis zur Zeit Pindars.* Hypomnemata 3. Göttingen.

——, ed. 1982. *Die Lieder des Bakchylides: Erster Teil, Die Siegeslieder.* Mnemosyne Supplement 62. 2 vols. Leiden.

Mangelsdorff, E. A. 1913. *Das lyrische Hochzeitsgedicht bei den Griechen und Römern.* Hamburg.

Marrou, H. I. 1956. *A History of Education in Antiquity.* London.

Martin, R. P. 1984. "Hesiod, Odysseus, and the Instruction of Princes." *TAPA* 114:29–48.

——. 1989. *The Language of Heroes: Speech and Performance in the Iliad.* Ithaca, N.Y.

Mauss, M. 1967. *The Gift.* Trans. I. Cunnison. New York.

Mazon, P., ed. 1928. *Hésiode: Théogonie, Les travaux et les jours, Le bouclier.* Collection des Universités de France. Paris.

Mazzarino, S. 1947. *Fra oriente e occidente: Ricerche di storia greca archaica.* Florence.

Meillassoux, C. 1968. "Ostentation, destruction, reproduction." *Economies et Sociétés* 2:759–772.

Merkelbach, R., and M. L. West. 1967. *Fragmenta Hesiodea.* Oxford.

Meuli, K. 1935. "Scythica." *Hermes* 70:121–176.

——. 1941. "Der Ursprung der Olympischen Spiele." *Die Antike* 17:189–208.

Meyer, E. 1901. *Geschichte des Altertums*. 4 vols. Stuttgart.

Mezger, F., ed. 1880. *Pindars Siegeslieder*. Leipzig.

Miller, A. M. 1981. "Pindar, Archilochus, and Hieron." *TAPA* 111:135–143.

———. 1983. "N. 4.33–43 and the Defense of Digressive Leisure." *CJ* 78:202–220.

Molyneux, J. H. 1971. "Simonides and the Dioscuri." *Phoenix* 25:197–205.

Morris, I. 1986a. "Gift and Commodity in Archaic Greece." *Man* 21:1–17.

———. 1986b. "The Use and Abuse of Homer." *CA* 5:81–138.

Mossé, C. 1969. *La tyrannie dans la Grèce antique*. Paris.

Most, G. W. 1982. "Greek Lyric Poets." In *Ancient Writers: Greece and Rome*. Ed. T. J. Luce. Vol. 1. New York.

———. 1985. *The Measures of Praise: Structure and Function in Pindar's Second Pythian and Seventh Nemean Odes*. Hypomnemata 83. Göttingen.

———. 1987. "Two Leaden Metaphors in Pindar P. 2." *AJP* 108:569–584.

———. 1988. "Pindar I.1.67–68." *RhM* n.f. 131:101–108.

Muir, E. 1981. *Civic Ritual in Renaissance Venice*. Princeton, N.J.

Mullen, W. 1967. "Place in Pindar." *Arion* 6:462–491.

———. 1982. *Choreia: Pindar and Dance*. Princeton, N.J.

Nagy, G. 1979. *The Best of the Achaeans*. Baltimore.

———. 1982. "Hesiod." In *Ancient Writers: Greece and Rome*. Ed. T. J. Luce. New York.

———. 1985. "Theognis and Megara: A Poet's Vision of His City." In *Theognis of Megara: Poetry and the Polis*. Ed. T. J. Figueira and G. Nagy. Baltimore.

———. 1986a. "Ancient Greek Epic and Praise Poetry: Some Typological Considerations." In *Oral Tradition in Literature: Interpretation in Context*. Ed. J. M. Foley. Columbia, Mo.

———. 1986b. "Pindar's Olympian 1 and the Aetiology of the Olympic Games." *TAPA* 116:71–88.

———. 1990. *Pindar's Homer: The Lyric Possession of an Epic Past*. Baltimore.

Nassen, P. 1975. "A Literary Study of Pindar's Olympian 10." *TAPA* 105:219–240.

Newman, J. K. 1982. "Pindar, Solon, and Jealousy: Political Vocabulary in the Eleventh Pythian." *ICS* 7:189–195.

Newman, J. K., and F. S. Newman. 1984. *Pindar's Art: Its Tradition and Aims*. Hildesheim.

Nilsson, M. P. 1968. *Geschichte der griechischen Religion*. Vol. 1. 3d ed. Revised by H. Bengtson. Munich.

Nisetich, F. J. 1975. "Olympian 1.8–11: An Epinician Metaphor." *HSCP* 79:55–68.

———. 1977a. "Convention and Occasion in Isthmian 2." *CSCA* 10:133–56.

———. 1977b. "The Leaves of Triumph and Mortality: Transformation of a Traditional Image in Pindar's Olympian 12." *TAPA* 107:235–264.

———. 1980. *Pindar's Victory Songs*. Baltimore.

Norwood, G. 1915. "Pindarica." *CQ* 9:1–6.

———. 1945. *Pindar*. Berkeley, Calif.

Ober, J. 1989. *Mass and Elite in Democratic Athens: Rhetoric, Ideology, and the Power of the People*. Princeton, N.J.

Onians, R. B. 1951. *The Origins of European Thought*. Cambridge.

Page, D. 1955. *Sappho and Alcaeus: An Introduction to the Study of Ancient Lesbian Poetry*. Oxford.

———. 1962. *Poetae melici graeci*. Oxford.

———, ed. 1972. *Aeschyli Septem Quae Supersunt Tragoedias*. Oxford.

Pavese, C. 1966. "Χρήματα χρήματ' 'Ανήρ ed il motivo della liberalità nella seconda Istmica di Pindaro." *QUCC* 2:103–112.

Peek, W., ed. 1955. *Griechische Vers-Inschriften*. 1. *Grab-Epigramme*. Berlin.

Pelliccia, H. 1987. "Pindarus Homericus: Pythian 3.1–80." *HSCP* 91:39–63.

Peron, J. 1974. *Les images maritimes de Pindare*. Paris.

———. 1976. "Pindare et la victoire de Télésicrate dans la IXe Pythique (v. 76–96)." *Revue de Philologie* 3d ser., 50:58–78.

———. 1986. "Pindare et la tyrannie d'après la XIe Pythique." *REG* 99, nos. 470–471:1–21.

"Philologus." 1844. "Conjecture on a Passage in Aeschylus." *Classical Museum* 1:267.

Pickard-Cambridge, A. 1968. *The Dramatic Festivals of Athens*. 2d ed., revised by J. Gould and D. M. Lewis. Oxford.

Pleket, H. W. 1969. "The Archaic Tyrannis." *Talanta* 1:19–61.

———. 1974. "Zur Soziologie des antiken Sports." *Medelingen van het Nederlands Institut te Rome* 36 (=n.s. 1):57–87.

———. 1975. "Games, Prizes, Athletes, and Ideology: Some Aspects of the History of Sport in the Greco-Roman World." *Stadion* 1:49–89.

Polanyi, K. 1968. *Primitive, Archaic, and Modern Economies: Essays of Karl Polanyi*. Ed. G. Dalton. Garden City, N.Y.

Poliakoff, M. 1982. *Studies in the Terminology of the Greek Combat Sports*. Beiträge zur klassischen Philologie 146. Hain.

———. 1987. *Combat Sports in the Ancient World: Competition, Violence, and Culture*. New Haven, Conn.

———. 1989. Review of D. C. Young, *The Olympic Myth of Greek Amateur Athletics*. In *AJP* 110:166–171.

Price, S. R. F. 1984. *Rituals and Power: The Roman Imperial Cult in Asia Minor*. Cambridge.

Puelma, M. 1972. "Sänger und König: Zum Verständnis von Hesiods Tierfabel." *MH* 29:86–108.

Race, W. H. 1982. *The Classical Priamel from Homer to Boethius*. Mnemosyne Supplement 74. Leiden.

———. 1983. "Negative Expressions and Pindaric Ποικιλία." *TAPA* 113:95–122.

———. 1987. "Pindaric Encomium and Isokrates' *Evagoras*." *TAPA* 117:131–155.

Radt, S. L. 1958. *Pindars zweiter und sechster Paian*. Amsterdam.

Raschke, W. J. 1988. "Images of Victory: Some New Considerations of Athletic Monuments." In *The Archaeology of the Olympics: The Olympics and Other Festivals in Antiquity*. Ed. W. J. Raschke. Madison, Wis.

Redfield, J. 1975. *Nature and Culture in the "Iliad": The Tragedy of Hector*. Chicago.

———. 1982. "Notes on the Greek Wedding." *Arethusa* 15:181–201.

Renehan, R. 1969a. *Greek Textual Criticism: A Reader*. Cambridge, Mass.

——. 1969b. "Conscious Ambiguities in Pindar and Bacchylides." *GRBS* 10:217–228.

Risch, E. 1974. *Wortbildung der homerischen Sprache*. Berlin.

Robbins, E. 1978. "Cyrene and Cheiron: The Myth of Pindar's Ninth Pythian." *Phoenix* 32:91–104.

Robert, L. 1967. "Sur des inscriptions d'Ephèse." *Revue de Philologie* 3d ser., no. 41:7–84.

Robinson, E. S. G. 1951. "The Coins from the Ephesian Artemision Reconsidered." *JHS* 71:156–167.

——. 1956. "The Date of the Earliest Coins." *NC* 6th ser., 16:1–8.

Rose, H. J. 1931. "Iolaos and the Ninth Pythian Ode." *CQ* 25:156–161.

Rose, P. W. 1974. "The Myth of Pindar's First Nemean: Sportsmen, Poetry, and *Paideia*." *HSCP* 78:145–175.

——. 1982. "Towards a Dialectical Hermeneutic of Pindar's Pythian X." *Helios* 9:47–73.

Rösler, W. 1980. *Dichter und Gruppe: Eine Untersuchung zu den Bedingungen und zur historischen Funktion früher griechischer Lyrik am Beispiel Alkaios*. Munich.

Rubin, N. F. 1980. "Olympian 7: The Toast and the Future Prayer." *Hermes* 108:248–252.

Ruck, C. A. P. 1968. "Marginalia Pindarica." *Hermes* 96:132–142.

——. 1972. "Marginalia Pindarica" *Hermes* 100:143–153.

Rumpel, J. 1883. *Lexicon Pindaricum*. Leipzig.

Rusten, J. S. 1983. "Γείτων Ἥρως: Pindar's Prayer to Herakles (N.7.86–101) and Greek Popular Religion." *HSCP* 87:289–298.

Sahlins, M. 1972. *Stone Age Economics*. New York.

Sansone, D. 1988. *Greek Athletics and the Genesis of Sport*. Berkeley, Calif.

Saussure, F. de. 1974. *Course in General Linguistics*. Glasgow.

Schadewaldt, W. 1928. *Der Aufbau des pindarischen Epinikion*. Darmstadt.

——. 1932. "Der Kommos in Aischylos *Choephoren*." *Hermes* 67:312–354.

Schmidt, V. 1975. "Zu Pindar." *Glotta* 53:36–39.

Schmitt, R. 1967. *Dichtung und Dichtersprache in indogermanischer Zeit*. Wiesbaden.

Schulze, W. 1968. "Tocharisch *Tseke Peke*." In *Indogermanische Dichtersprache*. Wege der Forschung 165. Ed. R. Schmitt. Darmstadt.

Segal, C. 1967. "Pindar's Seventh Nemean." *TAPA* 98:430–490.

——. 1976. "Pindar, Mimnermus, and the 'Zeus-Given Gleam': The End of Pythian 8." *QUCC* 22:71–76.

——. 1981. "Myth, Cult, and Memory in Pindar's Third and Fourth Isthmian Odes." *Ramus* 10:69–86.

——. 1985. "Messages to the Underworld: An Aspect of Poetic Immortalization in Pindar." *AJP* 106:199–212.

——. 1986. *Pindar's Mythmaking: The Fourth Pythian Ode*. Princeton, N.J.

Sheppard, J. T. 1922. "Pind. Nem. ii.1." *PCPS* 121–123:6–8.

Simpson, M. 1969a. "The Chariot and the Bow as Metaphors for Poetry in Pindar." *TAPA* 100:437–473.

——. 1969b. "Pindar's Ninth Olympian." *GRBS* 10:113–124.

Slater, W. J. 1969a. *Lexicon to Pindar*. Berlin.

——. 1969b. "Futures in Pindar." *CQ* 19:86–94.

——. 1971. "Pindar's House." *GRBS* 12:141–152.

——. 1972. "Simonides' House." *Phoenix* 26:232–240.

——. 1979a. "Pindar and Hypothekai." *Proceedings, Second International Conference on Boiotian Antiquities*: 79–82.

——. 1979b. "Pindar's Myths: Two Pragmatic Explanations." In *Arktouros: Hellenic Studies Presented to Bernard M. W. Knox*. Ed. G. W. Bowersock, W. Burkert, and M. C. J. Putnam. Berlin.

——. 1981. "Peace, the Symposium, and the Poet." *ICS* 4:205–214.

——. 1984. "Nemean One: The Victor's Return in Poetry and Politics." In *Greek Poetry and Philosophy: Studies in Honour of Leonard Woodbury*. Ed. D. E. Gerber. Chico, Calif.

Smyth, H. W. 1956. *Greek Grammar*. Revised by G. M. Messing. Cambridge, Mass.

Snell, B., and H. Maehler, eds. 1970. *Bacchylidis Carmina cum Fragmentis*. Leipzig.

Snell, B., and H. Maehler, eds. 1975. *Pindari Carmina cum Fragmentis, Pars II: Fragmenta, Indices*. Leipzig.

Snell, B., and H. Maehler, eds. 1987. *Pindari Carmina cum Fragmentis, Pars I: Epinicia*. 8th ed. Leipzig.

Snodgrass, A. 1980. *Archaic Greece: The Age of Experiment*. London.

Starr, C. G. 1961. *The Origins of Greek Civilization*. New York.

Stein, R. 1965. "*Megaloprepeia* bei Platon." Inaugural diss., University of Bonn.

Steiner, D. 1986. *The Crown of Song: Metaphor in Pindar*. New York.

Steinkopf, G. 1937. "Untersuchungen zur Geschichte des Ruhmes bei den Griechen." Inaugural diss., University of Wittenberg.

Stengel, P. 1920. *Die griechischen Kultusaltertümer*. 3d ed. Munich.

Stenzel, J. 1926. Review of F. Taeger, *Thukydides*. In *Göttingische Gelehrte Anzeigen*. 188:193–206.

——. 1934. "Philosophie der Sprache." In *Handbuch der Philosophie*. Munich.

Stoddart, R. C. 1981. Dissertation Abstract. *HSCP* 84:313–315.

——. 1990. *Pindar and Greek Family Law*. New York.

Stoneman, R. 1976. "The 'Theban Eagle'." *CQ* n.s. 26:188–197.

——. 1979. "The Niceties of Praise: Notes on Pindar's Nemeans." *QUCC* n.s. 2:65–77.

Svenbro, J. 1976. *La parole et le marbre: Aux origines de la poétique grecque*. Lund.

Tarditi, G. 1984. "Alceo e la volpe astuta." In *Lirica greca da Archiloco a Elitis: Studi in onore di Filippo Maria Pontani*. Padua.

Thomas, R. 1989. *Oral Tradition and Written Record in Classical Athens*. Cambridge.

Thummer, E. 1957. *Die Religiostät Pindars*. Commentationes Aenipontanae, 13. Innsbruck.

——, ed. 1968. *Pindar: Die Isthmischen Gedichte*. 2 vols. Heidelberg.

Todorov, T. 1978. *Les genres du discours*. Paris.

Trexler, R.C. 1973. "Ritual Behavior in Renaissance Florence: The Setting." *Medievalia et Humanistica* n.s. 4:125–144.

Tugendhat, E. 1960. "Zum Rechtfertigungsproblem in Pindars 7. nemeischen Gedicht." *Hermes* 88:385–409.

Turner, V. 1974. *Dramas, Fields, and Metaphors: Symbolic Action in Human Society.* Ithaca, N.Y.

Ure, P. 1962. *The Origin of Tyranny.* New York.

Van Groningen, B. A. 1960. *Pindare au banquet.* Leiden.

Verdenius, W. J. 1969. "Νόστος." *Mnemosyne* 4th ser., no. 22:195.

——. 1976. "Pindar's Seventh Olympian Ode: Supplementary Comments." *Mnemosyne* 4th ser., no. 29:243–253.

——. 1983. "Pindar, Pythian 8.67–72." *Mnemosyne* 4th ser., no. 36:367–368.

——. 1987. *Commentaries on Pindar, Volume I.* Mnemosyne Supplement 97. Leiden.

Vermeule, E. 1979. *Aspects of Death in Early Greek Art and Poetry.* Berkeley, Calif.

Vernant, J.-P. 1976. "Remarks on Class Struggle in Ancient Greece." *Critique of Anthropology* 7:67–81.

——. 1980. *Myth and Society in Ancient Greece.* Trans. J. Lloyd. Brighton, Sussex.

——. 1982. "From Oedipus to Periander: Lameness, Tyranny, Incest in Legend and History." *Arethusa* 15:19–38.

——. 1983. *Myth and Thought among the Greeks.* London.

Vernant, J.-P., and P. Vidal-Naquet. 1969. "Tensions and Ambiguities in Greek Tragedy." In *Interpretation: Theory and Practice.* Ed. C. S. Singleton. Baltimore.

Vernant, J.-P., and P. Vidal-Naquet. 1981. *Tragedy and Myth in Ancient Greece.* Trans. J. Lloyd. Atlantic Highlands, N.J.

Von der Mühll, P. 1964. "Weitere pindarische Notizen." *MH* 21:168–172.

——. 1968. "Weitere pindarische Notizen." *MH* 25:226–230.

Wackernagel, J. 1916. *Sprachliche Untersuchungen zu Homer.* Göttingen.

Wade-Gery, H. T. 1932. "Thucydides the Son of Melesias." *JHS* 52:205–227.

Waring, P. 1982. "Pindar, Nemean 1.24—Smoke without Fire." *CQ* 32:270–277.

Wasserstein, A. 1982. "A Gamma in Pindar, OL. 13.3." *CQ* 32:278–280.

Watkins, C. 1989. "New Parameters in Historical Linguistics, Philology, and Culture History." *Language* 65:783–799.

Welcker, F. G. 1834. "Ibykos." *RhM* 2:211–244.

West, M. L., ed. 1971–1972. *Iambi et elegi graeci.* 2 vols. Oxford.

——. 1973. "Greek Poetry, 2000–700 B.C." *CQ* 23:179–192.

——, ed. 1978. *Hesiod: Works and Days.* Oxford.

——. 1985. *The Hesiodic Catalogue of Women: Its Nature, Structure, and Origins.* Oxford.

——. 1989. "The Early Chronology of Attic Tragedy." *CQ* 39:251–254.

Whitehead, D. 1983. "Competitive Outlay and Community Profit: Φιλοτιμία in Democratic Athens." *Classica et Mediaevalia* 34:55–74.

Wilamowitz-Moellendorff, U. von., ed. 1896. *Orestie: Griechisch und deutsch. Zweites Stück: Das Opfer am Grabe.* Berlin.

——. 1922. *Pindaros.* Berlin.

Wilhelmi, G. 1967. "Untersuchungen zum Bild vom Fließen der Sprache in der griechischen Literatur." Inaugural diss., University of Tübingen.

Will, E. 1955. *Korinthiaka: Recherches sur l'histoire et la civilisation de Corinthe des origines aux guerres médiques.* Paris.

Willcock, M. M. 1982. "Second Reading of Pindar: The Fourth Nemean." *Greece & Rome* 2d ser., 29:1–10.

Williger, E. 1928. *Sprachliche Untersuchungen zu den Komposita der griechischen Dichter des 5. Jahrhunderts.* Göttingen.

Woodbury, L. 1947. "Pindar, Isthmian 4.19f." *TAPA* 78:368–375.

———. 1968. "Pindar and the Mercenary Muse: Isthm. 2.1–13." *TAPA* 99:527–542.

———. 1979. "Neoptolemus at Delphi." *Phoenix* 33.95–133.

———. 1981. "The Victor's Virtues: Pindar, Isth. 1.32ff." *TAPA* 111:237–256.

———. 1982. "Cyrene and the *Teleuta* of Marriage in Pindar's Ninth Pythian Ode." *TAPA* 112:245–258.

Yates, F. A. 1966. *The Art of Memory.* London.

Young, D. C. 1968. *Three Odes of Pindar: A Literary Study of Pythian 11, Pythian 3, Olympian 7.* Mnemosyne Supplement 9. Leiden.

———. 1970a. "Pindaric Criticism." In *Pindaros und Bacchylides.* Wege der Forschung, 134. Ed. W. M. Calder III and J. Stern. Darmstadt.

———. 1970b. "Pindar Nemean 7: Some Preliminary Remarks (vv. 1–20)." *TAPA* 101:633–643.

———. 1971. *Pindar Isthmian 7: Myth and Exempla.* Mnemosyne Supplement 15. Leiden.

———. 1983. "Pindar Pythians 2 and 3: Inscriptional ποτέ and the 'Poetic Epistle.'" *HSCP* 87:31–48.

———. 1984. *The Olympic Myth of Greek Amateur Athletics.* Chicago.

Zeitlin, F. 1986. "Thebes: Theater of Self and Society in Athenian Drama." In *Greek Tragedy and Political Theory.* Ed. J. P. Euben. Berkeley, Calif.

Index Locorum

Pindar (*cont.*)
 9.104–105, 73; *9.105–125*, 133; *9.117–118*, 132
 Pythian 10, 11, 21n.17, 50n.29, 53n.37, 163n.1; *10.4*, 250n.25; *10.5–6*, 54; *10.8*, 158n.48; *10.11–16*, 20n.14; *10.28–30*, 22n.25, 53, 215; *10.48*, 53; *10.51–54*, 12, 53; *10.55–58*, 54, 141; *10.63*, 143, 147n.26; *10.63–68*, 141
 Pythian 11, 20n.17, 38, 229; *11.11–14*, 215; *11.12*, 142n.13; *11.13–14*, 20n.14; *11.28–30*, 215; *11.29*, 195n.1; *11.41–44*, 243; *11.43–50*, 20n.14, 215; *11.46–48*, 215; *11.50b–58*, 214–218; *11.54*, 237n.29; *11.55–58*, 35, 79, 261; *11.56–58*, 230; *11.58*, 38
 Pythian 12, 155; *12.4–6*, 205; *12.5*, 209; *12.5–6*, 20n.14
 fragments, *fr. 43 SM*, 73n.36; *fr. 94a.14–20 SM*, 63; *fr. 94b.31–41 SM*, 58n.45; *fr. 109 SM*, 183n.43; *fr. 123 SM*, 252n.33; *fr. 124ab SM*, 252n.33, *fr. 181 SM*, 86; Δ. *2.27*, 124n.46; *Paean 4.4*, 118; Παρθ. *2.36*, 76n.42; *2.48*, 105n.68; *12.17*, 79n.47
Plato
 Apology 36d, 170n.19
 Phaedo 115d, 44n.20
 Republic 560d8–561a8, 178; *564b4–5*, 178; *566a2–7*, 178
 Symposium 212d2–213a1, 152n.33
Plutarch
 Life of Kimon 10, 172
 Life of Lysander 1.1, 190
 Life of Nicias 3.1–3, 174

Quintilian
 Inst. 11.2.11–16, 59n.47

Sappho
 fr. 112 LP, 124n.45
SIG 1219.10, 44n.20
Simonides
 584 PMG, 123n.43
Solon
 fr. 4W.9, 210n.31; *fr. 4W.32–39*, 212n.33; *fr. 9W.5*, 210n.31; *fr. 23W*, 88
Sophocles

 Ajax, 552, 123n.43
 Antigone, 600, 75n.40; *661*, 30n.41; *1161*, 123n.43; *1187*, 30n.41; *1249*, 30n.41
 Electra, 145–146, 44n.20; *1027*, 123n.43; *1113*, 42n.14; *1354–1355*, 75n.40
 OC, 765, 30n.41; *943*, 123n.43; *OT: 29–30*, 239n.33; *1162*, 30n.41; *1526*, 123n.43
 Philoctetes, 414, 44n.20
 Trachiniae, 757, 30n.41
Strabo
 Book 9.3.4, 190n.51

Theocritus
 Idyll 18.16–20, 124n.45
Theognis
 15–18, 157n.44; *83–86*, 254n.36; *117–128*, 142n.15; *149–150*, 254n.36; *173–174*, 254n.36; *189–192*, 254; *315–322*, 254n.36; *415–418*, 142n.15; *449–452*, 142n.15; *455*, 123n.43; *463–464*, 254n.36; *499–502*, 142n.15; *523–526*, 254n.36; *683–684*, 254n.36; *699–718*, 254n.36; *751–752*, 254n.36; *1009*, 229n.13; *1061–1062*, 254n.36; *1117–1118*, 254n.36
Theopompus
 FGrH 2 F89, 179n.35
Thucydides
 Book 1.9, 30n.41; *1.68–78*, 164n.7
 Book 2.40, 30n.41; *2.51*, 30n.41; *2.65.8*, 210n.31
 Book 6.12.2, 171–173; *6.15.2–4*, 176–177; *6.16*, 198n.9; *6.16.1–3*, 171–172; *6.16.3–6*, 181–182; *6.16.5*, 204n.21
 Book 8.86.5, 210n.31

Valerius Maximus
 1.8.Ext. 7, 59n.47

Xenophanes
 fr. 2 DK, 170n.19
Xenophon
 Anabasis 2.4.1, 44n.19
 HG 1.4.17, 44n.19
 Oeconomicus 2.1–8, 225; *2.5–7*, 168; *9.10–13*, 38n.8; *9.11–13*, 11n.37; *9.18*, 30n.14; *11.8–9*, 167; *11.9*, 230n.14

General Index

Adkins, A. W. H., 163, 175
Agalmata, 95–96, 104–105, 118, 126, 139, 145, 155–159, 190–191, 259
Aganōr, 97, 102–103
Agōgē, 125, 127–128
Aiakidai, 37, 49, 50–52, 55–58, 79n.47, 178, 190, 198–200, 232
Alcaeus, 1, 6, 241, 245, 249, 252–253
Alcibiades, 171–173, 176–177, 181, 183, 186
Alkmeonidai, 15, 173, 178–180, 191–192, 196
Amachania, 101
Anacreon, 241, 245, 254
Anageomai, 56–57
Anagō, 54–55
Anathemata, 169, 188–192, 204, 214. *See also* Dedications
Ancestors, 15–18, 37–49, 69–70, 73–82, 97, 114, 132–133, 146–148, 172, 202–203
   tombs of, 15–16, 46, 60, 240
Aphrodite, 241, 254
Apoina, 92, 106–117, 134, 135, 139, 146. *See also* Recompense
Apollo, 116, 126–130, 132–133, 145–146, 150, 151–153, 189, 191, 219
Archilochus, 100–101
Aretē, 4, 47, 65, 72, 81, 97, 99n.51, 102, 122, 159n.49, 182, 184, 185n.46, 188, 202–203, 223–224, 231–232, 235–236, 250
Aristocracy, 2, 4–6, 9, 85, 87–92, 102–104, 106, 108–111, 113, 116–118, 122, 125, 134, 136, 139–140, 142, 167–170, 172,

173, 193–194, 196, 211–212, 217, 228–229, 232, 239, 240, 242, 252–256, 258–260
Athena, 5, 17, 28, 46, 257
Audience, 1, 5–6, 10–12, 87, 89, 101–106, 108, 110, 112–113, 122–125, 136–139, 163, 195–239, 241, 255–260
Austin, M. M., 193

Banking, 232
Bathus, 33–34, 51–52, 145
Becker, Otfrid, 22, 32, 39, 60n.51
Benveniste, Emile, 9n.27, 205–206
Birth, 21, 56, 62–64, 70–82, 259
Blame, 86, 99–100
Bohringer, F., 207n.25
Bourdieu, Pierre, 8, 26n.33, 36, 71n.31, 93, 96, 261
Bowra, Maurice, 223, 254
Boxing, 110–111
Bride, 114, 118–129, 131–133, 240
Brown, Christopher, 119, 121
Bundy, Elroy, 9–10, 19, 97, 102, 211, 217n.42, 238
Burckhardt, Jakob, 16
Burkert, Walter, 62
Bury, J. B., 41, 58, 112, 145n.22, 190n.54, 191, 238n.30

Campbell, J. K., 36
Carey, Christopher, 20n.16, 113n.13
Carne-Ross, D. S., 52n.34
Carson, Anne, 34n.46, 127, 129n.55, 130n.57, 132n.60, 183nn.43–44, 236n.26

283

Library of Congress Cataloging-in-Publication Data
Kurke, Leslie.
  The traffic in praise: Pindar and the poetics of social economy / Leslie Kurke.
    p.   cm. — (Myth and poetics)
  Includes bibliographical references (p.   ) and indexes.
  ISBN 0-8014-2350-3 (cloth: alk. paper)
    1. Pindar—Criticism and interpretation.   2. Laudatory poetry, Greek—History and
criticism.   3. Political poetry, Greek—History and criticism.   4. Literature and society—
Greece.   5. Odes—History and criticism.   6. Social values in literature.   7. Praise in
literature.   I. Title.   II. Series.
PA4276.K87   1991
884'.01—dc20
                                                                            90-55722